FOREIGN CULTS IN ROME

FOREIGN CULTS IN ROME

Creating a Roman Empire

ERIC M. ORLIN

OXFORD
UNIVERSITY PRESS

2010

OXFORD
UNIVERSITY PRESS

Oxford University Press, Inc., publishes works that further
Oxford University's objective of excellence
in research, scholarship, and education.

Oxford New York
Auckland Cape Town Dar es Salaam Hong Kong Karachi
Kuala Lumpur Madrid Melbourne Mexico City Nairobi
New Delhi Shanghai Taipei Toronto

With offices in
Argentina Austria Brazil Chile Czech Republic France Greece
Guatemala Hungary Italy Japan Poland Portugal Singapore
South Korea Switzerland Thailand Turkey Ukraine Vietnam

Published by Oxford University Press, Inc.
198 Madison Avenue, New York, New York 10016

www.oup.com

Library of Congress Cataloging-in-Publication Data
Orlin, Eric M.
Foreign cults in Rome : creating a Roman Empire / Eric Orlin.
p. cm.
Includes bibliographical references and index.
ISBN 978-0-19-973155-8
1. Rome—Religion. I. Title.
BL805.O74   2010
292.07—dc22   2009045003

9 8 7 6 5 4 3 2

Printed in the United States of America
on acid-free paper

To my life's partner

Acknowledgments

Many, many years ago, this book had its genesis on a site visit to Veii as part of the inaugural Summer Program in Archaeology, organized by the American Academy in Rome. I am extremely grateful to the Academy and to the directors of that program, Malcolm Bell, Lisa Fentress, and Darby Scott, for the work they put into that program and for opening my eyes to issues of Romans and Italy that I had not previously considered. I also want to express my gratitude to the Samuel H. Kress foundation for a grant that made that trip possible for me.

The journey toward completion of this project could not have been completed without assistance from many friends and colleagues. I want to express my appreciation to Judy Barringer, Jon Brockopp, Brad Clough, Judy Gaughan, Mary Jaeger, J. H. W. G. Liebeschuetz, Molly Pasco-Pranger, Beth Severy, Barbette Spaeth and Marco Zangari for their support and interest in furthering this project. My colleagues at the University of Puget Sound—David Lupher, Ili Nagy, Aislinn Melchior, and Bill Barry—have provided encouragement and a supportive environment in which to work. I am grateful to the university for a Martin Nelson Junior Sabbatical grant that enabled me to complete work on several chapters, as well as for research grants to enable travel to Italy.

The ideas in this book were refined during a National Endowment for the Humanities seminar in 2002 on "Roman Religion in Its Cultural Context." I want to thank Karl Galinsky for his able leadership of that seminar, as well as the thoughts he shared with me during that summer and subsequently on this project. That seminar was a particularly fruitful moment, not least for the many colleagues in both Classics and Religion who talked with me about this specific project as well as broader issues of Roman religion. In particular I want to thank Jeff Brodd, Nicola Denzey, Georgia Frank, Ed Gutting, Jonathan Reed, and Greg Snyder.

Stefan Vranka at Oxford University Press has been very helpful throughout this process, as indeed has been the entire staff at the press. The anonymous readers enlisted by the Press suggested revisions both large and small that ultimately made this manuscript better, for which I wish to express my appreciation. In several instances I have made conscious choices not to follow their advice, so whatever mistakes remain truly are my own.

While I am appreciative of all these people, I would be remiss beyond words if I did not reserve special gratitude to four individuals. Erich Gruen remains for me the model of what a person pursuing career in academia should aspire to be: using his wisdom to create space for others to succeed, and unfailingly present with support and advice when asked. I feel privileged to have him as a friend and colleague. My children, Sam and Ben, have lived their entire lives to date with this book, and their excitement as the book neared completion provided the last boost of energy necessary to reach the finish line. And my wife, Kathleen, without whom none of this— the book, the children, the career—would be either possible or enjoyable.

Contents

Note on Abbreviations		XI
Introduction		3
1	Foreign Cults in Rome	31
2	Cult Introductions of the Third Century	58
3	Foreign Priests in Rome	86
4	Prodigies and Expiations	111
5	*Ludi*	137
6	Establishing Boundaries in the Second Century	162
7	The Challenges of the First Century	191
Conclusion		215
Bibliography		221
Index		241

Note on Abbreviations

The abbreviations of the names of ancient authors and their works and modern reference works in the notes below follow the practice of the Oxford Classical Dictionary, 3rd edition (Oxford, 1996).

FOREIGN CULTS IN ROME

Introduction

The Ausonian tribes
shall keep the speech and customs of their sires;
the name remains as now; the Teucrian race,
abiding in the land, shall but infuse
the mixture of its blood. I will bestow
a league of worship, and to Latins give
one language only. From the mingled breed
a people shall come forth whom thou shalt see
surpass all mortal men and even outvie
the faithfulness of gods; for none that live
shall render to thy name an equal praise.

Vergil, Aeneid 12.823–28

The willingness of the Romans to incorporate new cults and foreign traditions within their religious system has become one of the most frequently noted aspects of religion in Rome. During the first three hundred years of the Republic, numerous cults and practices—first from neighboring communities and then from farther abroad—found a home in the city. Cults such as Hercules suggest that this willingness to adopt foreign cults extended back into the regal period as well, and this progression continued with such divinities as Castor and Pollux and Ceres, both of whose temples are said to have been dedicated in the

490s.[1] The openness manifested on the religious level matched the openness expressed in political terms as well, as many people living outside the city of Rome became Roman citizens. Rome incorporated numerous people from neighboring communities into the state as citizens, either with or without the right to vote, and planted many colonies of Roman citizens in different parts of Italy, so that by 250 B.C.E. a substantial number of Roman citizens lived more than a day's journey outside the city. This policy, which might be called the "ideology of the open city," contributed heavily to the Romans' success in building a hegemonic rule that at the end of the third century withstood the determined efforts of Hannibal to unravel it.

A second point that has become axiomatic among scholars of Roman religion is that religion was embedded in Roman society, that religion and politics were inextricably linked.[2] The addition of new cults has therefore been viewed in the light of the growing Roman power, an expansion of the divine pantheon to match the expansion of territory and citizens.[3] The process of assimilation and incorporation was not automatic, however, on either the divine or the human level; not every foreign religious cult or practice became part of the Roman religious system, just as not every community was admitted to citizenship. The Romans made conscious choices about how to act in individual cases. Politically, this behavior is seen most easily in the Roman actions following the suppression of the Latin Revolt in 338, when some communities were granted citizen rights while others were punished severely for their role in the uprising, and the choices made at this time can help us explore Roman policy toward the integration of Latium and subsequent other regions.[4] This point should remind us that the Roman religious system was not a hodgepodge, a mere accretion of cults and practices, but that decisions were made to create a sense of direction for the Roman religious system. The choices that the Romans made in the adoption and treatment of religious practices have not yet been fully explored, especially in regard to their implications for Roman policy. Exploration of this behavior will show that the decisions the Romans made in the religious sphere, just as with their political decisions, were tied to their attempts to incorporate new territories and new peoples within the body politic of the Roman people.

1. Castor and Pollux: Livy 2.42; Ceres: Dion. Hal., *Ant. Rom.* 6.17. All dates are B.C.E. unless otherwise noted.

2. E.g., Wardman (1982); Beard, North, & Price (1998); Scheid (2003); Warrior (2006); Rüpke (2007).

3. North (1979), 9–11.

4. See Livy 8.11 for the settlement after the Latin Revolt.

The encounter with foreign and ultimately subjugated peoples created issues for the Romans not only in terms of deciding how to treat the new-comers but also in its effects on their own society. The decision to accept so many elements from other cultures—people, cults, practices—into Roman society posed potential problems of social cohesion and identity by blurring the distinction between what was Roman and what was not. "Foreign" elements were now "Roman" as well. This problem was compli-cated further by the presence of so much Greek culture in Italy, both at Rome and elsewhere, for as we shall see, Greek culture could represent both foreign and Roman.[5] In the early Republic, these problems were less acute: the Roman community was largely contained within the walls of the city and its surrounding environs, the concerns were largely local, and the continuous skirmishes with other inhabitants of central Italy provided the necessary social cohesion. Those fighting for Rome were clearly members of the community, and the boundaries between Roman and non-Roman were vividly represented by city walls. The civic identity—those citizens living in and around the *urbs*—may well have been suffi-cient, as it generally was for Greek *poleis* such as Athens. But with the conquest of Italy and the dissolution of the Latin League, the situation changed. Many who were not Roman citizens now fought on Rome's behalf, and the city walls, while still present, were no longer necessary to separate the Romans from their enemies; neither of these elements was sufficient to define Roman identity.[6] When Rome became too large for the immediate interaction that might help to define a civic community, her policy of welcoming foreigners left her without an obvious means by which to define the community in other terms. At the beginning of the second century, in the wake of her transformation from city-state to the dominant power in the Mediterranean basin, Rome faced what might be called a "crisis of identity" (Map 1).[7]

5. Since the publication of *Hellenismus in Mittelitalien* in 1976, scholars have accepted that the presence of Greek culture in Italy was not always connected with the imposition of Roman power. This observation has led to further discussions of whether one should speak of the Romanization of Italy or its Hellenization. See Zanker (1976), 11–20 and the recent comments by Wallace-Hadrill (2008), 17–28. As the present study concerns itself with Roman self-definition rather than with actual developments in Italy, these questions will play only a minor role here.

6. The point is driven home when one considers the next time that walls did again play a military role for the Romans: against Hannibal. The distinction made by the walls is now between Rome and the invader from across the sea, but no longer between Rome and her Italian allies, who were so crucial to Rome's victory in that war.

7. Cf. Habinek (1998), 34–37.

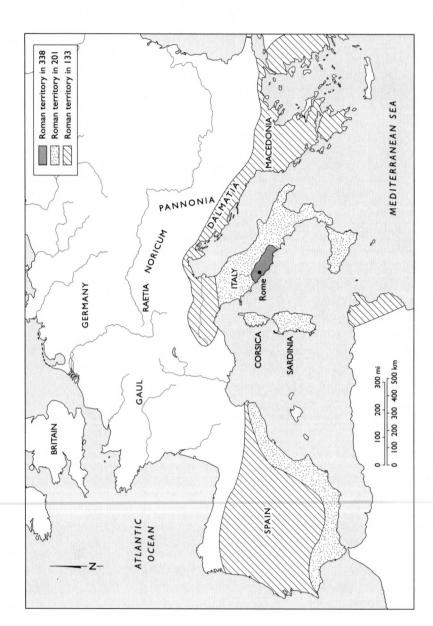

Map 1: Roman expansion to the second century B.C.E.

Roman territory in 338
Roman territory in 201
Roman territory in 133

MEDITERRANEAN SEA

PANNONIA

DALMATIA

MACEDONIA

NORICUM

RAETIA

GERMANY

ITALY

Rome

CORSICA

SARDINIA

GAUL

BRITAIN

ATLANTIC
OCEAN

N

SPAIN

0   100   200   300 mi
0   100 200 300 400 500 km

This crisis of identity is visible in many aspects of Roman society, including religious practice, hardly a surprising development in light of the aforementioned connections between religion and the res publica. A number of high-profile episodes involving religion in the late third and early second century, such as the actions taken against the worship of Bacchus in 186, have been viewed as a conservative reaction against the policy of openness, a symbolic closing of the gates in an effort to maintain a core of Romanness against the onrushing innovations.[8] The present study, however, will argue that this supposed religious conservatism does not indicate a fundamental shift away from the ideology of openness, but rather is part of a concerted attempt to define a traditional Roman way of doing things where none may have existed previously. Rome continued to be open to foreigners through the end of the Republic and under the emperors, and the notion of openness became an important part of Roman ideology that played a significant role in holding the Empire together for more than five hundred years.

At the heart of this study lies the question: what did it mean to be Roman in the Middle and Late Republic? How Romans defined their sense of cultural identity has been a major issue for historians of Rome for more than a decade, and religion, especially the response to foreign cults, has played a significant role in these discussions.[9] But the full implications of this issue have yet to be explored; if religion was embedded in Roman society, discussions of religious actions need to be considered broadly in the context of Roman religion and culture, not treated as isolated incidents. How were issues of Roman identity reflected in religious activity, and how did religious activity affect the development of Roman identity? Many studies have focused on life in the Roman provinces during the Imperial period and caused us to rethink the process of Romanization and even question the appropriateness of that term to describe what is now, and more properly, viewed as the negotiation between Roman culture and local culture.[10] These studies often take the concept of Romanness, against which local customs can be compared, for granted, since their primary focus often lies with how

8. E.g., Dumézil (1996), 512–525.

9. Dench (2005), Gruen (1992), Lomas (1993), Giardina (1997), Torelli (1999), Bradley (2007), Wallace-Hadrill (2008).

10. E.g., Millett (1990), Woolf (1998), Laurence and Berry (1998), Keay and Terrenato (2001), Wallace-Hadrill (2008). See also the essays in Bradley, Isayev, and Riva (2007). In the sphere of religion, attention has focused on *interpretatio Romana*, a phrase used by Tacitus (*Germania* 43.3), but whose meaning is just as slippery as Romanization. Cf. Girard (1980); Beard, North, and Price (1998), 313–319 and 339–348; Ando (2008), 43–58.

a given community reconciled its own identity with its new status as part of the larger Roman world. Yet it is a question that is fundamental: what does it mean to be a Roman? What is the standard of Romanness to which other customs should be compared, and how did those practices come to represent Romanness? What does it mean to speak of Roman religion, at a point when the term can no longer refer simply to religious rituals performed in the city of Rome?

A central problem in approaching this issue is that we have few or no contemporary texts to provide us with insight as to what Romans of the time deemed important to Roman identity; rather, we have Livy and other first-century authors, writing long after the period in question and reflecting back on that era through the lens of how Romans of their own day grappled with these issues, not necessarily what their forebears thought about them. Livy's text frequently betrays a concern about what it meant to be a Roman in the age of Augustus, and recent scholarship has highlighted the ways in which Livy's text, especially the first pentad, revolves around the issue of Roman identity, whether the question concerns the degree to which the plebeians belong in the Roman state or the status of individuals who either move to Rome from abroad or are forced out of Rome into exile.[11] Nowhere is this concern more evident than in the historian's references to religious activity. Religion plays a central role in Livy's text, as the historian frequently recounts religious events and includes in his annalistic record notices of both temple foundations and prodigy reports. Livy's concern with a proper Roman way to worship the gods should, however, be seen as a product of the Augustan era and its concerns with what it meant to be Roman. Indeed, Livy explicitly indicates, in his discussion of the *devotio* of Decius Mus, that his concern is for religious practice in his own day:

> Even if the memory of all divine and human customs has been lost through our preferring everything new and foreign to our old and ancestral customs, I considered it scarcely a departure from my subject to record them in the very words in which they were handed down and vowed.[12]

Livy was not alone in his concern to establish what constituted proper Roman religious practice for his own day, for other authors of the same

---

11. E.g., Miles (1995), Jaeger (1997), Feldherr (1998).

12. Livy 8.11: *Haec etsi omnis diuini humanique moris memoria aboleuit noua peregrinaque omnia priscis ac patriis praeferendo, haud ab re duxi uerbis quoque ipsis, ut tradita nuncupataque sunt, referre.*

period aimed at categorizing and regularizing the understanding of Roman rites. For instance, Verrius Flaccus offered a definition of *sacra peregrina* as those for gods who came to Rome that are performed according the custom of the people from whom they were received, one of a number of definitions offered by Flaccus that seem intended to make sense of the variety of religious practice in Rome.[13] Both Flaccus and Livy were preceded by the polymath M. Terentius Varro, whose efforts to create clear categories for Roman religion are well known; while Varro's view of foreign cults is not preserved, his statement that the Roman worship for 170 years without images of the gods was "more pure" reveals his attempt to assert an "original" Roman religion, one perhaps uncontaminated by later anthropomorphic practices.[14] It is therefore not surprising to find Livy concerned with the issue of foreign elements in Roman religious practice. But it is important for us not to be misled into retrojecting Livy's attitude back onto the Romans of the early or middle Republic and simply to accept his conception of "foreign."

We must also beware of incorporating Livy's often negative view of religions he deemed to be foreign and their impact on Roman practice. One of Livy's core operating principles, that the res publica had declined over a long time from a period of "purer morality and richer in good examples" to one in which "avarice and luxury have made their inroads," carried over into his treatment of religion, for the historian often depicted Roman religion as being polluted under the influence of foreign practices.[15] A good illustration comes from the first pentad, in the context of a severe drought that caused a plague in Rome in 428 B.C.E.:

> Pretended soothsayers went about introducing new modes of sacrificing, and did a profitable trade amongst the victims of superstition, until at last the sight of strange foreign (*peregrina*) modes of propitiating the wrath of the gods in the streets and chapels brought home to the leaders of the commonwealth the public scandal which

---

13. Festus (p. 268, Lindsay): *peregrina sacra appellantur, quae aut evocatis dis in oppugnandis urbibus Romam sunt coacta aut quae ob quasdam religiones per pacem sunt petita, ut ex Phrygia Matris Magnae, ex Graecia Cereris, Epidauro Aesculapi, quae coluntur eorum more, a quibus sunt accepta.* See Ando (2003), 195–196 for similar thoughts on Flaccus.

14. Varro, cited in Augustine, *De Civ. D.*, 4.31.

15. Livy, *praefatio*. Livy's presentation of Roman religion undoubtedly lies behind some of the misleading modern studies that try to find an originally "pure" Roman religion discussed previously.

was being caused. The aediles were instructed to see to it that none but Roman deities were worshipped, nor in any other than the established fashion.[16]

It is revealing of Livy's mind-set that he explicitly compared the involvement with foreign superstitions to the disease that sprang up as a result of the drought: "Nor was it only the body that was affected by the pest, the minds of men also became a prey to all kinds of religious feeling, mostly foreign ones."[17] Similar editorial comments can be found scattered throughout the entire text that has survived, including examples from more historically reliable eras.[18] These sections frequently conclude, as the previous passage does, by citing the actions that attempt to restore Roman practice and insisting that only Roman deities be worshipped and only in the fashion established by the Senate.[19] This passage forms part of Livy's approach to this issue, insisting that there *is* a proper Roman way to worship the gods. This presentation is seen most clearly in the great speech of Camillus that caps Book Five, in which Camillus asserts that Roman religion, and thus Roman identity, are inextricably linked to the site of Rome.[20] But this attitude need not be representative of Roman attitudes earlier in their history, or even of Livy's own day, and it is precisely the exploration of those varying attitudes that is under investigation here.

16. Livy 4.30: *novos ritus sacrificandi uaticinando inferentibus in domos quibus quaestui sunt capti superstitione animi, donec publicus iam pudor ad primores civitatis pervenit, cernentes in omnibus vicis sacellisque peregrina atque insolita piacula pacis deum exposcendae. Datum inde negotium aedilibus, ut animadverterent ne qui nisi Romani di neu quo alio more quam patrio colerentur.*

17. *Nec corpora modo adfecta tabo, sed animos quoque multiplex religio et pleraque externa invasit.*

18. For another example of a Livian criticism of foreign practices in close proximity to his acknowledgment of the acceptance of innovation approved by the Senate, see the episode in 212 involving the *carmen Marciana* and the introduction of the *ludi Apollinares* (25.1, 25.12), in which *vates* also play a prominent role. See also Livy's treatment of the Bacchic incident, 39.8–19.

19. Davies (2004), 78–82, suggests that Livy was more concerned to protect Rome from foreign *rites* than from foreign cults, though his own acknowledgment (82) that Livy recognized the value of some foreign rites undermines this claim.

20. The twin destructions of Veii and Rome itself provide the backdrop to this speech, and Kraus (1994) noted the many resonances between these two sacks and the most famous sack of a city for Roman history, the sack of Troy. She argues that Livy's account is designed to demonstrate how the Romans needed to move beyond their Trojan past and forge a new identity for themselves.

One ironic aspect of Livy's criticism of foreign religious practices is that Livy himself is often the source for our knowledge of the introduction of foreign practices and especially foreign cults. Livy's reliability on religious and other matters has often been the focus of study and so will not be treated in depth here; the dates of temple foundations and other facts concerning religious activity in Rome have generally been accepted, even if commentators have disagreed on how and why Livy shaped his account.[21] The incident cited previously from 428 provides a prime example, for three years prior to the drought, Livy reports that plague had struck the city, and in response a temple had been dedicated to Apollo.[22] Livy reports the dedication of this temple, and in this case he does so without a hint of censure, just as he reports many other cases of temple foundations or other religious actions without making negative comments. Although recent work has emphasized the ways in which Livy shaped his narrative to present a coherent picture of Roman religion and to assert that the Romans' religious piety or lack thereof was a direct contributing factor in their success or failure, his account still provides the crucial foundation for any study of Republican religion.[23] The essential data on religious actions undertaken by the Romans provided by Livy may be accepted from Livy's account, even while we must always remain aware of Livy's selection of specific religious incidents for elaboration in accord with his historiographic purposes.

Even if we accept the outlines of the data provided by Livy, the historiographic issues still present a significant challenge for a study of the response to foreign religious elements in Rome: how exactly should we define 'foreign' in regard to the religious elements that will form the object of our study? Flaccus' definition cited above, that foreign rites are those for gods who came to Rome performed according the custom of the people from whom they were received, provides no assistance, for not only does it, like Livy's account, date from the Augustan period, but it also defines any cult that came to Rome and utilized Roman rites as not foreign; our concern, however, lies precisely with how the Romans treated cults of foreign origin, so the fact that some cults continued to use the rites from their country of origin while others used Roman rites is a phenomenon to be studied, not

21. On Livy's reliability as a historian, see Cornell (1995), who broadly accepts Livy's account; Walsh (1961); and Luce (1977). The prodigy lists have perhaps been subject to the most challenges but have been defended by Rawson (1971), MacBain (1982), and more recently Rasmussen (1998), with prior bibliography.

22. Livy 4.29.

23. On religion in Livy, see Levene (1993), Davies (2004).

defined out of existence.[24] The difficulty modern scholars have faced in defining Roman and foreign cults in Rome suggests that the Romans never formalized the distinction as modern scholars, myself included, attempt to do, though the Romans clearly recognized a difference between such cults as Jupiter Optimus Maximus and the Magna Mater. Standard Roman governmental practice called for each situation to be treated on an individual basis, and I suggest we need to do the same in regard to foreign cults. Each case where the evidence preserves a strong indication of the origin of the cult outside Rome, either through archaeological remains or literary traditions, will have to be considered on its merits. As the ensuing study shows, there are enough straightforward cases, such as Juno Regina or Aesculapius, to enable us to observe how the Romans treated foreign cults as they built their territorial hegemony and then rebuilt their notion of Romanness.

Identity and Ethnicity

Scholarly literature from a variety of disciplines, including anthropology, political science, and sociology, that treat issues of identity and ethnicity has generally paid scant attention to the ancient world, though discussion of these topics has begin to filter into studies of the classical world.[25] While it is beyond the scope of this study to enter fully into the debates that have

24. Geiger's entry in Pauly-Wissowa exemplifies the problem, for he argued that cults of Italic origin or Greek cults that had been Romanized would have counted as *sacra Romana*; the term *sacra peregrina* was meant to distinguish these cults from the "wholly different foreign cults" (*grundsätzlich abweichenden fremdartigen Kulte*). The assumption that the Romans created gradations of foreignness is not supported by the sources. On the problems of defining "foreign cults," see further Orlin (2002).

25. Ancient Greece has been a fruitful place to study such issues, in part because of the abundance of material, literary, linguistic, and archaeological data that can be plumbed in the search for answers. See, e.g., Hall (1997) and (2002); McInerney (1999); Malkin (2001); Dougherty and Kurke (2003). The very term "the Greeks" begs for elucidation, since it serves as an identifying term more for classroom instruction and modern research than it ever did for the inhabitants of the ancient Greek world. An inhabitant of what we now call ancient Greece might identify himself or herself as an individual, a member of a certain family, a member of a tribe, a citizen of a given *polis*, or a member of a larger "ethnic" group such as the Dorians or Ionians, but only in exceptional and transitory circumstances, such as wars against the Persian king, would the "national" identity of a Hellene have come into play. To discuss the Greeks thus means to discuss the groups encompassed by the terms and the interplay between them, and one of the advantages of studying identity in the Greek world is precisely that so many communities exist, with the result that there are many levels at which identity might be explored—panhellenic, ethnic (in the sense of Dorians and Ionians), civic (in the different city-states).

emerged concerning ethnicity, the concepts raised by these studies prove useful in exploring the problems of Roman identity in the late third and early second century B.C.E., precisely because they focus on issues of collective identity.[26] Questions of how an ethnic group constitutes itself or how a nation may be created from a seemingly disparate group of people provide useful models as one ponders how the Romans refashioned the res publica and their own identity in the wake of their dramatic expansion. While we must be wary of importing anachronistic notions and models into the study of antiquity, the categories of analysis provide a useful framework that helps to illuminate developments in the Roman world.

The most important observation of these studies has been to suggest that ethnic groups are socially constructed and subjectively perceived.[27] It was long thought that ethnic identity was based on an objective criterion, an actual physical difference between one group and another, and the element most frequently invoked to distinguish ethnic groups was blood, or genetics. People derived from the same putative kin, sharing certain physical characteristics, were held to constitute an ethnic group. This notion of inherited and ineradicable physical differences fell into disrepute after World War II, partly on political grounds in light of the tragic way this theory was employed by the Nazis. But it was also challenged on intellectual grounds and scientific grounds; for instance, modern genetics has demonstrated that the genetic differences between accepted members of the same group can be as great as or greater than those between members of distinct groups.[28] It is not possible to identify a single characteristic or a certain bundle of shared traits that might define an ethnic group, leaving us with the conclusion that ethnic groups lack an objective basis, even while most ethnic groups believe that they do have an objective core. Although some scholars have suggested that this lack of an objective basis meant that ethnic groups would cease to exist, ethnic groups continue to exist, just as they have existed for hundreds of years.

The solution suggested for this conundrum is that groups set their own criteria for membership in the group and police its boundaries. The group is real, but the criteria are decided by the group, and the perception that someone

---

26. One of the major debates on ethnic groups revolves around whether ethnicity is primordial or instrumental, whether it reflects long-standing and natural ties among members of a community or is a symbol of association exploited by groups to serve their political or economic interests. For an introduction to this discussion, see Glazer and Moynihan (1975); Horowitz (1975); Smith (1986), 9–12.

27. See De Vos and Romanucci-Ross (1995), 350; Hall (1997), 19.

28. See Cole (1965), Neel (1970), and more recently Diamond (1994) for a discussion of genetics.

is a member of the group is perhaps the key to defining membership. This line of thinking was sparked by Fredrik Barth's observation that the content of a given group, the bundle of traits used to define membership, is less important that its ascriptive boundaries, the ability of the group to define that bundle of traits.[29] The key to ethnic identity, as Barth saw it, was the maintenance of a boundary between groups based on some chosen criterion that allowed a clear distinction to be made. For instance, language might appear as a marker of social group status if the group in question decided to make language a defining characteristic of the group; other groups might choose to emphasize physical characteristics or other traits. Barth noted that the boundaries need not remain static but can shift over time and thus include or exclude new cultural elements; the group, however, must continue to enforce a sense of boundary, or the solidarity among the ethnic group may begin to fade. This approach allows one to acknowledge that ethnic groups exist and focus on an existing cultural or physical commonality, while recognizing that there are no universal objective criteria to define ethnic groups. The observation that ethnic identity is subjective and constructed by the group itself has shifted the focus of study from isolating the supposed objective elements that constituted an ethnic group to analyzing the group itself and the choices made in determining which elements to emphasize as criteria for membership within that ethnic group.

If ethnic groups are socially constructed and subjectively perceived, one is faced with the question of what separates ethnic identity from other types of identity. As long as ethnic groups were thought to be based on an objective criterion such as blood or descent, the use of that criterion marked ethnic identity from other types of groups; with the observation that ethnic groups lack an objective core but are socially constructed, they were no longer automatically distinguished from other forms of social groups. In response to this problem, A. D. Smith proposed six characteristics of an ethnic group: (1) a collective name, (2) a common myth of descent, (3) a shared history, (4) a distinctive shared culture, (5) an association with a specific territory, and (6) a sense of communal solidarity.[30] Among the items on this list, Smith and others single out the myth of shared ancestry as *the* crucial factor in defining an ethnic group; one can think of many groups that share a collective name, a history, or even a sense of solidarity that one would not want to call an ethnic group, but the belief in common descent is distinctive.[31] Note that the use of this criterion does not imply a

29. Barth (1969), 14.
30. Smith (1986), 22–30.
31. Smith (1991), 22; Horowitz (1975).

genealogical approach to group formation precisely because it is a myth; it is not a shared genealogical lineage but the *belief* in a shared lineage that is essential for the construction of ethnic identity.[32] For instance, the Hebrew Bible, offering stories that provide myths of shared descent, continues to be a contributing factor in the shaping of ethnic identity; the salient point is that theoretically all Jews believe they are descended from Abraham, Isaac, and Jacob, regardless of whether they actually are so descended. Myths of descent thus provide a basis around which to construct a sense of ethnic identity.

The strongly subjective aspect of the elements proposed by Smith and the fact that they are cultural rather than physical or biological illustrate the concept that ethnic identity is subjectively perceived. The stories that people tell and the way they attach themselves to the land, rather than the land itself, reveal their connections to each other. Only the distinctive shared culture includes what might be considered objective elements, such as language, religion, food, or dress. But subjectivity plays a large role here as well, for these attributes do not have independent significance; they become important for group membership only when the group invests them with the power to distinguish between in-group and out-group members. As Smith comments, "it is only when such markers are endowed with diacritical significance that these cultural attributes *come to be seen* as objective, at least as far as ethnic boundaries are concerned" (italics mine).[33] Here again we are brought back to boundaries; for an ethnic group to exist, it must create and maintain boundaries that separate its culture from that of other cultures. Because cultural elements may appear the most objective and because cultural elements are the most liable to change over time, the policing of the boundaries of the distinct shared culture assumes a greater importance over time.

Of particular importance for our purposes is the stress that has been placed on religion as an important component of ethnic identity. Analyses of ethnic groups and nations often focus on the role of religion in creating and/or maintaining bonds among the members of the community.[34] For example, organized religion is among the three factors that Smith has posited as crucial to the formation of such identities.[35] Smith suggests that the

32. Hall (1997), 25.

33. Smith (1991) 23.

34. E.g., O'Brien (1988); Brass (1991); Hastings (1997).

35. Smith (1991), 26. The other two are state making and military mobilization, for obvious reasons. The existence of a unified polity and warfare against a hostile enemy obviously facilitate the development of a broad sense of community. See also Smith (1986), 32–41 and 119–125.

reasons for the importance of religion might be both spiritual and social. Myths of shared descent, the crucial building block for ethnic identity, often have a distinctly religious overtone, involving creation stories or at least some type of divine intervention. The sense of shared origins and shared destiny creates a powerful bond for members of the ethnic group, and the history of the group is often connected with its myths; for many groups, the historical records may even be kept by the religious authorities. And of course, religion itself is a form of cultural practice, so that communities can be distinguished not only by their myths and their histories but also by their ritual practices: prayers, sacrifices, festival calendar, and more. While religious groups and ethnic groups are not necessarily coterminous, the role played by religion in the formation of an ethnic identity has often proved fundamental.

Herodotus' famous formulation of Greekness provides an excellent opportunity to illustrate the application of these concepts to the ancient world. The ways in which the Persian Wars acted as a catalyst for the formation of a common Greek identity opposed to the barbarian Other has received much attention in recent studies, as has the way the text of Herodotus, by providing ethnographic comparisons for Greek practices, itself contributed to this process.[36] After Herodotus narrates the Athenian rejection of renewed Persian overtures of alliance in 479, he reports a speech in which they expressed their displeasure with the Spartans for even thinking that the Athenians might accept the offer, noting many reasons they did not do so:

> Again there is our Greekness (τὸ ἑλληνικόν), being our common blood and common language, common shrines of the gods and places/customs (ἐθέα) for sacrifices, and common way of life.[37]

The Athenian speaker, demonstrating his sense of Greek solidarity, focuses on the elements that he deems important for determining Greekness and who should be included within its boundaries, and the Greeks are represented as an ethnic group in precisely the terms outlined previously.[38] He first mentions common blood, recognizing the myth of shared descent from the hero Hellen as the most important bond among those he would define

36. See for example E. Hall (1989); P. Cartledge (1993); on the "mirror" of Herodotus, see Hartog (1988).

37. Herodotus 8.144.

38. It makes no difference here whether this statement was formulated by an Athenian in 479 or by Herodotus in the middle of the fifth century. In either case, the words represent a Greek's understanding of the elements important to defining Greekness.

as Greeks.[39] Hellen also provides them with the collective name Hellenes or, as here, "Hellenicness." The speaker goes on to mention three areas of distinctive shared culture: language, religious practices, and "way of life." Language has often been viewed by scholars of ethnicity as a key characteristic of an ethnic group, and the importance of language to Greek identity has long been recognized.[40] The Athenian's inclusion of religion among his items of distinctive shared culture illustrates the importance of religion outlined here; even if most anthropological studies focus on monotheistic religions with shared belief systems, the Greeks also recognized in their religion a common feature distinctive to them and of great importance for their self-identity.[41] By singling out these features, the speaker indicates precisely the objective differences between Greek and Other that have been invested with the ability to define Greek identity. The Lydian king Croesus might consult the oracle at Delphi but did not speak Greek, did not share in the regular worship of Apollo, and did not share the Greek way of life, and so he was not to be considered Greek. In their own words, the Greeks appear as an ethnic group in precisely the terms outlined here, bearing a common name, defending their homeland, and sharing a common history and myths of descent, as well as distinctive cultural characteristics.[42]

39. The importance of myths of shared descent for providing the basis of group identity in ancient Greece has long been recognized, not only for the Greeks as a group but also for Dorians and Ionians, and even for individual *poleis*. For a treatment of Greek myths of ethnic origins, see Hall (1997), 40–51, with literature on understanding Greek myth in general located in n. 65.

40. Language has sometimes been considered the determining factor for ethnic identity, e.g., by Renfrew (1987); while closer examination reveals that linguistic groups do not map directly onto ethnic groups, the importance of language as an identifying factor, an *indicium* of ethnic identity, should be recognized. In ancient Greece, the importance of language can be seen in the word *barbaros*, which derived from a linguistic connotation, as well as from the eligibility requirement for initiates into the mysteries at Eleusis that they be able to speak Greek. See Hall (1989), 9–11.

41. Hall (1997), 45, points out that Herodotus innovates by including religion among the features that define Greekness, considering the great diversity in the specific cults and practices of individual *poleis*. But there are many other indications of the importance of religion to Greekness; the requirement to speak Greek for initiation at Eleusis has already been mentioned, and only Greeks, this time defined by supposed shared ancestry, could participate in the Olympic games, which we must remember was a religious festival.

42. Since this study has employed Smith's definition of an ethnic group, it is not surprising to find Smith (1991), 8, speaking of the Greeks as a "cultural and ethnic community." It is interesting to note that some translations of this passage (e.g., Aubrey de Sèlincourt in the Penguin edition) employ the "the Greek nation"

The Romans and Ethnicity

These perspectives are of tremendous value in exploring the concept of Romanness and Roman identity under the Republic. It was once fashionable to search for the "original" Roman culture in the mists of archaic Latium, before Roman culture was tainted with admixtures from abroad. In no field was this more true than in Roman religion; much effort was expended in a futile attempt to weed out later accretions to the Roman religious system to find the original and "pure" Roman religion.[43] But as noted previously, Roman religion was always open to influences from abroad, and in fact, the defining feature of the Roman religious system may be precisely its willingness to adopt and adapt foreign practices and cults within its confines. Adopting the principles of boundaries, however, frees us from the fruitless search for an original Rome and to focus instead on the boundaries of Romanness. As Barth suggested, the content of what might count as Roman might change over time, but the maintenance of a clear sense of Roman identity depended on the maintenance of a clear boundary between what was Roman and what was not. Our focus, therefore, needs to be not on the search for some purely Roman characteristics, but on how the Romans created and maintained a distinct shared culture.

Defining Romanness for the late third and early second centuries presents a far more difficult challenge than defining Greekness in the fifth century. Since Rome was a single city, citizenship might seem to be the most obvious mechanism for defining social identity, as it was for the majority of *poleis* in Greece. Rome's expansion into an empire challenged that sense of identity and demanded a broader construction of the community, a challenge not faced in Greece. Athens, the Greek state that built an empire most similar to that of the Romans, does not provide an appropriate comparandum, for three reasons: Athens controlled a smaller and more culturally homogeneous empire, she controlled it for a much shorter time, and

---

for τὸ ἑλληνικόν, which I have rendered as "Greekness." This translation, despite its literal inaccuracy, may convey a broader truth in acknowledging the existence of smaller ethnic groups in ancient Greece (e.g., Dorians and Ionians) and searching for a larger collective term. Modern authors, both classicists and scholars of nationalism, have been loath to call the Greeks a nation because that term implies a sovereign political community, and outside the Persian Wars, the Greeks seldom acted as a unified political community.

43. Scheid (1987) has ably discussed the problems in the historiography of Roman religion.

perhaps most important, she had a much more restrictive citizenship policy.[44] An additional problem for the Romans is that the cultural basis for a broader identity was not as easily available to them as it was for the Greeks: there was no common language, common way of life, or pan-Italic religious festivals or sanctuaries along the lines of Delphi or Olympia. Nor does there seem to have been any overarching sense of cultural unity in Italy, or even in Latium, along the lines of what Herodotus describes that the Romans might use to build a broader sense of community. The expansion of Rome and her willingness to welcome foreigners and foreign cultural elements left her without a well-defined social or cultural core, even as the *urbs* provided a geographical center. The vibrant mix of influences that had been essential to Roman growth left her without the clear sense of boundaries necessary for maintaining group identity at precisely the moment when she became too large to maintain a purely civic community.

Paradoxically, Rome's generosity with citizenship meant that citizenship did not provide the most useful way to define the Roman community. In a certain sense, of course, anyone granted citizenship would be a "Roman," but phrased in that way, the definition is tautological and so has limited usefulness.[45] Possession of Roman citizenship does not mean that others would have viewed the holder as Roman, nor does it mean that the holder would have identified himself as Roman. Put another way, legal rights do not of themselves create a sense of community, a social identity. The point can be grasped quite easily in the fact that neither Romans nor modern scholars hold that being Roman consisted simply of being a Roman citizen. It may be that this state of affairs is a particular function of the Roman style of citizenship, where citizen status conveyed a bundle of rights but not necessarily an obligation or even an ability to influence political affairs.[46] Thus one could be a Roman citizen without necessarily identifying as a Roman; Roman citizenship could be exercised without ever journeying

44. See Gauthier (1974). Indeed, the Athenians increased the restricted nature of their citizenship precisely when their empire had expanded to its greatest extent; in the middle of the fifth century, they passed a law requiring that both parents, not just the father, be Athenian citizens for the child to be a citizen.

45. Roman citizenship has been well studied in the past; the necessary starting point is Sherwin-White (1973).

46. One might usefully compare it with citizenship in a Greek *polis*, where citizens were expected to participate fully in the running of the state. Indeed, according to Aristotle, the definition of a citizen is one who "shares in the administration of justice, and in offices" (*Politics* 1275a 22–23). This close correlation makes legal rights a potentially more useful way to consider identity in a Greek *polis* than in Rome. On the contrast between citizenship in Greece and Rome, see Gauthier (1974).

to the city itself or becoming part of the Roman community in any but a technical sense. While citizenship may create a political and legal identity, it does not advance very far the discussion of the social or cultural identity of being a Roman, and it was precisely the latter that became harder to define as the former became spread over a wider geographical area and as foreign people and foreign cultural elements came to Rome. Rome needed to create a new community with a new collective identity, and over the course of the second and first centuries B.C.E., what emerges in many ways might be considered as an ethnic community, no longer just a *polis*-community. It was in fact the *creation* of this larger group community that enabled the Romans both to solidify their state and to build their empire.

The creation of a sense of ethnic identity was no easy matter for the Romans, for they lacked important elements of a cultural collectivity. The very notion of shared descent posed significant problems for the Romans. Roman myths, in their emphasis on the important role played by foreigners in the early history of the state, tended to stress the lack of shared ancestry among the members of the early Roman community. Although mythology eventually developed a blood relationship between the founder figures Aeneas and Romulus, Roman tradition continued to ascribe the first male population to Romulus' opening of an asylum on the Capitoline to all comers, including numerous unsavory characters. Similarly, the first female population was said to have been stolen from the neighboring Sabines.[47] Furthermore, Titus Tatius, Romulus' coruler, was a Sabine, as was Numa Pompilius, who held the throne following the death of Romulus and hailed from Cures, while the later king Lucumo/Tarquin immigrated from Etruria. These myths emphasized the openness of early Rome and offered an image of the Romans as a nation of immigrants; Roman authors, far from hiding this fact, displayed it proudly. Perhaps more significantly, one did not have to trace one's ancestors back to these primitive beginnings to be thought of as Roman, just as in the United States one does not have to trace ancestry back to the Mayflower; while it may have provided some cachet to certain families, it was not the defining feature of Romanness.[48]

47. Vergil's *Aeneid* is of course the *locus classicus* for the Aeneas narrative, but the legend had been popular in Rome since at least the third century B.C.E. See further Galinsky (1969); Wiseman (1995). Livy provides a connected narrative of the other stories of early Rome in Book I of the *Ab Urbe Condita*, but different pieces can be found in many other authors. It is worth noting that both Aeneas and Romulus are represented as refugees, as people bereft of family and relationships, and alone in a new land.

48. Indeed Gary Farney (2007) has argued that emphasizing one's Latin ethnicity was often used by leading families in the Late Republic as a strategy for political and social advancement.

Nonetheless, these stories of early Rome did provide access to myths of shared descent. Rather than emphasizing direct descent from specific individuals, Roman myths provided a sense of collective descent, which all Romans could share; all Romans, no matter their origins, were in a sense descended from Romulus. One might compare Athenian myths of autochthony, about which Alan Shapiro has written: "What autochthony implies, then, is that, in a collective sense, all historical Athenians are descended from the two founding heroes, even if (or perhaps because) no one Athenian family is descended from either of them."[49] The same might be said of the Romans; although some Roman families did trace their descent specifically from Aeneas, all historical Romans were considered to be descended from the two founding heroes. Livy, for example, indicates that the Romans considered Mars not just as the parent of Rome's founder, but of the Roman people themselves.[50] Commitment to the community allowed one to become part of that community; the moral most frequently attached by the Romans to Romulus' slaying of Remus—"so perish whoever else might cross my walls"—emphasized that loyalty to the group was more important than biological ties in the construction of Roman society.[51] Roman mythology thus provided for myths of shared descent in a figurative sense from both Aeneas and Romulus.

Because myths of shared descent serve as such a crucial building block for ethnic identity, the period when these myths developed offers an indication of when the Romans became concerned to articulate their sense of identity. Recent studies have argued that the two myths that came to dominate Roman thinking about their origins, those of Romulus and Remus and of Aeneas, have their genesis in the late fourth or early third century. T. P. Wiseman has argued that the story of Romulus and Remus dates only from the late fourth or early third century, although Romulus as a single figure may date from a slightly earlier period.[52] Wiseman connects this

---

49. Shapiro (1998), 131. The comparison between Athens and Rome in this regard is further strengthened by the fact that in several of Euripides' tragedies (*Suppliants, Medea*), Athens is portrayed as a home for refugees, just as we have seen that early Rome was portrayed. Myths of autochthony may thus have provided the sense of ethnicity for the Athenians that the myths of foreign arrivals provided for the Romans; Athens's more restrictive citizenship laws may account for the emphasis on myths of autochthony, which imply a closed system, while Rome, as we have seen, had a much more liberal policy on granting citizenship to foreigners.

50. Livy, *Praefatio 7: suum conditorisque sui parentem Martem potissimum ferat.*

51. For the moral, which Livy tells us was the *vulgatior fama*, see Livy 1.7.2.

52. Wiseman (1995).

development with the resolution of the conflict between the patricians and plebeians over the status of the latter; part of the question, which is clearly articulated by Livy in Book 4, involved defining the degree to which plebeians were to be included within the res publica.[53] This period also saw the beginnings of Rome grappling with the consequences of empire on Roman identity. By the end of the fourth century, Rome had extended her territorial control to include most of central Italy and had begun to send out citizen colonies, while the settlement following the suppression of the Latin Revolt in 338 had granted Roman citizenship to the inhabitants of several Latin towns, so that the city walls were no longer the boundaries of Rome. The story of Aeneas and his arrival in Italy was embraced by the Romans in the same period or even slightly later, as Rome expanded further toward Magna Graecia.[54] The myths of Romulus and Aeneas took hold and created a sense of common descent exactly in the period when Roman civic identity was just beginning to be challenged.

In fact, it is remarkable how Rome set about acquiring exactly the aspects of ethnic identity that she lacked at precisely the time that she expanded her territorial dominions. With the development of these myths of descent, by the middle of the third century, Rome possessed five of the attributes previously described by Smith: the myths of shared descent, a name, a history, a territory, and a sense of solidarity. The one feature considered essential to the formation of an ethnic identity that Rome still lacked was the existence not just of a shared culture, but of a distinctive shared culture, one that the differentiated the Romans from other peoples.[55] The word *distinctive* needs to be stressed, for it reminds us of the element of boundaries. It is not the elements that constituted Roman culture, but the ability of the Romans to define and maintain distinctive boundaries that allowed the Romans to be a cohesive social group. The absorption of outsiders into the group and of foreign cultural elements thus need not be seen as a threat to Roman identity as long as the Romans were able to draw distinctions and clearly define what was to be considered Roman. Since the myth of shared descent was by nature permeable in Rome, the ability to define a distinctive culture may have been a particularly important aspect of their identity, and Roman religion needs to be considered as a primary element of that distinctive and shared culture.

53. See for instance the speech of Canuleius, Livy 4.3–5.

54. Gruen, (1992), 28–29; Galinsky, (1969).

55. The term *culture* is, of course, extremely problematic, and I attempt to use it throughout in the relatively neutral sense of what characterizes a people. For a recent brief and cogent discussion of the term, with fuller bibliography, see Wallace-Hadrill (2008), 28–32.

What the late third and second centuries B.C.E. witnessed, then, was nothing less than the creation of a Roman sense of ethnicity. The conquest first of Carthage and then of Greece had dramatically transformed the nature of the Roman state and Roman society; the Senate no longer made decisions solely on Rome and her immediate neighbors, but decided world affairs. The sense of Rome as a small community on the banks of the Tiber was gone forever, and a new community needed to be imagined. A community faced with a change as dramatic as that which Rome faced at the beginning of the second century can head in one of two directions: the disruption can either destroy or renew the community's sense of itself. Anthony Smith has identified four characteristic mechanisms for ethnic self-renewal: (1) religious reform, (2) cultural borrowing, (3) popular participation, often in the form of social movements, and (4) myths of ethnic election, or chosenness.[56] It is remarkable that not just one or two of these mechanisms, but all four make an appearance in the course of the third and second centuries. These four mechanisms also highlight the central importance of religion in the formation of ethnicity; with the exception of the movement for greater popular participation initiated by the Gracchi, religion played a key role in each of these mechanisms at Rome.

It would be presumptuous, however, to claim that religion played the only significant role in shaping a clear sense of identity; other contributing factors are easily identifiable. Latin literature has its origins at exactly this time, and modern studies on nationalism have often emphasized the critical role played by literature in the formation of a national consciousness.[57] Personal habits and customs contributed to a new sense of identity as well; the toga as the quintessential Roman style of clothing becomes prominent in this period, and Andrew Wallace-Hadrill has noted a shift in the style of the toga to make it more distinctive from the Greek pallium that dates precisely from the Augustan period.[58] Beginning in the second century, the Romans also developed a new form of domestic living, the atrium house, which could again be used to distinguish Greek from Roman.[59] In practical

56. Smith (1991), p. 25ff.

57. See Anderson (1983); Hobsbawm (1990); and specifically on the origins of Latin literature, Habinek (1998), 34–68.

58. Wallace-Hadrill (2008), 40–51.

59. Zanker (1998), 16. The fact that the villa was meant to evoke connections with Greece indicates once again the openness of the Romans and their ability to adapt Greek culture for their own ends, yet it does not diminish the fact that this was a new and distinctly Roman form of architecture. Cf. also Wallace-Hadrill (2008), 190–196 on Vitruvius' discussion of the atrium house.

terms, the Romans became more concerned with who counted legally as a Roman; expansion of citizenship, which previously had been one of the cornerstones of Roman policy, seems to come to a halt after the grants to Arpinum, Fundi, and Formiae in 188.[60] These developments work in this same direction as the religious activity to be discussed in this study, also helping to create clearer boundaries between what was Roman and what was not, and thereby to define the Romans as an identifiable ethnic group.

Yet religion is a particularly appropriate area in which to explore the development of Roman identity, not only because religion is considered by modern scholars as a critical element of social group cohesiveness but also because the Romans themselves placed great emphasis on their religion. Religion was the sphere on which the Romans prided themselves the most and that distinguished the Romans from the rest of mankind. They believed that proper religious practice was the cornerstone of their success in conquering the world: their ability to maintain the *pax deorum* had led directly to their imperial success. In the Late Republic, Cicero gave voice to this notion in the following terms: "in piety and proper religious feeling (*religio*), and in that one wisdom which recognizes that everything is ruled and directed by the will (*numen*) of the gods, we have excelled all tribes and nations."[61] Elsewhere, Cicero defines *religio* as "the cult of the gods" and declares that in this the Romans are superior to all outsiders, even while admitting that the Romans may be inferior to outsiders in other spheres.[62] The Romans of the first century also considered that religion more than any other sphere needed to be free from foreign influences. Even Vergil in the *Aeneid*, which frequently glories in the mixed ancestry of the Romans, in the passage cited at the head of this introduction emphasizes the uniqueness of Roman religious practice. Unlike language or dress, Jupiter will not preserve indigenous Italian customs or mix it with the Trojan arrivals, but he will give the new people *mores* and *ritus* of their own. That this picture of unadulterated religious practice does not actually conform to reality is in itself significant. The attempt to create a tradition that all Roman practices were traditional reveals the tensions inherent in the Romans' new conception of themselves, tensions that Cicero, Vergil, and Livy all reveal were still

60. It is possible that we simply do not know about further extensions of the franchise because of the loss of Livy's text for the bulk of the second century. Yet there are no chance references to grants of citizenship in any other sources, and by the end of the second century, the lack of citizenship became a serious issue in Roman-Italian relations.

61. Cic. *Har. resp.* 19.

62. Cic. *Nat. D.* 2.8

present at the time of Augustus, and to which we shall return at the end of this study. For now, it is sufficient to observe that all three authors reveal how critical religion was to the Romans' understanding of themselves and their identity.

It should not be assumed that the Romans consciously manipulated their religious system to redefine Roman identity. Scholars of Roman religion have only recently and at long last demolished the notion that the Roman religion was exploited by a disbelieving aristocracy to maintain their control of the state, or that it was manipulated by individual politicians for personal political advantage.[63] It is not necessary to view politicians as motivated solely by crass political calculation of either personal or community advantage. Roman religion was embedded into the res publica, which means that religious actions had political effects, both for the state or for individuals, and vice versa. In making decisions and shaping Roman religion as they did, the Romans need not have been intentionally delineating a clear sense of Roman identity, but their actions, embedded in a political context, had that effect. The result of the cumulative Roman actions in regard to their religious system during the Middle and Late Republic was in fact to redefine their community from the local *urbs* to a larger ethnic community.

Roman Religious Practices of the Third and Second Century

Despite the changes in Roman society as Rome developed into a world power, Roman religious behavior over the third and second centuries shows a great deal of continuity with the archaic and early period, especially in her continued absorption of foreign cults and foreign influences, behavior that signals the continuation of the open door policy that is the hallmark of early Rome. During the course of the century, however, we can trace the emergence of a new movement that begins to stress the distinctiveness of Roman religious practice. This attitude made itself felt not in the complete rejection of foreign influences, although the number of innovations in the second and first centuries does seem to decrease. Rather, this shift is marked especially by the insistence on marking certain religious practices as either non-Roman or as quintessentially Roman. This practice allowed the

63. The older notion is particularly well expressed by Taylor (1949), 76–97. North (1976), among others, has been critical to displacing this model; now see especially Beard, North, and Price (1998), 114–156.

Romans to maintain the ideology of openness, which the outright exclusion of foreign influences would not, but it also allowed for the emergence of a clear sense of Roman identity by drawing distinctions between Roman and non-Roman practices. As the Romans came into increasing contact with the Greek cultural world and became more familiar with the often exclusionary practices of the Greek cities, the contrast between their approach and the more restrictive Greek approach may have become more evident. It has been suggested that the image of the incorporated outsider became increasingly popular throughout the second century B.C.E, at precisely the period under investigation here.[64] The contrast between Greek and Roman practice, and the effort to build a sense of identity around cultural distinctiveness but not around exclusion, helped the Romans build a solid foundation for their imperial edifice. The current study describes the development of Roman identity in the Republic in three phases: first, tracing Roman behavior in welcoming and incorporating foreign religious elements into their society (chapters 1 and 2); second, exploring how they sharpened and defined the boundaries of Romanness through the late third and early second centuries (chapters 3 through 6); and, third, discussing how those boundaries became blurred in the course of the civil wars of the Late Republic and were reestablished by the emperor Augustus (chapter 7).

Many studies of the openness of Roman religion focus most of their attention on the foreign gods and goddesses who came to Rome and were installed as part of the state religion, and indeed, as the most obvious manifestation of the presence of foreigners, this is a logical place to begin. Chapter 1 thus opens with a survey of the foreign divinities admitted to Rome in the fifth and fourth centuries, including those imported both from Italian cities and from Greece or other overseas territories. Although cults from around the Mediterranean have attracted more scholarly attention, subsequent historical developments should not mislead us into believing that other cities in Italy were sufficiently close to Rome so as not to be considered foreign. The *evocatio* of Juno Regina from Veii in 396 provides an unambiguous case of a foreign cult from Italy, since the *evocatio* ceremony at its core involves the transfer of the enemy's cult to Rome. Equally remarkable are the Roman actions in regard to religion at the conclusion of the Latin Revolt in 338 as the Romans set out to remake their relationship with Latium at this time. The Roman behavior of this early period, while often difficult to discern in detail, provides the essential background for their later activity.

64. Cf. the conclusions of Dench (1995), 108.

Chapter 2 focuses on the cults introduced to Rome between 338 and 201 B.C.E., from the moment when Rome established herself as a major power in central Italy to the time when she established herself as a world power with the successful conclusion of the Second Punic War. Roman expansion during this period brought the state into increasing contact with the Greek cities of southern Italy, Sicily, and the Greek East, and the cults introduced to Rome during this period reflect that geographical range. The incorporation of foreign divinities continued to help the Romans build connections between themselves and other peoples as they expanded their territorial control. The Greek cult of Aesculapius provided a means of reaching out to southern Italy, as did the *ludi Tarentini*, sacred to the underworld deities Dis and Proserpina and inaugurated in 249 B.C.E. during the closing stages of the First Punic War. At the close of the century, the importation of the Magna Mater, together with her special priests the *galli*, strengthened Roman links to the East at a critical moment and suggested continued Roman openness to foreigners, especially as her temple was located on the Palatine hill, traditionally the oldest part of the city. We will have occasion to return to this cult, for several aspects of this cult in Rome—the presence of the *galli* and the development of two sets of rites to celebrate the goddess, including the quintessentially Roman *ludi*, display not only the openness of Roman religion but also the attempt to distinguish Roman from non-Roman practices, and the subsequent chapters treat this phenomenon.

This concern to define Romanness that can be seen in these aspects of the cult of the Magna Mater begins earlier in the third century, and one place to observe this phenomenon is the Roman decision to incorporate not just cults from other cultures, but priests. In the course of the third century, the Romans installed three separate sets of priests from foreign religious traditions into the structure of the state religion, and chapter 3 explores this phenomenon. Etruscan haruspices begin to appear in a formal relationship with the Roman Senate, priestesses for new Greek rites of Ceres were brought up from southern Italy, and as noted previously, the *galli* appeared in Rome at the end of the third century to celebrate the worship of the Magna Mater. The adoption of priests from alien communities provides an unusual testament to the Roman policy, for few other states were willing to accept foreign practitioners of their own religious practice. At the same time, concerns with Romanness emerge in connection with these changes, both in the discourse concerning the nature of these priests and in the rights granted to them, for some of the priests were granted Roman citizenship and others were not. These examples thus provide the opportunity to explore the concerns for both openness and distinctiveness at the same time.

Two developments at the end of the third century during the period of the Second Punic War, both revolving around what modern scholars perceive as characteristic features of Roman religion, make the concern with openness and Romanness apparent. Chapter 4 focuses on the expiation of prodigies, the attempt by the Romans to repair a perceived rupture in their relationship with the gods. During the third century, and especially at the height of the threat posed by Hannibal, the Romans took it upon themselves to expiate not only prodigies occurring on Roman soil but also those occurring on the territory of their Italian allies. This mechanism reveals an important stage in the Roman assertion of a sense of community that included the cities of Italy; the Roman belief that portents occurring on foreign soil affected the Roman state marked that soil as part of the Roman community. The development of *ludi* as the quintessential form of Roman celebration forms the subject of chapter 5. Although *ludi* originated much earlier in Rome, the third century saw an explosion in the number of annual games in Rome, with the *ludi Plebei, Apollinares, Megalenses,* and *Ceriales* added in a twenty-year period at the end of the century, and the *Floralia* added a further twenty-five years later. The chapter explores how the Romans, in a pattern familiar to sociologists, took a practice that dated from their early history and invested it with additional significance to shape their identity. It is noteworthy that the cults given this new form of celebration were either foreign (Apollo, the Magna Mater) or had recently seen Greek-style additions to the original cult (Ceres, Flora), so that we are witnessing simultaneously the development of *ludi* as the quintessentially Roman form of celebration and an effort to Romanize foreign cults. The significance in this development lies less in whatever actual distinctions might exist between Roman and Greek practices than in the Romans' insistence that there was such a difference, because such insistence, as we have seen before, formed the basis of creating boundaries between Greek and Roman and thus maintaining a unique sense of identity.

The reshaping of Roman identity was thus well under way in the late third century B.C.E. as a result of military successes already by that time, but the success of the Roman enterprise in the Second Punic War and the rapid expansion into the Greek East posed additional challenges on this front. Chapter 6 explores several religious incidents of the second century that demonstrate both the Roman attempt to grapple with the relationship to Greece, in light of the increased pace of exchange with Greek culture, and the relationship with the Italian peninsula. These episodes include the notorious affair involving the worship of Bacchus in 186, as well as the burning of the supposed books of Numa in 181 and several incidents that involve banning foreign worship later in the second century. One common strand in these incidents is the symbolic value of declaring particular forms of worship as non-Roman. Similar concerns can be seen in several other developments over the same period, for example, the increasing use of the terms *Graecus ritus* to designate different styles of ritual practice.[65] The artificiality of the distinctions that the Romans drew in this case is particularly significant; the label created the distinction, which allowed the Romans to foster a sense of their identity, and the distinction drawn against another corporate group, "the Greeks," allowed the Romans to foster a sense of themselves as a larger corporate group. In this conception, the Roman community was not simply limited to Rome but to those who utilized the *patrius ritus* and hence could encompass other inhabitants of Italy. This new conception is thus a significant step on the road toward creating a new vision of the Romans, one capable of including other inhabitants of Italy. The process of incorporating Rome's Italian allies within the boundaries of Romanness was not always smooth or without conflict, but the developments of the second century show consistent movement in that direction.

While the Social War marks a critical stage in the redefinition of these boundaries, its impact was overshadowed by even more fundamental questions about Roman identity: who among the inhabitants of Rome was a true Roman, and more important, who decided this question? Chapter 7 examines the struggles of the late Republic and the degree to which the very definition of who might count as a Roman became a highly contested subject at this time, between Roman and Roman, as well as between Roman and other inhabitants of Italy. Without a clear sense of Roman identity, the religious activity of the Late Republic is perhaps a less useful tool for understanding the boundaries of Romanness, but the religious actions of the individual dynasts reveal precisely the grounds on which Roman identity was contested. All parties strove to present themselves as truly Roman and their opponents as the ones who should no longer be included within that community, and the frequent recourse to religious activity by the dynasts of the Late Republic attests to the central place of religion in helping to shape Roman identity. While the behavior toward a foreign cult or practice at this time thus cannot be taken as indicative of a collective Roman identity, it does point the way toward how that identity was conceived and reconceived by the different political leaders.

It is only with the triumph of Octavian that it is possible once again to look to religion for its role in reflecting and shaping Roman identity. The religious "reforms" of the first emperor, in particular regarding foreign

65. Scheid (1995).

cults, contributed to his efforts to rebuild Roman society and reconstruct Roman identity. While it has long been noted that the triumph of Augustus marked the triumph of the Italian communities, and that one of Augustus' accomplishments was to bring the towns of Italy into fuller participation in the Roman system, the role of the emperor's religious activities in this process has long been understated. From the continued adaptation of foreign cults to the reshaping of old rituals to the invention of traditions, Augustus bound together many developments that had occurred haphazardly over the past two centuries as he strove to include *tota Italia* within the boundaries of Romanness. The development of stronger polarities between Roman and Greek, and between Roman and Egyptian, strengthened the position of Italy as "Roman" while still including Greeks and even Egyptians within the framework of the empire. The patterns of behavior set during the third and second centuries B.C.E. were thus reformulated by Augustus and established a model for the incorporation of outside communities and the redefinition of Roman identity, a model that would set the tone for relations between Rome and the provinces for the *longue durée* of the empire. Understanding that behavior is crucial to an exploration of Roman identity, and it is to that exploration that we now turn.

1

Foreign Cults in Rome

It has become a commonplace to remark on the openness of the Roman religious system to foreign influences, and indeed, many foreign gods and goddesses did come to Rome and were installed on the public festival calendar. Yet despite the Romans' penchant for adopting foreign cults and practices, they did not simply accept any and every god they encountered, nor was there any methodical attempt to assemble all the chief deities of defeated towns. Many divinities were brought to Rome and installed as part of the Roman state religion, but a great many more were not. No city appears to have had more than one divinity adopted by the Romans, implying that the remainder of their pantheon was not brought to Rome. More significantly, many cities did not have any of their divinities or practices brought to Rome; over the course of her territorial expansion, down to 133 B.C.E., Rome fought approximately twenty major wars and defeated countless cities both large and small, yet her pantheon at the end of the Republic numbered approximately eighty divinities, and a number of these were based on abstract concepts such as Spes or Fides. Certainly, there may have been a practical aspect to limiting the number of new deities, as the pantheon and the religious calendar would quickly have become unmanageable otherwise, but the absence of so many deities means that the Romans' behavior cannot be ascribed to a theological desire to avoid incurring the wrath of any divinity they encountered during their expansion. There were many deities of whose existence they became aware and whom they did not choose to honor with a place in their official pantheon. The decision to erect a temple to any particular divinity thus represents a conscious choice on the part of the Romans. As John North phrased it in a seminal study of the expansion of the Roman pantheon, "Their actions related to specific circumstances and transactions, not to a general method," so our task becomes to illuminate those circumstances and transactions.[1]

While the introductions of foreign cults responded to a theological need on the part of the Romans, the embedded nature of Roman religion within Roman society means that religious activities had political and social consequences.[2] In many circumstances, we can observe that these cult introductions had strong geopolitical overtones; that is, the action had implications not only for the Roman people themselves but also for Rome's relationship with a foreign community, a people living outside Rome. Sometimes the Romans imported a divinity from a place where they were on good terms with the inhabitants, but many times the divinity adopted had been worshipped by a people the Romans had just defeated in battle. This particular behavior—adopting the gods of their enemies rather than attempting to eradicate them—was not common among the polytheistic societies of the ancient Mediterranean. Victory in war was viewed as a sign that one's own gods were more powerful than those of the enemy, which left little reason to worship the "weaker" god.[3] When the Romans imported the gods of their vanquished opponents, there are no indications that they treated these divinities as subject to the other gods in their pantheon; rather, they worshipped them on an equal level with their other divinities. The absorption of the deity of a defeated people may be seen, therefore, as less a sign of imperial conquest and more an indication of a religious bond between the two peoples: both the victor and the vanquished now worshipped the same deity, and the victor even accepted the authority of the deity of

1. North (1993), 136.

2. By "theological need," I aim to recognize that the Romans felt a legitimate religious need to invoke the power of a new god. While the point of the present study is to analyze the political and social functions that religious actions played in Republican Rome, this emphasis should not be taken to mean that the Romans consciously manipulated their religious system or accepted divinities in whom they did not believe as part of their religion solely for political reasons. The Romans acted in a way that was consistent with their belief structure, and if moderns have difficulty understanding the Roman mind-set, that is a problem for us to resolve. On connections between religion and statecraft in Rome, see, e.g., Wardman (1982) and Beard, North, and Price (1998); on the need to divorce ourselves from modern, often Christianizing assumptions about religion, see Scheid (1987).

3. Compare the Babylonians, who destroyed sanctuaries and carried gods off into "captivity" rather than worshipping them.

the vanquished people.[4] Although this type of imperialistic behavior may have been unusual for the ancient world, it is fully consistent with Roman behavior in other arenas; as has been noted many times, the Romans were much more liberal with grants of citizenship, even to defeated peoples, than other ancient communities.[5]

This habit of adopting foreign divinities that created or strengthened a bond between the Romans and the particular people or region who worshipped that divinity stretches back to at least the fifth century B.C.E. and continues through the Republican period and into the Empire. Reconstructing the religious development of archaic Rome is perhaps the most impossible task for the historian of Roman religion. The sources come from a much later period, when the Romans themselves were beginning to try to make sense of their religious tradition, and the gaps in the record are too numerous to allow us to be confident in the details of the picture. As time passed, the Romans became aware of the presence of foreign practices in their religious system and even more self-conscious about their adoption of foreign practices, as is demonstrated in subsequent chapters. Nevertheless, for the early period there is abundant evidence of cultural borrowing and the forging of links between Rome and other communities through religious observance. The Roman religious system, just like other elements of early Roman society, was open to elements from outside the city.

The cult of Hercules provides an early example of such cultural receptivity. Both literary and archaeological evidence suggest that Hercules, whose worship was widespread over the Mediterranean basin, was honored in Rome from the archaic period; his cult at the Ara Maxima near the Forum Boarium was his oldest in Rome. The literary sources, none of which is earlier than the second century B.C.E., connect the institution of this cult to the Arcadian king Evander, who wished to honor Hercules for subduing the monster Cacus.[6] While the story is obviously an aetiological myth that may

4. For an interesting comparison to the Romans, see Holloway (2001). Holloway demonstrates that the Neo-Assyrian Empire's treatment of foreign cults served as a means of exercising control over its territory, either through terror, in the form of the destruction of sanctuaries, the despoliation of images, or the installation of Assyrian images in foreign temples, or through "diplomacy," in the reconstruction of foreign sanctuaries or the participation of the Assyrian court in local sacrificial ceremonies. One significant difference between the behavior of the Romans and the Assyrians is that the latter do not seem to have installed local cults in Assur.

5. Cf. Gauthier (1974).

6. This essential fact remains part of all the accounts, though many details differ from author to author. Cf. Dion. Hal., *Ant. Rom.* 1.33; Livy 1.7; Verg., *Aen.* 8.267–279; Cassius Hemina, *Origins of the Roman Race* 6.7; Varro, in Macrob., *Sat.* 1.12.28; Plut. *Quaest. Rom.* 60; Prop. 4.9. On the different versions of the story, see Bayet (1926), 127–154. More recent treatments of particular aspects of these presentations include Fantham (1992) and Staples (1998), 17–24.

date back to only the fourth century, the connection to a pre-Romulean hero evokes the Roman sense of the great antiquity of the cult. Many archaic Roman institutions were assigned to one of the kings of Rome, but the worship of Hercules was associated with Evander, a Greek king supposedly living on the site of Rome at the time of Aeneas; Romulus was even supposed to have sacrificed to Hercules at the Ara Maxima.[7] This association may reflect a sense among the Romans that worship of Hercules was even older than other archaic institutions, and certainly pre-Republican. In this instance, the archaeological evidence lends support to this notion, for excavations in the Sant' Omobono sanctuary near the Forum Boarium have revealed a large quantity of Greek pottery from the eighth century.[8] These deposits provide strong evidence for Greek presence in Roman religion in the archaic period.

The Roman cult of Hercules possessed a strong Greek flavor, even if the deposits just mentioned may not be directly connected to a sanctuary of Hercules. The Roman legends about Hercules are shot through with elements that reveal the fundamental Roman conception that the cult of Hercules was Greek. As noted previously, the specific connection of Hercules to the Arcadian Evander may date back to only the fourth century, but the story of Cacus provides a clear connection to Greek culture, seen most clearly in the name of the monster (or bandit, depending on the version). This word is clearly a Latinized spelling of κακός, Greek for "evil one," providing an indication that the entire story was probably taken lock, stock, and bandit from a Greek version, perhaps one current in the Greek cities of southern Italy. Roman practice reflected the notion of Hercules as a Greek cult with the use of the "Greek rite" in performing the sacrifice.[9] While John Scheid has demonstrated that the "Greek rite" is a later invention by the Romans, its ascription to this cult indicates that the Romans felt the need to mark this cult as foreign.[10] The cult of Hercules demonstrates that the absorption of foreign cults was a part of Roman religion from the outset, even if neither we nor the Romans can specify the exact circumstances and reasons for the adoption of Hercules in Rome.

Archaeological evidence provides further proof that archaic Roman religion was receptive to Greek influences. The god Vulcan possessed a cult center at the base of the Capitoline hill, known variously as the *Volcanal* or the *area Volcani*, and Roman tradition ascribed the foundation of the open-air altar to Titus Tatius, the king of the Sabines who become coruler of Rome with Romulus in the wake

7. Livy 1.7.
8. La Rocca (1977).
9. Livy 1.7.
10. Scheid (1995).

of the Rape of the Sabine Women.[11] As noted with Hercules, the ascription by Roman tradition to a regal founder implies a foundation date no later than the sixth century, though not necessarily as early as the traditional mid-eighth-century date of Romulus. More significantly, however, excavations in the Roman forum have identified this early sanctuary of Vulcan and in a votive deposit discovered an Athenian black-figure vase with an image of Hephaestus.[12] The vase provides evidence of contact with mainland Greece, either directly or indirectly, and demonstrates that the identification of Vulcan with the Greek god of the forge had occurred already in the sixth century. Such evidence explodes the modern myth that the identification of Roman divinities with their Greek counterparts occurred only in the third century with the expansion of Roman territory and contacts with the East. As we will see soon, the effect of those later contacts is visible in religious developments of that period, but they were not a novel feature of Roman religious practice.

Similar receptivity to Greek religious influence can be seen from the very beginning of the Republic in the first decade of the fifth century through the end of the century. The temple of Ceres, Liber and Libera, apparently an Italic dyad in origin but later assimilated to the Greek divinities Demeter, Bacchus, and Kore, was built in 493; according to Pliny the Elder, the temple was decorated by the Greek artists Damophilus and Gorgasos.[13] The reference to Greek artists in Rome once seemed unlikely, despite Pliny's statement that the inscription referring to the two artists was visible in his own day, but it appears much more trustworthy in light of the evidence concerning Vulcan discussed earlier. Ten years later, Castor and Pollux received a temple in the Forum in the wake of the victory at Lake Regillus; the famous inscription from Lavinium reading *Castorei Podlouque qurois* by its transliteration from the Greek reveals the ultimate origins of this cult, though the degree to which the cult may have been mediated through southern Italy remains open to debate.[14] Although the cult of the Dioscuri developed in a distinctly Roman fashion, emphasizing Castor to the near exclusion of

11. Dion. Hal., *Ant. Rom.* 2.50.3; Varro, *Rust.*, 5.74.

12. Coarelli (1977). On Vulcan and Hephaistos, see Capdeville (1995), 271–287.

13. Plin. *HN* 35.154. For the temple's foundation, see Dion. Hal., *Ant. Rom.* 6.17. For discussion of the cult's origins, see Le Bonniec (1958), 292–305; Spaeth (1996), 1–11. See also Momigliano (1967), 310–311, who suggests that the cult may have had strong connections with the Greeks of southern Italy, a suggestion that conforms well with the argument presented here but that I regard as a bit too speculative for confidence.

14. See Weinstock (1960) for discussion of the Lavinium inscription. Inscriptional and literary evidence also reveals worship of Castor and Pollux at Tusculum; cf. *CIL* 14.2620, 2629, 2637, 2639, and 2918; Cic. *Div.* 1.98. On the origins of the cult, cf. Latte (1960), 173–176; Richard (1978), 510–511.

Pollux, Roman legend does recall the Greek origins of the cult through myth, which recounts the miraculous appearance at the battle of Lake Regillus of two horsemen, who then afterward watered their horses in the Forum at the site of their future temple.[15] Another Greek god, Apollo, was worshipped in Rome already by 449 and received his first temple in 431 as a response to a plague ravaging the city.[16] In mainland Greece by the fifth century, the healing aspect of Apollo had become sublimated to his prophetic and cultural aspects, which may suggest that this older version of Apollo also came to Rome indirectly through southern Italy, but from where remains a mystery.[17] With regard to all of the Greek cults that became part of the Roman state religion from the archaic period through the late fifth century, there is little to suggest that Roman imperialism is at work here. Rome had not yet succeeded in establishing herself as a power in Italy, and none of the traditions relating to these cults connects their arrival in Rome with military defeat of the cult's original home; indeed, only Castor and Pollux are connected to war at all.[18] The arrival of these cults and others in Rome reveals the permeability of Roman religious boundaries and the expansion of the Roman pantheon even before the expansion of Roman power.

With the expansion of Roman power, we can begin to trace the relationship between Roman imperialism and Roman religion. In the fourth century, the Romans continued to be receptive to the worship of foreign cults, but during this period their religious actions related more directly to their military successes as they established their hegemony over central Italy. Juno Regina, brought to Rome from Veii in 396 B.C.E., provides an appropriate place to begin our analysis of this period, both as the earliest foreign cult introduced as part of Roman imperialism and because it illustrates many of the important features of the process. Juno Regina is also one of the more famous foreign cults imported to Rome, as the clearest example of an *evocatio*, a ceremony that Livy reports in some detail.[19] In 396, on the verge of capturing the city of Veii after a long siege, the dictator Camillus invited the goddess to leave her current home and move to Rome:

15. The official name of the temple in Rome was apparently *aedes Castoris*, though *aedes Castrorum* is occasionally found; *aedes Castoris et Pollucis* is relatively rare. Cf. Platner and Ashby, 102–105, and also Schilling (1960). For the appearance of Castor and Pollux at the battle and after, see Dion. Hal., *Ant. Rom.* 6.13.

16. Livy 3.63; 4.20–25.

17. The classic work on Apollo is Gagé (1955).

18. In Livy's version, the cult is a result of a vow made at the battle of Lake Regillus against a combined Latin force, while Dionysius of Halicarnassus tells the aetiological fable of miraculous horsemen appearing to announce the results of the battle.

19. Livy 5.21–23; 5.31.

"Juno Regina, you who now inhabits Veii, I pray that you will follow us as victors to our city, soon to be your city, where a shrine worthy of your majesty will receive you."[20] Chosen youths from the Roman army, purified and dressed in white garments, then obtained the consent of the goddess to transport her statue to Rome, where it was brought to the Aventine hill and eventually installed in a temple constructed there and dedicated in 392 B.C.E.[21] Although Juno had been worshipped in Rome since 509 as part of the Capitoline triad, possibly with the epithet Regina, the goddess introduced in 396 was an entirely separate deity, stated from the outset to have come from a foreign town and housed in a separate shrine on the Aventine hill, with her own festival day on the calendar.[22] The cult brought to Rome in 396 had certain non-Roman elements, and the goddess was probably an Etruscan Uni, the chief female deity of the Etruscan pantheon.[23] As a result of the Roman action, with the destruction of the town and the transport of the goddess to Rome, the cult at Veii ceased to exist, but the Romans ensured that the cult would continue to receive worship, and a memory of the cult's origins as an Etruscan cult was preserved.[24]

This incident has received much attention from modern scholars as the best attested and most fully described *evocatio*, a ceremony often considered to have been illustrative of Roman behavior and to have been repeated on numerous occasions.[25] The performance of this ritual reveals an ancient theology that believed that the state was defenseless without the help of its god. The Roman emphasis on maintaining the *pax deorum* indicates that they shared in this belief, and several imperial texts describe the mysterious name of Rome that was not to be uttered, for its discovery by enemies would leave Rome at their mercy.[26] Analysis of the importation of Juno Regina is complicated by the historiographical overtones of this incident, including the emphasis on the *evocatio*. Roman literary tradition likened the siege of Veii to the siege of Troy; Livy has Appius Claudius Crassus

20. Livy 5.21: *Iuno regina, quae nunc Veios colis, precor, ut nos uictores in nostram tuamque mox futuram urbem sequare, ubi te dignum amplitudine tua templum accipiat.*

21. Livy 5.22.

22. On the Capitoline Juno, see Palmer (1974), 22–23. For the later identification as Juno Regina, see Val. Max 5.10.2; Cic. *Scaur.* 47; and Livy 3.17.3.

23. Bloch (1972), 392–393; Palmer (1974), 21–29.

24. On the preservation of the memory that Juno Regina originated in Etruria, see p. 90–92, 126–30.

25. On *evocatio*, see Basanoff (1947), LeGall (1976); more recently Blomart (1997) and Gustafsson (2000), who offers a lengthy discussion of the Veian episode on pp. 83–105.

26. Plut., *Quaest. Rom.* 61. Plin. *HN*, 3.65; 28.18.

explicitly compare the two campaigns, and the siege of Veii lasts ten years, as did the Trojan War.[27] By the Late Republic, the tradition that Troy fell only after the Palladium had been stolen from the citadel at Troy was well established at Rome, and the similarity between that incident and the evocation of Juno Regina from Veii needs little elaboration.[28] The key theological difference between the two stories is that the Palladium was stolen by Odysseus, according to most traditions, while in the *evocatio* as Livy presents it, Juno Regina *voluntarily* chose to leave her besieged city in favor of the attackers. This element points out that the *evocatio* had two purposes: to deprive the town of its tutelary deity and so make its capture easier (or possible) and also to establish worship of the deity by the victor. Juno Regina was not "captured" as the Palladium was. The difference here highlights exactly the difference between the Roman attitude of adopting foreign deities and the more usual Mediterranean behavior of capturing and destroying cult places. While there is clearly literary embroidery in Livy's account, the important fact for our purpose is that the Romans introduced the worship of the leading goddess of their enemy's pantheon into their religious system at the same moment as they conquered the city of Veii itself.[29]

Livy's account, precisely because it offers an educated Roman's view of the importation of Juno Regina, provides a good starting point for an understanding of this incident. In Book 5, the historian is deeply

27. Appius Claudius: Livy 5.4.11–12. Ten years' duration: Livy 5.22.8 See Kraus (1994), 271–273, and Ogilvie (1970) for further parallels.

28. Kraus (1994), 272, also calls attention to the religious overtones of the fall of Troy in Livy's account of the capture of Veii.

29. The very fact that Livy presented the transfer of Juno Regina to Rome as an *evocatio* may have been intended precisely to emphasize her "foreignness"; the nature of the ritual, performed on the tutelary deity of her enemy, is such that it could be performed only on a goddess whom the Romans considered foreign. Gustafsson (2000) has discussed the ritual of *evocatio* from a historiographical viewpoint and suggested (82) that *evocatio* "has been emphasized, accentuated, and theologically elaborated, or may even be a fiction, in connection with certain important milestones in Roman history." It is noteworthy that the other goddess most frequently asserted as coming to Rome via *evocatio* is Juno Caelestis of Carthage, the other most potent enemy of Rome during the Republic. Even if one assumes that the entire ceremony of *evocatio* was embroidered by Roman sources, that embroidery points to a recognition of the deities involved as clearly foreign, perhaps even "more foreign" than other deities, and thus highlights even more strongly the Roman openness by their willingness to adopt even the tutelary deity of a mortal enemy. On the possible *evocatio* at Carthage, see Macrob. *Sat.* 3.9.7; Serv. *Ad. Aen.* 12.841; Wissowa (1912) 312–13; Basanoff (1947) 63–66, and now Gustafsson(2000), 59–60, 71.

concerned with the question of Roman identity and its survival, and Veii plays a prominent role in his approach.[30] The Etruscan city is assimilated to the paradigmatic *urbs capta*, Troy, the mother city of Rome, and an example to which Rome will be compared when she herself is captured by the Gauls.[31] At two separate points in his narrative, proposals are put forth to move the population of the city to Veii: once after the conquest of Veii, when the plebeian tribunes suggested dividing the population in half and inhabiting two cities that might form one state, and again after the Gallic sack, when the tribunes proposed moving the entire population to Veii rather than rebuilding Rome.[32] We need not believe that such proposals were seriously put forward at this time, but they raise the question of whether Rome would still be Rome if it were located at Veii, and so they are central to Livy's project in Book 5. Livy addresses this question directly with the climactic speech of Camillus at the end of the book, which outlines his view of what it means to be Roman: a move to Veii or anywhere else would make the city no longer Rome, for it is necessary to celebrate Roman rites at Rome in the place where they have always been worshipped. In its assertion that Roman gods can be worshipped only at Rome, Camillus' speech implies that Juno Regina is no longer a Veian goddess. The goddess worshipped in Rome is uniquely Roman, because she is worshipped at Rome by Roman magistrates and her festival falls on the Kalends of September in the Roman religious calendar; were she still an Etruscan divinity, she would still receive worship in Veii from Etruscan priests. Furthermore, Livy makes a point of noting that by Etruscan usage, the statue of Juno Regina in Veii was touched only by the priests of one particular house; when the Roman youths laid hands on the statue to move it to Rome, that physical action, inconsistent with Etruscan practice, demonstrated that the cult was already being treated as Roman.[33] The change of name, from the Etruscan Uni to the Roman Juno Regina, further symbolizes the change from an Etruscan to a Roman goddess.[34] These elements certainly point to an aspect of "religious imperialism" involved with the transfer of the goddess to Rome.

30. On this topic, see Kraus (1994), 278–282.

31. Kraus (1994), 270–278.

32. Livy 5. 24–25, 29–30, 49–50.

33. Cf. Livy 5.22.

34. This may explain why Livy never complains that Juno Regina was a foreign goddess; he considered her a Roman goddess on par with the other divinities in the Roman pantheon. While the name change could be seen as merely another instance of *interpretatio Romana*, other divinities who came to Rome were worshipped without changing their names, such as Apollo or Aesculapius.

Nonetheless, the goddess continued to receive worship, in contrast to her hapless former worshippers, and Camillus' speech again provides clues to understanding Roman attitudes. Camillus suggests that if the Romans ever were to move from their current physical location, it would have been preferable to do so from a position of strength following Rome's triumph over Veii rather than in the wake of her defeat by the Gauls:

> For we will seem not to have left our fatherland as victors, but to have lost it because we were vanquished; it will seem as though it was the flight at the Allia, the capture of the City, the beleaguering of the Capitol, which imposed a necessity upon us to desert our household gods and to decree for ourselves exile and flight from a place which we were not able to defend.[35]

Although there is a certain tendentiousness about Camillus' argument against the plebeians here, his argument is fully consistent with Roman notions of the importance of victory. Applying his attitude to the arrival of Juno Regina, we note that the Veian goddess similarly acted from a position of strength; the *evocatio* presupposes that she *chose* to leave Veii, rather than being forced out by a defeat.[36] She might then be honored fully in Rome with a brand new home, "a shrine worthy of [her] majesty" (Livy 5.21) on the Aventine hill, in contrast to the surviving human inhabitants, who resisted and whose homes were therefore leveled before they themselves were sold into slavery and exile. The contrast between the treatment of Veii's divine inhabitant and her human inhabitants discloses a crucial point of the Roman ideology: those who are willing to add their strength to the Roman side will be welcomed and given a place within the Roman community, while those who are not will be treated harshly. An important principle in Roman expansion is that individual treatment was meted out to different communities based on their behavior, and in

---

35. Livy 5.53: *Non enim reliquisse uictores, sed amisisse uicti patriam uidebimur: hoc ad Alliam fuga, hoc capta urbs, hoc circumsessum Capitolium necessitas imposuisse ut desereremus penates nostros exsiliumque ac fugam nobis ex eo loco conscisceremus quem tueri non possemus.*

36. While it might seem to us that Veii was on the point of defeat, and so the goddess was merely anticipating the inevitable, that interpretation responds to our modern skepticism about ancient religious beliefs. The *evocatio* or similar ceremonies held meaning for the ancients because of the importance of the gods to victory; for a believer, the city would not have fallen without evoking the goddess, and thus theologically the goddess possessed a free choice to either defend her original homeland or agree to move to a new home.

this regard gods and humans are no different. In the context of the destruction of the city, the Romans made a point of respecting the statue of the goddess and chose to incorporate her cult within their religious system rather than subjugate or destroy it. This willingness to accept Juno Regina within the Roman state, especially at a moment when the Romans had proven themselves superior militarily and thus religiously, provided a means to demonstrate the openness of the Roman state to those who were ready and able to bring aid, in this case a goddess who brought victory to Rome.

The next goddess to receive a temple in Rome was Juno Lucina, whose shrine was dedicated on the Esquiline on March 1, 375, though she may have been worshipped in a grove in Rome prior to this date. Livy, focused on the Struggle of the Orders, does not mention the founding of this temple, a salutary reminder to us that the historian does not record the foundation of every temple in Rome. The date is known from Pliny the Elder, whose primary concern is with the lotus tree that stood in the *area Lucinae* and who remarks only in passing on the temple founded in 375 B.C.E.[37] The Praenestine calendar provides some additional information: a notice from Verrius Flaccus claims that the temple was dedicated by married women following a vow by the wife (or possibly the daughter) of Albinus for a safe childbirth.[38] The story is patently an aetiological fable intended to explain the maternal connections to this temple, particularly the Matronalia held annually at the temple.[39] Other early temples connected with women have similar aetiological stories, such as the temple of Fortuna Muliebris, supposedly founded as a result of the intervention of Coriolanus' wife and mother in averting his attack.[40] These stories serve to assert the patriarchal vision of the proper behavior of Roman women, but it is extremely unlikely that the legend passed down by Flaccus has any connection to the actual circumstances in which Juno Lucina was granted a temple.

All is not lost, however, in attempting to glean some understanding of the foundation of a temple to Juno Lucina. Robert Palmer has drawn attention to

37. Plin. *HN* 16.235. Pliny's discussion creates the impression that a precinct to Lucina had existed before the temple, but Pliny's derivation of "Lucina" from *lucus*, "grove," may have led him to retroject the existence of the cult. "Lucina" appears to have been derived from *lux*, "light," for the goddess who helps babies see the light of day. Cf. Palmer (1974), 19–21.

38. Cf. Palmer (1974), 19–20.

39. Palmer (1974), 20.

40. On the temple of Fortuna Muliebris, see Livy 2.40.1–12; Dion. Hal., *Ant. Rom.* 8.55; Plut. *Coriolanus* 37. See also Champeaux (1982), 335–374; Mustakallio (1990).

a pair of inscribed cippi found in the vicinity of Capua and dedicated centuries after the introduction of Juno Lucina in Rome.[41] They read: *[Herc]ole
[Tusc]olana sacra* and *Iunone Loucina Tusculana sacra.* These inscriptions
indicate the existence of a "Tusculan rite" for these dedications to Hercules
and to Juno Lucina, though we know nothing else of the rite or even when
it may have come into existence. Another group of inscriptions, also of the
imperial period, indicates the existence of *sacerdotes Tusculani*, priests who
apparently concerned themselves with Tusculan rites, perhaps of the sort
indicated on the inscribed cippi. These inscriptions thus suggest a connection
between Juno Lucina and Tusculum, as well as between Rome and Tusculum,
and these connections may be useful in understanding the arrival of Juno
Lucina in Rome, particularly in light of the history of Tusculum's relationship with Rome. Under the year 381, Livy recounts the rather unusual way in
which Tusculum was brought under Roman hegemony; having incurred the
wrath of the Roman Senate for authorizing some soldiers to fight alongside
the Volscians, the people of Tusculum chose not to engage the Roman army
in battle. Rather, they opened the city gates to Camillus, journeyed to Rome
to beg the forgiveness of the Senate, and were rewarded with peace and soon
after with full citizenship.[42] The chronological proximity of the settlement
with Tusculum and the construction of a temple to Juno Lucina create strong
grounds for positing a connection between the two events: as the Romans
incorporated Tusculum within the state, they also brought Juno Lucina into
her pantheon.[43] The differences between the arrival of Juno Lucina and Juno
Regina could not be starker; in the case of the former, there was no need for
an *evocatio*, because the Romans and Tusculans settled their differences without resorting to arms. Nor did the cult of Juno Lucina cease to exist outside
Rome, as the inscribed cippi show. In this instance, it is difficult to support a
thesis of religious imperialism, since the Tusculans were not deprived of their
cult; rather, the erection of a temple to this goddess in Rome created a parallel
between the human and the divine spheres. As the Tusculans were granted
citizenship in the Roman state, Juno Lucina was granted an official place in
the Roman pantheon.

The most interesting set of religious actions taken by the Romans during
the fourth century followed the final defeat of the Latin League in 338, perhaps the seminal event in the development of Roman power in Italy. After

41. Palmer (1974), 21. The cippi can be found in *CIL* 12.1581–82 = Dessau, *ILS*
3099–3099a.

42. Livy 6.25–26.

43. Palmer (1974), 21, puts this relationship in the strongest terms: "The annexation
of Tusculum in 381 and the Roman dedication of a temple to Juno Lucina in 375 should
be related to each other."

their victory, the Romans were faced with the problem of how to treat the rebel states, and their response was to deal with the Latin states on an individual basis, according to what the Romans felt was appropriate for each, rather than to treat the entire league as a unity.[44] This approach is already evident in the fourth century, as we have seen with Veii and Tusculum, and became the standard Roman modus operandi in dealing with conquered territory and, indeed, the key to successful Roman expansion. Thus, the Veliterni, whom Livy describes as *veteres cives Romanos*, were severely punished because they had often revolted: their walls were leveled, their Senate relocated, and their land given to Roman colonists. The Tiburtes and the Praenestines were deprived of territory, while most of the Latins were deprived of the *ius conubium* and the *ius commercium* and prohibited from holding *concilia*. On the other hand, the Campanians, Fundani, and Formiani were granted *civitas sine suffragio* for refusing to join the Latins and for providing safe passage through their territory.

More interesting for our purposes are the arrangements made by the Romans regarding the town of Lanuvium. Despite the fact that the inhabitants of this town had participated in the revolt up to the very end, resuming fighting after the defeat at Trifanum in 340, Livy reports that "Lanuvium received the full citizenship and the restitution of her sacred things, with the proviso that the temple and grove of Juno Sospita should belong in common to the Roman people and the citizens living at Lanuvium."[45] That the *sacra* needed to be restored implies, of course, that the Romans had taken these when they conquered the city, but that they should have decided to return them to this town, alone of the towns mentioned, is curious. Furthermore, contrary to the other cases examined in this chapter, the Romans did not bring Juno Sospita to Rome at this time, but rather left the goddess in Lanuvium and undertook to share the worship of the goddess in Lanuvium.[46] While these arrangements make explicit a link between the religious actions of the Romans and their political actions—granting citizenship on condition of the sharing of a cult—it is not clear from Livy why Lanuvium

44. For these dispositions, see Livy 8.14.

45. Livy 8.14: *Lanuvinis ciuitas data sacraque sua reddita, cum eo ut aedes lucusque Sospitae Iunonis communis Lanuvinis municipibus cum populo Romano esset.* The Aricini, Nomentani, and Pedani were given citizenship on the same basis as the Lanuvians, but apparently without any stipulation about their gods; while Livy's language states that these towns were given the same legal status as Lanuvium (*eodem iure quo Lanuvini in civitatem accepti*), no religious proviso is mentioned.

46. A temple to Juno Sospita was eventually built in Rome in 194 B.C.E., a circumstance to be examined later, but the evidence indicates that worship continued in Lanuvium even after the temple in Rome was dedicated.

was singled out for this treatment.[47] We know of no particular association between the Romans and Lanuvium or Juno Sospita that might explain why they chose to single out this goddess and this city for special treatment. We do, however, know of the existence in Rome of *sacerdotes Lanuvini* from imperial inscriptions, just as we know of *sacerdotes Tusculani*, that attest to the importance of the continuation of Lanuvian religious activity into the Empire.[48] The curious phrase "holding the cult of Juno Sospita in common (*communis esset*)" with the people of Lanuvium may be at least partly explained by a reference from Cicero; in the *Pro Murena*, he indicates that the Roman consuls made an annual visit to Lanuvium to sacrifice to Juno Sospita.[49] Unlike with Juno Regina, therefore, the Romans assumed responsibility to sacrifice to the goddess of an enemy town in her own sanctuary, without moving her to Rome and without excluding the original worshippers from the sanctuary. The Roman action here is even more noteworthy than in regard to Veii, and yet this incident has attracted far less scholarly attention and has yet to be satisfactorily explained.

The decision to worship Juno Sospita at her sanctuary in Lanuvium was a mark of high honor, as can be best illustrated by the other instances in which Roman magistrates with *imperium* traveled outside the city to perform ceremonies of a religious character: the *feriae Latinae* on the Alban mount and annual sacrifices to the Penates at Lavinium. Roman magistrates presided over the *feriae Latinae* on the Alban mount; they performed the sacrifices there and divided the meat among the representatives of the Latin towns.[50] The *feriae Latinae* began on a *dies conceptivus*, that is, not on the same day but on a day fixed for its celebration; by the middle Republic, the Roman pontiffs had the responsibility for setting the date, usually early in the year.[51] The other religious obligation for Roman magistrates outside the city

47. For one attempt at an explanation, see Chiarucci (1983), 27–34.

48. On these *sacerdotes Lanuvini*, see Gordon (1938), 46–48. For suggestions on these priests, and others with similar names such as the *sacerdotes Tusculani*, see Mommsen (1887), III.579, n. 4; Wissowa (1912), 520–521.

49. Cicero, *Mur.* 90. It is certainly possible that Livy's phrase encompassed more than just this one annual sacrifice.

50. The most detailed description comes from Dion. Hal., *Ant. Rom.* 4.49; though he (falsely) ascribes the foundation of the festival to Tarquin the Younger, his description of the rituals may be accepted as valid at least for his own day, for he remarks that they were still being performed, and other authors make allusions to elements noted by Dionysius. Cf. Varro, *Ling.* 6.25; Cic., *Planc.* 23 (with *Schol. Bob.*); Cic. *Div.* 1.11.18. Livy several times makes mention of the portions belonging to each city, e.g., 32.1; 37.3.

51. See, e.g., Cic. *Div.* 1.11.18, who notes the presence of snow on the Alban mount when he performed the rite in 63.

also took place at the beginning of the year, for as soon as they entered into their office, they made a journey to Lavinium in order to sacrifice to Vesta and to the Penates, the household gods whom, according to legend, Aeneas had painstakingly rescued from the destruction of Troy and brought to Italy.[52] Despite the fact that these rituals took place outside the city, the Romans considered these ceremonies a necessary part of the rituals that must be performed by magistrates every year, and failure to perform them properly could have dire consequences for the state, just as any other ceremony of the state religion. A magistrate who failed to perform them risked rupturing the *pax deorum* and was considered as not vested with legitimate authority. Among the charges leveled against C. Flaminius in challenging the legitimacy of his authority in 217 was that he had not celebrated the Latin Festival, nor offered the sacrifice on the Alban Mount, and the subsequent disaster at Lake Trasimene was ascribed to this fault.[53] On other occasions when it was felt that the *feriae Latinae* had not been properly celebrated, the Romans might order *instaurationes* in order to avoid a rupture in the *pax deorum*, just as they would for a religious ceremony in Rome.[54] Livy makes clear the centrality to the Roman state of these ceremonies taking place outside Rome through the great speech of Camillus at the end of Book Five, which provides a capsule view of the historian's stance on Roman religion: Camillus remarks that the Romans' ancestors left to them "certain rites which must be performed on the Alban Mount or at Lavinium."[55] Nor was the performance of these rituals limited to the Republic; both ceremonies continued to be performed into the Empire. These two sets of ceremonies provide the context within which to understand the Roman behavior in holding the sanctuary of Juno Sospita in common with the people of Lanuvium.

The importance of the ceremonies at Alba Longa and at Lavinium in the Late Republic can be easily understood from their respective roles in the Romans' myth-history about their origins. In the developed version, seen in the Augustan-era texts of Livy and Vergil, Aeneas arrived as a fugitive from Troy and founded Lavinium upon his arrival in Italy. Thirty years later, his son Ascanius left Lavinium and founded the city of Alba

52. Macrob. *Sat.* 3.4.11: *consules et praetores seu dictatores, cum adeunt magistratum, Lavinii rem divinam faciant Penatibus pariter et Vestae.* Cf. also Varro, *Ling.* 5.144; Serv. *Ad Aen.* 2.296; Asc. *Sc.* 19. The sacrifice to the Penates is to be distinguished from the annual renewal of the treaty between Lavinium and Rome that took place on the tenth day following the *feriae Latinae*, as recorded by Livy, 8.11; cf. Thomas (1990), 156.

53. Livy 22.1.

54. E.g., Livy 32.1; 37.3; 40.45; 41.16

55. Livy 5.52: *illi sacra quaedam in monte Albano Lauiniique nobis facienda tradiderunt.*

Longa, from whose royal line three hundred years later the twins Romulus and Remus, the actual founders of Rome, were born. This rather complicated genealogy—the foundation of a colony by a Trojan exile, followed by the foundation of an intermediary city before the eventual foundation of Rome itself—emerged as a means of reconciling competing versions of Rome's origins and reconciling the chronological difficulties involved in having a Trojan War hero be responsible for a city that was believed to have been founded in the eighth century.[56] It is extremely unlikely that these stories of Aeneas and his descendants preserve an accurate memory of Rome's actual colonization from Lavinium.[57] Rather, these legends provided a mythological means of expressing Rome's heritage, and connecting Rome at her origins with other developed civilizations—Latin, Trojan, and Greek—and the rituals performed at Alba Longa and at Lavinium, the two main cities in the narrative, provided a religious means of expressing that same identity and cementing those same connections. But while the prominence of Alba Longa and Lavinium as Rome's "mother-city" and "grandmother-city" may suffice to explain the importance of those rites over this extended period, this explanation cannot extend to the treatment of Juno Sospita, for Lanuvium has no role to play in the stories that have survived concerning Rome's foundation. We must dig deeper to understand the decision of the Romans to make an annual visit to Lanuvium.

The complexity of the Roman mythological genealogy that connected them with Alba Longa and Lavinium offers a clue through which to approach this problem. As noted, the definitive version of Rome's origins is clearly an amalgamation of several stories that had developed as Rome grew to prominence. Despite the many issues surrounding our understanding of these legends, a few aspects can perhaps be established with reasonable confidence. The notion that Aeneas was the ultimate founder of the Roman people is the element that required the genealogical hijinks to cover the chronological gap between the end of the Trojan War and the founding of Rome. The earliest extant source associating

56. The stories of Rome's origins have naturally been the subject of numerous studies. Among the most prominent recent studies, see Galinsky (1969); Cornell (1975); Horsfall (1987); Bremmer (1987); Dubourdieu (1989); Gruen (1992), 6–51; Cornell (1995), 57–68.

57. As suggested by Dubourdieu (1989), 367–368, among others. As Cornell (1995), 70–71, points out, "on this point, tradition is disproved by the facts." Poucet (1989), 247–249, shows how the Greek model of colonization may have been utilized to explain the Romans' strange practice of sacrificing at other cities and thus played a role in these legends of colonization.

Aeneas with the founding of Rome, however, comes from Alcimus in the second half of the fourth century.[58] This version was merely one of many competing legends that touched on Rome's origins, some of which ascribed Rome to Greek founders and others that utilized Trojan ancestry but omitted Aeneas entirely.[59] Even versions that named Aeneas did not include all the elements that became part of the canonical myth; for instance, in Alcimus' version, there is no mention of Lavinium, and the generations between Aeneas and the foundation of Rome have been dramatically reduced. Even at Lavinium, the one site in Italy that Aeneas himself founded, it is not certain that the Trojan legend dates back beyond the fourth century; Timaeus, who might be dated to as early as 315 but more likely to the early third century,[60] is the first extant author to connect Aeneas with Lavinium, describing sacred objects in a sanctuary at that city as the Penates brought by Aeneas from Troy.[61] While some have speculated that the connection of Aeneas with Lavinium might go as far back as the sixth century, it is only with this reference from Timaeus that we are on solid ground in making this assertion.[62] The reference from Timaeus suggests that by the end of the fourth century, the main elements of the story of Rome's Trojan origins, including Lavinium and Alba Longa, have begun to come together.

The significance of this fact for our investigation should not be overlooked; while in the Late Republic, the ceremonies at Alba Longa and at Lavinium may have celebrated Rome's Trojan origins, these rituals must have held a different significance in the period before the legend of Trojan origins had yet to take hold. Although the myth of Alba Longa as Rome's mother city may explain why the Latin festival held such a prominent position in the Late Republic among Rome's religious responsibilities, the myth does not explain the original connection between Rome and the *feriae Latinae*. The story of the conquest and destruction of Alba as told by Livy offers further reason to believe that legends of consanguinity between Rome and Alba Longa did not exist

58. Festus 326, 328, L: *Alcimus ait, Tyrrhenia Aeneae natum filium Romulum fuisse, atque eo ortam Albam Aeneae neptem, cuius filius Rhomus condiderit urbem Romam.*

59. For Greek founders, cf. Aristotle's version preserved in Dion. Hal., *Ant. Rom.* 1.72; cf. also a number of accounts offered by Plut., *Romulus* 2. For Trojan ancestry that omits Aeneas, cf. the account of Callias, a Sicilian of c. 300, also preserved in Dion. Hal., *Ant. Rom.* 1.72.

60. Alföldi (1965), 248, offers 315, while Horsfall (1987), 19, suggests the 260s. Gruen (1992), 28 n. 100, prefers the latter.

61. Dion. Hal., *Ant. Rom.* 1.67.

62. Alföldi (1965), 255–255, pushed strongly for the existence of the Aeneas myth in sixth-century Lavinium, but the argument relies too much on speculation, despite the

in the archaic period. Although the historian, under the influence of the later mythologizing tradition about Rome's origins, does his best to present the conflict as a civil war and the forced transfer of the Alban people to Rome as the reuniting of a single people, he preserves traces of a tradition hostile to Alba in his presentation of the Alban king Mettius Fufetius, who in decidedly un-Roman fashion possessed neither courage nor fidelity.[63] And in his rather pathetic description of the destruction of Alba, Livy describes the Albans leaving their household gods behind, viewing their temples occupied by armed troops, and feeling that they were leaving their gods behind as if captured; given the importance of the Penates to the Romans, this representation must surely be read as the destruction of one people, not a merger of two peoples.[64] Despite the best efforts of the ancient authors, who assert that the religious bonds between Rome and the ceremonies at Alba Longa and Lavinium date back to the regal period, it is clear that these links postdate the establishment of the Republic.[65]

In fact, the *feriae Latinae* appear to have been founded by the Latins as a common festival in the archaic period, and the Romans became involved only at a later date, though identifying the specific date remains controversial.[66] The myth, in turn, may have settled on Alba Longa as a site of

efforts of Dubourdieu (1989), 307–317, to reinforce it. Even Cornell (1995), 68, who believes that it is "probable that Lavinium was among the first of the Latin cities to lay claim to a Trojan origin" and who wants to see the Aeneas-Lavinium connection as predating the Aeneas-Rome connection, admits that "as things stand at present we cannot be certain that the Trojan legend was established there [Lavinium] before the fourth century BC."

63. Civil war: Livy 1.23 (*ciuili simillimum bello*). The reuniting of a single people: Livy 1.28. Mettius Fufetius: Livy 1.27 (*Albano non plus animi erat quam fidei*).

64. Livy 1.29: *larem ac penates tectaque in quibus natus quisque educatusque esset relinquentes exirent . . . obsessa ab armatis templa augusta praeterirent ac uelut captos relinquerent deos.*

65. The texts of Dionysius of Halicarnassus (*Ant. Rom.* 4.49) and Livy (1.49–53), which suggest that Tarquin the Younger founded the *feriae Latinae*, are riddled with problems and shot through with their authors' agenda. See Alföldi (1965), 29; Quinn-Schofield (1967a, 1967b); Liou-Gille (1996), 89–93. A scholiast on Cicero (Schol. Bob. *ad* Cic. *Planc.*, 23 [Stangl, p. 154]) offers further evidence of divergent accounts: *Nam Latinae Feriae a quo fuerint institutae dissentiunt plerique auctores. Alii ab Tarquinio Prisco, rege Romanorum, existimant, alii vero a Latinis Priscis.*

66. See Liou-Gille (1996), especially 88–90. For the date of the Roman involvement with the *feriae Latinae,* both Alföldi (1965), 29–31, and Degrassi (1947), 143, favor 451 B.C.E., based in part on notions of Roman expansion at that time, and also on the observation of Mommsen (1879), 100, that the list of Roman prefects for the *feriae* begins in that year.

importance for Rome's origins precisely because of its prominence as a religious center for Latium, rather than the other way around.[67] The precise nature of the festival prior to the Roman involvement is difficult to ascertain from our extant sources, but it is clear that the ceremonies on the Alban mount were of great importance to the communities of Latium. A sacred truce was observed during the period of the festival to enable cities to send delegations safely to Alba Longa; while this custom is attested only in later times, it appears to be a remnant from a period when no single state exercised hegemony over the festival.[68] Participation in the festival seems to have functioned as a sign of membership in the *nomen Latinum*, the traditional phrase in our sources for the Latin community. Each participating community was entitled to a share of the meat from the sacrifices as a mark of their belonging, and failure to obtain one's share could cause the entire ceremony to be repeated, as when Ardea complained in 199.[69] As Cornell phrases it, "there can be no doubt about the importance of this annual celebration in the ethnic consciousness of the Latins."[70] Roman involvement in the *feriae Latinae* served as a means of indicating this shared sense of kinship with the larger Latin community. The nature of the ceremonies required Rome to appear as one among equals; even after Rome took over supervision of the ritual, not only did each Latin state continue to receive its portion of the sacrificial meat but also magistrates from the Latin communities actually performed sacrifices as part of the ritual, as Livy's report for the year 176 indicates.[71] What is most striking is that the Romans chose to make this ritual declaration of sharing in the broader Latin community so central to their own sense of religious propriety. The pilgrimage of Roman magistrates to the Alban mount provided an annual reminder of the ethnic bonds between Rome and the other Latin states.

The situation at Lavinium presents certain similarities to that at Alba Longa as a site that played an important role in Roman mythology

67. Cf. Cornell (1995), 71.

68. For the existence of the truce, cf. Dion. Hal., *Ant. Rom.* 4.49; Macrob. *Sat.* 1.16.16. That the truce dates back to the archaic period is less certain, but cf. Alföldi (1965), 30.

69. The sacrifice and distribution of meat is noted by Dion. Hal., *Ant. Rom.* 4.49. The complaint of Ardea can be found in Livy 31.1; for another instance, cf. Livy 37.3, a similar complaint from the Laurentes in 190.

70. Cornell (1995), 294.

71. Livy 41.16. We are informed about the procedure because the magistrate from Lanuvium actually made a mistake in reciting the vows prior to the sacrifice, leading the Roman pontiffs to declare an *instauratio* and require the Lanuvians to pay for the repeated ceremony.

as well as the location of an annual sacrifice by Roman magistrates. The literary sources indicate that Roman ties to Lavinium were reestablished annually by two ceremonies, one religious and one civil: when the magistrates entered their office, they made a pilgrimage to Lavinium to sacrifice to the Penates and to Vesta; then on the tenth day after the *feriae Latinae*, they renewed the treaty of alliance between Lavinium and Rome.[72] These ceremonies, like those on the Alban mount, were considered a primary responsibility of the Roman magistrates, and failure or alleged failure to carry them out properly had serious repercussions for the state and/or for the magistrates involved.[73] These responsibilities appear to date back to the aftermath of the Latin Revolt in 338, when, according to Livy, "an order was made for the treaty with the Laurentes to be renewed, and from that time it has been renewed annually on the tenth day after the Latin Festival."[74] The renewal of the treaty was important enough into the empire that when Lavinium had ceased to be a functioning town, special magistrates from outside the city were appointed *patres patrati* to act on behalf of Lavinian citizens at the renewal ceremony.[75] These ceremonies apparently took place on separate occasions, the sacrifice to the Penates and Vesta when the magistrates took office and the renewal of the treaty in mid-spring, following the *feriae Latinae*.[76]

72. Sacrifice to Vesta and the Penates: Macrob. *Sat.* 3.4.11; Serv. *Aen.* 2.296; Serv. auct., *Aen.* 3.12; Schol. Veron. *Aen.* 1.239. Treaty: Livy 8.11; Varro, *Ling.*, 6.25; Macrob. *Sat.* 1.16.6.

73. Cf. the cases of C. Mancinus in 137 (Val. Max. 1.6.7) and Aemilius Scaurus in 104 (Asc. *Scaur.* 18–10 (p. 21, Clark).

74. Livy 8.11: *extra poenam fuere Latinorum Laurentes Campanorumque equites, quia non desciuerant; cum Laurentibus renouari foedus iussum renouaturque ex eo quotannis post diem decimum Latinarum.* While this notice indicates that a treaty had existed between Rome and Lavinium prior to this time, it also suggests that the relationship was placed on an entirely different footing in 338. The nature of the earlier treaty is open to speculation, especially since Polybius (3.22) mentions "Laurentium," often emended to Lavinium, in the first treaty between Rome and Carthage, dated to 509. Whether the original treaty was an individual treaty between Rome and Lavinium (often ascribed to Romulus, as in Livy 1.14) or the *foedus Cassianum*, dramatically altered to the benefit of Lavinium in the aftermath of the Latin Revolt, is less relevant for our purposes than the fact that Rome's relationship with Lavinium was dramatically altered in 338. Cf. Alföldi (1965), 263–65; Castagnoli (1972), 103–104; Saulnier (1984), 522–524.

75. These magistrates, apparently part of a corporation of Roman knights known as the *Laurentes Lavinates*, are known from *CIL* X.797. See, most recently, Saulnier (1984).

76. Thomas (1990), 156ff., argues in favor of two separate ceremonies, while Dubourdieu (1989), 345, sees these as a single event.

As at Alba Longa, the early history of these ceremonies is difficult to discern, but the initial connection seems not to have been occasioned by the mythological role of the city in the story of Rome's founding. Roman tradition certainly retrojected ceremonies at Lavinium back to the distant past; a story found in several sources even connects Ascanius and his founding of Alba Longa with the establishment of the annual religious pilgrimage to Lavinium.[77] These stories again operate within the Lavinium-Alba-Rome mythological triad; they illustrate the importance of the Penates and of the concept of place to Roman religion, like the speech of Camillus from Livy recounted earlier, but are not helpful in locating the initial Roman interest in the site. Better evidence is often sought in the archaeological evidence from Practica di Mare, generally identified as ancient Lavinium, where excavations revealed a tumulus that covered a seventh-century burial chest, with the area extensively remodeled in the fourth century.[78] The tumulus has been interpreted as the hero-shrine dedicated to Pater Indiges mentioned by Dionysius, who proceeds to equate Aeneas with this figure.[79] This identification, however, has not been fully accepted, and even for those who accept the connection, it seems more likely that an original shrine was remodeled into a heroon for Aeneas in the fourth century.[80] Given that the myths linking Rome and Troy, or even Lavinium and Troy, had yet to become fully established in the fourth century, it is difficult to ascribe Roman interest in Lavinium in the wake of the Latin revolt to the stories of Rome's origins.

The other significant discovery of the excavations at Practica di Mare may be more helpful in understanding the Roman relationship with Lavinium: a series of thirteen altars aligned in a row just south of the city and just west of the tumulus, with the first altar dating to the middle of the

---

77. See Livy 1.14; Dion Hal., *Ant. Rom.* 1.67; Val. Max. 1.8.7.

78. See Sommella (1972).

79. Sommella (1972) and (1974) initially proposed the identification of the tumulus with the shrine mentioned by Dionysius at *Ant. Rom.* 1.64.5; see also Livy 1.2 for the worship of a Jupiter Indiges at Lavinium whom he identifies with Aeneas. The identification was accepted by Castagnoli (1982), 12–13, and Holloway (1994), 138; objections have been raised most strongly by Cornell (1977), 78–81, and Poucet (1979), 181–183.

80. Cf. Liou-Gille (1980), 99. Cornell (1995), 68, notes the lack of evidence for Aeneas in the seventh century, and even Holloway (1994), 138, seems to accept that the heroon was connected with Aeneas only in 338: "A tumulus only 250 years old could be taken for the tomb of Aeneas."

Figure 1.1: Sanctuary of the Thirteen Altars, Lavinium

sixth century (fig. 1.1).[81] Additional altars were constructed in the fifth and early fourth centuries, and in the later fourth century, a major refurbishment took place. Activity at the altars lasted to the end of the third century, when the entire area fell into disuse. These altars have been interpreted as part of a major federal sanctuary, but the identity of the divinity to whom the sanctuary was dedicated has been widely debated; the Penates, the Dioscuri, and Venus have all been suggested.[82] That the altars represent a

81. The excavations were published by F. Castagnoli in two volumes, the second of which (1975) focuses entirely on the thirteen altars. Other important discussions of the sanctuary include Dury-Moyaers (1981); *Enea del Lazio* (1981); Torelli (1984). Holloway (1994), 129–134, offers a succinct summary in English.

82. Alföldi (1965), 265–267, saw the sanctuary of the thirteen altars as that of the Penates, a suggestion tentatively adopted by Cornell (1995), 66. Dubourdieu (1989), 251–53, objected, largely on the basis of the location of the sanctuary outside the city

federal sanctuary seems certain, but barring further discoveries, it is unlikely that we will be able to definitively identify the primary divinity honored there. The important point, however, is that the early date of the initial altars, in the sixth century, reveals that Lavinium, like Alba Longa, was a site of regional religious importance even before the Romans became attached to the site of Lavinium. Furthermore, it is hard to avoid the conclusion that 338 marked a defining moment in the history of Lavinium and of Rome's relations with the city; the evidence from Livy suggests as much, and both the tumulus and the sanctuary of the thirteen altars show major changes in the late fourth century.[83] Over the ensuing decades, as the legend of Rome's origins and Lavinium's role in the legend became more elaborate and more widely established, Lavinium grew in importance, but this connection cannot explain the transformation of Rome's relationship with Lavinium in 338. Once again, it seems that the elaboration of the myth relating Lavinium and Rome followed the change in the relationship between the two cities, and perhaps was caused by it, rather than preceding it.[84]

This brief review of the ceremonies performed at Lavinium and at Alba Longa suggests that the importance of these sites in the period prior to the

---

walls and on the fact that the sanctuary fell into disuse in the third century B.C.E. while the Roman sacrifices to the Penates continued into the Imperial period. Weinstock (1960) argued for the Dioscuri based on the fact that the inscription mentioned earlier (see p. 35) was found near altar 8; Holloway (1994), 134, accepts the identification of the Penates with the Dioscouri but is careful to identify the sanctuary only as "the Thirteen Altars." Castagnoli (1977); Dury-Moyaers (1981), 221–226; and Dubourdieu (1989), 285–292 are less convinced. Dubourdieu (1989), 254–257, favors Venus, based on Strabo 5.232 and picking up on a suggestion from Castagnoli's original publication (1975).

83. Cf. Dubourdieu (1989), 380. In recognizing the speculative quality of many of her conclusions, she remarks that the only point that seems assured is that the fourth century was marked by considerable changes in the history of Latium and Rome, changes that manifested themselves in the religious architecture of the religious metropolis of Lavinium. But it is not only the nature of the changes that are important, but the reason that Lavinium was affected in one way while other cities, even of religious importance (such as Ardea), were affected in other ways. As she writes, "Le seul point qui nous semble à peu près assuré, c'est que le IVe siècle a marqué des changements considérables dans l'histoire du Latium et de Rome, changements qui se manifestent dans l'architecture de la métropole religieuse de Lavinium, mais dont il est difficile d'apprécier la portée exacte."

84. So, for instance, the heroon described by Dionysius was, as noted previously, originally dedicated to a *Pater Indiges* figure but may have become associated with Aeneas under the influence of the Trojan myth. If the heroon discovered at Practica di Mare is indeed this monument, it would be a remarkable sign of this development. As Holloway (1994), 138, says, "The hero shrine of Lavinium shows the reflection of this first chapter in Roman antiquarianism among the Romans themselves."

Latin Revolt—and prior to the development of the canonical myth of Rome's origins—may be best explained by the status of these two communities as regional religious sanctuaries. The literary sources indicate that Lavinium was home to a federal sanctuary of Venus, a sanctuary whose regional importance is further underlined by the fact that it was actually administered by the city of Ardea. The sanctuary of the Thirteen Altars reveals a federal sanctuary in use from the sixth century down to the end of the third, whose continued importance can be seen in the numerous renovations of the sanctuary over those three hundred years. If the sanctuary of the Thirteen Altars is not in fact that sanctuary of Venus, then Lavinium must have hosted at least two sanctuaries of regional importance. Similarly, Alba Longa was the site of the regional celebration in honor of Jupiter Latiaris, the eponymous divinity of the Latin people. The Roman actions in singling out these two sites, especially in aligning herself closely with Lavinium at the time of the Latin Revolt, should be seen as a recognition of the importance of these religious centers.[85] In the wake of the Roman defeat of the Latin League, the reaffirmation of the openness of Roman society, of a broad view of Roman identity, by fostering connections with both cultural centers, takes on added significance.

These conclusions have direct relevance for our understanding of the Romans' decision to hold the shrine of Juno Sospita in common with the people of Lanuvium. Juno Sospita was the most important divinity at Lanuvium, and although there is no evidence that this shrine was a federal sanctuary, Juno Sospita was a goddess of widespread importance in early Latium, perhaps the most famous Juno in Latium.[86] Her iconography was widely known; Cicero describes her as appearing regularly with "a goat-skin, a spear, a shield, and broad sandals," and this description matches her appearance on a long series of Roman Republican coinage.[87] But her appearance in prominent places was not limited to Rome; temple antefixes displaying the image of a divinity with this iconography, which has become known as the Juno Sospita type, have been found on a number of temples in Latium, at Falerii, Norba, Satricum, Antemnae, and even Lavinium, in addition to Rome.[88] Imperial sources continue to mention the importance of the cult of Juno at Lanuvium; Silius Italicus called Lanuvium *Iunonia sedes*, and Ovid notes that several Italian towns, including

85. Cornell (1995), 71, suggests further that the prominence of Alba Longa and of Lavinium in the developed mythological tradition originated from their historical importance as religious centers.

86. Gordon (1938), 24.

87. Cic., *Nat. D.*, 1.82. For the coinage, see Sydenham (1952), #598, 722, 771–773, 915, 964, 1054.

88. Andren (1940). On the iconography of Juno Sospita, cf. Dury-Moyaers (1986).

Lanuvium, had a month named *Iunonius*.[89] The decision to hold the sanctuary of Juno Sospita in common with the Lanuvians held importance beyond the two cities involved.

By leaving intact the worship of Juno Sospita and sharing the worship with the Lanuvians, the Romans demonstrated respect for an important local deity, an action that would be repeated frequently throughout the course of her history, and one that might be especially effective in smoothing over lingering discontent over the outcome of the war. On the one hand, the Roman presence in the sanctuary of Juno Sospita at Lanuvium undoubtedly served as a reminder of Rome's military preeminence in Latium. At the same time, however, the Romans symbolically indicated an equal status with the Latins in regard to the worship of the goddess; significantly, the Romans undertook to sacrifice at the shrine of Juno Sospita in Lanuvium, rather than transporting the goddess to Rome, as they had done in the case of Juno Regina from Veii. The contrast between the two divinities is instructive and may owe something to the roots of one cult in Latium as opposed to the other in Etruria; if the acceptance of Juno Regina in Rome suggested that Rome was open to Etruscan peoples, then worshipping Juno Sospita at Lanuvium might indicate a deeper sense of shared identity with the Latins who shared in the worship of an important cult. This paraded notion of equality might have been particularly important in the case of a recalcitrant state such as Lanuvium, a state that had been a major participant in the revolt against Roman hegemony. The Roman decision not to overtly insist on her superiority was part of her use of the individualized carrot-and-stick approach that became evident in 338 and that the Romans became adept at employing. The Roman settlement provided favorable treatment for some cities alongside severe punishment of other Latin towns, and the religious treatment of Lanuvium was an important part of those calculations. In this particular case, the religious actions of the Romans were explicitly linked with their political actions: the Lanuvians were given citizenship on the condition that the cult of Juno Sospita be held in common with the Romans. The symbolic equality on the divine level was thus matched by a symbolic equality on the political level and with a physical superiority on the military level. This juxtaposition was to become a recurring motif in Roman behavior.

The significance of the Roman action at Lanuvium should not be underestimated. It is only at Lanuvium that the literary sources explicitly remark on the religious action of the Romans; while it seems likely to us that the Romans would have assumed greater control over the *feriae Latinae* at this time and instituted changes at Lavinium, these conclusions are suppositions based on likely scenarios. For Alba Longa, we are told nothing at all at this time,

89. Sil. *Pun.* 8.360; Ov., *Fast.* 6.60.

while for Lavinium, we are told only about the institution of the annual treaty renewal, to which moderns have often connected the sacrifice to the Penates or the modifications revealed by excavation. But Livy, following his annalistic sources, only preserved a record of the changes at Lanuvium, which might warn us that although the ceremonies at Alba Longa and Lavinium *became* more important to the Romans, *at the time* the involvement with the shrine at Lanuvium may have seemed the more significant for creating and sustaining links with the Latin communities.

The comparison of Roman behavior at Lanuvium with that regarding Alba Longa and Lavinium also illuminates clearly the distinctions drawn by the Romans in their treatment of outside religious practices. On the Alban mount, the Romans assumed full responsibility for the sacrifices, from setting the date for the festival to ensuring that it was properly carried out. This position symbolically reinforced the Roman position of dominance over the Latin communities. At Lavinium, the Romans sacrificed directly to the Penates on their own behalf; these gods were specifically claimed to be the patron deities of the Roman state, and the Latin communities, and even Lavinium, apparently did not take part in this ceremony. This sacrifice reflected the mythological links between Rome and Lavinium, but it was only the annual treaty renewal that provided the connections to the larger Latin community. It was only at Lanuvium that the Romans "shared" a sanctuary, consciously placing themselves on an equal level with the Lanuvians in their worship of an important Latin goddess in her most important shrine. As noted before, this may well have been the most important religious action undertaken by the Romans in the wake of the Latin Revolt.

The fourth century thus saw several instances where the Romans incorporated a religious tradition from outside their territory into their own religious calendar as they expanded their power over central Italy. The procedure was not exactly the same for each divinity, as in each instance the Romans utilized a mechanism that best reflected the relationship between themselves and the other town; thus Juno Regina was "evoked" from Veii while the Romans themselves journeyed to Lanuvium for sacrifices to Juno Sospita. The result in each of these cases, however, was that a goddess the Romans identified as Juno came to be worshipped by the Romans and thus created a religious link between the Romans and the neighboring city.[90] The Roman behavior in 338, as they began

90. The most complete treatment of these Italian Junos is that of R. E. A. Palmer in his essay "Juno in Archaic Italy" (1974), 3–56. In an earlier work (1970), 167–169 and 180–181, Palmer argued that each of the curial Junos must have been evoked from another community to Rome to bind the new community to Rome. Although this would strengthen my argument in this section, that the Romans occasionally imported foreign gods in a federative effort, the evidence available for Palmer's thesis does not seem sufficient to draw such conclusions with confidence.

to evolve institutions to maintain their hegemony over Latium, suggests that the Romans had become more self-conscious of their treatment of foreign divinities. While the first decades of the Republic display the Roman openness to foreign religious influence, at that time this openness manifested itself primarily in the simple decision to institute cult worship in Rome for a new divinity. By the end of this period, more nuances had emerged in Roman behavior, as divinities continued to be accepted at Rome, but the more active involvement of Rome in the religious life of neighboring Latin communities suggests a greater self-awareness of the importance of religion in fostering relationships with the communities of central Italy. As we turn our attention to the Roman expansion further afield in Italy and then overseas, we will see that the Romans employed this same mechanism for fostering relations with peoples inhabiting these areas, areas that were more culturally linked with the Greek world and the East than those the Romans had previously encountered.

2

Cult Introductions of the Third Century

Historians are accustomed to see the events of 338 as a significant watershed in Roman history. From the beginning of the Republic, it took the Romans 170 years to establish their leadership in central Italy, yet within the next 70 years she extended her hegemony to all of peninsular Italy, and 100 years after that, she was the unquestioned power in the entire Mediterranean basin. Moreover, the pattern established in the wake of the Latin revolt became the operative model for Roman hegemony. The Romans treated individual cities or territories each on their own terms, based on their individual characteristics, rather than creating a league with herself at the head in which all the allies (or subjects) were treated in the same fashion.[1] This individualized treatment provided direct motivation for Rome's associates to behave as Rome wanted them to, in terms of both rewards for appropriate behavior and punishment for failure to comply with Roman demands. Yet the repercussions of this consolidation of Roman power in Latium were, of course, not immediate. While Rome after 338 was more powerful than her immediate neighbors, the city was by no means free from

---

1. Rich (2008) has recently argued that Rome's relationships with the cities and towns of Italy were based on *deditio* and not on alliances of a theoretically equal nature. His argument raises important considerations, but the ultimate solution to this question is not relevant here; either as allies or as subjects, Rome did not apply the same blanket provisions to each Italian city but tailored her treatment toward specific local considerations.

military threats, as the subsequent campaigns against the Samnites would show. Although the transformation of Rome may have begun, in the short term the continuities were more significant than the changes, and well into the third century, Rome resembled a city-state more than an imperial power.

The religious sphere shows a similar continuity in Roman behavior in the period following the defeat of the Latin Revolt, with the differences caused more by the pace and scope of Roman expansion than by changes in fundamental principles. The Romans continued to incorporate foreign aspects into their religious system, just as they had in the preceding century and a half. The accelerating growth of the Roman state certainly led to accelerated growth in the Roman pantheon, as the late fourth and early third centuries saw a dramatic increase in the number of new temples constructed in the city of Rome. Furthermore, many new additions in this period came from further afield, southern Italy or even overseas rather than central Italy. While the Romans continued to be fundamentally open to the incorporation of foreign elements within their religious system, they also showed themselves increasingly aware of the importance of religion in fostering connections as they moved onto the world stage. Just as in 338, their actions enabled the Romans to present themselves as sharing in a larger central Italian culture, so the adoption of cults and practices from the Greek East, such as Aesculapius, the Secular Games, and the Magna Mater, allowed the Romans to present themselves as members of the larger Hellenistic world. Roman behavior in regard to foreign religious traditions in the third century helped them carve out a place for themselves as their geopolitical concerns forced them to cope with the challenges of the Hellenistic world.

The increasing awareness of their place in the Hellenistic world is immediately apparent in the new cults the Romans inaugurated during the first decade of the third century. This period is the most prolific in Roman history in terms of the rate of temples built, with eight temples either built or vowed in the stretch from 296 to 291 B.C.E., and the better part of these looked to the Hellenistic world.[2] The influence of Greek culture can be easily seen in the adoption and adaptation of the concept of Victory evident in several of the

2. For some of the temples dedicated in this period, we are not informed of the circumstances of the original vow, and similarly for some temples vowed in this period, we are not informed of the date when the temple was eventually dedicated. Accounting for those two factors would obviously stretch the time period involved on either end, but nonetheless the spate of temple building at this time is impressive: only fourteen public temples had been dedicated in the first two hundred years of the Republic, and these eight were then built within the next twenty years (allowing a conservative estimate for the completion of all temples).

temples built during this boom. In the Greek world, cults related to victory had existed for many years; the temple of Athena Nike on the Athenian acropolis is a good example, built in the early stages of the great Peloponnesian War.[3] Personifications of this concept were widespread in the art and literature of the fifth and especially the fourth century, not only on mainland Greece, where the Nike of Paionios at Olympia dating to the last quarter of the fifth century is the most famous example, but also in Magna Graecia. Tarentum in southern Italy possessed its own statue of Nike, this one by a disciple of Lysippus, and Nike also appears on Tarentine coinage throughout the fourth century.[4] The theological implications of victory were greatly expanded by Alexander the Great, to whom the Athenians apparently dedicated a statue as "the Invincible God"; the concept was perpetuated by Seleucus I, who adopted the surname Nikator.[5]

Cults and objects along these lines are conspicuously absent from Rome prior to the third century; Jupiter Optimus Maximus was the primary Roman cult concerned with victory. But new cults related to Victory sprang up as if fully formed at the beginning of the third century. In 295, at the battle of Sentinum, Q. Fabius Maximus vowed a temple to Jupiter Victor, and in 294 L. Postumius Megellus dedicated a temple to Victoria on the Palatine hill, the first temple to Victoria in Rome, that he had begun while serving as curule aedile some years previously.[6] Furthermore, in that same year of 294, a statue of Jupiter in a quadriga was placed on the roof of the Capitoline temple; imagery on later Republican coinage suggests that the chariot was driven by a personification of Victory.[7] Livy also notes that in 293, "for the first time, palms were given to the victors after a custom borrowed from Greece."[8] As Rufus Fears remarked, "This combination of events cannot be fortuitous."[9] The introduction into the Roman state religion of cults related to Victory—what Fears calls the "theology of Victory"—was a direct

3. On the temple of Athena Nike, see most recently Mark (1993).

4. For the statue, see Wuilleumier (1939), 284. For coins and a fuller discussion of the Nike iconography, see Weinstock (1957).

5. For the statue of Alexander, see Hyp., *Or.* 1, 32.5: $\dot{\alpha}\nu\dot{\iota}\kappa\eta\tau\sigma\varsigma$ $\theta\epsilon\dot{\sigma}\varsigma$. Cf. Dio Cass. 43.45.2 for a similar honor apparently offered to Caesar. See Weinstock (1957), 212–213, for fuller discussion and more examples of the use of this term by the Diadochoi.

6. For Fabius' vow, see Livy 10.29.14; for Postumius' dedication, Livy 10.33.9 The date of Postumius' aedileship is not known for certain; Broughton, *MRR* suggests 307, on the assumption that his aedileship should come before he first held the consulship in 305.

7. For the statue, see Livy 10.23.12. For the coinage, see Crawford (1983), 715 and n. 2.

8. Livy 10.47: *palmaeque tum primum translato e Graeco more uictoribus datae.*

9. Fears (1981), 774. Fears himself points out that Weinstock's article in *RE* VIII A 2, 2501–2542, had already noted the significance of this unusual concurrence of events.

consequence of the expansion of Roman horizons beyond Italy. Within a short time of encountering these ideas in the Hellenistic world, the Romans imported them to Rome, incorporating this newly popular contemporary conception into their own religious system.[10] The Romans' willingness to speak the religious language current in the Hellenistic world reveals the continuation of openness visible in the fourth century and earlier and undoubtedly facilitated the expansion of their control beyond central Italy.[11]

In welcoming this "theology of Victory," the Romans did not merely adopt this conception wholesale but adapted it to their own religious needs and to the shape of their own system. This "adopt and adapt" approach is one that was to be repeated over and over as the Romans expanded further and introduced more foreign elements into their religion. As noted earlier, in 294 the Romans dedicated a temple to Victoria as a goddess in her own right. This action seems to have been in itself an innovation, because there are no known cults or temples to the personification of Victory alone in Greece before this time.[12] As demonstrated by the items cited here, the concept was known and had developed in importance, but Victory had apparently not been given her own cult worship until she came to Rome. In the 290s, personifications were not as common in Rome as they would become later in the third century (Spes, Fides, and Honos all received temples in the middle of the century), but a temple to Salus had been dedicated in 302, so the practice had recently made an appearance in Rome. The temple to Victoria is thus not a simple transplant from Greece to Rome, but the adaptation of a theological notion from Greece and Magna Graecia onto the Roman scene. A similar adaptation can be seen in the cults of Hercules; the *fasti* indicate that this hero had multiple cults in Rome, beginning with the very old cult at the Ara Maxima and ultimately including

10. Wallace (1990), 286, downplays this degree of Hellenization, suggesting that these temples signify nothing "more than an effort to gain the assistance of the gods, sometimes new and powerful gods, in a dangerous military crisis." But the Romans did not always respond to military crises with temples, nor with temples to such a suggestive set of divinities; as noted in chapter 1, they made decisions on which gods to import, and those decisions should be seen as possessing some significance. For a further critique, see the response of Torelli to Wallace in the same volume.

11. Fears (1981), 774, argues that the introduction of this theology of Victory was part of the "state propaganda in order to justify Roman expansion." While this is a possible motive, many of Fears's examples of divine justification for imperial expansion date from the middle of the third century or later. Certainly, the Romans may have wanted to utilize the imagery of Victory on their own behalf, but to argue from there to a conscious promotion of an imperial ideology at the beginning of the third century stretches the available evidence.

12. Cf. Weinstock (1957), 218.

multiple separate cults to Hercules Victor and Hercules Invictus.[13] Again, these cults seem to be Roman innovations; cults to Herakles Kallinikos or to Herakles Aniketos did exist in Greece, but not very often and not with the popularity that these cults attained in Rome. Although it is not possible to date the first appearance in Rome of these particular manifestations of Hercules, the earliest manifestation of Hercules in Rome was connected with merchants and wayfarers. The connection to generals and to victory, including a late tradition that generals dedicated a tithe of their booty to Hercules, seems more likely to have arrived in conjunction with the "theology of Victory" in the third century.[14] Here again the Romans applied a conception they had received from the Greek East and applied it in their own way. While employing an idea adopted from a foreign culture might have made the Romans seem less foreign to those outsiders, the Romans also put a distinctive mark on the notion as practiced in Rome, allowing them to carve out space for themselves within the broader Hellenistic world.

If this process is visible with regard to the introduction of a broad theological concept from the Hellenistic world, it can also be seen in the more direct importation of a single cult. In 293, contemporaneously with the arrival of the theology of Victory, they imported a god of great popularity in fourth-century Greece, the healing god Asklepios, or Aesculapius as he became known in Rome. Aesculapius was the first Greek deity imported since the early fifth century, so his introduction is clearly part of the renewed attention paid to the Greek world; although the Romans did have a tradition of introducing Greek elements into Roman religion, as we saw in the last chapter, the fourth century was primarily occupied with Italian Junos. The story of the introduction of Aesculapius is known mostly from Valerius Maximus, as the text of Livy breaks off just at the point when the decision had been made to summon Aesculapius.[15] In 295, a pestilence had struck Rome, tempering the celebration of the decisive Roman victory at Sentinum in that same year. Most likely

13. At least two temples for both Hercules Victor and Hercules Invictus are attested in Rome. The stone calendars of Rome indicate a celebration for Hercules Invictus at the Circus Maximus on August 12; this temple was apparently located in the Forum Boarium in the vicinity of the Ara Maxima (Livy 10.23.3; Macrob. *Sat.* 3.6.10). On August 13, the *fasti Antiates maiori* indicate a festival for Hercules Victor, and the *fasti Allifani* indicate one for Hercules Invictus at the Porta Trigemina, apparently a separate cult of Hercules Invictus since the *Allifani* also record the celebration on the twelfth. And finally, Dessau, *ILS* 20 reveals that in 142 L. Mummius dedicated a temple to Hercules Victor, probably on the Caelian, judging by the find spot of the inscription.

14. Cf. Weinstock (1957), 222–223.

15. Val. Max. 1.8.2; Livy 10.47 and ep. 11. See also Ov., *Fast.* 1.291–2 and *Met.* 15.622–744; *De Viris Illustribus* 22.

on account of the pestilence, the prodigies that occurred in this year provoked a consultation of the Sibylline Books, although Livy does not record a response.[16] Two years later, the pestilence was severe enough to be considered a prodigy in its own right, and the Sibylline Books were again consulted. This time the books recommended the summoning of Aesculapius from Epidaurus to Rome, but as the consuls were busy in the field, nothing was done about it until the following year. An embassy was then sent to Greece under the leadership of Q. Ogulnius. After their arrival at Epidaurus, a snake that was thought to represent the god slithered on board the Roman ship and curled up in the quarters of Ogulnius. The Romans set sail and, after a three-day stop in Antium, where the snake visited his shrine there, the embassy returned to Rome. On arrival, the snake slithered off the ship and onto the Tiber Island and immediately brought a halt to the plague. A temple was duly built and dedicated to Aesculapius in 291 on the spot that the god himself had so obviously indicated. Such is the story handed down by the ancient tradition.

A closer look at the timing of the events surrounding this cult's introduction offers some understanding of the purposes that the introduction of Aesculapius may have served besides bringing an end to the pestilence. The plague had been raging since 295, and the books were even consulted in that year, yet it is only in 293 that the order was given to summon Aesculapius from Epidaurus. One might attempt to explain the delay by arguing that it was precisely the length of the plague that required extraordinary measures. But the consultation of the books in itself was an extraordinary measure; taking that step in 295 indicates that the Romans already considered the plague serious enough to warrant action. If the intention all along had been to introduce Aesculapius, the decision to wait until the devastation reached alarming proportions seems inexplicable from a purely religious standpoint. The lapse of time suggests that initially the Romans had no plans to import Aesculapius from Greece, but a change in Roman circumstances led to a change of course. The intimate connection between religion and politics at Rome encourages us to consider what might have changed in the political context between 295 and 293 that made the decision to import Aesculapius the appropriate response to this crisis.

The first decade of the third century saw the waging of the Third Samnite War for supremacy in central Italy. The critical battle of this campaign was fought in 295 at Sentinum, where the Roman forces under Fabius Rullianus and Decius Mus defeated the combined forces of the Samnites, Gauls, and Umbrians. In the following year, the Romans received the surrender of several Etruscan cities that had defected to the Samnite confederacy. These

16. Livy 10.31.8.

actions put an end to any chances for eventual Samnite victory, although the Samnites continued to be a thorn in the Roman side for another thirty years.[17] In this situation, with the outcome of the war essentially decided, the Romans may have turned their thoughts forward, toward the direction they would take after the fighting was completed, rather than focusing exclusively on the task at hand. Even as Roman forces were employed in finishing off the Samnites, the attention of the Senate may have been engaged elsewhere. It can hardly be coincidental that at the time of the importation of Aesculapius, the Romans began moving in the world known as Magna Graecia, the part of southern Italy that was littered with Greek colonies. Although no cult of Aesculapius is known archaeologically in Italy prior to the one at Rome,[18] these colonies, through their overseas trade, would surely have been aware of the cult; the mention of Antium in the story of the cult's transfer from Greece implies the presence of a cult of Aesculapius in that city, although no traces of a sanctuary have been discovered to date. The adoption of Aesculapius by the Romans would have been a signal that the Romans did not intend to stamp out Greek culture in Italy, but rather sought to enter their world. As J. Scheid has remarked, "The cult of Aesculapius was able to play the role of federator and integrator for the cities of Magna Graecia."[19]

The particular timing of the introduction of Aesculapius, just at the turning point of the Samnite War, confirms the significance of this action. The Romans made this overture to Magna Graecia at a key juncture in their relations with southern Italy. The Roman campaigns against the Samnites had brought them in contact—and, indeed, into conflict—with the prosperous town of Tarentum in the southernmost part of Italy. An attempt at rapprochement during the Second Samnite War had come to nothing. That the Romans expected trouble from this quarter may be seen from their establishing a particularly large

17. One might compare Sentinum with Metaurus, the battle that effectively decided the outcome of the Second Punic War, even as the actual fighting stretched on for several more years.

18. Archaeological evidence of an Asclepeion has been discovered in Latium at Fregellae, but the earliest phase is dated to the beginning of the second century. It appears that the cult reached Fregellae without coming through Rome. See Coarelli (1986) and Musial (1990), 234–5.

19. Scheid (1985), 97–98. This role has been denied by Musial (1990), 233, who argues that no ancient source gives us clear information on this subject. While that may be true, no ancient source tells us that there were ulterior motives behind the introduction of the Magna Mater, yet such ulterior motives in that case seem impossible to deny.

colony at Venusia, on the borders of Lucania, at the conclusion of the Samnite Wars.[20] The extent of the wars with Pyrrhus was certainly not envisioned at this time, but conflict with Tarentum seemed likely. In this situation, Roman diplomatic overtures to the Greek colonies of southern Italy take on an added significance. The introduction of Aesculapius to Rome was not meant merely as a general token of Roman attitudes, but perhaps also as specific preparation for a possible conflict in which the support of the Greek towns could be decisive. The importance that the Romans attached to this project can be seen in the speed with which they constructed the temple. The Sibylline Books urged the adoption of Aesculapius in 293, and already in 291 a temple was dedicated. This compares favorably with other temples; four years elapsed after the *evocatio* of Juno Regina in 396 before the construction of her temple, and almost a century later, thirteen years were allowed to pass following the arrival of the Magna Mater before her temple was dedicated. In the latter instance, the goddess was received into the temple of Victory on the Palatine, so perhaps less urgency was felt in building the temple; a clear indication of acceptance had already been made. There was no such temporary housing for Aesculapius, and so the quick completion of the temple reveals how important the importation of Aesculapius was to the Romans. The severity of the plague cannot be considered justification for the speed of construction, for according to our sources, the plague ceased on the arrival of Aesculapius. Even granting that the tale has been embroidered to make Aesculapius look even more efficacious, the text shows that Aesculapius' arrival was held to be the key moment in taming the pestilence; the construction of the temple was secondary. The alacrity with which the Romans erected the temple for Aesculapius was not necessary on strictly "religious" grounds, but it was essential to a successful diplomatic overture.

The identity of the leader of the embassy to Epidaurus, Quintus Ogulnius, offers other clues that may lead to additional conclusions from this episode. This is the same man who, as tribune with his brother in 300, proposed and succeeded in enacting the *lex Ogulnia*, which increased the number of members in the pontifical and augural colleges and reserved half the spaces for plebeians.[21] As aediles in 296, they also erected a

20. This point is also noticed by Altheim (1938), 283, in connection with the introduction of Aesculapius.

21. Livy 10.6.3–7. Henceforth, there were to be eight pontiffs and nine augurs, with a plebeian as the extra augur.

representation of Romulus and Remus being suckled by the wolf at the *ficus Ruminalis*, the statue of Jupiter in a four-horse chariot described previously, as well as other more ordinary dedications.[22] Several attempts have been made to connect these three known actions, but most founder by emphasizing one of these actions as definitive for a supposed program without considering all three equally. So for instance, the Ogulnii have been seen as the champions of the plebs in a late stage of the Struggle of the Orders, on account of the *lex Ogulnia*, or as champions of introducing Hellenic culture into Rome, on account of the cult of Aesculapius.[23] Neither hypothesis stands up to scrutiny, for a variety of reasons. The cult of Aesculapius is not known to have held particular appeal to the plebs, so even if the model of patrician-plebeian conflict was useful in understanding the Ogulnii, it would not help us understand the introduction of this cult.[24] And while the early third century was a time of increasing adoption of Hellenic culture at Rome, it is no more possible to ascribe all of this activity to a single family in the third century than it is to ascribe it to the Scipios in the second. The dedication by the Ogulnii of the Romulus and Remus image, a "Roman" symbol, should dispel any notion that the Ogulnii were Hellenizers par excellence.

It may, however, be useful to consider the *lex Ogulnia*, the dedication to Romulus and Remus, and the introduction of Aesculapius as items connected in a larger context. As noted earlier, at the beginning of the third century B.C.E., Rome was drawing into closer contact with the Greek world. To the upsurge of Greek elements in Roman religion already discussed can be added other signs of Greek civilization in Rome. Dedications to Alcibiades and Pythagoras were erected in the Forum during the Samnite Wars; according to Pliny, Pythian Apollo ordered statues erected to the bravest and wisest of the Greeks.[25] J. Gagé has suggested that these actions reflect an attempt on the part of the Romans to find a means of

22. Livy 10.23.11–13. Their other activities included adding brazen thresholds and silver vessels to the temple of Jupiter and paving the road from the Porta Capena to the temple of Mars.

23. Ogulnius as a champion of the plebs is inferred from his role in extending to the plebs the right to sit in the pontifical and augural colleges. The argument of Ogulnius as the champion of Hellenization was made most strongly by Münzer (1920), 83–89; see also his article in *RE*, s.v. *Ogulnius*, col. 2066–2068. His arguments are accepted by Altheim (1938), 283, and by Gagé (1955), 152–153. Altheim also credits Ogulnius with the introduction of silver coinage to Rome, which he takes to be another Greek element.

24. Musial (1990), 238, notes that "the god of Epidaurus was not the object in Italy of a popular cult," undercutting the notion that the introduction of Aesculapius might be connected to the Struggle of the Orders.

25. Plin., *HN* 34.26.

appealing to a broader group of people who are now involved with Roman public life, particularly Italian allies and residents of Magna Graecia.[26] Through them, the Roman governing class recognized that contributions were possible, or even necessary, from those outside the traditional circle of power, and the *lex Ogulnia* similarly allowed participation, in this case specifically in religious affairs, from a wider group than the patrician aristocrats. Opening the door to wider involvement from outside groups, however, may also have led the Romans to begin to articulate a clearer vision of their origins as a means of distinguishing themselves with their own unique identity as they encountered a broader world. T. P. Wiseman has shown how the myth of Romulus and Remus came to be developed during this period; Wiseman suggests that the story of the two founders speaks to the division between plebeians and patricians.[27] The Ogulnii are implicated both with the myth and with plebeian-patrician issues, for in addition to the passage of the *lex Ogulnia*, they were the ones who erected the statue of the twins at the *ficus Ruminalis* in 296, as noted before. These statues, emphasizing the unique Roman origin myth, also served as a counterpart to the statues of the historical Greek figures and to the cult of Aesculapius, emphasizing the distinct nature of the Romans at the same time as demonstrating the open nature of Roman society.[28] The actions of the Ogulnii may thus be seen as part of an effort to present the Romans as open to the involvement of outsiders while continuing to stress their own unique sense of identity.

In the middle of the third century, a new ceremony dedicated to the gods of the underworld allows us to glimpse another Roman religious action with similar overtures. This ceremony became known as the *ludi saeculares*, a ceremony marking the end of one age and the beginning of the next, and is most famous for the celebration held by Augustus in 17 B.C.E.[29] However, the Augustan observance involved significant alterations to the ceremony, and the Augustan desire to project good Republican precedents makes it difficult to determine the nature of the Republican festival, and even its initial celebration. Despite the fact that a number of sources claim that the celebration was held every 100 or 110

---

26. Gagé (1955), 224–225.

27. Wiseman (1995), esp. 103–128.

28. Cf. Gagé (1955), 151, who notes the interest in a "national tradition" at this time, perhaps capable of creating a union for most of the Italic peoples, and the role of the Ogulnii in creating a balance between that impulse and Hellenism.

29. The sources relating to the *ludi saeculares* have been collected by G. B. Pighi (1965).

years, and that the Augustan celebration was the fifth in the series, the year 249 seems the most likely date for the first celebration of this ceremony.[30] The ceremony may not even have been part of a recurring cycle at the time of their foundation but was reinterpreted in that light by later sources under the influence of the Augustan celebration.[31] Indeed, Varro's account of the foundation of the games does not call them *ludi saeculares* but *ludi Tarentini*, a reference that has naturally focused attention on the town of Tarentum, in the boot of Italy.[32]

The aetiological story for the foundation of this rite found in Valerius Maximus and Zosimus offers further reason to focus on Tarentum.[33] When the children of a Sabine named Valesius fell ill and no cure could be found, a voice told Valesius to sail down the Tiber as far as Tarentum and have them drink water from the Tiber, boiled in a kettle on an altar he would find there dedicated to Dis and Proserpina. This seemed an awfully long way to go to the father, and he despaired of finding Tiber water in southern Italy, but nonetheless he set off from his village and made it as far as the Campus Martius before night fell. Upon disembarking, he learned that there was a spot nearby called Tarentum, and seeing smoke rising from the earth, he lit a fire there, boiled some water, and gave some to his children.

30. For the ancient sources pertaining to the first celebration of this ritual, see Censorinus, *DN* 17.8–10; Livy, *Per.* 49; Zos. 2.4.1–2; August., *De Civ. D.* 3.18. Verrius Flaccus, in Pseudo-Acro *Schol. on* Horace *Carmen Saeculare* 8. For 249 as the most likely date, see Wagenvoort (1956), 196; Wuilleumier (1938), 143; and most recently Bernstein (1998), 136. Palmer (1974, 102–104) preferred 456. Taylor (1934, 108–110) argued for 348, although she acknowledged (120) that the date 249 would be "the proper one for the formal inclu- sion of the *ludi saeculares* in the cult of the state"; only at that point was provision made for the regular repetition of the games. Brind'Amour (1978) attempted to completely discard the ancient chronology in favor of an elaborately constructed system of his own that has won few, if any, adherents. See also Cooley (2006) on the impact of Augustan concerns on the ceremony and our understanding of its history.

31. Weiss (1973); Schnegg-Köhler (2002), 158–161.

32. See Censorinus *DN*, 17.8: When there were many portents occurring, and the wall and tower which lay between the Colline gate and the Esquiline were struck by lightning, and for that reason the quindecemviri consulted the Sibylline Books, they announced that Tarentine games (*ludi Tarentini*) should be held in the Campus Martius to father Dis and Proserpina for three nights, and black animals should be sacrificed, and that the Games should be held every hundred years. (*Cum multa portenta fierent, et murus ac turris, quae sunt inter portam Collinam et Esquilinam, de caelo tacta essent, et ideo libros Sibyllinos XV viri adissent, renuntiarunt, uti Diti patri et Proserpinae ludi Tar- entini in campo Martio fierent tribus noctibus, et hostiae furvae immolarentur, utique ludi centesimo quoque anno fierent.*)

33. Val. Max. 2.4.5; Zos., 2.4.1–2. Cf. the discussion in Wuilleumier (1932), 131–139, and Wagenvoort (1956), 196–197.

They were cured on the spot. A divine figure then appeared to the children in a dream, which commanded Valesius to sacrifice black animals on the altar of Dis and Proserpina and to hold games in the Campus Martius. While digging the foundations for his new altar, Valesius found one already in the earth twenty feet below ground, and dedicated, according to the inscription Valesius found, to Dis and Proserpina. Valesius promptly offered his sacrifice on the newly uncovered altar.

The foundation legend thus serves to complicate what seems otherwise like a straightforward connection to Tarentum. The myth is at pains to insist that the *ludi Tarentini* derived their name from a spot in the Campus Martius, an important piece of Roman real estate, even while indicating its awareness of the southern Italian town.[34] The gods honored by the ritual also seem to have southern Italian connections; Dis and Proserpina are not attested as recipients of cult in Rome prior to this time, but a number of artifacts from Tarentum itself and from other towns in Magna Graecia indicate that cults devoted to these underworld divinities were thriving in this area at this time.[35] Kurt Latte, who insisted on taking a cautious approach and not postulating that the Secular Games were brought lock, stock, and barrel from Tarentum, suggested at least that "this much should be taken for certain, that the gods are of south Italian origin and possibly also the nocturnal ceremonies were brought from there."[36] Without positing a direct connection between the *ludi Tarentini* and the city of Tarentum, it seems clear that a cult of importance in Magna Graecia, and in Tarentum itself, found a home in Rome in the middle of the third century.

The introduction of Dis and Proserpina to Rome fits the pattern seen in the introduction of Aesculapius in revealing the openness of the Roman state to outsiders at a key juncture in Rome's history, while at the same time insisting on a clear sense of Roman identity. In 249, the outcome of the First Punic War was still very much in doubt; the Roman invasion of Africa had turned into a debacle, and a successful attack on Panormus had been offset by the failed siege of Lilybaeum. The Romans' naval supremacy, which they had maintained since the battle of Mylae in 260, was threatened by losses near Drepana both to the Carthaginian commander and to a gale at sea. At this juncture, the loyalty of Rome's south Italian associates was a matter of no small consequence to the

34. The location of the Tarentum in the Campus Martius has been a matter of some discussion among modern scholars, which it is not necessary to resolve here. See, e.g., Wuilleumier (1932); Taylor (1934); Castagnoli (1984).

35. Cf. Wuilleumier (1932), 139–140. An inscription (*IG* 14.630–631) from Locri, where a sanctuary for Hades and Persephone has been discovered, provides further evidence of the pair of underworld deities in southern Italy. Cf. Latte (1960), 248, n. 1.

36. Latte (1960), 247–248.

Romans; the Tarentines in particular had contributed ships in the early part of the war, precisely the area of Rome's most glaring weakness in 249.[37] Fifty years earlier, the adoption of Aesculapius may have helped win support against potential hostilities from Tarentum; now that Tarentum and the rest of southern Italy had been incorporated into the Roman polity, the tables were turned, and Rome attempted to cultivate the support of those same towns in a similar fashion. The introduction of an elaborate festival in honor of the underworld couple showed a considerable commitment on the part of Rome toward the sensibilities of the towns of southern Italy. Considering that the conquest of these towns was still relatively fresh, this goodwill expressed by the Romans in this act may have been doubly important. The institution of *ludi* dedicated to Dis and Proserpina took a significant step in that direction.

At the same time, the aetiological story insists upon the essential Romanness of this celebration. The Romans had *not* taken the cult from Tarentum, but the cult derived its name from a location in the Campus Martius.[38] Indeed the myth, like many other Roman stories, insists on the sacredness of that particular place; the children were cured simply from drinking the water, and an altar to Dis and Proserpina had existed in that spot all along, except that no one had known about it until Valesius came along. Valesius himself is a suspicious figure, with a name easily connected to the suffect consul of 509, P. Valerius Publicola, a fact that made it easy for later Romans to project the origins of the *ludi saeculares* back to the first year of the Republic.[39] While the historicity of this claim has been rejected, the attempt to synchronize these two events reveals the attempt to link it to the founding of the Republic and thus establish the essential Roman nature of the festival, just as the temple of Jupiter Optimus Maximus was said to be dedicated in that year. Even as Rome demonstrated that Tarentum and

37. Polyb. 1.20.13.

38. Curiously, the original place name seems to have been *Terentum* rather than *Tarentum*; the former is the form used by both Festus (478.15, s.v. Tarentum) and Servius (*Ad Aen.* 8.63), as well as Pseudo-Acro (on Horace, *Carmen Saeculare* 8) and Paulus Diaconus (479.6 L). Scribal error, of course, cannot be excluded, but modern scholars have generally agreed that Terentum was the original form, quite possibly changed under the pressure of the *ludi Tarentini*. See Wuilleumier (1932), 127–133; (1938); J. Gagé (1934); Wagenvoort (1956), 197–204; G. B. Pighi (1965). Erkell (1969), 173, argued most strongly for a link with Tarentum: "the Secular Games should still actually have come from south Italian Tarentum to Rome, and in connection with it *Terentum* changed to *Tarentum*." See also Wuilleumier (1938), 143–145. But contra, see Palmer (1974), 101, who believes it unlikely that the Romans would have used the name of a Greek town in this way.

39. Cf. Pighi (1965), 4–5; Taylor (1934), 111–112.

the other cities of southern Italy were no longer considered enemies but valued friends, elements of the mythmaking make clear the Romanness of the new cult.

Venus Erycina provides another example, again set against the backdrop of a Punic War, of how the introduction of a new cult might serve to strengthen ties with potential friends and at the same time strengthen a sense of Roman identity. Venus Erycina was the Venus from Mount Eryx, a hilltop town on the western, Punic, side of Sicily.[40] The Romans had become acquainted with this goddess during the First Punic War, when she had proven to be of great assistance. In 248, after the Romans had lost two fleets and control of the sea to the Carthaginians because of a storm, the consul L. Junius seized Eryx in an effort to regroup, controlling both the temple on the top of the mountain and the town on its flank.[41] For the next several years, the forces of Junius were able to hold off Hamilcar's attempts to retake the citadel, although the Carthaginian did capture the lower town. Polybius provides an image of the intensity of the combat around Eryx by comparing it with a boxing match between two champions and with a life-and-death struggle between gamecocks.[42] Eventually, the Roman victory at the Aegates Islands cut off the supplies of the besieging Carthaginians, forcing them to sue for peace. The Roman ability to hold on to Mount Eryx thus contributed in no small way to the eventual Roman victory, and Venus Erycina, the patron goddess of this mountaintop, earned the gratitude of the Romans for her support during the extended struggle against the Carthaginian attackers. An inkling of the strong Roman feeling on her behalf may be seen in the severe Roman punishment of Gauls who had pillaged her sanctuary during the war.[43] The Romans' acquaintance with Venus Erycina in the First Punic War set the stage for their importation of Venus Erycina to Rome during the Second Punic War.

In 217, as part of the religious response to the crisis brought on by Hannibal's invasion, the Romans decided to introduce Venus Erycina to Rome. Late in the previous year, a Roman army had been destroyed at Trebia, and early in that year, another was cut to pieces at Lake Trasimene. Following this second disaster at Trasimene, the Romans appointed a dictator, Q. Fabius Maximus, whose first act was to persuade the Senate that "the gods themselves ought to be consulted as to what expiations there were for the anger of the gods."[44] This consultation stands out as an unusual

40. The best treatment of this goddess is by R. Schilling (1954), especially 233–266.
41. Polyb. 1.55.
42. Polyb. 1.57, 1.58.7–9.
43. Polyb. 2.7.
44. Livy 22.9.

event, because consultation of the books was a step usually taken only following portents or natural disasters. Fabius apparently persuaded the Senate that the disaster at Trasimene should be perceived as evidence that the gods were angry at the Romans and thus treated as a portent, so the Roman response must be religious as well as military. Thus the decemviri consulted the oracular books and reported that the following steps must be taken: an earlier vow to Mars had not been properly performed and must be performed again, on a larger scale; *ludi Magni* were to be vowed to Jupiter; temples were to be vowed to Venus Erycina and to Mens; a *supplicatio* and a *lectisternium* were to be held; and a *ver sacrum*, a Sacred Spring, should be vowed, if the state proved victorious. This is an impressive list. Multiple expiations had been ordered before, but never had the list contained so many major vows: games, two temples, and a Sacred Spring, in which all livestock born during a designated period in the spring were given over to the gods. This last was a vow of such magnitude that it was deemed necessary to take a vote of the people before it could be legally undertaken.[45] The books ordered that he whose authority was highest in the state should undertake the vow to Venus Erycina, and the temple was duly vowed by Fabius Maximus. The following year, although he was no longer in office, Fabius asked the Senate for permission to dedicate the temple, which was now nearing completion. The Senate responded by decreeing that the consul designate for 215, Tiberius Sempronius, should propose to the people that Fabius should be appointed a duumvir for the purpose of dedicating the temple as soon as he entered office.[46] Accordingly, Fabius was made a duumvir and dedicated the temple on the Capitoline in 215.[47] It is worth noting that the temple to Venus Erycina was only one of a number of steps taken to combat the wrath of the gods, but several details concerning its construction attest to the importance that the Romans attached to this action. For the temple of Venus Erycina, the highest magistrate in the state was ordered to make the vow, in this case the dictator Fabius. The expedited construction compares favorably with most other temples and, indeed, matches that of the temple of Aesculapius discussed earlier. The temple was located on the Capitoline hill, separated by only a short distance from the temple of Jupiter Optimus Maximus, the religious center of the city. And rather than taking the chance that the fulfillment of the vow might have any improprieties (and thus according to Roman standards be considered null and void), Fabius was appointed duumvir to dedicate the temple.

45. Livy 22.10.
46. Livy 23.30.
47. Livy 23.31.

In part, this appointment may be due to a Fabian family connection with the goddess Venus, as Fabius' ancestor Q. Fabius Gurges had dedicated the first temple to Venus in Rome in 295. But it also enabled the man who made the vow to personally fulfill the vow, so there could be no doubt that the vow had been properly fulfilled. This action, building a temple to a foreign goddess in the heart of the city in a very short period of time, is sufficiently remarkable to warrant special attention.

One might understand this action in part by focusing on the military nature of the goddess and the extreme Roman needs at this juncture. As the Romans learned during the First Punic War, one aspect of Venus Erycina was military and defensive in nature, and after her arrival in Rome, this was the aspect of the goddess that the Romans most emphasized. Coins of the first century B.C.E. depict Venus Erycina with laurel wreath and diadem, while Victory appears in a quadriga on the reverse. Lest one suppose that the Romans invented this martial aspect, coins from Eryx also depict Victory in a quadriga on the reverse, although the goddess does have a different set of attributes on the obverse of the Sicilian coins.[48] After several crushing defeats at the hands of Hannibal, the Romans had good reason to have recourse to a goddess who would be thought to bolster their military forces. Furthermore, since Venus Erycina had been of great assistance in their first struggle with the Punic enemy, the Romans had every reason to believe that she would be just as helpful in another campaign against the same foe.[49] And since the theater of war in the second conflict was Italy, not Sicily, it was logical to bring the goddess from Sicily to Rome to provide assistance. While these considerations may explain part of the motivation for the adoption of Venus Erycina, the emphasis put on the construction of her temple suggests that other factors may be at work as well.

Like the foreign religious traditions previously discussed, the introduction of Venus Erycina to Rome may have been intended to secure human as well as divine aid. The mechanism in this instance involved the legend of Aeneas as the founder of the Roman people, although this tradition had been established only in the past hundred years.[50] Most versions of Aeneas' travels throughout the Mediterranean involve a stopover in Sicily and a visit to Mount Eryx; Diodorus Siculus held that the eponymous founder of

48. Roman coins: *BM Coins, Rep.* 3830–3832; 4087–4090. Eryx coins: Rizzo (1946), pl. 64.12. Cf. Schilling (1954), 243–244; Galinsky (1969), 186.

49. This idea may have been reinforced by the fact the Carthaginian commander in the Second Punic War was the son of the commander whom Venus Erycina had helped repel during the First Punic War.

50. On the development of the Trojan legend in Rome, see Galinsky (1969); Gruen (1992), 31.

Eryx, also a son of Aphrodite, had founded the shrine and that Aeneas embellished the sanctuary during his visit, while Vergil claims that Aeneas actually dedicated the sanctuary.[51] Vergil's version is likely to have been conditioned by his particular concerns to construct a genealogy for the Romans and for the Augustan family, but in so doing, Vergil reveals how Venus Erycina had come to be viewed not as a foreign cult, but as a matron deity who was counted on to help her descendants. In adopting the Venus from Mount Eryx, the Romans could be seen as reaching back to their roots and emphasizing the divine nature of their heritage, not adopting some strange polyglot goddess from a remote part of a foreign land. The use of claimed kinship links in conducting diplomacy in the ancient world was an established custom in the Hellenistic world, and its use by the Romans confirms their ability to maneuver smoothly in that milieu.[52]

The introduction of Venus Erycina thus appears to have had diplomatic overtones, through the connection to Aeneas, as the Romans attempted to create bonds between themselves and another people. Sicily, of course, had been the major theater of war in the First Punic War and had been a Roman possession for barely twenty years at the outbreak of the Second Punic War. While some cities such as Segesta may have welcomed the Roman presence, the Romans had good reason to be apprehensive about their position on the island. The western part of Sicily, including the area around Mount Eryx, had been a Carthaginian possession for a significant period prior to the First Punic War, and even the cult of Venus on Mount Eryx was essentially Punic, as noted before. There was no reason to think that the states there would not defect to Carthage when given the chance. Bringing the goddess to Rome and adopting her as part of the Roman state religion made a significant statement to the inhabitants of northwest Sicily. By welcoming the primary deity of that area into their own home, the Romans publicly affirmed the kinship between the two peoples, a kinship that had only recently been discovered. By this act, the Romans may have hoped that those states would be bound more tightly to them and maintain their allegiance to Rome during the coming struggle.

At the same time, the connection to Aeneas as the nature of the cult of Venus Erycina in Rome reveals the same efforts to establish a sense of Roman identity that we have seen with the other cults introduced earlier in the third century. The importation of Venus Erycina marks the first occasion, to the best of our knowledge, on which the Romans themselves had used the Trojan legend to foster connections between themselves and other cities. The connection had been used against the Romans by Pyrrhus in 281 B.C.E. in seeking to rouse

51. Diod. Sic., 4.83; Verg., *Aen.* 5.759.
52. On kinship diplomacy, see Jones (1999).

animosity toward Rome on the basis of the old enmity between Greeks and Trojans, and it had been used by states seeking alliance with Rome on the basis on consanguinity, such as when Segesta defected to the Roman side during the First Punic War on the basis of the claimed common ancestor, Aeneas.[53] Here the myth was consciously exploited by the Romans as a part of their self-representation to the outside world, especially to the residents of Sicily, and the location of the cult on the Capitoline hill may well have been intended to suggest the centrality of this mythological connection. Elements of the cult in Rome further suggest that this cult was conceived in Roman terms. The dedication of the temple to Venus Erycina took place on April 23, the day of the Vinalia Priora. This dedication parallels that of Venus Obsequens, the first temple dedicated to Venus in Rome, which was celebrated on the day of the Vinalia Rustica, August 19.[54] The nature of the cult in Rome was also different from the Sicilian counterpart. The cult in Sicily had many oriental or Phoenician aspects, the most prominent being the attachment of sacred prostitutes to the cult and the annual ritual of *anagogia* and *katagogia*, in which sacred pigeons were released and then returned after nine days.[55] Even Roman magistrates visiting the temple in Sicily, "putting off the austerity of their authority, enter into sports and have conversation with women in a spirit of great gaiety."[56] In Rome, however, there is no indication that the goddess was worshipped there in such fashion, but the Roman cult was altered to conform to traditional Roman norms.[57] Plutarch attests that the connection with wine suggested by the Vinalia was apparently maintained in the Roman ritual, but there is no sign of sacred prostitution or the *anagogia*.[58] Schilling has captured the essence of the Roman treatment of Venus Erycina:

> Far from feeling discomfort from the "Punic monopolization" of the Erycina, they wonderfully exploited the Trojan milieu of the land of the Elymi to reverse the situation. By virtue of the Trojan legend, they were able to claim Venus Erycina as *their* goddess.[59] (Italics original)

53. For Pyrrhus, see Paus. 1.12.1; cf. Gruen (1992), 44–46. For Segesta, cf. Zon. 8.9.12; and also Diod. Sic. 23.5. Segesta also minted coins depicting Aeneas carrying Anchises on his back: *BM Coins, Sicily*, 59ff.

54. Schilling (1954), 249.

55. For a fuller description of the Phoenician cult, see Schilling (1954), 242–248. See also Galinsky (1969), 71–72.

56. Diod. Sic. 4.83.

57. Schilling (1954), 248–254, provides a good overview of the cult as celebrated on the Capitoline.

58. Plut., *Quaest. Rom.* 45.

59. Schilling (1954), 244.

In sum, the Romans treated the Capitoline Venus Erycina "not as a stranger, but as a national divinity."[60] The transformation wrought in the cult of Venus Erycina highlights an important feature of the Roman treatment of foreign cults, and one that we have seen earlier in regard to Juno Regina and other cults. In importing foreign religious traditions, the Romans had no compunction about making changes in the original cult to adapt them to their own system; the openness to foreign traditions was indicated by the welcoming of certain practices, not necessarily by their wholesale implementation. This "adopt and adapt" behavior allowed the Romans to express their openness to foreigners and simultaneously maintain a sense of Romanness in their religious practices. The introduction of Venus Erycina thus stands in the tradition of Aesculapius and the Italian Junos, and it laid the foundations for the subsequent introduction of the Magna Mater in 205 by publicly proclaiming Rome's Trojan roots.[61]

At the other end of the Second Punic War, in circumstances very different from those surrounding the arrival of Venus Erycina, the Romans turned east to welcome another goddess with links to their Trojan past. In 205 B.C.E., frequent showers of stones led the Romans to consult the Sibylline Books, where an oracle was found recommending that "when a foreign enemy should bring

---

60. Schilling (1954), 249.

61. One unusual aspect of the importation of Venus Erycina is that a second temple was dedicated to the same goddess less than thirty-five years after the first. During the Ligurian War, the consul Lucius Porcius Licinus vowed this temple, and it was dedicated by his son in 181 outside the *porta Collina*. This cult was apparently closer to a reproduction of the Sicilian cult, for Strabo (6.272) calls it an ἀφίδρυμα a daughter cult, and Ovid (*Rem. am.* 549; *Fast.* 4.865–872) refers to the gathering of prostitutes in the vicinity of the temple. The Praenestine *fasti* even refer to the day of the temple's founding as *dies meretricum*, though the dedication date, like the first temple of Venus Erycina, was April 23.

The reasons for the introduction of two cults of Venus Erycina are not entirely clear. It may be, as Galinsky (1969, 186–187) suggests, that the Capitoline Erycina, as a foundation by the Senatorial aristocracy for political purposes, enjoyed little popularity with the broad masses, though other cults introduced by the Senate for "political" purposes, such as Aesculapius, do seem to have held appeal for the Roman populace. Furthermore, members of the ruling class were responsible for almost all the cults introduced to Rome during the Republic, and it is difficult to separate political and nonpolitical temples, given the close connection between religion and politics in Rome. While it would certainly be attractive to view the Capitoline temple as serving the needs of the aristocracy while the Colline temple met the needs of the populace for a more emotional outlet, this view seems too simplistic and too reliant on the old paradigm of "popular religion" filling the emotional and spiritual gap that the state religion failed to address. Elsewhere, I have suggested that this temple was meant as a sign in the wake of the Bacchanalia controversy that the Romans were not in principle opposed to foreign cults, but that the Senate needed to demonstrate its control over foreign cults. See further Orlin (2000).

MATRIDEVMETNAVISALVIAE
SALVIAE VOTO SVSCEPTO
CLAVDIA SYNTHYCHE
D· D

Figure 2.1: Marble Altar with Claudia Quinta pulling the Magna Mater to Rome, first century C.E.

war to Italian soil, he may be driven from Italy and defeated if the Idaean mother should be brought from Pessinus to Rome."[62] In pursuance of this oracle, the Romans sent an embassy to King Attalus of Pergamum, with whom they had recently entered into friendly relations in a joint effort against Philip V. The embassy first stopped at Delphi to inquire about the success of the mission and, upon receiving a favorable response, proceeded to Pergamum. Attalus welcomed the ambassadors and escorted them to Phrygia, where he handed over the black stone that was considered to represent the goddess. The embassy then returned to Rome, where it was greeted, as directed by the Delphic oracle, by the best and noblest of the Romans, P. Scipio. With great pomp and fanfare, and according to some versions a miraculous intervention on the part of the goddess (fig. 2.1), the stone was safely introduced into Rome and lodged in the temple of Victoria on the Palatine hill until a new temple could be built expressly for her; this temple was eventually dedicated in 191 B.C.E.[63]

62. For the events described here, see Livy 29.10.4–29.11.8; 29.14.5–9; 29.37.2; 36.36.3–5.
63. The "miraculous intervention" referred to here consists of the story of Claudia Quinta. When the ship bearing the black stone became stuck in the mud of the Tiber, Claudia stepped forward and demonstrated her chastity by escorting the ship safely to the dock. See Ovid, *Fast.* 4.305–348; Suet. *Tib.* 2.3; Lactant. *Div. inst.* 2.8.

While one might be tempted to look on the importation of the Magna Mater simply as reaching out to a patron deity to help finish off Hannibal, just as the Romans had reached out to Venus Erycina at the beginning of the war, the circumstances and timing of this episode suggest that the introduction of this goddess also held further implications. A critical point is that the Romans willingly chose to import this goddess from the East; no calamity either political or religious urged them on. By 205, the Second Punic War was winding its way to a definitive conclusion; the battle at the Metaurus in 207 had eliminated the possibility of major reinforcements reaching Hannibal and so had effectively ended the threat that the Carthaginians might triumph.[64] Though Hannibal might still hope for some reinforcements, the initiative had clearly passed to the Romans, who were no longer seeking only to defend themselves from Hannibal's onslaught and were now trying to find a way to evict Hannibal from Italy and finish the war. No crisis in the war with Hannibal precipitated the introduction of this cult, unlike the numerous cult activities and innovations of 218 and 217, and, one might argue, no crisis existed at all. The religious grounds on which the introduction of the cult was based betray this lack of crisis: the consultation of the Sibylline Books was occasioned only by frequent showers of stones.[65] Showers of stones (perhaps meteorites) were a common prodigy in the Republic and were most often expiated by means of a *novemdiale sacrum*, but prior to 205, showers of stones by themselves are never recorded as the sole cause of a Sibylline consultation.[66] Showers of stones are attested as part of a larger group of prodigies that led to the consultation of the Sibylline Books, such as in 344, when it was reported along with an eclipse, or in 218, with a whole series of other prodigies in the wake of the battle at Trebia.[67] The latter example makes clear that the *novemdiale sacrum* was the normal expiation for showers of stones, for Livy reports that a *novemdiale* was celebrated on account of the shower of stones, while the decemviri *sacris faciundis* were ordered to consult the Sibylline Books on account of the other prodigies. It is therefore impossible to see the importation of the Magna Mater as driven primarily by religious pressures. Indeed, seen in the context of other prodigies that drove religious actions during the Second Punic War, it

64. This point is argued strongly by Gruen (1990), 6–7, though it is rejected just as strongly by Burton (1996), 39–41. Roller (1999), 266, accepts that "the arrival of the Magna Mater had little to do with the Carthaginian Wars." See also Lambrechts (1951), 46–47.

65. Burton (1996), 42, correctly recognizes the shower of stones as the prodigy that prompted the sequence of events leading to the introduction of the Magna Mater but fails to note the extraordinary nature of this response to that particular prodigy.

66. Livy 1.31 provides the initial report of this type of prodigy; while unsure of the origins of this practice, the historian remarks that "certainly the rite remained that whenever the same prodigy was reported, a festival was observed for nine days."

67. 344: Livy 7.28. 218: Livy 21.62.

almost appears that the Roman Senate was looking for an excuse to import the Magna Mater to Rome, rather than being coerced into it by an unfavorable military or political situation.[68] The determination to consult the Sibylline Books in 205 rather than celebrating a *novemdiale*, in the absence of prodigies that were more significant or an imminent crisis, strongly suggests that other considerations loomed large in the decision-making process.

A beginning to the explanation may be found by considering the locations where the Magna Mater had been worshipped prior to her introduction to Rome. Cybele had been important goddess in Asia Minor from the Bronze Age, with several important cult sites throughout the region.[69] Roman sources split on the site from which the Romans obtained the goddess; although Livy reports that the Romans fetched Cybele from Pessinus in Galatia, he also refers to the goddess as the Idaean mother, a reference to Mount Ida in the Troad, site of another important cult to the Great Mother.[70] Cicero, like Livy, calls her the Idaean mother in one text but refers to Pessinus as her home in another.[71] Of the other sources who mention the arrival of the Magna Mater, many allude to Pessinus, with one major exception: Ovid in his *Fasti* focuses exclusively on the Idaean connection.[72] Each of the literary sources is particularly open to challenge in this instance. Ovid, in a work that emphasized the Julian family, may well have favored a home that allowed him to connect the Mother with Rome's Trojan origins and hence the divine ancestry of the Julii. On the other hand, Pessinus appears to have been the most prominent cult location in Asia Minor in the first century B.C.E. and later, the period in which Livy, Cicero, Strabo, and Diodorus were writing, but it appears to have become prominent only in the Hellenistic period and especially under the influence of the Pergamene kings, so these later sources may have been swayed by the position of Pessinus in their own day.[73] Historically, there is reason to think that Pergamene authority did not extend to the interior of Phrygia as early as 204, and Livy's report of the campaign of Manlius Vulso in Galatia in 189, when the *galli* of Pessinus came out to meet his troops and prophesy victory, leaves the impression that the Romans had not yet been in contact

68. Lambrechts (1951), 48.

69. Cf. Vermaseren (1977), 24–32, and more fully Roller (1999).

70. Livy 29.10; 29.14.

71. Cic. *Har. resp.* 27–8; *Sen.* 45.

72. Those mentioning Pessinus include Strabo 12.5.3; App. *Hann.* 56; Val. Max. 8.15.3; Diod. Sic. 34/35.33.2; *De Viris Illustribus* 46; Dio Cass. fr. 57.61, and Amm. Marc. 22.9.5. For Ovid, cf. *Fast.* 4.249–272.

73. Cf. Roller (1999), 269; for the discussion of Pessinus in the Hellenistic era, see her discussion on 192–194 and sources cited there.

with the shrine there.[74] Furthermore, evidence from the cult in Rome, including large numbers of votive deposits to Attis found in the sanctuary on the Palatine hill, suggest a cult that was more Hellenized than Phrygian and so again points away from Pessinus as the cult home.[75] This evidence suggests that Mount Ida is a more likely source for the cult of the Magna Mater that came to Rome, a point perhaps confirmed by the official name of the goddess in Rome: *mater deum magna Idaea*.[76] Certainly, that association loomed largest in the Roman imagination, as the confusion in both Livy and Cicero suggests that they recognized the importance of the connection to Mt. Ida.[77]

The significance of this locale should not be overlooked: this is the Mount Ida that overlooks the Trojan plain, and the goddess invoked was the primary divinity of the Troad. As with Venus Erycina, the Romans again capitalized on the legend of Aeneas as the founder of the Roman people; there could hardly be a more public endorsement of this legend by the Romans than the introduction of this goddess. This interpretation is clearest in Ovid's account, for the goddess is made to say that she almost followed Aeneas to Rome but "felt that the Fates did not yet demand her presence in Latium," while Attalus, who initially resists the move, finally agrees, saying that "Rome ascribes her ancestors to the Phrygians."[78] Just as with Venus Erycina, the Magna Mater came to be viewed not as a foreign deity, but as the old patron deity of the Romans' Trojan ancestors. This notion seems to have been present not just in the Augustan age, but from the moment the cult was introduced, as may be inferred from the location of the temple: on the Palatine hill, which the Romans considered

74. Cf. Gruen (1990), 16; Roller (1999), 268–269. For the incident with Manlius Vulso, see Livy 38.18.9–10.

75. Roller (1999), 271–278. The sanctuary of the Magna Mater on the Palatine was first excavated by Romanelli (1963); summaries of more recent work at the site can be found in Pensabene (1982, 1985).

76. The name appears on the *fasti Antiates maiores*, from the 60s B.C.E., as well as on other stone calendars. Cf. *Inscr. Ital.* 13.2, 127. Gruen (1990), 15–19, argued for Mount Ida as the source for the cult, while Roller (1999), 269–271, following a note in Varro (*Ling.* 6.15), preferred Pergamum, while noting that Ida lay well within Pergamene control and so also made a possible source. Cf. contra Burton (1996), who follows many earlier commentators in supporting Pessinus as the home of the Roman goddess.

77. Even Burton (1996), 56–57, while arguing for the cult's home in Pessinus, nonetheless agreed that the association with the Troad was the operative connection for the Romans.

78. Ovid, *Fast.* 4.253–254: *nondum fatis Latio sua numina posci senserat*; 4. 272: *in Phrygios Roma refertur avos*.

the oldest part of the city, the site of their origins. During the Republic, very few new temples were constructed on the Palatine hill, and the location testifies to the importance of this cult and the relationship that Troy's descendants saw between the goddess and the foundation of their city.

The connection between the Magna Mater and Rome's Trojan origins provides the link that helps explain why the Romans decided to introduce the cult of the Great Mother at this particular moment, with no apparent religious or military crisis present. Another event of the year 205 is often overlooked against the backdrop of the Punic War: the conclusion of the First Macedonian War, which ended less than satisfactorily for the Romans with the Peace of Phoenice. The Roman image and reputation in the East had been tarnished by her failure to commit more than token forces to the war and by the rapacious behavior of her troops.[79] Some attempt at reconciliation was desirable, even if it was only a symbolic gesture. The introduction of a cult that was known throughout the region advertised Roman sensitivity to local traditions. By publicly proclaiming their Trojan roots, the Romans were also declaring their intention to play a significant role in that part of that world. This message, of continued Roman interest in the East, may have been directed as much to Philip as to Rome's Greek allies. These sentiments, expressed through the incorporation of the Magna Mater, might help to resuscitate the Roman name in the East. In this regard, it is important to recall that the Romans did not attempt to fetch Cybele themselves, but rather through the offices of King Attalus of Pergamum. All sources are agreed on this, and Varro even suggested that Pergamum was the home of the goddess.[80] By having Attalus serve as an intermediary, the Romans clearly announced their continuing support for a key ally in the area and thus their intention not to abandon the eastern Mediterranean to the wishes of Philip.[81] Not only is the Roman adoption of the Magna Mater an acknowledgment of the permanent relationship between the Romans and Phrygians but also an important Greek king publicly approved and acknowledged this deed. The acceptance of the Roman claim by one of the leading powers in the region can only have helped Rome to win over any doubters. If Attalus was unsure about linking himself so closely with Rome,

79. See Polyb., 9.37.5–8, 9.39.1–3, 11.5.4–8; Livy 29.12.1, 31.29.1–15, 32.21–22. For a fuller treatment of the Roman motives here, see Gruen (1990), 27–33.

80. Varro, *Ling.* 6.15.

81. Even Burton (1996), who generally downplays the foreign policy implications of the advent of the Magna Mater, acknowledges the link to Attalus and admits (62) that this action "coincided nicely with Roman foreign relations at this time."

the approval of the Delphic oracle, to which the Roman embassy directed a question before arriving at Attalus' court, would have provided him with divine sanction for this action. So the Roman adoption of the Magna Mater helped the cause of Roman diplomacy in three ways: it reaffirmed the alliance with Attalus, it reassured the Greek states of the area, and it warned Philip that the Romans were not about to disappear from this region. This model, of religious activity carrying broader cultural and political messages, should be familiar from previous Roman actions throughout the fourth and third centuries.

Those earlier actions also showed the Romans taking simultaneous steps to ensure that a clear definition of Roman identity remained intact, even as they incorporated cults from beyond their city, and the case of the Magna Mater is no different. As with the importation of Venus Erycina, the Romans again placed an emphasis on their Trojan heritage through this cult and underscored this point by erecting the temple of the Magna Mater on the Palatine hill, traditionally considered the home of Romulus, founder of the city. The location of this cult inside the *pomerium* is also significant; even if no rule banned foreign cults from the city, traditionally most such cults did find themselves outside the religious boundary line.[82] In other ways as well, such as with the inauguration of *ludi* and the treatment of the priests of the Magna Mater known as the *galli*, subjects that will be treated in subsequent chapters of this book, Roman actions served to welcome the foreign goddess into the heart of Roman religion while simultaneously marking out what was Roman and what was non-Roman. These twin results were the hallmark of the Roman religious response to foreign cults. The case of the Magna Mater at the end of the century, whose arrival was precipitated by a "manufactured" crisis, reveals most clearly the Romans' increasing self-awareness of the manner in which the religious actions might foster links between themselves and other peoples and simultaneously delineate their own sense of Romanness.

The purpose of the discussion in this chapter is not to suggest that the Roman actions relating to religion in this period were intended to induce the non-Romans to accept a Roman hegemonic position, or that they were sufficient to create bonds between the Romans and others. We are extremely ill equipped to understand the reaction of the other party to these Roman initiatives, but under any circumstances, a single action does not suffice to build a lasting relationship. Rather, these actions are important for what they reveal about the Roman mind-set; as the Romans expanded, they often sought to present themselves as partaking

82. See Orlin (2002).

of the local culture, rather than seeking to impose their own practices on a subjugated people. Although the Romans certainly indicated their superior position, both by installing these practices in Rome and modifying them as they saw necessary, what is remarkable compared with their contemporaries is that they chose to incorporate these practices in the first place. The willingness to find a place for foreign practices within the Roman religious system is symptomatic of the willingness to find places for foreign people within Roman society, and this readiness to incorporate foreigners, rather than to solely subjugate them, is a key element in understanding the Roman success in building their hegemony.

The incorporation of foreign elements into Roman religion was not, however, completely unproblematic for the Romans. With the arrival of so many elements from outside the state, the boundary between Roman and non-Roman became blurred, but maintaining a clear sense of that boundary was vital in order to define Romanness, and the question of what constituted Roman practice thus became an increasing area of concern. In the religious sphere, some of the cults and rituals now practiced at Rome differed tremendously from practices they had previously utilized, and similar changes are visible throughout Roman society. As we saw, the response is visible with the influx of the first Greek elements at the beginning of the century, for the introduction of Aesculapius was accompanied by several other actions that focused attention on the mythical founders of Rome, emphasizing Rome's Italic roots at the same moment as a new wave of Hellenic culture arrived in Rome. Further initiatives that brought foreign elements into Roman society as the century progressed were accompanied by further steps taken by the Romans to emphasize their own identity. As they expanded their territorial holdings, the Romans were faced with the twin challenges of continuing to remain open to foreign influences and people while still retaining a clear sense of Roman identity. Roman religion, by virtue of its central place in Roman society and its intimate connections with the political structure, provides a valuable means of examining the tensions caused by the Roman expansion and the incorporation of foreign elements into the system.

It is often overlooked that the Roman activity during the third century marks the first direct sustained encounter with Hellenic culture, as the Greek elements arriving in the archaic period appear to have been mediated through Italian cities both in Magna Graecia and farther north in central Italy. Modern discussions of the Roman relationship with the Greek world have tended to focus on the second century, following upon the numerous treasures of Greek art brought to Rome by M. Claudius Marcellus following the sack of

Syracuse.[83] Yet despite the paucity of sources, it is important to look back to third century to understand the Roman encounter with Hellenic culture; from Aesculapius at the beginning of the century to the Magna Mater at its close, an increasing number of the cults and religious practices introduced in Rome in the third century were no longer mediated through mainland Italian towns. Nor was religious practice the only place where Hellenic influence made itself felt. Livius Andronicus introduced Greek literature to Rome, through his translation of the Odyssey in 240 and subsequent Latin plays, and Fabius Pictor, in addition to writing in Greek, adopted the very notion of history writing from Greece.[84] During this period, the Romans showed no fear or hesitation concerning foreign culture, but welcomed these practices and displayed little discomfort in making them part of Roman culture, even installing two of the cults on the two most religiously important hills of Rome: Venus Erycina on the Capitoline and the Magna Mater on the Palatine. The sustained and direct Roman encounter with Hellenism began in the third century; the nervousness about Greek culture that became part of the subsequent historiographical tradition at Rome is in part a response to these earlier developments as well as to the events of the second century.

The examination of the introduction of new cults and rites during the third century points the way toward a pattern that can be seen in other aspects of Roman religion, both in the third century and afterward. Moving forward, an exploration of how the Romans treated foreign religious traditions, not just at the initial moment of acceptance but over the ensuing generations, reveals how the Romans continued to balance their inclination for openness with the need for boundaries. While some actions served to mark out the Romans on the world stage as a clearly distinguishable people, the growth of Rome's power throughout the Mediterranean basin often led to a sharpening of distinctions between those living overseas and

83. E.g., Colin (1905); Saunders (1944), Petrochilos (1974), Ferrary (1988); MacMullen (1991). Gruen (1992), 230–235, does note an expansion of interest and competence in Greek during the third century but then devotes the bulk of his discussion (241–269) to the second century and later. This focus on the second century may be in part a product of our sources, who focus on the changes wrought on Roman society in the second century by the influx of Greek culture, and who often blame this influx for the weakening of Roman society, as they saw it, which culminated in the civil wars of the first century. For instance, Livy (39.6.7) emphasized the significance of Manlius Vulso's triumph in 187, and Sallust focused upon the destruction of Carthage in 146.

84. Andronicus apparently hailed from Tarentum in southern Italy, another example in this case of Greek culture mediated through Magna Graecia. The fact that direct encounters with Greek culture began at the beginning of the third century does not mean that all subsequent encounters followed that model.

those inhabiting peninsular Italy. The attentiveness to the status of the Italians can be seen in many initiatives of the later third and second centuries, especially as the manpower of Italian cities played such a crucial role in the military conflicts of this period. The process of maintaining a sense of Romanness and identifying those who belonged continued to evolve throughout the Republic, ultimately, as we will see at the conclusion of this book, finding some resolution under the emperor Augustus, who consolidated many of the developments of the previous two hundred years. It is to those developments that our attention must now turn.

3

Foreign Priests in Rome

One of the most noteworthy aspects of the Roman willingness to incorporate foreign elements within their religious system is the fact that in several cases they brought the foreign priests associated with that cult into their system as well. The significance of this behavior has seldom been fully recognized: priests of a foreign nationality were engaged on behalf of the Roman state on a regular basis, a situation for which there is no parallel in the ancient world (or even the modern world).[1] The nature of the Roman religious system makes this action even more remarkable. First, since one of the primary functions of the Roman state religion was to safeguard the well-being of the state, this action had the even more momentous consequence of placing the welfare of the state at least partly in the hands of foreigners. Second, because of the emphasis in Roman religion on the proper performance of ritual (orthopraxis), rather than on belief (orthodoxy), a foreign-born priest could not integrate simply by adopting the belief system of the home community.[2] The inclusion of foreign priests within their religious system therefore required the Romans to accept the rituals performed by those priests rather than requiring the priests to adopt Roman behavior. Examining the particular places in which foreign priests

1. MacBain (1982), 43, is one of the few to notice the extraordinary nature of this situation.
2. Scheid (2003), 18–21, provides a succinct summary of the major principles of Roman religion, including the emphasis on orthopraxis in Rome.

made their appearance in the Roman religious system reveals to an even greater degree the Roman openness to foreigners that was evident in the cults introduced during the third century.

Priesthood in the Roman Republic differs greatly from modern notions of priesthood in several important ways.[3] Religious authority was not located in a single place but was diffused across a wide spectrum of persons, a feature very much in keeping with the principles by which the Roman aristocracy governed the state. The Senate, ostensibly an advisory body on matters of state, always met in a religiously demarcated location and wielded great authority on religious affairs, to the point that it has been suggested that the Senate served as the primary locus of mediation between the divine and the human in Rome.[4] Alongside the Senate were a host of religious colleges, each charged with a different set of responsibilities, although the lines demarcating the responsibilities of each group could become blurred. The pontiffs, headed by the titular head of Roman religion, the *pontifex maximus*, officiated at some state festivals, as well as holding a general supervisory role over Roman religion. The augurs were charged with defining sacred space on earth and ascertaining the will of the gods for political and military actions, while the *decemviri sacris faciundis*, expanded to fifteen under Sulla, had custody of the Sibylline Books, a collection of oracles that prescribed remedies for ruptures in the *pax deorum*. The Vestal Virgins played a role in a number of rituals throughout the year, though their main task was to guard the sacred hearth of the city and to ensure that the fire in the temple of Vesta did not die out. Other groups had lesser roles: the *septemviri epulones* organized ritual meals for the gods, the *salii* performed a ritual dance through the city twice a year, and the *fetiales* supervised the religious aspects of declaring war and making peace treaties with Rome's external foes. Membership in each group was for life, barring some disqualification, but not hereditary. Members were chosen by a variety of mechanisms, but members tended to also be members of the Senate or the ruling aristocracy. As a rule, Romans served on only one college, which both created opportunities for more Romans to serve and contributed to the diffusion of religious power across the colleges.

In addition to these groups of priests who concerned themselves with religion in Rome as a whole, individual Roman cults were generally served by an individual priest or priests. The most important of these was the *flamen Dialis*, who was attached to the cult of Jupiter Optimus Maximus. This particular office, whose holder was directly chosen by the *pontifex maximus*, was so hedged about with religious taboos that, unlike other Roman priests, a normal

3. See Beard (1990), and also Beard, North, and Price (1998), passim.
4. Beard (1990).

senatorial career was all but impossible; among other restrictions, he was not allowed to see the army arrayed outside the *pomerium*, and he was not allowed to be away from his own bed for three consecutive nights, both of which prevented him from carrying out the normal duties of most Roman magistrates. Other flamines included the two other "major" ones, those attached to Quirinus and Mars, as well as twelve "minor" flamines, of which we know the names for ten only: *Carmentalis, Cerialis, Falacer, Floralis, Furrinalis, Palatualis, Pomonalis, Portunalis, Volcanalis*, and *Volturnalis*. The obscurity of some of these cults has led to the widespread assumption that these priests and cults are among the oldest in Roman religion, dating back before the beginning of the Republic. These are merely the best known examples of priests attached to individual Roman cults; each Roman temple apparently had its own personnel, whose responsibilities lay primarily in presiding over the rites held at the temple, particularly on its *dies natalis*. When a new temple was constructed in Rome, it thus created a need for an additional priest to officiate at the temple. Studying the place of priests, especially foreign priests, in the Roman religious system has the advantage of revealing Roman behavior toward these individuals over a period of time, rather than simply at the moment of inclusion. While at the beginning the Romans may have projected the attitude of openness, the passage of time allows us to see a growing attentiveness to defining a sense of Romanness and developing a sense of Roman identity among the presence of so many foreign elements. The treatment of foreign priests in Rome displays how the Romans attempted to balance these two concerns.

Perhaps the most unusual example of the Roman acceptance of foreign priests is the addition not just of a single priest to minister to a single cult, but of an entire college of priests: the haruspices from Etruria. Bruce MacBain has already discussed the presence of the haruspices in Rome, emphasizing the uniqueness of allowing priests of foreign nationality, and even of a former bitter enemy, to serve in such an important position, so here it is necessary only to touch on the key points.[5] Haruspices appear as a group acting in a formal relationship with the Roman state for the first time in 278 B.C.E. Earlier appearances of the haruspices in certain episodes appear either to be apocryphal, such as the haruspex present at the *devotio* of Decius in 340, or to be limited to informal appearances on an ad hoc basis, as with the presence of these priests in Rome during the reign of the Tarquins, an Etruscan family. As MacBain notes, it is "impossible to believe that she [Rome] allowed the Etruscan enemy access to the political and religious machinery of the State" during the time when

5. For the overall discussion of MacBain (1982) on the presence of haruspices in Rome, see pp. 42–59.

Rome and Etruria were locked in their struggle for supremacy of central Italy.[6] The incident in 278 provides a secure starting point, as consultation of the haruspices—in order to locate the head of Jupiter, which had been blasted from a temple pediment by bolt of lightning—resulted in the construction of a temple to the Etruscan god of night lightning Summanus, an event that is firmly anchored. From this point forward, the Romans invited the haruspices to offer their opinions, at first tentatively but with increasing frequency from the late third century onward, to the extent that by the 130s, the haruspices were consulted more frequently than the *decemviri sacris faciundis*. In light of the Roman religious actions of the third century discussed in the previous chapter, it should not be surprising to see the Romans beginning to utilize the Etruscan haruspices in a formal way in 278, at almost exactly the moment when hostilities with Etruria were finally drawing to a formal close, with *foedera* concluded with many Etruscan cities.[7] The inclusion of the haruspices within the Roman religious system reflects part of the Roman attempt to include the inhabitants of Etruria within the res publica.[8]

Some scholars have suggested that the haruspices were never fully accepted into Roman religion and that a rivalry existed between the decemviri and the haruspices over the expiation of prodigies, but the evidence points toward cooperation rather than competition.[9] We must remember that for either group to become involved in an expiation, the Senate had to formally ask for their assistance. It is difficult to imagine that the Senate would continue asking the haruspices for their advice if they had felt uncomfortable with using Etruscan methods of interpretation. It is equally difficult to imagine a continued rivalry between the decemviri and the haruspices, especially considering that

6. MacBain (1982), 46. For the *devotio*, see Livy 8.9.1. Other apocryphal instances noted by MacBain include the snake gliding out of a wooden column during the construction of the temple of Jupiter Optimus Maximus, which led to the equally apocryphal embassy to Delphi in which Brutus kissed the earth, his mother (Livy 1.56).

7. Cf. MacBain (1982), 47, who is careful to note that the first *recorded* appearance of the haruspices in Rome may not be their first actual appearance but still finds it "difficult to overlook the coincidence of the final political settlement of Etruria in, or shortly before, 278 with the first fully believable notice of the activity of the *haruspices* in Rome." On the *foedera* confirming peaceful relations with Etruria between 280 and 278, see Harris (1971), especially chapters 2 and 3.

8. MacBain (1982), 46, suggests that the invitation to the haruspices reflects an effort by the Roman state to cement relationships with the Etruscan aristocrats who made up the bulk of these priests and who might exercise control over their cities. While this appeal undoubtedly played a role in the Roman actions, the significance should not be limited to the aristocratic class.

9. E.g., Bloch (1963); Gagé (1955).

the decemviri were themselves members of the Senate who would have to vote to consult their supposed rivals. We should therefore not expect to find continued contentiousness between the two groups, and the evidence drawn from expiations of the second century offers no indication of such a view. Rather, the androgyne expiation of 207 provides a telling indication of the degree of cooperation and coordination between the decemviri and the haruspices in successfully expiating prodigies. When the androgynous child was first discovered, the haruspices declared that it was a dire portent and must be banished without touching Roman soil.[10] The pontifices then decreed that twenty-seven virgins should sing a hymn through the city, and when lightning struck the temple of Juno Regina while they were practicing, both the haruspices and the decemviri prescribed further expiatory measures. The haruspices declared that the goddess should be appeased with a gift, while the decemviri set aside an additional day for the procession. The details of this event recorded by Livy leave no doubt that the whole celebration was carefully orchestrated, probably by the decemviri, since in the performance of the ritual they first accompanied the procession with the maidens and the gift to the temple and then sacrificed the two white heifers to Juno Regina themselves. The decemviri were thus intimately involved with many aspects of the performance of the expiation, while the haruspices' role was to pronounce on the meaning of the prodigy and the broader direction of the expiation. Similar androgyne expiations were performed many times over the next hundred years, and the continued recourse to a ritual that involved both haruspices and decemviri is one indication that these groups worked in concert with each other, not against each other.[11]

Examples of coordination from ceremonies other than androgyne expiations can also be found. One such instance dates from 172 B.C.E., when a column on the Capitol was shattered by a bolt of lightning.[12] Both the decemviri and the haruspices must have been consulted, for both weighed in on the response: the decemviri prescribed a *lustratio, supplicatio,* sacrifices, and *ludi* as expiations; the haruspices announced that the omen portended the expansion of Roman frontiers and the destruction of Rome's enemies, a response that was most welcome and appropriate, as the war with Perseus loomed. We should not see the responses of the two groups as hostile or in

10. See Livy 27.37 for the narrative of events.

11. See MacBain (1982), 127–135, for a discussion of all the androgyne expiations. The major elements of the ritual were repeated on further occasions when androgynous births were reported, in 200, in 133, in 125, in 119, in 117, in 97, and in 92 B.C.E.; on other instances, the sources report the announcement of an androgyne birth but do not explicitly state that the full expiation, including the procession of chanting maidens, was performed.

12. Livy 42.20.

conflict with each other,[13] but rather the different responses symbolize the different types of responses that the Senate might get from the Roman and Etruscan sources. The Roman priests outlined a series of rituals to expiate the prodigy, and the Etruscan priests indicated what the omen portended for the future. Rather than competition, the episode thus reveals how the priestly groups in Rome that dealt with portents might complement each other, as each group offered a response based on its own style of divination. While some rivalry may have existed between the groups, the Senate clearly valued the input from both groups, which militates against seeing the haruspices as not fully accepted into the Roman religious system.

Another example of cooperation provides an additional piece of evidence for seeing cooperation between the haruspices and the Roman priestly groups, and also perhaps a partial explanation. In 191, the Senate decided that two oxen who had climbed the stairs onto the roof of a building should be treated as a prodigy; in response, the haruspices ordered that the oxen should be burned, and the decemviri ordered that several showers of stones and lightning strikes in separate locations should be expiated with sacrifices and the institution of the *ieiunium Cereris*. Although Livy's report presents these as separate prodigies with separate expiations, it is noteworthy that lightning, the area of traditional Etruscan expertise, was named as one of the prodigies, although expiated by the Roman priests. One might suggest that here we have evidence that the Roman priests had developed some expertise from their contact with their Etruscan counterparts, but at the very least, we see here another example of complementarity: both haruspices and decemviri involved in expiating a series of prodigies. It may in fact be more significant that the haruspices were *not* involved with the lightning expiation in this episode. Although they may have been engaged by the Roman state initially on account of their expertise with fulgural lore, their opinion came to be sought on other matters as well, even, as in this instance, when there was also a lightning prodigy demanding attention.[14] Similar episodes can be found at other times in the second century; in 199, they were consulted concerning

13. In this conclusion I follow MacBain (1982), 59: "it seems unnecessary to read competition and acrimony into the episode."

14. MacBain (1982), 118–120, has discussed the prodigy types that seem to be more or less characteristic of the haruspices. Lightning strikes are one obvious example; monstrous births, both androgynes and otherwise, and sex changes in humans also seem to be characteristic for the Etruscan diviners. MacBain includes animals behaving in strange fashion, such as talking, on this list, but his evidence shows that Roman priests were as likely as the haruspices to be involved in expiating such animal prodigies, so it may be difficult to class these as characteristic for the haruspices.

laurel leaves that were growing from the stern of a ship; in 192, they were consulted about a talking ox; and in 182, a severe storm that blew down doors and statues led to their involvement.[15] Perhaps more interesting is the fact that the haruspices on several occasions prescribed remedies that seem uncharacteristic for the haruspices but are very characteristic for Roman religion. The prodigy of the laurel tree in 199 was expiated by a *supplicatio*, as was an instance of a bull mounting a bronze cow in Syracuse in 177. In 102 B.C.E., the haruspices ordered a *lustratio*, the ritual purification of the city that followed every census, and in 65 B.C.E. they prescribed *ludi*, a typically Roman ceremony, as we shall see later.[16] The haruspices clearly adapted themselves to the Roman religious system, just as the Romans made room in their system for the haruspices and integrated them fully, to the point where they were not merely used as specialists for certain "Etruscan-style" portents.

In light of the Roman habit of adopting foreign cults and foreign rituals, which were not always linked solely to the aristocratic class, the incorporation of the haruspices into the Roman religious system may speak to relations with Etruria more broadly. The Romans had previously incorporated cults from individual cities in Etruria, including most famously the *evocatio* of Juno Regina from Veii after a supposed ten-year siege. These actions are double-sided: on the one hand, they demonstrate the hegemony of the Romans over their defeated foes, as even the gods of the defeated people have been moved to Rome. But on the other hand, the installation of a foreign deity within the Roman pantheon is a mark of respect and honor; in these cases, the Romans chose not simply to terminate the worship of the divinity by the local population but to take that obligation onto themselves. Juno Regina, who was discussed earlier, was of course imported from the Etruscan city of Veii and provides an instructive example; the Roman sources indicate that she was worshipped in a temple "worthy of [her] majesty," hardly a sign of disrespect.[17] The same principle can be applied to the adoption of rituals from foreign territories; the decision to adopt such rituals is an indication of respect for the ritual and for the people who practice it, and a sign of a cultural affinity between the two peoples. In the case of haruspicial activity, this statement is even more remarkable, because the Romans not only began to use the *Etrusca disciplina* but also actually brought in Etruscan priests to do so. That they began to do so at almost exactly the moment when hostilities ceased between the two sides provides an astonishing example of the Roman

15. 199: Livy 31.1.10–14; 192: Livy 35.21.2–5; 182: Livy 40.2.1–4.

16. 177: Livy 41.13.1–3. 102: Obsequens 44 and 65; Cic. *Cat.* 3.19–20. For *ludi*, see chapter 5.

17. Livy 5.21.3. See Orlin (2002).

tendency to extend their hegemony not by military power alone, but by creating cultural links and by incorporating significant elements of the defeated culture into their own community.[18]

The details of how the haruspices the Roman state employed were selected and organized, while not known clearly, provide enough outlines to allow a better understanding of the relationship of the Roman state to the Etruscans. Imperial inscriptions indicate that there existed an *ordo haruspicum LX*, not exactly like a Roman college but similar in that there was a clearly defined group the Romans consulted. The date when this formal order came into existence is a matter of some controversy, though a *terminus ante quem* can be established by the *elogia Tarquienensa*. This inscription seems to indicate that the *ordo*, which is mentioned in the document, must date earlier than the 80s B.C.E., for the text includes a reference to the *decemviri sacris faciundis*; this group of priests expanded to fifteen members under Sulla, so a reference to the college as having only ten members must predate the dictator.[19] It is possible that a formal organization goes back even earlier, for in the *De Divinatione*, Cicero remarks that "in the days of our ancestors (*apud maiores nostros*)" the Senate had passed a decree providing for the setting aside of Etruscan youths to ensure proper training in this skill.[20] Exactly what Cicero means by "the days of our ancestors" is unclear; he defines it as the time when the Senate's power was flourishing, which clearly intends a contrast to the setting of the dialogue in 45 B.C.E. This reference may not mean that a formal process for training youths, which presupposes a formal group of priests, can be projected back to the third century when consultation of the haruspices became more regular, but it does confirm that a formal organization existed in the Republican period. Cicero's notice also indicates that the *ordo* was drawn from multiple cities; considering that the *ordo* contained sixty members, it is a reasonable conjecture that these consisted of the *duodecim populi Etruriae*, as sixty members would allow for five

18. MacBain (1982), 60–79, has pointed out how the Romans continued to make statements of cultural affinity with Etruria, particularly at moments when Etruria was threatened, for instance in 207, when the haruspices are involved in the elaborate expiation directed at Juno Regina (from Veii) in that year, or in 104 and 103, in response to the great defeat at Arausio.

19. Inscriptions: *CIL* VI.2162, XI.3382. For the *elogia Tarquienensa*, see Torelli (1975), 105–135, who offers a fuller list of haruspices and the inscriptional evidence on pp. 122–124. The expansion of the *decemviri sacris faciundis* to fifteen is first attested in a letter of Cicero dated to 51 B.C.E. (*Fam* 8.4.1) but is usually ascribed to Sulla based on a passage in Servius (*Aen.* 6.73).

20. Cic. *Div.* 1.92.

members per city.[21] The fact that there were sixty members of the *ordo* is significant, for this is not a number found in any other Roman religious organization, and so attests the degree to which the organization of the *ordo* was based on Etruscan rather than Roman customs. Although it is unclear exactly how and when these arrangements were formalized, it seems fair to assert that there was a formal organization for the haruspices when the Roman state first began consulting them on a regular basis and that the original haruspices were drawn from multiple Etruscan cities.

Since the haruspices were not associated with any individual city but with the Etruscan people as a whole, it seems clear that this move toward incorporation was directed not at any individual city but at the whole community of the Etruscans. The Etruscans were treated here as a defined group, as an ethnic group, distinct from the Romans.[22] Previous religious borrowings had involved Rome and another city, such as Veii, revealing a conception of Rome as a city of the same type as her Etruscan counterpart, albeit one that was militarily superior. But this instance, involving Etruria as a whole, created a polarity between the Romans and the Etruscans as two groups, defined in part by their religious practices. The shift, from a city to an ethnic group, seems to reflect the beginnings of a shift in the way the Romans thought of themselves, no longer merely as people inhabiting a single geographically defined city, but as a *populus* that extended beyond the boundaries of the city into the surrounding region and was held together by religious practices, among other traits.

It should not be entirely surprising that the beginnings of this shift in self-perception began at this time, considering the events of the previous fifty years. A key turning point in Roman history, as noted earlier, came in 338, when the Romans finally cemented their hold on Latium with the defeat of the Latin League. In the aftermath, Roman colonies were founded in numerous locations, first in central Italy (e.g., Suessa, Saticula, and Interamna in 312), but moving progressively further afield, to the northern Adriatic Coast with Hadria in 289, Sena in 284, and Ariminum in 268, and to the south with Luceria in 314, Venusia in 291, and Paestum in 273. The primary demand of the Roman state, both with colonies and with the nominally independent states with whom the

21. Cicero says that six Etruscan youths were chosen from each tribe, but this number appears to be corrupt. Valerius Maximus (1.1.1) reports that ten youths were designated, and the emendation from *sex singulis* to X *ex singulis* is fairly straightforward. If 10 youths were handed over to each of the 12 *populi* of Etruria, 120 youths would be trained, of whom half would then become members of the haruspicial *ordo*. See MacBain (1982), 49–50.

22. Cf. also Cic. *Cat.* 3.19, where he notes that the haruspices were drawn *ex tota Etruria*: not from a single city but "from all Etruria."

Romans concluded treaties, was provision of manpower to the Roman army; every time a Roman army took the field after 338, it contained large numbers of non-Romans fighting on behalf of the Roman state, fostering the notion of a *populus* that was not bounded by the walls of Rome.[23] Moreover, the colonies contained many people who were originally Roman citizens, and their new cities were mostly granted Latin status; the inhabitants of these colonies thus maintained a position that was clearly privileged in regard to other residents of Italy, even if they were not quite fully Roman. The significance of this behavior for how the Romans thought about themselves has seldom been fully appreciated; by reinterpreting a term previously designating a geographical area and the ethnic group inhabiting that territory into a juridical status with a defined relationship to the Roman state, the Romans made a conceptual leap from thinking of themselves as a single city to seeing themselves as a larger community. As Emma Dench noted, "This is the sort of conceptual leap upon which changing ideas of the Roman citizenship, and Roman identity itself, will be based."[24] As noted in chapter 1, the religious actions of the Romans at this time reveal the beginnings of this reconception by the Romans, with the commitment to direct and participate in two annual ceremonies outside the city (the *feriae Latinae* and the sacrifice to Juno Sospita at Lanuvium). The decision to welcome the haruspices to Rome, drawn not from a single city but from Etruria as a region, shows the Romans continuing to move in the direction of acting on the level of a broader ethnic community rather than as a single city. The difference between the Roman actions in the fourth and third centuries can be seen by considering the acceptance of Juno Regina in 396 and the welcoming of the haruspices after 278. The former involved two important cities, Rome and Veii, and the latter revolved around two peoples, Romans and Etruscans. The Roman utilization of Etruscan haruspices may thus be seen in the same light as earlier incorporations, as a sign of continued openness on the part of the Romans toward bringing foreigners within the Roman res publica, but at the same time it suggests ways in which the Romans were establishing a sense of their own identity as they began to build an empire.

The establishment of this identity may also be seen in the traces that the literary tradition has preserved of negative responses to the presence of haruspices in the Roman religious system. Several stories have been preserved that seem intended to demonstrate that the haruspices, and perhaps the Etruscan

---

23. Cornell (1995), 365–366, calls attention to the numbers of allies in the Roman army, noting that by 264 more than 150 communities had *foedera* with Rome, and that at Sentinum in 295, Livy (10.26) reports that the allies provided more troops than the Romans themselves did.

24. Dench (2005), 123.

people in general, were devious, untrustworthy, or even perfidious. The clearest example, preserved only in the *Attic Nights* of Aulus Gellius, recounts how the haruspices were consulted on how to expiate a bolt of lightning that had struck a statue of Horatius Cocles in the *comitium*.[25] The story, which Gellius claims he found in Book Eleven of the *Annales maximi*, as well as in Book One of Verrius Flaccus, claims that the haruspices intentionally gave false directions to relocate the statue in a place with no sunshine, but that their treachery was discovered and the haruspices involved were executed. Every scholar examining this story has noted that it has a particularly invented quality, which is especially clear toward the end of the account, where Gellius discusses the ritual chant to which this episode supposedly gave birth. Attempts to date the invention of this story have not met with any success, but it must go back to at least the second century B.C.E., prior to the publication of the *Annales Maximi* circa 120, and quite possibly into the third.[26] A second story, and a more famous one, involves Olenus Calenus, the wisest haruspex of Etruria, and the discovery of a head on the Capitoline hill; versions are found in Dionysius, Livy, and Pliny, among other sources.[27] Recognizing that the omen presaged that the spot where the head was found would be the head of the world (*caput rerum*), Olenus tried to capture it for the Etruscans by suggesting to the Roman ambassadors that they needed to reveal the location where the head was found before he could read the omen properly. The Roman ambassadors recognized that Olenus was trying to get them to say that the omen was found "here" (i.e., in Etruria), but they persisted in stating that the omen was found in Rome and so kept the omen for the Romans. MacBain comments that the myth is "principally a cautionary tale on the craftiness and hostility of the *haruspices*" and suggests that it must postdate the Pyrrhic wars.[28] These two stories, both intended to show that the Etruscan haruspices are not to be trusted, might offer some sense of the tension within the Roman aristocracy about utilizing a foreign practice and foreign practitioners on behalf of the state, but a closer reading reveals deeper meaning here.

25. Gell. *NA* 4.5.1.

26. MacBain (1982), 55, believes a date in the early to middle of the third century is "quite plausible," on the grounds that Book Eleven of the Annales Maximi cannot describe the fifth century or the late second century. Walbank (1957), 1.636, had argued for a late-second-century date on the basis that a story involving the Horatius legend presupposes the text of Polybius; Gagé (1973) argued for a fifth-century date based on the credulity of the Roman audience as compared with other legends.

27. Dion. Hal. *Ant. Rom.* 4.59–61; Livy 1.55.5–6 (*caput rerum*); Plin. *HN* 28.15. See also Arn. *Adv. nat.* 6.7; Serv. *ad Aen.* 8.345; Zonar. 7.11; and Isid. 15.231.

28. MacBain (1982), 53.

Several curious details suggest that these stories involve more than simply an anti-Etruscan viewpoint or an attack of the position of the haruspices. In the story of the Capitoline head, it is the son of Olenus, naturally also an Etruscan, who saves the Romans by warning them of his father's trick. The son is sufficiently versed in Etruscan divinatory lore to realize that an omen could be captured in the way his father was attempting, and yet he comes to the aid of the Romans. Clearly, not all Etruscans were as devious as Olenus or as loyal to the Etruscans (and thus disloyal to the Romans) as the haruspices of the Horatius Cocles story. The point of the Olenus story therefore cannot be one of simple opposition, but perhaps one of stereotyping, as many of the anecdotes preserved for us by Roman sources reveal the Etruscans as cunning and devious. From a Roman perspective, it might even be difficult to view Olenus' son in a favorable light, despite his action on behalf of the Romans; if the father is duplicitous in trying to capture the omen from the Romans, the son is disloyal to the father in revealing the plan. Deviousness and perfidy are thus presented as Etruscan character traits; such behavior is almost expected of the Etruscan. These Etruscans thus provide a clear foil for Roman character traits. Roman sons who displayed the lack of filial piety exhibited here by the Etruscan are regularly presented in Roman myths as paying dearly for their transgression, such as Titus Manlius.[29] Such stories make it clear that such behavior was not acceptable for a Roman, even if the end result was positive for the state. The Romans preferred to think of themselves as succeeding through bravery and strength, through *virtus* rather than through devious tricks.[30] So the haruspices can be presented as representatives of non-Roman character traits, even while they form part of the Roman religious system.

Roman practice confirms the impression that a memory of the foreignness of the haruspices and the *Etrusca disciplina* was always present, despite their acceptance into the Roman religious system. The haruspices were never organized into a college along the lines of the Roman priests discussed previously. Rather, they seem to have been consulted by the Romans as needed,

29. See Livy 8.7, where Manlius killed the enemy commander in single combat, yet was put to death by his father, in command of the Roman army, for disobeying both the authority of the consul and the authority of a father.

30. One might compare Vergil's representation of Greeks in the *Aeneid*, and especially the lying Sinon in Book 2, with Livy's Etruscans in the early books of his history. The Romans were, of course, not above utilizing devious tricks themselves on occasion; the story of the Sabine cow (Livy 1.45), where the Roman priest sends the Sabine farmer down to purify himself in the river so that the Romans can capture the omen of the cow, is a good example.

with the *decemviri sacris faciundis* perhaps providing the point of contact. The *Elogia Tarquiniensa*, which has been dated by Torelli to earlier than 51 B.C.E., contains the following line: *sub decemviros ea discipulin[a relata est].*[31] In light of the restoration at the end of the line, one should not insist that this epigraphical evidence proves that the decemviri were the conduit through which the *Etrusca disciplina* was passed to Rome, but it does confirm a relationship between the decemviri and the Etruscans in their operations.[32] Further, the particular expertise of the haruspices, as repeatedly noted in Roman sources, lay in their expiation of lightning prodigies. The incident of 278, which seems to mark the beginning of the formal relationship between Romans and haruspices, was a lightning prodigy, and the haruspices were involved in expiating ten of the thirteen lightning prodigies for which our sources preserve a recollection of the means of expiation.[33] The Romans themselves recognized the Etruscan preeminence in this field; Cicero remarked that "Etruria has considered most scientifically the things that fall from the sky," and other Roman sources also analyze Etruscan fulgural lore, indicating it was a particular specialty.[34] The Roman sources even offer cautionary tales about Romans who try to make use of this Etruscan discipline, in particular Tullus Hostilius, who was struck by lightning himself when he incorrectly performed the ritual.[35] Roman practice thus confirms the attitude seen in the stories about devious Etruscan haruspices, underscoring differences between Roman and non-Roman practices while simultaneously expanding the Roman repertoire on both the human and divine levels. This phenomenon—accepting a foreign element as Roman in a technical sense, as a valued part of the religious system, and at the same time utilizing it as a cultural foil and presenting it as non-Roman in a social sense—recurs repeatedly in regard to the Roman treatment of foreign religious traditions.

One final story about involving the haruspices that has no relation to prodigies serves to highlight this very point about the place of the Etruscan priests in the Roman state. In the *De Natura Deorum*, Cicero has the Stoic Lucilius tell a story that dates to 163 B.C.E.[36] According to Cicero, Tiberius

31. Torelli (1975), 108, 133.

32. Admittedly, this reading depends on assuming that the decemviri involved are the Roman decemviri, but this is the conclusion reached by Torelli (1975) and MacBain (1982).

33. MacBain (1982), 50–51.

34. Cic. *Div.* 1.92; Diod. Sic. 5.42; Plin. *HN* 2.138–144; Sen. *Q. Nat.* 2.39–51.

35. Plin. *HN* 2.140. Livy (1.31) has Tullus make mistakes while attempting secret rites in honor of Jupiter Elicius, serving as a cautionary tale both about lightning and about performing rites in secret.

36. Cic. *Nat. D.* 2.4.10–11.

Gracchus as consul was conducting the election when the first *rogator* suddenly died on the spot. Gracchus eventually referred the incident to the Senate, which decided that the matter ought to be referred "to those who usually took cognizance of such affairs [*senatus quos ad soleret, referendum censuit*]." The haruspices were called and pronounced that the elections had not been conducted by a proper *rogator*, whereupon Gracchus flew into a rage: "Am I not thus proper, who am consul and augur and properly auspicated? And shall you, who are Tuscans and barbarians, have the right of the auspices of the Roman people, and be able to be the interpreters of our assemblies?"[37] After expelling the haruspices from the Senate, Gracchus departed for his province, where he realized that he in fact was not a proper *rogator*; he had pitched his tent illegally, and he had crossed the *pomerium* in order to hold a senate meeting but had failed to reauspicate upon departing across the *pomerium*. He wrote to the college of augurs, who referred the matter to the Senate, which decided that the consuls should in fact step down and new elections be held.

This story is an incredibly rich source for understanding the place of the haruspices in the Roman state and their place in Roman religion, especially since Gracchus' speech explicitly raises the question of the Etruscans' ability to act in matters of Roman religion. The first noteworthy point is that when the Senate decided to refer the matter to those who were accustomed to deal with such matters, they chose the haruspices. It is not at all clear in what sense the haruspices could have been the customary body here; it is difficult to imagine that they were the usual body to consult in cases of vitiated elections, though that seems to be the plain reading of the text. Perhaps the sudden death of the *rogator* was perceived as a prodigy with which they were most familiar, but as Gracchus' criticisms make clear, we find the haruspices here acting on an issue at the very heart of the Roman political system, the election of new consuls. This in itself is a remarkable statement of their position, not on the margins of the Roman state, but very much on the inside. Gracchus, of course, brings up the issue of whether this in fact should be the proper role, denying that foreigners can possibly serve as interpreters of the auspices or arbiters of Roman elections. While Gracchus' bluster does carry the day in the Senate, the haruspices turn out to be right; Gracchus was not a *iustus rogator*. On one level, therefore, the haruspices have been vindicated, but Gracchus' response goes further. In admitting that the elections were invalid, Gracchus does not cite the death of the *rogator* but refers to the Roman law of the *pomerium* as invalidating his *auspicia*, entirely

---

37. *Itane vero, ego non iustus, qui et consul rogavi et augur et auspicato? An vos Tusci ac barbari auspiciorum populi Romani ius tenetis et interpretes esse comitiorum potestis?*

separate grounds from what the haruspices had apparently cited. And the letter acknowledging his mistake was sent to the college of augurs, the Roman college concerned with elections and proper auspices. So on the one hand, we see the haruspices comfortably installed as a fully functioning part of the Roman religious and political system, and we see that a challenge to that position comes to nothing, as the resolution of the situation bears out the haruspices' interpretation. On the other hand, the story provides several reminders of the haruspices' foreignness, both in the speech of Gracchus and in his insistence that the *vitium* was not the one the haruspices had isolated and that the augurs were the priests who should ultimately decide the fate of the recently elected consuls. And finally, in light of what we have said about cooperation between the haruspices and the Roman priests, although Gracchus might have seen an opposition between these two groups, Cicero did not. The point of the story, as Lucilius introduces it, is that both the augurs and the haruspices are true interpreters: "Events themselves have proven the discipline both of our augurs and of the Etruscan *haruspices*."[38] The foreign aspect of the haruspices may be remembered, or even paraded at times, but they remained a vital component integrated into the heart of Roman religion.

The same paraded foreignness is evident with another set of priests connected to a foreign religious tradition that was brought to Rome in the third century B.C.E., the *galli* of the Magna Mater. The previous chapter discussed the circumstances and events of the cult's introduction into Rome, beginning with the consultation of the Sibylline Books by the *decemviri sacris faciundis* on account of the frequent showers of stones in 205.[39] Despite the controversy over the exact location of the cult's origin, all sources are agreed that the cult came from Asia Minor and that the goddess was symbolized by an aniconic black stone that was brought to Rome with the help of Attalus of Pergamum. As intriguing as it is to consider the circumstances of the cult's introduction into Rome, here our focus turns to consider the Roman treatment of this cult, and especially its priests, after it arrived in Rome. The sources note that the Magna Mater was served by special priests, known as *galli*, and that these priests came to Rome along with the cult to serve the Magna Mater. Although prior to the third century we have no evidence for the presence of foreign priests in Rome, the *galli* make a second group of foreign priests to

38. *Atqui et nostrorum augurum et Etruscorum haruspicum disciplinam P. Scipione C. Figulo consulibus res ipsa probavit.*

39. For the narrative see Livy 29.10.4–29.11.8, 29.14.5–9, 29.37.2, 36.36.3–5, and the earlier discussion.

be installed as a regular part of the Roman religious system, and as with the haruspices, their presence allows us to observe how the Romans continued to maintain their policy of openness to foreigners while at the same time developing a sharper sense of themselves.

Even more than with the Etruscan haruspices, the Romans paraded the foreignness of the priests of the Magna Mater. The *galli* wore brightly colored garments, and in procession they danced through the streets accompanied by the music of tambourines and flutes. In contrast to Roman festivals, which were often the occasion for distributions to the spectators, the *galli* begged for alms *from* the bystanders.[40] Most significantly, the *galli* were eunuchs, who may even have castrated themselves in a state of ritual frenzy during the festival. Roman texts consistently highlight this point in mentioning the *galli*, not only Republican authors such as Catullus and Lucretius but also Imperial ones; authors such as Martial and Juvenal harp not only on the fact of castration but also upon the point that the *galli* continued to indulge in sexual relations despite their lack of "proper" equipment.[41] As Beard points out, this marks a double transgression: not only do the *galli* not fit into Roman gender categories, being neither male nor female, but also they violate sexual categories, taking an active (male) penetrating role, but having to use the tongue rather than the penis.[42] In light of their transgressive nature, it is perhaps not surprising to hear from Valerius Maximus of a case in which Genucius, a *gallus*, was not allowed to inherit under Roman law on the grounds that he was "neither man nor woman."[43] The *galli* stand out in the Roman imagination precisely because they are so "non-Roman."

The Roman authorities erected barriers to ensure that the non-Roman status was evident to all. The case of Genucius has just been mentioned, nor can we put it down as an isolated incident. Dionysius of Halicarnassus has

40. The description here refers to those ceremonies that we can confidently date to the Republican period; these rituals are attested by Lucr. 2.610–628 and Dion. Hal. *Ant. Rom.* 2.19. Although the latter wrote during the Augustan age, his account appears to reflect Republican practice, as similarities between his account and Lucretius suggest.

41. On the *galli*, see Lucr. 2.610–628; Catull. 63; Juv. 6.511–516; Mart. 3.81. Ovid's treatment at *Fasti* 4.193–244 is not negative in its tone but does still highlight both the castration of the *galli* and the clamor made by musical instruments during the procession.

42. Beard (1994), 175. On gender categories and sexual categories in ancient Rome, see now Hallett and Skinner (1997), especially the contribution of Holt Parker. See also Williams (1999), who discusses the Roman attitudes toward oral sex on 197–203.

43. Val. Max. 7.7.6.

preserved a series of regulations pertaining to the cult of the Magna Mater that show how broad the Senate intended to make the distinction between Roman and non-Roman:

> By a law and decree of the Senate, no native-born Roman either acts as a begging priest of Cybele [μητραγυρτῶν] or walks in procession through the city playing the flute and dressed in a colored robe or celebrates [ὀργιάζει] the goddess with Phrygian rites [ὀργιασμοῖς].[44]

As Dionysius remarks just prior to this quote, it is a Phrygian man and a Phrygian woman who serve the priestess, while the Roman praetor makes sacrifices to her and organizes games "according to the Roman custom." The priests of the Magna Mater were thus kept firmly outside the Roman state, and as a further sign of their marginalization, the *galli* were confined to the precinct of their temple.[45] They were permitted outside only for the processions during the *dies natalis* and for the *ludi Megalenses*.

Interpretation of these restrictions on the *galli* presents us with some difficulty.[46] It has been common among scholarly assessments of the cult of Magna Mater in Rome to see these measures as a sign of the Roman discomfort with the cult. On this view, the Romans imported the cult only under pressure from the Second Punic War, and upon discovering the distasteful nature of the rites, they passed restrictive measures as a means of protecting the purity of their religious system.[47] Yet this hypothesis relies more on assumptions, often based on modern notions of what is distasteful, and a number of elements argue against this hypothesis.[48] We have seen here that the Romans *chose* to import this goddess, and they spent an entire

---

44. Dion. Hal., *Ant. Rom.* 2.19: Ῥωμαίων δὲ τῶν αὐθιγενῶν οὔτε μητραγυρτῶν τις οὔτε καταυλούμενος πορεύεται διὰ τῆς πόλεως ποικίλην ἐνδεδυκὼς στολὴν οὔτε ὀργιάζει τὴν θεὸν τοῖς Φρυγίοις ὀργιασμοῖς κατὰ νόμον καὶ ψήφισμα βουλῆς. It is unclear what Dionysius means by "native-born" here; as Beard, North, and Price (1998), 97 n. 90 point out, this is not a recognized category in Roman legislation. It is more likely that Dionysius is here using an odd locution for Roman citizens, and thus that the Senate directed this legislation at the citizen body, but we can not completely discount the possibility that the legislation was directed at the narrower category.

45. Graillot (1912), 76.

46. The following discussion of the position of the Magna Mater in Rome owes much to the stimulating discussion by M. Beard (1994).

47. E.g., Vermaseren (1977), 96; Scullard (1981), 98–99.

48. Cf. Lambrechts (1951), 47.

year just in the process of making the transfer; considering that the Roman Senate in general carefully weighed its decisions, particularly in religious matters, it is difficult to believe that they were wholly unprepared for what they received. The pomp with which they received the cult, sending the *optimus vir* to meet the statue, assisted by the Vestal Virgins and a throng of citizens, hardly conforms to a picture of fear and marginalization. And while the *galli* may have been restricted to their temple precinct, we need to remember that this precinct was on the Palatine hill, at the heart of the city. The temple, and even the priests, would have been visible, and audible, to the members of the Roman aristocracy who lived there, as well as to their *clientes* who came to their houses for the morning *salutatio*. Fragments of one of Varro's Menippean Satires emphasize the noise of the cymbals as one passed by the precinct of the goddess, as well as the throng of *galli* at the temple.[49] Several *monetales*, by definition members of the aristocracy, put images of the Magna Mater on their coins alongside images of Roma, and some families, such as the Julii, linked themselves even more closely to the Magna Mater.[50] Roman aristocrats formed special *sodalitates* to hold special banquets in honor of the goddess during her festival, and the state established the *ludi Megalenses* in her honor.[51] On this basis, Pierre Lambrechts has argued that even prior to the time of Augustus, the Magna Mater was treated as an ancestral deity and not as a foreigner.[52] While we may not wish to go this far, the evidence clearly demonstrates that the Magna Mater was not relegated to the edges of Roman religion but was incorporated firmly within the heart of the Roman state. Rather than ignoring those elements that do not fit smoothly into a picture of a Rome uncomfortable with the Magna Mater and her priests, a better understanding of the cult can be gained by including, and even focusing on, all of the available evidence about the cult.

The tension between the apparent rejection of certain elements of the cult and its incorporation into the Roman religious system may best be seen as part of a discourse on the nature of Romanness.[53] It seems clear that, as with the Etruscan haruspices, the Romans were intent on parading the foreignness of the priests of the Magna Mater, even while they firmly accepted the cult within their religious system. The *galli*, and the style of worship they represent, are

---

49. Varr. *Eum.* fr. 16 Cèbe. Cf. fr. 18 and 24.

50. Lambrechts (1951), 50–51.

51. For the *sodalitates*, see Cic. *Sen.* 45; Ov. *Fast.*, 4.353–356. See also the *Fasti Praenestini* for April 4 (*Inscr. Ital.* 13.2, p. 127). See further chapter 5.

52. Lambrechts (1951).

53. Beard (1994).

identified as non-Roman in every way. This representation begins with the person of the priest himself; as eunuchs, they occupy a category that has no place in the Roman construction of gender. It extends to the rite itself, as this type of singing and clashing of cymbals, the spilling of blood, and the begging for alms from the observers are thus located outside the boundaries of what the Romans deemed to be proper religious behavior. Yet this should not be taken to imply that the cult was not welcomed at Rome; after all, the Romans built a public temple to the goddess, set aside seven days on the calendar for her, and imported priests to perform the rites. The location of the cult on the Palatine hill and the accompanying restriction of the priests to their precinct may best be understood in this light. The cult itself is welcomed to the very oldest part of the city and placed among the noblest houses of the Roman aristocracy, as a constant visual reminder of the presence of the cult within the Roman religious system. But that reminder is double-edged, for the restriction on the movement of the priests remained as a marker of the cult's foreignness; the cult was to be seen and yet at the same time not seen. Choosing to have the priests remain outside the boundaries of Roman citizenship makes a statement about the style of worship, not the cult itself or the goddess. To emphasize this point, the Roman aristocracy celebrated the festival of the goddess in a more "Roman" style, with *ludi* and with banquets sponsored by the *sodalitates*. The Romans could thus incorporate the goddess within their religious system while simultaneously making clear where the boundary lay between a Roman and foreign style of celebration. While the Roman state remained open to the incorporation of foreigners and of foreign cultural elements, the maintenance of a sense of Roman identity demanded a continual process of demarcating boundaries between the Roman and the foreign, and this process is precisely what we see at play in the case of the Magna Mater and the *galli*.

The Romans did not insist on parading the foreignness of every cult imported to Rome, for the line between Roman and non-Roman might be drawn differently in different contexts, as yet another example from the third century reveals. At some point prior to 216 B.C.E., the Romans made several innovations in the cult of Ceres at Rome, which amounted to the establishment of Greek rites in honor of the goddess. Ceres had been worshiped in Rome since the early fifth century B.C.E., and despite some Greek influence, probably from Magna Graecia, the cult introduced traditionally in 493 B.C.E. was based essentially on Italic precedents.[54] Although the cult may have slowly become Hellenized over the next two centuries, as increasing contacts with

---

54. Spaeth (1996), 7–8; Le Bonniec (1958), 292–305. The Greek influence is deduced from the decoration of the temple by the Greek artists Damophilos and Gorgasos, as reported by Plin. *HN* 35.154.

Magna Graecia diffused knowledge about Greek Demeter, the literary sources indicate that a significant addition took place at some point during the second half of the third century B.C.E.[55] Unfortunately, the changes are reflected in our sources only indirectly, so that it is difficult to speak with precision about the nature of these changes to the cult or even their exact dating, but they are important enough to our investigation to be worth a closer look.

The evidence for the third-century addition of "Greek rites" in honor of Ceres is varied but secure. A *terminus ante quem* for the innovation is provided by Livy, for in his report of the Roman response to the battle of Cannae in the year 216 B.C.E., the historian notes that the *sacrum anniversarium Cereris*, the yearly rite in honor of Ceres, was interrupted because of the mourning imposed on the women of Rome by the disastrous result of the battle. In consequence, the Senate ordered that mourning be limited to thirty days to ensure that neither public nor private rites would be neglected, a detail also noted by Valerius Maximus.[56] Festus, though a much later source, adds the detail that this festival, which he names as the *Graeca sacra festa Cereris*, was celebrated "on account of the finding of Persephone" and was imported "from Greece," thus explicitly linking this festival with Greek mythology and with one of the Greek cults of Demeter and Kore.[57] In contrast, the fifth-century cult of Ceres in Rome had placed more emphasis on Liber and relegated Libera, who came to represent Persephone, to a secondary (or tertiary) position.

Additional evidence may allow us to specify further the nature of the changes to the cult and offers important other details. In the *De Legibus*, Cicero makes an explicit allowance for initiation into the "Greek rite of Ceres," and further along during his commentary on this provision, he states that it should be most carefully done in order that "the clear light [of day] should guard the reputation of the women with the eyes of many [watching], and that they [the women] be initiated with that rite of Ceres with which they are initiated at Rome."[58] Cicero thus confirms that Greek rites of Ceres were celebrated in Rome and adds the detail that this rite was celebrated by the women of Rome and involved initiation. The reference to the Greek rite and to the role of women indicates that this celebration is the same as that to which Livy referred. These elements of the rituals connected with this cult of Ceres, as well as the association of the myth of Demeter and Persephone, suggests that the cult introduced in the third century may be most closely

55. For a historical overview of the cult of Ceres in the Middle Republic, see Spaeth (1996), 11–16.

56. Livy 22.56.4; Val. Max. 1.1.15.

57. Festus, s.v. Graeca sacra (p. 97 Müller).

58. Cic. *Leg.* 2.21: *Cereri Graeco sacro.* Also 2.36–37: *mulierum famam multorum oculis lux clara custodiat initienturque eo ritu Cereri quo Romae initiantur.*

connected to the Greek Thesmophoria.[59] In Greece, the Thesmophoria has been understood as a fertility festival, apparently celebrated only by married women; the festival seems to focus on the opposition between the two roles women were allotted in ancient Greece, those of fertile mother and of chaste daughter.[60] Evidence from Rome, such as the references to *matronae* in Livy's account as the celebrants of this ritual and Ovid's complaint of his girl's chastity during the yearly festival, confirms that the Roman festival operated using these same themes, even if evidence for specific rituals in Rome is lacking.[61]

More interesting for our discussion of priests is the fact that the Romans imported priestesses from outside the state to preside over this cult. Cicero provides us with the clearest statement about this aspect of the changes in the cult of Ceres. In his speech defending Cornelius Balbus from the charge of falsely claiming Roman citizenship, the orator offers the following example of foreigners who were granted citizenship:

> Our ancestors, O judges, wished that the rites of Ceres should be performed with the very strictest religious reverence and ceremony. These rites, as they had been originally derived from the Greeks, had always been conducted by Greek priestesses, and were called Greek rites. But although they chose a woman from Greece who might show us that Greek rite and perform it, nevertheless they wished that a citizen should perform the rite on behalf of other citizens, in order that she might pray to the immortal gods with foreign and external knowledge, but with the feelings of one of our own family and of our citizens. I see that these priestesses were for the most part Neapolitans or Velians, without a doubt federate cities.[62]

Cicero goes on to cite the case of Calliphana, a woman from Velia, on whose behalf the praetor C. Valerius Flaccus submitted a motion to the people for the express purpose of making her a Roman citizen, and concludes by asking

59. Spaeth (1996), 108.

60. Zeitlin (1982).

61. Spaeth (1996), 108–112. Cf. Ov. *Am.* 3.10. Ritual chastity was part of the Greek cult of the Thesmophoria as well and is one of the elements that led scholars to focus on the fertility aspect of the rite.

62. Cic. *Balb.* 24.55: *Sacra Cereris, iudices, summa maiores nostri religione confici caerimoniaque voluerunt; quae cum essent adsumpta de Graecia, et per Graecas curata sunt semper sacerdotes et Graeca omnino nominata. Sed cum illam quae Graecum illud sacrum monstraret et faceret ex Graecia deligerent, tamen sacra pro civibus civem facere voluerunt, ut deos immortalis scientia peregrina et externa, mente domestica et civili precaretur. Has sacerdotes video fere aut Neapolitanas aut Veliensis fuisse, foederatarum sine dubio civitatum.*

rhetorically whether there is anyone who might deny that the priestess was made a Roman citizen.

The decision to make the priestesses of Ceres citizens provides a direct contrast to the treatment of the Etruscan haruspices and the priests of the Magna Mater. In the case of the haruspices, who entered into a formal relationship with the Roman Senate early in the third century, the issue of citizenship seems to have been ignored; the diviners were neither made citizens as a group nor forbidden to become citizens. At some point probably later in the century, priestesses from Magna Graecia were granted citizenship specifically because of their role in the Roman religious system. But then at the end of the century, or perhaps early in the second century, the Roman Senate prevented Roman citizens from becoming *galli*. Cicero's explanation for the citizenship granted to the priestesses of Ceres—that the Senate felt it necessary for citizens to perform rites on behalf of citizens—obviously cannot be accepted at face value, for the Senate did not insist that the haruspices become citizens in order to read omens on behalf of citizens, nor the *galli*. Cicero's reading of the Senate's action probably derives from the exigencies of his case for Balbus and from his own sense of how Roman religion should operate, rather than an actual motivation of the third century.

How, then, are we to explain the apparent inconsistency of these choices? An easy and definitive answer eludes us, but some lines of approach can be suggested. One answer is practical, and here the gender of the celebrants in question is relevant. The fact that those associated with the cult of Ceres were female may have made it easier to grant them the status of citizens, for such status in the case of women would be largely symbolic. Citizenship conferred far fewer benefits on females than on males, as the former would not be exercising their citizenship in the *comitia*, for instance. While males living in Rome would find themselves enrolled in a tribe and eligible to participate in all aspects of running the Roman state, these women would still find themselves restricted to the religious sphere. The significance of the grant of citizenship should not be underestimated; it was an important marker of their acceptance into the Roman state and one entirely consonant with Roman practice. The fact that citizenship for these priestesses was largely symbolic may even make it more important as a symbol, as Cicero clearly recognized two hundred years later.

Not only does the gender of the priestesses call attention to the symbolic nature of the grant of citizenship but also it may be part of the explanation for the grant of citizenship. As we have seen, the century prior to the notice of the change in the cult of Ceres was already a time of great change for the Roman state. Internally, conflict between patricians and plebeians had intensified toward the end of the fourth century, culminating with the passage of the *Lex*

Hortensia in 287 that gave legislation of the *concilium plebis* the status of law for the whole community. Externally, victories over Samnium and Etruria led to the establishment of Roman colonies in various parts of Italy, and the end of the First Punic War saw the expansion of Roman power to Sicily. Women as well as men took part in these developments and were affected by the results. The foundation of a cult of Plebeian Chastity to match the cult of Patrician Chastity reveals the continuing tension between the classes over the issue of intermarriage.[63] Other issues revolving around marriage and chastity appear to have been prominent in these years, for in 295 the aedile Fabius Gurges built a temple to Venus Obsequens out of the proceeds of fines collected from women convicted of *stuprum*.[64] In the same period, Appius Claudius Caecus wrote a treatise known as *Interruptions*, in which he discussed the *trinoctium*, a means by which women could avoid coming under the *manus* of their husband, and the censors of 307 expelled a man from the Senate for divorcing his wife without first calling a *consilium amicorum*.[65] These incidents indicate that the traditional familial roles of women were already coming under pressure, perhaps in part as a result of military campaigns that extended further afield.[66] An indication of these changes can be seen clearly in the story of Claudia, sister of P. Claudius Pulcher, who lost a Roman fleet at the battle of Drepana in 249. Three years later, Claudia was held up by a throng leaving the games, leading her to wish aloud that her brother were still alive to lose another fleet; on those grounds she was convicted of *maiestas*.[67] The story preserves an indication of continuing tension between patricians and plebeians, but it is most noteworthy that Claudia was convicted of *maiestas*, a purely political charge. Charging a woman on grounds not related to her familial role indicates clearly how Rome's new circumstances had begun to create pressures on traditional female roles already by the middle of the third century.

It may be possible to understand the innovations in the cult of Ceres as at least in part a response to these changed circumstances. As noted earlier,

63. The story is recounted in Livy 10.23.

64. Livy 10.31. Bauman (1992), 16, suggests that *stuprum* in this context refers to repeated offenses and not the occasional adultery, so the women involved may have been acting as prostitutes.

65. Censors' action: Val. Max. 2.9.2. Appius: *Dig.* 1.2.2.36. Cf. Bauman (1983), 22, on Appius.

66. Evans (1991) has suggested that the extended overseas campaigns of the second century B.C.E. created profound challenges for women and brought about significant changes in their position in Roman society. There is no reason to believe that this process did not start even earlier than the second century, if on a smaller scale.

67. Various elements of the story can be found in Livy *Per.* 19; Val. Max. 8.1d4; Suet. *Tib.* 2; Gell. *NA* 10.6. Cf. Bauman (1992), 20.

the cult of the Thesmophoria in Greece was a women-only festival that emphasized civic virtues, as defined by the males of the society: chastity, motherhood, and fertility. These are virtues that the Roman aristocracy would have wanted to emphasize as much as their Greek counterparts.[68] If, as Burkert suggested, the Greek festival allowed women to demonstrate "their independence, their responsibility and their importance for the fertility of the community and the land," then it may have provided an ideal vehicle for the Senate to redirect the attention of the Roman *matronae*.[69] The Senate's decision to import this Greek cult of Ceres may have been driven in part by a desire to affirm both the importance of women in Roman society and their appropriate place in that society.[70] Granting citizenship to the priestesses of the cult—placing the priestesses inside the Roman state— served as a further marker of the centrality of women, in their proper place, to the success of the Roman state.

Gender issues alone, however, do not suffice as the entire explanation for the reforms in the cult of Ceres during the third century, for the Greek element demands consideration as well. If granting citizenship to the priestesses of the cult serves to emphasize the place of women in the Roman state, the fact that the priestesses came from Greece must be significant in a similar fashion. If the Romans refused to let the haruspices and the *galli* become citizens but paraded the differences between Etruscans and Phrygians on the one hand and Romans on the other, the decision to make the priestesses of Ceres into citizens marks Greek practice as lying within the boundaries of Roman religion. We might almost say that the Romans here paraded the *Romanness* of the foreign cult, rather than the foreignness of the Roman cult. This action may speak to a fundamentally different attitude toward Greek culture on the part of the Romans during the third century, as they did not at this point feel the same need to differentiate their own behavior from Greek practices as they did from Etruscan or Phrygian. Perhaps this stems from the long familiarity of the Romans with Greek culture, back to the sixth century, but the Romans had an equally long acquaintance with Etruscan culture. More plausibly, during the first three hundred years of the Republic, the Romans did not engage in extended military conflict with the Greeks, and so may not have developed a view of the Greeks as the enemy or the Other against whom the Romans needed to define their identity; the duplicitous Etruscans or the exotic Easterners could play that role.

68. On these virtues associated with Ceres, see Spaeth (1996), 113–119.
69. Burkert (1985), 245.
70. Cf. the comments of Spaeth (1996), 113.

In the religious field, the difference between Roman and Greek practice is consistently represented as much less than between Roman and other foreigners. In the case of Ceres, the third-century changes made by the Romans adopted not only Greek practitioners and a Greek ritual but also the ideology and values behind that ritual. The fact that this ideology concerning the proper roles for women in the state was so similar to that held by the Roman aristocracy surely made the incorporation of the entire cult, complete with practitioners, easier for the Romans. But the decision to include these priestesses within the boundaries of the state also speaks to a larger sense of identification and comfort with Greek culture.[71] If at the beginning of the third century the Romans were just beginning to present themselves to the Greeks on the world stage, by the end of the century they had achieved a degree of self-assurance in their dealings with the Greek world.

The inclusion of foreign priests within the Roman religious system allows us a deeper glimpse into Roman attitudes than the inclusion merely of a cult. The notion of openness to foreigners is maintained, and even extended, by offering a place in Rome to these individuals and, in the case of the priestesses, making them citizens. At the same time, the treatment of these individuals subsequent to their arrival in Rome reveals the Romans drawing cultural lines to distinguish for themselves what it means to be Roman. The haruspices, the *galli*, and the priestesses of Ceres all provide valuable foils for the Romans to stake claims as to the appropriate behavior of Romans and non-Romans, of men and women, at precisely the moment when the expansion of the Roman state is causing changes in the traditional notions of those roles. Increasingly, as the third century progressed, the Romans began to think in terms not just of a single city-state, but of a broader entity comprising first Latium and eventually most of peninsular Italy. The development toward thinking of Italy as a part of the Roman res publica is visible elsewhere in the religious developments of the late third century, as the next chapter explores.

71. One should note here remarks that the Romanization of Italy might more properly be called the Hellenization of Italy, as the culture spread by the Romans owes as much to Greek culture as to indigenous Roman practice. See especially the collection *Hellenismus in Mittelitalien*, edited by Paul Zanker (1976); more recently, Bilde, Nielsen, and Nielsen (1993) and Curti, Dench, and Patterson (1996).

4

Prodigies and Expiations

The expiation of prodigies, which appears as one of the most character-istic procedures of Roman religion, provides a further glimpse of the relationship of Rome to outside communities. For the Romans, the occur-rence of a prodigy signified a break in the *pax deorum*, a rupture in their relationship with the divine, such that the impending wrath of the gods needed to be averted through the proper performance of expiatory rites.[1] What counted as a prodigy was essentially left to the Senate to decide, for it was the Senate's task both to accept the report of a prodigy and then to approve the expiatory rites, often after consulting one of the priestly col-leges in Rome.[2] Reported prodigies range from either human or animal unusual births, such as hermaphrodites and animals born with too many or too few limbs, to visual or auditory apparitions, to persons, buildings, or statues struck by lightning.[3] The common link among events the Romans

---

1. On prodigies and their expiations, see Wülker (1903), Bloch (1963), MacBain (1982), and the more recent studies of Rosenberger (1998) and Rasmussen (2003).

2. Rasmussen (2003), 53–116, provides an exhaustive listing of prodigies, which offers an idea of the wide range of events accepted as prodigies. See also MacBain (1982), 118–119.

3. Any discussion of prodigies in Rome must enter into the thorny issue of the reliability of the prodigies that have been reported to us in our sources, primarily Livy and the book of prodigies compiled, apparently from Livy's text, by Julius Obsequens probably in the fourth century C.E. Rawson (1971) is perhaps the most critical of the prodigy reports, arguing that the lists as we have them were not derived from the

counted as prodigies was that the Romans believed that each event must have been caused by a supernatural power and that the event indicated the gods were angry at the Romans.[4] Consistent with this reasoning, the Senate might on occasion consider an especially disastrous military defeat as a prodigy in itself, believing that only the gods could have brought about such a disastrous defeat.[5] If victory in battle was ascribed to the favor of the gods, then defeat in battle might similarly be ascribed to the wrath of the gods, and the proper response was to redouble efforts on both the human and divine levels.[6] At a basic level, the Romans believed that prodigies were one of the primary means of communication from the gods to themselves.

The reporting of prodigies was thus a regular occurrence during the Roman Republic.[7] During the years of the middle Republic for which Livy's text survives, prodigies are reported nearly every year; for only seven years of the fifty-two between 218 and 167 B.C.E. are there no reports of prodigies. It is likely that our poor sources for the preceding and succeeding periods account for the lesser records for those years, though we still do have some records of prodigy reports. The prodigies that have survived

---

Annales Maximi and that rewriting, corruption, and selection from specialized sources have deeply distorted the surviving material. MacBain (1982), while admitting that the lists are incomplete and may contain doublets and other types of minor errors, has defended the general reliability of the prodigies that have been reported. I agree that the lists as we can put them together are clearly incomplete, so that any conclusions based on comparing what we see with what we fail to see would be imprudent. But the argument that the records for prodigies that we do have are so distorted as to render any analysis meaningless is not compelling; MacBain, 8–24, has demonstrated that sources lying behind our prodigy reports may be reliable, and such distortion as has clearly occurred does not vitiate the overall picture provided by the surviving sources. Rasmussen (2003), 15–23 and 35–52, also accepts the reliability of the prodigy reports, including even some material rejected by MacBain.

4. Cf. Rosenberger (1998), 97–126, and especially his comments on ἀδύνατα on 103–107.

5. In 215, the first act of Q. Fabius Maximus, appointed dictator after the disaster of Cannae, was to discuss religion and convince the Senate that the defeat had been the result of neglect of the gods, rather than poor generalship. As Livy states (22.9), "He succeeded in getting a decree passed that the *decemviri* should be ordered to consult the Sibylline Books, a course which is only adopted when the most alarming portents have been reported."

6. On the Roman response to defeat, see Rosenstein (1990).

7. Both ancient and modern scholars have noted that prodigy reporting falls off dramatically after the assumption of power by Augustus, though occasional reports are still known. Considering the close relationship between religion and politics, the decline is undoubtedly due to the changes in the form of Roman government. Rosenberger (1998), 233–240, touches on this issue, but it is worth further study.

in our sources prior to the outbreak of the Second Punic War are frequently spectacular in some way, either a major crisis such as a plague or an expiation that resulted in an innovation to the religious system, such as the construction of a temple to Apollo in 433 or the introduction of *ludi scenici* in 364. Although the information for the period after 167 is preserved only in late compilations such as that of Julius Obsequens, it seems to reflect the better nature of the sources for that period, for prodigy reports are preserved for more than half of the years between 167 and the end of the Republic, and many of these seem more typical: strange births, lightning strikes, and others.[8]

The recent study of prodigies by Veit Rosenberger has pointed out the liminality of most of the prodigies observed during the Roman Republic.[9] Many of the items the Romans accepted as portents represent a transgression of normal boundaries. Hermaphrodites represent perhaps the most spectacular example; as human beings who were neither male nor female, they existed in the liminal space between the two recognized gender categories in ancient Rome. Similarly, animals with more than the usual number of heads or feet embodied a transgression, and the appearance of wild animals (e.g., wolves) in an urban setting violated the boundaries between nature and civilization. Lightning strikes provide another means of considering the liminality of prodigies, for most often the occurrences accepted as portents struck a liminal spot. Forty-three lightning strikes are recorded on temples, a liminal space between humans and the gods, and a further twenty-two are recorded on walls and gates; these two categories represent almost two thirds of all lightning strikes accepted as prodigies.[10] The occurrence of prodigies indicated not only a rupture in the *pax deorum* but also, by challenging the way in which the Romans understood the workings of the world, represented a rupture in the very fabric of Roman society. Such threats to the underlying structure of the community could not be ignored. The transgression of boundaries helps to explain why prodigies played such a central role in the Republican religious system and, as we shall see, have particular relevance for a study of the development of Roman identity.[11]

8. See Wülker (1903), 86–92, for a chronological listing of prodigy reports, with source references.

9. For a fuller discussion of the points presented in this paragraph, see Rosenberger (1998), 97–126.

10. See Rosenberger (1998), 116, for a table listing the occurrences of lightning strikes.

11. Cf. the comments of Rasmussen (2003), 241–246, on portents and the construction of Roman identity, especially on the way in which the established procedures linked past, present, and future into one continuous entity.

One aspect of these prodigy lists that has occasioned much discussion from modern scholars has been the presence of numerous prodigies from outside Rome itself. Theodor Mommsen was troubled by the notion that events accepted as *prodigia publica* for the Roman state might occur on land that was not *ager publicus* of the Roman people but was forced to devise exceptional reasons to accept them.[12] Elizabeth Rawson, on the other hand, suggested that the prodigy lists themselves were compiled after the Social War, when the legal distinctions between peregrine and Roman were less evident, due to the extension of the franchise.[13] Bruce MacBain, however, has effectively countered these arguments, arguing that by the Hannibalic War at the latest, the Romans could react to religious events outside the *ager Romanus* if they chose to do so, and so a public prodigy was any prodigy the Senate chose to recognize.[14] This explanation brings the recognition of prodigies in line with standard Roman governmental practice: far from having a written constitution that carefully delineated the powers of the Senate or of the various magistrates, the Romans acted on an ad hoc basis, most often following an established precedent but deviating from it whenever they felt it necessary to further their interests. We should not arbitrarily assume either that the Senate could not recognize prodigies occurring outside Rome or that these prodigy reports are spurious, but attempt to explain what looks like an anomaly to us.

These reports of prodigies thus pose a question related to our study: why should the Romans have accepted events occurring in non-Roman territory as prodigies affecting the Roman state? MacBain has suggested that just as prodigies and their expiations served as a form of communication between the Romans and the divine community, they might serve as a means of communication between the Romans and other political communities. His suggestion was that prodigies acted as a signaling system whereby the Roman Senate, by accepting as *prodigia publica* those reported from the non-Roman towns of Italy, could acknowledge the anxieties and identify with the religious sensibilities of Italians, particularly at times of severe stress on the whole fabric of the confederacy.[15]

This interpretation of prodigy expiation offers many similarities to other Roman religious responses to foreigners, such as adoption of foreign cults discussed earlier. Again, the interdependence of the religious and political spheres is visible, such that we need not assert that the

12. Mommsen (1912), 168ff.

13. Rawson (1971), 164.

14. MacBain (1982), 25–33. MacBain's position is supported by Rasmussen (2003), 219–231.

15. MacBain (1982), 7–8.

Romans were manipulating religion for political purposes, but that religious and political motives might blend seamlessly. The tension between "religious imperialism" on the part of the Romans, whereby they took over responsibility from local communities, and Roman respect for local traditions is also present, as with the adoption of foreign cults. A close examination shows that Roman actions frequently imply that respect for local traditions was operative more often than an aggressive hegemonic stance and that these religious actions often contributed to building a sense of community between Roman and Italian.[16]

Viewed from these perspectives, the timing of the first recorded prodigies accepted from outside Rome is suggestive. These date to 269 B.C.E., when lightning struck the walls at Formiae in Latium, and fire burst from the earth at Cales, a Latin colony in Campania. Though the poor quality of our sources for the third century should make us wary of placing too much emphasis on this particular date as the first-ever occurrences of the phenomena, it is not surprising to find these reports in the early third century B.C.E. This is the same period, following the expansion of the Roman state into all of Italy and the settling of numerous groups of Roman citizens outside Rome, that saw the Roman religious system beginning to incorporate more elements from other areas of Italy.[17] This action may have been in part a practical reaction to the Pyrrhic war, which created strains on the new Roman confederacy.[18] It also helped to define the relationship between the Romans and the peoples of Italy as the Romans took increasing control over the peninsula. The recognition of prodigies from peregrine territories diminished the distinction between Roman and non-Roman in an effort to create unifying bonds, since the Romans treated a prodigy occurring on its territory just as they did a prodigy on the *ager Romanus*. These first two peregrine prodigies come from Formiae, an ancient city in Latium that had taken no part in the Latin Revolt and had been rewarded with Roman citizenship, and from Cales, a colony in Campania founded in 331 B.C.E. The

16. MacBain (1982), 8, suggests to the contrary that the Romans "by appropriating the responsibility to expiate non-Roman prodigies at Rome with Roman priests, could assert Roman hegemony over Italy in the religious sphere parallel to its assertion of hegemony in the temporal sphere." This analysis, however, undervalues the Roman willingness not only to accept prodigies from foreign locales, but actually to perform expiations outside Rome. This point is further discussed later.

17. These include the formalization of the relationship with the Etruscan haruspices in 278 (cf. chapter 3), the Hellenizing reforms in the cult of Ceres (cf. chapter 3), and earlier, the adoption of the cult of Juno Sospita in common with the people of Lanuvium (cf. chapter 1).

18. MacBain (1982), 31–32.

former was geographically close and shared close cultural bonds and legal rights; the other, while geographically more distant, was founded just after the Latin settlement as the first colony to receive the Latin status, whereby its citizens enjoyed the same rights as the seven towns that had remained Latin colonies after the Latin war.[19] The recognition of a prodigy from this town served as another indication of this community's status as Roman in an important religious matter and so furthered the overall bonds between this community and the Romans. Over the course of the next two hundred years, the Romans continued to recognize prodigies from peregrine communities, with approximately half of the total number of prodigies accepted occurring outside the *ager Romanus* (map 2).

The recognition and acceptance of prodigies from religious sanctuaries in Italy provided a particularly effective way for the Romans to signal their religious communality with Italian peoples. These actions, relating to shrines of either local or regional importance, underscored the religious nature of the connection between the Romans and the local community. By assuming responsibility for a message that the local divinity had conveyed, the Romans acknowledged that the divinity was communicating with them, as well as with the local community, and thus placed both groups in the same position. On many occasions, the sanctuary involved held regional importance, as for instance the oracular sanctuary at Caere, where the lots shrank in 218; the grove of Feronia at Capena, where the statues were seen sweating in 210; or the temple of Mater Matuta in Satricum, struck by lightning in 206.[20] The recognition of these prodigies allowed the Romans to express their religious solidarity not just with a single town, but with the entire community of worshippers to that shrine, wherever they might live. These actions were thus particularly effective in expressing the notion that membership in a community did not depend merely on residence and citizenship. Anyone who worshipped Feronia, for example, would be concerned that the goddess was properly propitiated, and by accepting the unusual event as a *prodigia publica*, the Romans could express that the entire Roman state formed part of that community. In other instances, the sanctuary involved does not appear to have had wider significance than the local community, such as the grove of Marica in Menturnae or the temple of Jupiter at Formiae.[21] These instances may be seen

19. MacBain (1982) notes the significance of Cales as the site of the first peregrine prodigy, though he ignores the prodigy at Formiae in the same year. On the status and significance of Cales, see Salmon (1970), 55–57.

20. Caere: Livy 21.62. Capena: Livy 27.4. Satricum: Livy 28.11.

21. Menturnae: Livy 27.7.3; Formiae: Livy 32.1

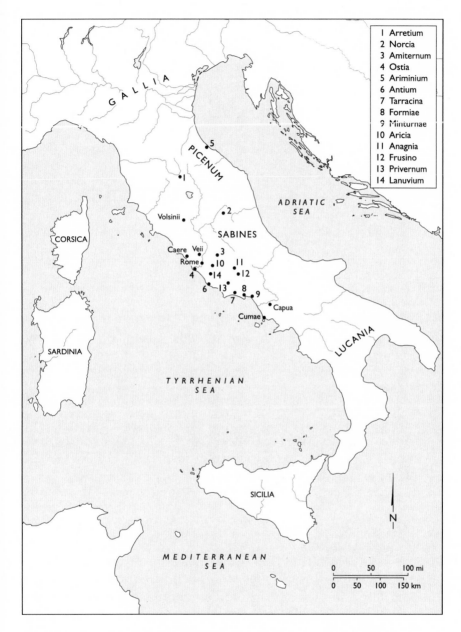

Map 2: Locations in Italy (including regions) with four or more prodigies accepted in Rome

as a heightened form of accepting a prodigy from the community in general, recognizing a religious solidarity in the common need to appease the wrath of the local divinity.

Two other types of sanctuaries should be considered in the context of the recognition of prodigies. One type is those sanctuaries with which the Romans had long-standing associations even prior to recognizing a prodigy from it. The Alban Mount, site of the temple of Jupiter Latiaris and the annual *feriae Latinae*, is a good example, as four prodigies are reported from it. Only one of these prodigies is known to have come from the temple of Jupiter, while one came from a temple of Juno, and the other two were celestial occurrences and so not related to a specific building in the sanctuary.[22] The temple of Juno Sospita at Lanuvium is the other sanctuary of this type. As discussed earlier, the Romans had held this sanctuary in common with the Lanuvians from the end of the Latin War in 338. This relationship probably explains why more peregrine prodigies are reported from Lanuvium than from any other single locale, fifteen. Six of those prodigies were reported from the sanctuary of Juno Sospita itself; only twelve other communities have as many prodigies as just the sanctuary in Lanuvium. This point suggests that holding the sanctuary in common with the people of Lanuvium included assuming more responsibility for extraordinary occurrences in the sanctuary. Prodigies are reported from the sanctuary of Juno Sospita in 218, at the outbreak of the Second Punic War, and three additional prodigies from the sanctuary were recognized during the war, in 215, 214, and 204.[23] Prodigies continue to be reported from the sanctuary of Juno Sospita down to 99 B.C.E., but perhaps more interesting is that after the Second Punic War, prodigies begin to be reported from locations other than the sanctuary of Juno Sospita, first from the temple of Jupiter, struck by lightning in 198, and then apparently from the town itself, which reported a shower of stones in 193.[24] The willingness to expand the range of acceptability from a sanctuary for which the Romans formally accepted some responsibility to a temple where the Romans had no formal connections and then to the town as a whole offers a prime example of the processes we have been examining. Through a link developed by sharing a religious sanctuary, the Romans developed a sufficient relationship with the people of Lanuvium that they accepted a prodigy occurring at a different sanctuary as affecting the entire Roman populace. By

---

22. Lightning struck the statues of Jupiter in 209 (Livy 25.7), and the temple of Juno, set on a platform, mysteriously turned northward at night in 56 (Dio Cass. 39.20). In 212, two days' rain of stones was reported (Livy 27.11), and in 113 the sky was reported on fire at night (Obsequens 38).

23. Livy 21.62; 23.31; 24.10; 29.14.

24. 99: Obsequens 46; 198: Livy 32.9; 193: Livy 35.9.

affirming their religious unity with Lanuvium on a broader scale and after the war, the Romans indicated that their unity with the town was not dependent on exigent circumstances. Although the Romans may have had power over the sanctuaries at the Alban mount and at Lanuvium, which may account for the frequency of the prodigies recognized at them, we should remember that these sanctuaries did have federative roles. Accepting a prodigy from these sanctuaries conveyed a message of shared responsibility that responding to a prodigy from Rome itself did not.

The willingness to expand the range of responsibility beyond the main cult of a sanctuary is evident in the other group of prodigies attested from sanctuaries in Italy. The Romans accepted prodigies from several cities that served as the home to important regional sanctuaries, but in these instances, the Romans are not known to have accepted prodigies from the city's major sanctuary, but from other places within that town. For instance, the Romans accepted six prodigies from Aricia, which was the home of a famous grove to Diana, but the only prodigy from a sanctuary recorded from Aricia is a lightning strike on the temple of Jupiter in 213.[25] Similarly, Tarracina, a center for the worship of Feronia, witnessed eleven prodigies, but the only three known to involve sanctuaries in that city did not involve the sanctuary of Feronia; rather, two lightning strikes on the temple of Jupiter and the death of three women in the temple of Minerva in 166 were accepted as prodigies by the Romans.[26] It may be that the "religious ambience" of these towns accounted for the relatively high numbers of prodigies accepted, as an effort to foster positive religious connections with a town whose religious importance was known far and wide.[27] The absence of prodigies reported from the major sanctuaries in these towns should not cause great concern, as our lists are certainly incomplete, and the human population could not dictate where a prodigy might occur; if lightning struck the temple of Jupiter rather than the grove of Diana, the Romans could decide whether to accept the lightning strike as a prodigy, but they could not cause the lightning to strike in the grove of Diana. But it may in fact be of greater significance that the Romans chose to recognize prodigies from these towns but not from the major sanctuary, expressing interest not just in a single deity of importance but with the entire community. The acceptance of

25. Livy 24.44.

26. The lightning strikes occurred in 206 (Livy 28.11) and 179 (Livy 40.45); for the prodigy at the temple of Minerva, see Obsequens 12.

27. It should be noted that Ardea, site of a major pan-Italic sanctuary to Aphrodite, saw only two prodigies, including a lightning strike on the temple of Hercules in 198 (Livy 32.9); not every town that contained a major sanctuary saw an unusually high number of prodigies accepted by the Romans.

prodigies from outside Rome thus served as another means of expressing religious communality with wide groups of people inhabiting the Italian peninsula.

The appearance of a prodigy is, however, only part of the communication process between the Romans and the divine; since prodigies served to indicate divine displeasure with the Romans, the Romans needed a means to communicate in return in an effort to earn back the favor of the gods, and this effort took the form of expiatory rituals. Once a prodigy had been accepted by the Senate, the response invariably was to perform a ritual that would attempt to appease the wrath of the gods. Expiations of all types were performed in all types of crises; reading Livy's account of the early second century gives one the impression that they were performed just about every year, regardless of how severe the prodigy might seem to modern scholars. Some prodigies, such as a shower of stones, which we might understand as a meteor shower, seem to have had a regular expiation ritual, in this case a *novemdiale sacrum*, nine days of sacrifices; human hermaphrodite births also seem to have occasioned a regular set of practices. Many times, a priestly college simply directed a particular set of sacrifices, while on some occasions a specific one-time gift or ritual was performed at a specified sanctuary. As a rule, the Romans seem to have been less concerned with interpreting the specific content of the gods' message than with finding the proper ritual to regain the favor of the gods.

While the theological function of the expiatory rituals was to communicate the proper obedience to the gods and reestablish a harmonious relationship with them, these rituals also communicated messages to the members of the human community. Expiatory rites worked on at least two levels: on the one hand, they demonstrated to the Roman populace that the favor of the gods was being restored, and on the other hand, they reestablished the bonds of the community in the face of a crisis. On the most obvious level, the system of public divination in Rome functioned to reassure the Romans that each action they undertook had the blessing of the gods; in this way, divination was an essential part of the Romans' belief that they were the most religious of all people and therefore had a special connection to the divine.[28] But more interesting for our purposes, expiatory rites also represent the community coming together to combat a danger to society, rather than allowing the community to dissolve in a spate of blaming others or an "every man for himself" fatalism. In anthropological terms, this social function of expiation may be considered a subcategory of rites of passage known as rites of intensification; such rites are

28. On this aspect of divination at Rome, see Liebeschuetz (1979), 8–10. On the Romans' special connection to the divine, see earlier, p. 24–25.

held whenever there is a threat to the equilibrium of a society, and they serve to solidify and reestablish the social order.[29] The rupture in the *pax deorum* may be seen as rupturing the fundamental order of the Roman state, casting the society back into a transitional or liminal state, "a time and place of withdrawal from normal modes of social action," according to Victor Turner, and hence "potentially a period of scrutinization of the central values and axioms of the culture in which it occurs."[30] Ritual behavior in such moments has the ability to generate social change and, in particular, to bring to an otherwise structured society a greater degree of undifferentiated and equalitarian relations between humans, what Turner calls *communitas*: "symbolic behavior actually 'creates' society for pragmatic purposes—including in society both structure and *communitas*."[31] Turner thus asserts that ritual does not merely bring a return to the status quo ante, but brings fundamental change even as it reestablishes the social order.

Using anthropological models along these lines, Rosenberger has analyzed the Roman material and observed that expiations appear as a symbolic reerecting of boundaries, just as the prodigies themselves were often transgressions of boundaries.[32] Rosenberger categorized expiatory rites as having four major variants: the removal of the object that was treated as prodigy beyond the boundaries of the state; its preservation, carefully controlled, within the boundaries of the state; the renewal and cleansing of Roman boundaries (for instance, by a *lustratio*); and the expansion outward of the boundaries of the Roman community. Several points are worthy of special emphasis for our purposes. For one, Rosenberger stresses the importance of the visibility of the expiatory rituals; the public performance of the expiatory ritual, even the public nature of the Senate meeting at which the matter was discussed, served as an essential element in binding the community together through the sharing in the ritual.[33] Second, as Rosenberger notes, "expiatory rites are regarded as 'rites of aggregation,' in which Rome and her citizens were defined against an area of 'the outside,' against the 'Other,' so that a ritual self-definition of the state was achieved."[34] Since the maintenance of a community's sense of identity depends on a continued maintenance of the boundaries between itself and others, the reerection of boundaries in the wake of a prodigy is thus an essential element in the definition of the Roman community.

29. See Chapple and Coon (1942).
30. Turner (1969), 267.
31. Turner (1974), 56.
32. Rosenberger (1998), 131–154. For his view of prodigies as boundary transgressions, see the earlier discussion of the liminality of prodigies, p. 113.
33. Rosenberger (1998), 154–157.
34. Rosenberger (1998), 141; cf. also 152. Cf. Rüpke (1990), 141, for a similar self-definition in military rituals.

In fact, prodigies and their expiation provided a regular mechanism by which the Roman state could express its sense of identity. Following the work of Turner outlined previously, these expiatory rituals might not merely restore the preexisting sense of community, but might bring about changes to that community even while reestablishing it.

In this regard, it is striking that so many prodigies and their related expiations involved foreign religious traditions. On most occasions, the means of expiations was determined by a foreign element, either the Etruscan haruspices, whom we discussed in the previous chapter, or the Sibylline Books, which are agreed by all sources ancient and modern to have come to Rome from the outside, although the precise source of the Sibylline Books was a matter of debate among the ancient sources and continues to be so for modern scholars.[35] More than 90 percent of the recorded expiations during the Republic involved one of these two sources, while the pontiffs, the quintessentially "Roman" priests, were involved in only approximately 20 percent.[36] More strikingly, on occasion the Roman Senate directed that expiations be carried out not in Rome but at a sanctuary or other location outside Rome. Furthermore, many of the expiations carried out in Rome were performed to foreign divinities already incorporated into the Roman religious system. This trend was particularly marked during Rome's most severe national crisis, the Second Punic War. In view of the fact that prodigies were considered to indicate a rupture in the relationship between the Romans and their gods and that expiations were meant to heal those rifts, the involvement of so many foreign elements at this critical juncture that threatened the very existence of the Roman state deserves closer scrutiny.

The year 218 was a prodigious year in the wake of Hannibal's invasion of Italy, with twelve prodigies reported from districts all over the peninsula,

35. The story of the purchase of the Sibylline Books by Tarquinius Superbus from a mysterious old woman is told in Dion. Hal., *Ant. Rom.* 4.62; Gell. *NA* 1.19.1; Lactant. *Div. inst.* 1.6.10–11. Where the ancient sources speculate about the woman, they name her as one of the nine Sibyls and assign her a home in either Etruria or Cumae. Modern scholars are therefore divided as to whether the Sibylline Books were Etruscan or Greek; see Wissowa (1912), 461–469; Hoffmann (1933); Latte (1960), 160–161; Dumézil, (1996), 601–602; Orlin (1997), 76–115.

36. For the involvement of the different priestly colleges in expiations, see the index of prodigies given by MacBain (1982) 82–104; several colleges might be involved in the expiation of some prodigies, so the percentages do not add to one hundred. While the exact percentages should be treated with some caution, since there are many expiations where no priestly groups are explicitly mentioned and it is possible that that the involvement of one of the colleges has been overlooked by our sources, it is unlikely that that the picture is dramatically different from that suggested here. The pontiffs clearly were not as involved in expiations as the *haruspices* and the *decemviri* were.

including Etruria, the Sabine territory, and Picenum, in addition to Latium.[37] Among these were two prodigies from sanctuaries as previously discussed, one from Juno Sospita in Lanuvium, when the spear of Juno shook of its own accord and a crow flew into the sanctuary and lit upon a couch, and the other from Caere, where the oracular tablets shrank. Since Hannibal's early success was taken by the Romans to be a sign in itself that their relationship with the gods was amiss, and since maintaining unity in their confederation was clearly an important element in the response to Hannibal, both the total number of prodigies and the number of peregrine prodigies cannot be considered surprising. What is more noteworthy are the numerous expiations ordered at the time. Many rituals were performed at Rome: a *novemdiale sacrum* in response to the shower of stones at Picenum, a *lustratio* of the city, a *lectisternium*, and an *intercessio*, as well as sacrifices to a variety of deities. But in addition to these ceremonies carried out in Rome, the decemviri decreed that the Romans should make an offering of forty pounds of gold to Juno Sospita in Lanuvium, celebrate a *lectisternium* at Caere, and perform a *supplicatio* to Fortuna on the *mons Algidus*. On this occasion, the Romans not only recognized a prodigy that occurred on foreign soil but also directed that expiations should be carried out on foreign soil, a dramatic extension of the relationship. Bringing an expiatory offering, especially such a costly one, from Rome to the sanctuary at Lanuvium moves the relationship with Juno Sospita well beyond recognition of her importance; it makes her a goddess of the Romans to be propitiated in exactly the same way as a divinity whose home lay in the city. Moreover, the ceremony brought not only the Roman populace together in an effort to strengthen societal bonds through a communal action but also brought the Romans and Lanuvians together. At the same time, the procession from Rome to Lanuvium, which accompanied the gift, made a visible statement to the other Latin communities about the Romans' willingness to acknowledge that union publicly. To underline the message, the Romans erected the bronze statue in Rome on the Aventine hill, the traditional location for welcoming foreigners to Rome.[38] This statue apparently marked the first physical presence of Juno Sospita in Rome; her temple in Rome would not be erected until 194. By not only accepting the prodigy occurring in Lanuvium but also celebrating the expiation there, Juno Sospita was treated as a Roman cult rather than as a foreign cult worthy of special treatment by the Romans. The expiatory rites thus provided a means for the Romans to express or even create a greater degree of community with the people of Lanuvium. This unity of Rome with her Italian allies formed an important part of the Roman response to Hannibal's invasion.

37. Livy 21.62.
38. Orlin (2002).

The expiation of the prodigy that occurred at Caere indicates that the Roman behavior at Lanuvium cannot merely be ascribed to Rome's special relationship with Juno Sospita. Not only did the Romans decide that the shrinking of tablets at Caere should be expiated but also they did so with ceremonies both in Caere and at the shrine of Fortuna on the *mons Algidus* in Latium. This action is perhaps more remarkable, since the Romans ordered a celebration here not only at the site of the prodigy but also at a different cult site to the same goddess.[39] We thus have a prodigy occurring in Etruria being expiated in Latium. We know remarkably little about this shrine of Fortuna at Algidus; in fact, this incident is the only recorded notice of the shrine. The particular site here may not be of primary importance; though the site commanded a pass along the Via Latina south of Rome, its strategic value against an invader coming from the North would have been minimal. But these expiations may be significant in terms of Rome's attempts to foster a sense of unity against the Carthaginian invader. Worship of Fortuna as a goddess was ancient in Rome, with a temple to Fors Fortuna on the bank of the Tiber ascribed to Servius Tullius.[40] But her cult was also widespread not just in Latium, where she had major shrines at Tusculum, Praeneste, and Antium in addition to Algidus, but throughout peninsular Italy, with shrines known at Capua, Beneventum, Cales, and along the Adriatic coast.[41] By ordering expiations at cults of Fortuna outside Rome, the Romans signaled that cults of Fortuna outside Rome were on the same level with cults inside the city in terms of securing the *pax deorum* and the welfare of the state. The simultaneous expiations, both north and south of Rome, highlighted a common cultural feature against the Punic foe and thus promoted a sense of unity among Rome, Latium, and Etruria, just as the rites at Lanuvium promoted that sense.

Even more remarkable than the expiations of 218 were the Roman actions in the following year, when Roman armies were defeated at Lake Trasimene, the year that, not coincidentally, saw the highest number of

---

39. The sources do not specifically state that the prodigy occurred in a shrine of Fortuna at Caere, but other oracular sanctuaries using lots are known to have been dedicated to Fortuna, most famously at Praeneste. Considering that the expiation took place at a sanctuary of Fortuna, it is most likely that the oracular tablets at Caere were located in a shrine of Fortuna.

40. Varr. *Ling*. VI.17; Dion. Hal. *Ant. Rom.* IV.27. Another temple to this goddess was apparently built by Sp. Carvilius in 293 B.C.E.; cf. Livy 10.46.14.

41. On these "secondary" centers of Fortuna's cult, see Champeaux (1982), 182–191; she concludes that "the accumulation of facts encourages us to go beyond what we know with certainty of the Latinity of Fortuna, to envisage, as a highly probable conjecture, her Italicity."

prodigies recognized in a single year.[42] In response to prodigies from as near as the Appian Way and as far away as Sicily and Sardinia, the Senate prescribed a wide series of expiatory measures, including an apparent reform of the Saturnalia. Most interesting for our purposes are the expiations that the decemviri again directed to be made on non-Roman soil: sacrifices to Juno Sospita at Lanuvium, as well as in the forum of Ardea. These expiations were ordered even though neither Lanuvium nor Ardea witnessed a prodigy in 217; peregrine prodigies from Latium in 217 came from Praeneste and Antium. In this year, the Romans carried their relationship with Juno Sospita another step forward; in offering sacrifices to Juno Sospita despite the fact that she herself had not communicated any disfavor, the Romans further assimilated her as a state goddess of the Roman people. The sacrifice of "greater victims" was made to her in Lanuvium, just as sacrifices of greater victims were made in Rome to Capitoline Jupiter and other Roman divinities. The Roman decision to expiate prodigies from all over Italy at the shrine of Juno Sospita significantly reduced whatever distinctions remained between Roman and non-Roman. Even though there was as yet no temple to Juno Sospita in Rome—one would be erected in 194—Juno Sospita at Lanuvium effectively became a Roman goddess, one who might be propitiated on behalf of the Romans even when she herself had not indicated displeasure with the Romans. As we will see, the Romans continued to honor this goddess throughout the war and eventually constructed a temple to her in the Forum Holitorium after the war, thus expanding their relationship with the entire community of Lanuvium, both religious and human.[43]

If the offerings to Juno Sospita in 217 can be partly understood in the light of the existing relationship between the Romans and this goddess, the sacrifices performed at Ardea present a more complicated picture that points in the same direction. Ardea had been founded as a Latin colony in 442 and upon the conclusion of the Latin War had maintained its status as

---

42. Livy 22.1.

43. Fowler (1911), 354, n. 7, first suggested that the construction of the temple in Rome was actually meant to reduce the number of portents stemming from the temple in Lanuvium, and his suggestion was taken up by Gordon (1938), 32. However, prodigies continued to be reported from Lanuvium, including from the sanctuary of Juno Sospita, periodically throughout the second century and into the first century B.C.E., and prodigies are not specifically reported from the temple of Juno Sospita in Rome, so it is difficult to maintain this thesis. The continued acceptance of prodigies from Lanuvium provided a means for the Romans not only to reaffirm their unique relationship with Juno Sospita but also to build on that relationship to create religious and political links with the entire community of Lanuvium.

a Latin colony, bound directly to Rome rather than to the now-dissolved Latin League. The city was also the site of an important pan-Latin cult of Aphrodite, and the Ardeates also controlled the temple of Aphrodite at Lavinium.[44] In 217, the decemviri directed that sacrifices should be offered at Ardea, despite the fact that the city had not witnessed a prodigy, just as Lanuvium had not.[45] The connection of Ardea to Venus and to Lavinium may offer a partial explanation for the Roman decision to involve this apparently unrelated town in the religious activities of this year, for the Romans appear to have been capitalizing on their mythical origins at this time; several months later, they would vow a temple to the Venus from Mount Eryx in Sicily, another place connected with Aeneas legends, in response to the defeat at Cannae.[46] But the Romans did not direct that the sacrifices be made at the sanctuary of Aphrodite or at any other shrine in the city, but in the forum at Ardea. The connection of the religious to the political is hard to miss: in the political heart of an important Latin city, the Romans came and performed rites to expiate prodigies from all over Italy.

Two other actions from the set of expiatory activities from the year 217 deserve attention, for both are concerned with maintaining the Roman community at the outset of the Second Punic War. In addition to the afore-mentioned sacrifices at Lanuvium and at Ardea, the decemviri decreed that the Romans should offer sacrifices to Juno Regina in her temple on the Aventine hill and that the matrons of Rome should collect money to be given to Juno Regina. Juno Regina on the Aventine was originally a foreign goddess; she had arrived in Rome in 396 B.C.E. following her *evocatio* from Veii.[47] Just as the expiations at Lanuvium and Ardea looked toward the inte-gration of those communities, the Romans here emphasized the importance of a foreign goddess who had been integrated into the Roman state. As noted earlier, the temple of Juno Regina on the Aventine hill was located outside the *pomerium*, the sacred boundary of the city; from a religious perspective, sacrifices at her temple might be considered as taking place outside the city, just as those at Lanuvium and Ardea did. The Aventine had traditionally served as the location for outsiders who had been incorporated into the Roman state, so this location makes the Roman action all the more signifi-cant: far from closing their doors at this time of crisis, Rome's boundaries on the divine level and on the human level remained open, even in times of national trauma.

44. Pliny *HN* 3.57; Mela 2.71; Strabo 5.3.5. Cf. MacBain (1982), 36–37.
45. Ardea would not witness a prodigy recognized at Rome until 198 B.C.E.
46. Livy 22.9. Cf. chapter 2.
47. Livy 5.21–23. Cf. chapter 1.

The expiations of 217 also included a directive that the freedwomen of Rome should make an offering according to their means to Feronia, another foreign goddess. Feronia was an ancient deity, a warrior goddess as well as a goddess of the harvests and a protector of freedmen, worshipped especially by the Sabines and Latins; her popularity is attested by major sanctuaries both in Tarracina in southern Italy and at the foot of Mount Soracte near Capena in Etruria.[48] The cult site at Capena, also known as the *lucus Feroniae*, was apparently the site of an annual festival—Roman legend connected it with the rape of the Sabine women—and was sufficiently important that by 211 it had accumulated enough silver and gold that Hannibal despoiled the sanctuary on his retreat from Rome.[49] The presence of significant amounts of uncoined bronze attests to the antiquity of the sanctuary at Capena. The offering in 217 to this divinity, worshipped by Sabines and Latins in Etruscan territory, again emphasized the unity of the Roman enterprise in the face of Hannibal's threat. The expiation further recognized the importance of Rome's Etruscan allies, those most directly affected by the arrival of Hannibal in the first two years of the war. At the same time, the offering demonstrated the social unity at Rome, for the contribution made by the freedwomen of Rome specifically paralleled them with the freeborn *matronae*: the latter were making their offering to Juno Regina while the former were making theirs to Feronia.[50] The inclusion of both groups within Roman society was thus demonstrated by their active participation in winning back the favor of the gods, just as the inclusion of the Italian allies was demonstrated by the choice of deity. Several years later, the Romans made an even stronger statement of affinity with Feronia, an action undoubtedly related to the despoliation of the sanctuary by Hannibal's army. In 210, the year after Hannibal's depredation, statues near the grove of Feronia were seen sweating, and the pontiffs decided that a *supplicatio* should be performed, first at Rome and then at the sanctuary in Capena.[51] The mere acceptance of a prodigy emanating from the sanctuary offered an important recognition from the Romans that the sanctuary continued to function despite Hannibal's depredations, and it also implied that the sack of a non-Roman sanctuary had affected the Romans' relationship with their gods. Although we do not hear specifically about

48. Cf. Bloch and Foti (1953), utilizing inscriptional evidence from Capena.

49. Annual festival: Livy 1.30; Dion. Hal. *Ant. Rom.* 3.32. Hannibal: Livy 26.11; Sil. *Pun.*13.83–90.

50. Cf. Rosenberger (1998), 183, commenting on the roles of patricians and plebeians, free and slave, men and women in the activities of 217.

51. Livy 27.4.

restorations made to the grove of Capena, the sanctuary continued to function into the second century, and the Romans recognized at least one additional prodigy from the sanctuary after the conclusion of the war.[52] The decision to perform expiatory rites both in Rome and in Etruria in 210 further expressed the solidarity of the Romans with the people of southern Etruria; at both locations, the exact same ceremony was to be performed. The choice of ceremony, the *supplicatio*, was made by the Romans and conformed to Roman practice, now spreading outside the walls of the city; the dual ceremonies signal the broader acceptance of the importance of the Etruscan sanctuary and the people who worshipped there.

It is remarkable that such important expiatory rites were performed to foreign gods. This action explicitly makes those gods Roman and demonstrates that the success of the Roman enterprise is as dependent on these recent arrivals as on traditional Roman gods. At the same time as the decemviri directed these four expiatory actions involving foreigners, they also recommended that a golden thunderbolt be given to Jupiter, and gifts of silver to Juno and Minerva, making explicit the parallel between the Capitoline triad and these foreign—or originally foreign—elements. The message, doubly important in a time of crisis, may in part serve as a reminder that these gods now act on behalf of the Romans, but it also embraces these gods by reminding the community that these originally alien divinities were so deeply a part of the Roman system that they were invoked in times of greatest crisis. These expiations at the very outset of the war are thus remarkable acts of religious and political unity and began a pattern of religious activity by which the Romans sought to unite themselves more closely with their Italian allies. As discussed earlier, expiatory rites serve to unite the community in the face of a threat to its existence, so the ceremonies at Lanuvium and particularly in the forum of Ardea indicate that the Romans considered these communities a part of the res publica. Ardea, in fact, provided an ideal complement to Lanuvium; the latter community was a *municipia cum suffragio* with long-standing political and religious ties to Rome, and so the Roman action may have reassured her of her place within the Roman alliance, while the former was a Latin colony, technically non-Roman and independent with armed forces of her own, where the Romans demonstrated that these cities, too, were considered as one with themselves. By going to these towns to make the sacrifice, the Romans acknowledged the power and importance of their Italian allies and their essential unity with them. And since both towns served as sites for important regional sanctuaries, the message may have aimed at a wider audience and been disseminated more widely. This demonstration of

52. In 196 (Livy 33.26).

oneness with her Latin allies offers insight into how Rome was able to hold that alliance together at the critical moment in her imperial expansion.

The Roman focus on maintaining unity with her Italian allies during the latter part of the Second Punic War can also be seen in the extraordinary expiation performed in 207 B.C.E. In that year, a child the size of a four-year-old was born in Frusino, but more ominously, it was uncertain whether the child was male or female.[53] The Etruscan haruspices were consulted and declared that the child should be cast into the sea, and they themselves put it alive into a box and threw it in the sea, while the pontiffs declared that twenty-seven maidens should walk through the city chanting a hymn. However, while the maidens were in the temple of Jupiter Stator rehearsing the hymn, written incidentally by Livius Andronicus, lightning struck the temple of Juno Regina on the Aventine. In response to this second prodigy, the haruspices declared that Juno Regina must be appeased with a gift from the *matronae* of Rome, so the curule aediles supervised collections, and the decemviri then led a procession in which the maidens chanted their hymn and wound their way to the temple of Juno Regina, where the gifts were presented and sacrifices made. Bruce MacBain has offered an analysis of this complex set of rituals, noting several key points that undermine previous interpretations of this expiation.[54] First, we should notice that this is a rare instance where virtually all of the religious colleges of Rome, not to mention a group of "secular" magistrates, were involved in a single set of ritual acts, thus placing tremendous authority behind these rites.[55] The ritual activity, moreover, was possessed of a strong Etruscan flavor; the haruspices were consulted twice, once for the initial prodigy that was expiated by "an exclusively Etruscan technique," the casting of the item into the sea, and the second time for the subsequent lightning strike, for which Etruscan expertise in fulgural lore was at hand. And the expiatory rites were directed toward Juno Regina, who, as we saw before, had already been the focus of expiatory activity in the war, in 217 B.C.E., as part of the general Roman effort to encourage the Italians to maintain their place within the Roman alliance. At the same time, the hymn of the maidens and accompanying dance appear to have been a ritual already familiar to the culturally Greek cities of southern Italy, and the involvement of Livius

53. Livy 27.37. On the topic of deformed births as prodigies, see Allély (2003).

54. MacBain (1982), 65–71. Earlier studies include those of Boyce (1937), Cousin (1942), and Gagé (1955).

55. MacBain (1982), 68–69, is surely right to see these groups cooperating with one another, rather than seeing the decemviri and haruspices as operating at cross-purposes. Cf. also Rosenberger (1998), 196. MacBain suggests, more speculatively, that the ultimate source for this set of expiatory rituals was the consul of 207, M. Livius Salinator, who was a member of the decemviral college, whose son was a pontiff and whose client, Livius Andronicus, composed the hymn for the occasion.

Andronicus points toward another Greek element of the ritual.[56] That the rituals of 207 were concerned with the support of the Etruscans, with their proximity to Hasdrubal's expected path, and of southern Italy, where Hannibal continued to maintain his forces, is also revealed by the timing of this expiatory activity. Two years earlier, in 209, Livy for the first time reports the birth of a child whose sex could not be determined, yet no special rite was performed in that year; the entire group of prodigies for 209 was expiated with sacrifice, *supplicatio*, and *obsecratio*.[57] That an elaborate ceremony was devised for the same prodigy two years later suggests that the surrounding context had changed such that the new rite was warranted. MacBain is undoubtedly right to suggest that Etruscan unrest at the approach of Hasdrubal and Roman fears about the loyalty of Etruria, should Hasdrubal march along the western coast of Italy, lay behind this extraordinary Roman activity, though the importance of maintaining the support of Campanian allies should not be overlooked.[58] By incorporating a new ritual into their system and paying new honors to the originally Etruscan Juno Regina, using both religious and nonreligious personnel, the Romans again emphasized their respect for the characteristics they held in common both with the Etruscans and with the Greeks of southern Italy. Just as Greek and Etruscan rituals and an Etruscan goddess were part of the Roman state and part of the religious effort against the Carthaginians, so, too, the Romans hoped that the cities of Etruria and southern Italy would see themselves as part of the Roman war effort.[59] A similar androgynous birth was reported among the prodigies just after the war in 200 and was expiated by the same means, reaffirming the position of the haruspices and the Etruscans more generally even after the immediate crisis had passed.[60]

The performance of so many expiatory rites in honor of foreign, especially Italian, gods and goddesses points to the importance of Italian support in the war effort against Hannibal. The Roman victory in the Second Punic

56. The Greek nature of the procession was first proposed by Diels (1890), 92, and accepted by Boyce (1937) and now Rosenberger (1998), 186.

57. Livy 27.11.

58. MacBain (1982), 67–69. On the turmoil in Etruria at the time, see also Van Son (1963). Rosenberger (1998), 194, notes the existence of enemies in both northern and southern Italy as part of the explanation for both Etruscan and Greek elements in the ritual.

59. As it turned out, Hasdrubal attempted to link his forces with Hannibal via the eastern route, along the Adriatic, so the loyalty of the Etruscans was not a decisive factor. Nevertheless, after the battle of the Metaurus, the consul Livius was sent to Etruria to investigate possible acts of treachery. Cf. Livy 28.10.

60. Schultz (2006a), 33–37, has emphasized the participation of women, both *matronae* and *virgines*, in these expiatory offerings, a salutary reminder of gender concerns evident in Rome at this time; cf. the discussion of the priestesses of Ceres in chapter 3.

War can be largely attributed to the decision by Rome's Italian allies not to abandon her for Hannibal, and the expiations of this period formed an integral part of the Roman strategy to persuade allies to remain on her side by highlighting an important cultural similarity in the face of an alien invader. The acceptance of prodigies from Italian cities demonstrated to the Italians that Rome was concerned for their welfare and shared their anxieties about the course of the campaign. The expiation of those prodigies, at times on foreign soil and frequently to divinities especially worshipped by Italic or Etruscan peoples, helped to demonstrate the unity of Roman and Italian in religious terms, worshipping the same divinities and respecting the same sanctuaries, even outside the city of Rome. The definition of the Roman community thus expanded under the pressure of the Second Punic War, as the Romans made a concerted effort to include the Italians in the Roman community. There is, of course, no way of gauging the impact of these actions, but the repeated Roman actions in this area indicate that the Romans at least felt that the activity was worthwhile. Even if the cities that chose to stand by Rome did so out of self-interest more than out of any emergent sense of pan-Italian consciousness, the Roman reminders of cultural connections and receptivity worked to contribute to the sense that those interests might be better served by remaining with Rome.

Expiatory activity, of course, continued after the war, just as it had proceeded during the war, and continued to serve as a means to define the Roman community. Although the total number of prodigies the Romans recognized declined after the war, the percentage of prodigies recognized from outside Rome remained approximately the same, just over half of all prodigies accepted. The geographical range from which prodigies were accepted continued to expand; in 199, a dispatch from P. Sulpicius, serving as proconsul in Macedonia, reported that laurel leaves had shot forth on the stern of a warship.[61] Curiously, the Senate itself ordered the consuls to expiate the other prodigies of that year but called in the haruspices for advice on the Greek portent. Otherwise, the prodigies and expiations for the twenty years after the war are unremarkable, from Rome as well as Italy, from sanctuaries as well as unconsecrated land. But in 181 comes an expiation unlike any other that had preceded it. In that year, the people of Lanuvium reported that the statue of Juno Sospita had shaken her spear and shed tears.[62] The frequency of prodigies occurring in the sanctuary of Juno Sospita has been discussed already, though it should be noted that by 181 the Romans had erected a temple to Juno Sospita in Rome, yet

61. Livy 32.1
62. Livy 40.19.

prodigies continue to be reported from Lanuvium. The Senate's response to this prodigy contains the remarkable element: following the advice of the decemviri, they decreed that a three-day *supplicatio* and *feriae* should be held *per totam Italiam*. This command may be seen as the logical outcome of the Roman actions taken during the Second Punic War, where the Romans took on themselves the responsibility to perform rites at foreign sites to expiate prodigies that occurred outside Rome. Here they directed local communities to take that responsibility upon themselves. This message is more forceful in its assertion of religious unity, as the Romans gave notice that a prodigy that affects the Roman state thereby affects *tota Italia* and must be expiated by the entire community of Italy. In this regard, it may be significant that the prodigy that led to this decree came from the sanctuary in Lanuvium rather than Rome itself. This sanctuary, as we have repeatedly seen, was held in common by the people of Lanuvium and the Romans. It had been an important pan-Latin sanctuary to which the Romans had attached themselves, and even in the second century, it was shared by the two communities. It thus might serve as a good example of the sharing of religious responsibility between the Romans and other non-Romans: just as the Romans and Laurentes shared responsibility for the sanctuary, the Romans and the inhabitants of Italy shared the responsibility to expiate prodigies from it.

The timing of this incident is again suggestive of larger Roman concerns. The twenty years following the conclusion of the Second Punic War had seen the Roman and non-Roman inhabitants of Italy working out their relationships in the wake of the Roman victory. Some towns had sought, and received, a higher status from the Roman government in the aftermath of the war: in 188, the towns of Arpinum, Formiae, and Fundi were admitted to the full Roman franchise. Other towns may have sought or even received similar privileges, but the promotions of these three towns to full citizenship are the last three instances attested in the sources prior to the Social War.[63] In the following year, Latin towns seeing a loss in population on account of migration to Rome, where the new settlers received full citizen rights, requested the Senate to send the emigrants back home, and the Senate complied, ordering 12,000 Latins who had already registered as Roman citizens to return home. The issues were not related merely to citizenship and settlement but might also touch on religious affairs. In reaction to the Bacchanalian affair of 186, the

63. The question of the enfranchisement of the Italian *municipia* prior to the Social War is a vexed question, but Sherwin-White (1973), 210–214, concludes, rightly in my opinion, that there are no grounds for assuming widespread grants of citizenship during the second century B.C.E.

Senate passed a decree both allowing Roman magistrates to arrest suspected members of the Bacchic cult and ordering Italian towns to institute certain regulations regarding cult practices related to Bacchus. In fact, investigations into the Bacchic cult had continued into 184 and 183, so the *supplicatio* and *feriae* of 181 may have been intended to bring closure to that episode, involving *tota Italia* in the effort to offer proper—that is, Roman-approved—rites to obtain the favor of the gods. In the early second century, as we will see in chapter 6, the Romans became concerned to define more clearly what it means to be Roman, and the decree to perform a *supplicatio* and *feriae* in response to a prodigy formed part of that effort.

This central message of a religious unity in Italy and Roman-defined rites was repeated in the following year. In 180, the severe pestilence that had been raging since the previous year carried off both the praetor and the consul for that year, and their deaths were considered to be a prodigy; in response the decemviri recommended that a *supplicatio* be held *per omnia concili- abula et fora* in Italy.[64] The Senate's action in this year must be regarded as a stronger restatement of the signal indicated in the previous year. Although the pestilence had been raging for a year and affected other areas of Italy as well as Rome, it was the death of two Roman magistrates that ultimately led the Senate to consider the pestilence as a sign from the gods, underscoring the role of Rome in determining what extraordinary occurrences should be defined as prodigies. The Senate also reasserted its role in expiating prodigies that might affect all of Italy, as it prescribed that the same ritual from 181 should be reenacted, further establishing the *supplicatio* as the Roman response to appease the wrath of the gods. The prodigies and expiations of these two years show all of Italy associated in performing the same ceremony in response to the same prodigy, albeit under Roman supervision. While in the third century the Romans had begun to take prodigies from outside Rome as indicative of a rupture in their own relationship with the gods, these incidents from the second century signal that the responsibility for appeasing the gods also falls on those living outside the city, even if the prodigy itself came from Rome. We may catch a glimpse of the results three years later, for in 177, when an osprey cut the sacred stone in Crustumerium, a *supplicatio* was performed on the spot in Crustumerium, not back in Rome with the other prodigies of the year.[65] Although we might take our analysis further if we knew whether the local population took the initiative to perform this ceremony on their own or whether the ritual was carried out at the behest of the authorities in Rome, in either scenario, we again see a prodigy

64. Livy 40.37.
65. Livy 41.13. Other prodigies for 177 are recorded by Livy at 41.9.

expiated outside Rome using the *supplicatio*. The prodigy-expiation complex continued to signal the bonds that linked Roman and non-Roman in the same religious position.

If prodigies served to indicate that particular communities belonged as part of the res publica, they might also serve to signal that a community was no longer to be considered Roman. In 169, Livy reports eight prodigies, including four from Rome and four from peregrine communities, but he also indicates that two additional reports of extraordinary occurrences were *non suscepta*: a spear that burned for two hours in the house of L. Atreius in Fregellae was rejected because it occurred *in loco peregrino*, and a palm tree that suddenly appeared in the *impluvium* of the house of T. Marcius Figulus in Rome was rejected because it occurred *in loco privato*.[66] Although some scholars have tried to turn these rejections into a general rule about the acceptance of prodigies from private property or from territory outside Rome, it is not possible to do so, for the Romans had previously accepted many prodigies both *in loco peregrino* and *in loco privato*.[67] In the case of the incident at Rome, both the announcement of the prodigy and its rejection were clearly politically motivated, as has often been noted.[68] The prodigy itself was intended to suggest that victory would come to the Marcii if they were assigned the command against Perseus, and the Senate's rejection indicated it was unwilling to sanction that statement, though it did ultimately assign the campaign to two Marcii.[69] The obvious political overtones of that rejection suggest that similar political overtones were at work with the Fregellan rejection. MacBain is undoubtedly right to suggest that if the "acceptance of non-Roman prodigies by the Roman Senate constituted a political act whose purpose was to assert the religious unity of Italy . . . , then, by the same token, the rejection of a peregrine prodigy might, in different circumstances, suggest itself as a means of signaling that the town in question was indeed foreign and beyond the pale."[70] Prodigies from Fregellae had been accepted twice during the Second Punic War, so the rejection here must signal a change in Roman attitudes toward the town. Fregellae is, of course, notorious for having unsuccessfully rebelled against Rome in 125

66. Livy 43.13.

67. See p. 114–20 and the references there. This incident has been studied by MacBain (1982), 28–31, who points out that the Romans continued to accept prodigies from *loco peregrino* and *loco privato* after 169. Indeed, in 166 a boy born at Teanum Sidicinum in Campania with four hands and four feet was declared a prodigy and expiated by a lustration of the city (Obsequens 12).

68. Cf. Münzer in *RE*, s.v. "Marcius."

69. Of course, ultimately it was Aemilius Paullus, not the Marcii, who gained the credit for triumphing over Perseus.

70. MacBain (1982), 28.

B.C.E., resulting in the city's complete destruction at the hands of the Romans, and the prodigy rejection incident suggests that already in the first half of the century, the Romans saw the Fregellans as not properly integrated into the Roman order and potentially disruptive.[71] Fregellae is not recorded as witnessing another prodigy until 93 B.C.E., just prior to the Social War, when the town had been converted to Roman public property.[72]

A sense of both the possibilities and the limitations of using the acceptance of prodigies to signal communality with non-Roman cities can be gained by considering the Social War. This war, which broke out in 90 B.C.E. as some Italian allies sought full citizenship from the Romans, reveals interesting divisions. The rebellion was strongest in Samnium and the Oscan territory, and these areas are the regions of Italy from which the fewest prodigies are recorded.[73] The lack of Oscan prodigies in particular is somewhat surprising, given its geographical proximity to Rome, but the hostility between the Oscans and Romans does not seem to have dissipated as easily as with some of Rome's other Italian rivals. The lack of prodigy acceptance may reflect the lack of comfort the Romans felt in expressing commonality with the Oscans, and that same lack of a sense of a shared enterprise was a key component in the Oscan resolution to take up arms against Rome. The Romans did accept a pair of prodigies from the Vestini in 94 and again in 91, on the cusp of the war's outbreak, but these may be best categorized as too little and too late; the Vestini were among the leaders of the Italian *socii* during the war.[74] The failure to succeed with the Vestini indicates that the acceptance of prodigies by itself and over a short period of time was not sufficient to create a sense of commonality. Nevertheless, the timing of these two prodigies, the only two accepted from a nonallied people of east-central Italy, suggests that the Romans intended the acceptance of peregrine prodigies to function simultaneously on the human and divine levels.

71. Another indication of Fregellae as not working within the system may be preserved in a report from 177 (Livy 41.8), when the Samnites and Paeligni complained that four thousand of their citizens had moved to Fregellae, but their own military contributions had not decreased, nor had that of the Fregellans increased. This incident is the second of two complaints by the Latin communities that the migration of their citizens was posing internal problems for them; see Livy 39.3 for 187. It is not clear from Livy's report why exactly Fregellae was singled out in 177; it may be that the historian, knowing about later rebellion, focused specifically on them, but it is also possible that the Fregellans were somehow exacerbating an already challenging problem in 177.

72. Obsequens 52.

73. MacBain (1982), 29.

74. For the prodigies, a shower of stones in each case, see Obsequens 51, 54.

On the other hand, the Social War did not make a deep impression in Etruria, and while a number of individualized reasons can be put forward as an explanation, the repeated acceptance of prodigies coming from Etruria and the employment of the Etruscan haruspices contributed to this outcome. As a rule, the Etruscan cities did not rush to join the war effort and were among the first to cease hostilities, suggesting that they felt themselves to be sufficiently a part of the Roman enterprise that revolt was not in their best interest. Religion was a significant part of the means by which the Romans made the Etruscans feel this way, both in the incorporation of the haruspices within the prodigy-expiation system and in the continued acceptance of prodigies from Etruria. Many scholars have pointed to a distinct upsurge in prodigies accepted from Etruria toward the end of the second century and the beginning of the first century, and it has been suggested that these prodigies represent an attempt by the Roman Senate to acknowledge the anxieties of the Etruscans and that the Etruscan detachment from the rebellion may be partly attributed to this Roman attention.[75] Unlike the Vestini, the Romans had cultivated the relationship with the Etruscans over many years and with a number of different religious actions, so that in this case the increased recognition of prodigies on the verge of the war contributed to maintaining the allegiance of this region.

In these cases, and in the other cases we have examined throughout this chapter, we should not imagine that the acceptance of prodigies was carefully calculated to produce the optimal political effect. We need not hark back to the view of Roman religion mercilessly manipulated by disbelieving political elites to understand Roman actions. The inseparability of religion and politics at Rome suggests that in Roman religious actions we may see reflected a mind-set that is as much politically conditioned as religiously correct. The Roman acceptance of prodigies from non-Roman towns (or rejection in the singular case of Fregellae) is not so much designed to convey the message that these places are, or are not, considered Roman; rather, that action reveals that the Romans may already consider these places in that light and are acting on that belief. The prodigy-expiation complex is so useful for understanding the Roman sense of community precisely because each accepted prodigy reveals an action that the Romans believed affected their own relations with the divine, and each expiation thus revealed their notion of how the Roman gods could be appeased. Both ends of the process contribute to creating the circle of Romanness.

75. MacBain (1982), 78–79.

5

Ludi

L *udi* have long been considered one of the quintessential Roman religious activities. Although the term is conventionally translated as "games," *ludi* comprised a broader set of religious rituals, beginning with a procession of both gods and humans and involving an elaborate sacrifice before proceeding to the main event: *ludi scenici*, theatrical presentations, and *ludi circenses*, chariot racing in the Circus Maximus. The proliferation of these games in the Late Republic and Empire is a well-known feature of Roman civilization, and modern scholars have developed numerous different lines of inquiry in studying them. One avenue concerns the role of *ludi* in politics; their importance in the Late Republic as a means for politicians to communicate with the *populus* or to curry favor with the electorate has been a frequent object of study, even controversy.[1] A second line of inquiry has focused on the possible Etruscan or Greek antecedents for the Roman *ludi*, which might reveal the degree of Etruscan or Greek influence on the development of Roman civilization.[2] Yet it is only recently that attention has been paid to the history of *ludi*

---

1. Cf., e.g., Scullard (1951), 24–25; Yavetz (1969); Tengström (1977); Nicolet (1980), 361–373; Veyne (1990), 212–213.

2. Ancient sources as well as modern disagree on this question. Livy 7.2; Val. Max 2.4.4; and Tert. *De. Spect.* 5.6 all look to Etruria for the origins particularly of the *ludi scenici*, while Dion. Hal. *Ant. Rom.* 7.71–73, naturally looks to Greece; Tac. *Ann.* 14.21, splits the difference by attributing the *ludi circenses* to southern Italy and the *ludi scenici* to Etruria. Cf. further

in Rome: not just to their origins but to their development and expansion.[3] Whether the games originally developed from Greek or Etruscan models, they clearly developed into a style of celebration that was distinctively Roman and acquired a symbolic significance that they possessed neither in Greece nor in Etruria. This aspect of their development has not received sufficient attention; while *ludi* came to be seen as a characteristically Roman form of worship, the process by which they achieved that position needs further investigation.

The critical period in this development is the late third and early second centuries B.C.E., when the number of annual *ludi* celebrated on the Roman religious calendar increased dramatically. This period, as has been repeatedly noted in earlier chapters, is precisely the time during which Rome was evolving from a traditional city-state into a world power, and the conjunction of these two developments is hardly a coincidence. The discussion in the earlier chapters has largely focused on how the Romans presented themselves as open to foreign cultures and how this openness helped them reach out especially to the other Italian communities. This approach, however, presents its own set of challenges, as the inclusion of so many foreign elements may cause difficulties in defining what was Roman about Roman religion. The inability to differentiate Roman from non-Roman would pose a significant threat to Rome's sense of identity, at precisely the moment when Rome's rapid geographic and cultural expansion had altered her traditional position, and her perceptions of that position, in the world. As discussed in the introduction, an essential element in maintaining a sense of identity was preserving a clear definition of Roman and non-Roman. Already in the discussion of foreign priests in Rome, we have seen the Romans make some efforts to distinguish between Roman and non-Roman, even as they accepted these priests as valued members of the Roman religious system. The establishment of *ludi* as a quintessentially Roman form of celebration formed another part of the Roman response to the challenges posed by her new hegemonic position and contributed to reshaping a clear sense of Roman identity.[4]

Thuillier (1985); Clavel-Lévêque (1986); Briquel (1986, 1993); Beaujeu (1988). Crowther (1983) is concerned primarily with athletic games, which will not be the subject of our investigation here. Dupont (1993) focuses on the ancient discourse concerning the origins of *ludi* rather than trying to penetrate the mist surrounding their actual introduction.

3. See most recently F. Bernstein (1998).

4. See the comments of North (1993). Bernstein (1998) also focuses on the third and second centuries, though his concern is less with the establishment of Roman identity than with the way in which the development of *ludi* reflects a renewed philhellenism on the part of the Roman nobility.

Reconstructing the origins and history of *ludi* in the Early Republic presents many uncertainties, but the available evidence does not suggest that *ludi* played an important role in the religious life of the city at this time. Much of the difficulty comes from having to rely on Roman tradition as filtered through Livy. The major developments reported by the historian are linked with major events in the myth-history of early Rome: the foundation of the city by Romulus, the reign of Tarquin the Proud, and the Licinian-Sextian reforms of the 360s. So, for instance, Livy suggests that *ludi* provide the backdrop for the rape of the Sabine women, for it was during the celebration at the Consualia that Romulus ordered the Romans to swoop in and make off with their brides.[5] Of course, one should not blithely accept the factual basis of Livy's account here, and the historicity of these games has been strongly challenged.[6] If indeed the details of this incident have been embroidered by Roman tradition, as seems likely, it might nonetheless be noted that *ludi* were considered the appropriate setting for this seminal event in the growth of Rome; connecting the founder of the city and the event by which Rome gained reproductive capability with the celebration of *ludi* serves to remind us of how central *ludi* were in the Roman imagination.

The second mention of *ludi* in Livy's account comes from his discussion of the reign of Tarquinius Priscus and presupposes the earlier celebration of *ludi*: Priscus is said to have celebrated games "more elaborate and more splendid than earlier kings had given."[7] These games are supposed to have marked the institution of an annual celebration known either as the *ludi Romani* or *ludi magni*.[8] The historicity of these games has also been challenged forcefully by Bernstein, who notes that the *ludi Romani* were closely connected with the temple of Jupiter Optimus Maximus; while Priscus is reported by the tradition to have vowed the temple, it was not actually dedicated until the first year of the Republic.[9] Furthermore, among the reforms in the practice of *ludi* that Livy ascribes to Priscus are setting aside the space that would become the Circus Maximus, setting aside seats for the senators and equites, and utilizing horses and boxers. As some of these reforms can clearly be seen as a retrojection of late Republican practices—for instance, the reservation of seats for senators at *ludi* began in 194, according to Livy's own testimony—the

5. Livy 1.9.6.
6. Bernstein (1997).
7. Livy 1.35.7–10: *opulentius instructiusque quam priores reges fecit.*
8. On the phrase *Romani magnique varie appellati*, see Quinn-Schofield (1967a).
9. See Bernstein (1998), 24–51.

historical value of this entire account is limited, though it has been the subject of much discussion.[10] Perhaps the only conclusion that may be safely drawn from these passages is to confirm the belief of later Romans that *ludi* date back to the regal period.

Modern scholars have generally concurred with the Roman belief that *ludi* do in fact find their origins in the archaic period, even though the evidence is too sparse to permit a firm conclusion of precisely when or where or under what circumstances the rite originated. Most recently, Frank Bernstein has suggested, relying on the observation that the *ludi Romani* and the *dies natalis* for the temple of Jupiter Optimus Maximus fell on the same day, that the *ludi Romani* should have been instituted by 509 (or 507) at the latest.[11] This hypothesis depends in part on positing an Etruscan origin for the games, which might explain the connection in the Roman tradition between the *ludi* and Tarquin, as well as Livy's report of the inclusion of boxers in Tarquin's games, for boxing as an athletic activity was particularly popular among the Etruscans.[12] It may not be possible to resolve the question of origins with sufficient certainty, but it may not be necessary to resolve the question of place to resolve the question of time; we have strong evidence of Roman cultural borrowings from both civilizations by this time, so that a date in the late sixth century is plausible, wherever the impetus may have come from.[13] As Bernstein put it, the evidence suggests "a certain probability" for the development of games in Rome by the foundation of the Republic.

While scholars tend to agree that the *ludi Romani* originated in the regal period, there is great controversy over the institution of the *ludi plebeii*. Three alternatives have been proposed: approximately contemporaneous with the *ludi Romani* in the late sixth or early fifth century, 366 with the creation of separate curule and plebeian aediles, or shortly before 220 with the construction of the Circus Flaminius. The argument in favor of the early date rests on suggestions in Valerius Maximus and a scholiast on Cicero that *ludi plebeii* were celebrated in the 490s, though the value of these pieces of

---

10. In addition to Bernstein (1998), see Quinn-Schofield (1967a, 1967b); Thuillier (1981). As so often, the terms of the debate were set down by Theodor Mommsen (1859), and much of the subsequent literature responds to his article. See Bernstein (1998), 31 n. 49, for references to this literature.

11. Bernstein (1998), 64.

12. On athletic activities associated with the Etruscans, see Thuillier (1985).

13. See Bernstein (1998), 24–30, for a sketch of the evidence, especially from Etruria, that gives the Roman development of games at this time.

evidence is dubious.[14] The date in the fourth century is connected by Livy to the Licinian-Sextian reforms and the first plebeian consul; since Roman historical tradition has a tendency to cluster reforms in the context of a larger institutional reform and to view all these events as part of the "Struggle of the Orders," this evidence must be viewed with skepticism. In 367, upon the resolution of the strife that followed the election of the first plebeian consul, Lucius Sextius, the Senate decided to give thanks to the gods for the newly found concord in the state by celebrating the *ludi maximi* and adding an extra day to the festival.[15] Livy goes on to relate how the plebeian aediles refused to supervise these games, whereupon patrician youths clamored for the chance to organize them; the next year was noteworthy not just for the first plebeian consul, but the first curule aedile as well.[16] The existence of separate aediles has contributed to the argument that there must have been separate sets of *ludi* from this time, since we know in the later Republic that the curule aediles organized the Roman Games while the plebeian aediles organized the plebeian games; the institution of the *ludi plebeii* is seen as an appropriate expression of the newly achieved plebeian equality.[17] Livy, however, makes no mention of this innovation; indeed, the *ludi* of 366 appear to have been special games vowed by the Senate as a direct response to the renewed harmony in the state following the Licinian-Sextian compromise, not a permanent institution.[18] In fact, Livy makes no mention of the *ludi*

14. Val. Max. 1.7.4, who identifies a celebration traditionally dated to 491 as *ludi plebeii*; pseudo-Asconius on *Verr.* 1.31 (217 Stangl), who connects them with either the liberty of the plebs after the expulsion of the kings or the reconciliation of the plebs after a secession. Wiseman (2005), 51, suggests that the games celebrated in this period might originally have been known as the *ludi plebeii*, and only after the institution of a separate celebration, which he places in 367 (see later), came to be known as the *ludi Romani*. But he does not posit two separate celebrations in the early fifth century.

15. Livy 6.42.12.

16. Livy 7.1.

17. For the later division of responsibility between curule and plebeian aediles, see, e.g., Livy 31.50. For the notion of a plebeian riposte to the *ludi Romani*, see Quinn-Schofield (1967b). The argument that the two sets of games date from this time has been made by Piganiol (1923), 84–90, esp. 85, and most recently Wiseman (2005), 50–52, who notes other similarities between the *ludi Romani* and *ludi plebeii* that in his view suggest an archaic origin for both celebrations. Bernstein (1998), 63–78, sees the expansion in the number of aediles as resulting in a change in the production of *ludi*, in which responsibility for these games was taken over by the aediles, but not in a second set of *ludi*.

18. Livy 6.42.12: *ita ab diutina ira tandem in concordiam redactis ordinibus, cum dignam eam rem senatus censeret esse meritoque id, si quando unquam alias, deum immortalium [causa libenter facturos] fore ut ludi maximi fierent et dies unus ad triduum adiceretur.* This point is noted by Taylor (1939), 197.

plebeii until the year 216, and although arguments from silence are always uncertain, the absence of a mention of *ludi plebeii* in the seventy-five years for which Livy's work survives, down to 293, provides the basis of the argument in favor of a third-century date. Livy's notice of the *ludi plebeii* for 216 implies that the celebration was not an innovation of that year, but since his account does not survive for the years 292 to 218, it is impossible to know exactly when the historian marked the introduction of the *ludi plebeii*, and neither the *periochae* nor other sources provide any assistance.[19] Valerius Maximus' account, although filled with its own anachronistic problems, suggests that the *ludi plebeii* were celebrated in the Circus Flaminius prior to the construction of the Circus Maximus, which would set the introduction of annual *ludi plebeii* between the construction of that venue in the 220s and the previously referenced celebration of 216.[20] On the whole, the evidence is insufficient to securely date the introduction of the *ludi plebeii*, but what does seem clear is that *ludi* do not seem to have played a major role in Roman religious practice at this time. At most, there seem to have been two sets of annual games and the occasional votive *ludi* in response to a specific crisis or event warranting thanksgiving to the gods, such as the *ludi* celebrated in 366 to celebrate the renewed concord in the res publica.[21] And even votive games disappear from the historical record between 358 and 218, as was observed long ago by Piganiol.[22] Whatever innovations occurred prior to the third century, *ludi* were not a significant element of the Roman religious landscape at this time.

One innovation that Livy does mention in the early Republic, and indeed in the very next chapter after describing the events of 366 and the creation of the curule aediles, is the introduction of *ludi scenici* to Rome. According to

19. Livy 23.30.16: *Plebei ludi aedilium M. Aurelii Cottae et M. Claudii Marcelli ter instaurati.*

20. Argued most recently by Bernstein (1998), 78–83 and 158–63. The suggestion was first made by Theodor Mommsen (1887), 2.1.519–20, and accepted by Quinn-Schofield (1967b), 678. See further p. 140 with additional references.

21. For other examples of votive *ludi* in the early Republic, see Livy 4.12, 4.35, 5.31, 7.15, and 10.23. Livy also relates a tendentious story (2.36) involving a slave who was beaten prior to the games and a plebeian who received a dream from Jupiter warning him that the "dancer" was displeasing. The plebeian feared to approach the patrician consuls until Jupiter paralyzed him, whereupon he relayed the message to the consuls, and all was well. The repetition of the games then provided the pretext for a Volscian attack on Rome; in a story laden with references to the rape of the Sabine women, the Romans refused to allow the Volscians to attend the games out of fear of violence, and the Volscians then used this insult as a reason to attack. This incident, with its obvious aetiological purpose, tells us little about the history of *ludi* in Rome.

22. Piagniol (1923), 78–79.

the historian, a plague had struck Rome in 365, carrying off one of the new curule aediles, as well as the great Marcus Furius Camillus, and even the celebration of the third *lectisternium* in Rome's history the following year failed to ease the pestilence. Livy continues: "When the strength of the plague was alleviated neither by human measures nor by divine aid, with their minds overcome by superstition, among other means of placating the wrath of heaven, scenic plays also are said to have been instituted, a new thing for a warlike people—for to this point there had been only the spectacle of the circus."[23] Livy goes on to describe the addition of dancers from Etruria, who were soon imitated by Roman youths, until eventually Livius Andronicus was the first to compose a play with a plot. This account of the origins of Roman drama has generated its full share of controversy, and certainty the date or manner of the introduction of *ludi scenici* may again be impossible to attain, though the fact that Livy connects the *ludi scenici* to a plague rather than to the Struggle of the Orders lends some credibility to the chronology of his account.[24] While Livy's accounts of *ludi* are sparse and the historian is far from clear on the subject, it seems clear that by the end of the fourth century *ludi* might include both contests in the circus and stage plays and were established as one form of Roman religious activity. However, the relative infrequency of *ludi* in this early period suggests that this ritual did not yet play the prominent role that it would in the Late Republic and Empire.

The critical period in the development of Roman *ludi* came in the late third century B.C.E., with the rapid introduction of a series of new votive games. The process may have begun with the first celebration of the *ludi Tarentini*, which, as discussed in chapter 2, probably occurred in the middle of the third century. Although these games were not annual, they did represent a significant innovation, and the close proximity to the games introduced toward the end of the century should not be overlooked. The date of the introduction of the *ludi Plebeii*, as noted before, is a notorious problem, but the most likely suggestion places it within this period. The *ludi Ceriales* also seem to have been introduced around this time, although determining the date of their first appearance in Rome is beset by problems similar to that of the *ludi plebeii*.[25] Again, Livy's first

---

23. Livy 7.2.3: *cum vis morbi nec humanis consiliis nec ope divina levaretur, victis superstitione animis ludi quoque scenici, nova res bellicoso populo—nam circi modo spectaculum fuerat,—inter alia caelestis irae placamina instituti dicuntur.* Compare the account of Val. Max., 2.4.4. A fragmentary passage of Festus, 436 L, that mentions aediles also appears to relate to the introduction of *ludi scenici*.

24. On the introduction of the *ludi scenici*, see Mommsen (1887), 2.483; Hanson (1959), 10–11; Gruen (1992), 185–186; Bernstein (1998), 119–129.

25. Livy 30.39.8: *Cerialia ludos dictator et magister equitum ex senatus consulto fecerunt.*

reference to these games comes only in the late third century, in 202 B.C.E. Again, the historian implies that these games were not an innovation of that year, but rather had been established previously, presumably during that part of the third century for which Livy's text in missing. In the case of the *ludi Ceriales*, we do have some additional evidence available, but that evidence has been the subject of much controversy in its own right. A denarius of C. Memmius, *triumvir monetalis* in 56 B.C.E., bears the legend MEMMIUS AED CERIALIA PREIMUS FECIT, commemorating an ancestor who was claimed as the first to do something at the Cerialia.[26] The identity of this earlier Memmius and whether he was the first aedile to celebrate the Cerialia or simply made an innovation to the festival have been the subject of much discussion. Other notices in Livy reveal the importance of the claim to have been the first to celebrate a festival in a certain way, but these claims do not always relate to the first ever celebration of the rite, but often to some innovation.[27] Nonetheless, Broughton suggested that the reference must be to the first *ludi Ceriales* and posited an unknown Memmius as aedile in 211, since the aediles for 210 through 202 are all known.[28] Bernstein has rejected Broughton's conjecture and offered 219 as the date for the first *ludi Ceriales*, aligning a famine known in the early years of the Hannibalic war with a note in Pseudo-Cyprian claiming a famine as the inspiration for the games to Ceres.[29] For our purposes, all the issues need not be resolved; while it would enable deeper analysis if we knew the exact context and content of the first Cerialia, it is sufficient to note the virtual unanimity that *ludi* in honor of Ceres were introduced in the last quarter of the third century B.C.E.[30]

More precision is possible with three additional sets of games inaugurated over the course of the next fifty years. The *ludi Apollinares* were celebrated for the first time in 212, and then each year for the next four years, apparently

26. Crawford (1983), I.451.

27. Cf. Livy 27.23.5, where in 208 P. Licinius Varus is noted as the first to celebrate the *ludi* to Apollo on a fixed day, or Livy 34.54.3 and 36.36.3, competing claims to be the first celebrate *ludi scenici* at the Megalesia. Cf. Wiseman (2005), 53–54.

28. Broughton *MRR*, 273, followed by Hayne (1991). Le Bonniec (1958), 320–332 suggested that the commemoration was of the first *ludi scenici* at the Cerialia and identified Memmius with the praetor of 172, but the coin alone does not present sufficient evidence to believe that *ludi scenici* and *ludi circenses* were introduced separately to the Cerialia.

29. Bernstein (1998), 163–166. For the famine, see pseudo-Cyprian, *De Spect.* 4.1.

30. To my knowledge, only Wiseman (2005), 52–53, would push the origins back to the fifth century, on the basis of several passages in Dionysius of Halicarnassus (*Ant. Rom.* 6.17.2–4; 6.94). Those passages, however, refer primarily to the foundation of the temple of Ceres, Liber and Libera; games are mentioned in the first of these passages only, and are not indicated as either being dedicated to Ceres *or* instituted on an annual basis.

vowed and celebrated anew every time; finally in 208 the *ludi Apollinares* were made an annual festival and became a permanent part of the religious calendar.[31] In 204, the black stone representing the Magna Mater was brought to Rome and installed in the temple of Victory on the Palatine hill until her temple could be constructed; a *lectisternium* and *ludi* were celebrated to mark the occasion.[32] By the end of the next decade, the Megalesian games had become an annual rite of the Roman state, though again there is some uncertainty as to the exact date, 194 or 191, when the games became annual.[33] Finally in 173, the *ludi Florales* were made an annual rite in honor of the goddess Flora, apparently an old Italic goddess who had long been worshipped in Rome.[34] Games in honor of Flora had apparently been celebrated at the dedication of her temple erected around 240, just before the explosion in the celebration of annual *ludi*, so there is a certain symmetry in noting that she was apparently the first deity of this group to receive *ludi* and then that she received the last set of annual *ludi* until the games of the military dynasts of the first century.

The addition of these sets of annual *ludi* deserves more attention than it has received; over a roughly fifty-year period, encompassing the last quarter of the third century and the first quarter of the second, *ludi* came to occupy a much more prominent place on the Roman religious calendar than they had previously held. While *ludi* had been celebrated in Rome since the regal

31. Livy 25.12 (212); 26.23.3 (211); 27.11.6 (209); 27.23.5–7 (208). There is some confusion in Livy's account, for in 211 he reports that the Senate decreed that the games should be vowed *in perpetuum*, while in his report for the year 208 he indicates that up until then the games had been vowed on an annual basis: *in unum annum vovebant dieque incerta faciebant*. It is generally thought that the decree of 211 was never carried out, so that 208 does in fact represent the institution of the games to Apollo as an annual festival, but it is possible that some other reform lies under Livy's laconic reports. See in general Gagé (1955), 270–286; Bernstein (1998), 171–186.

32. Livy 29.14.13–14.

33. The uncertainty is caused by two separate reports by Livy on the addition of *ludi scenici* to the Megalesia; either in 194 (34.54.3) or at the dedication of the temple in 191 (36.36.4, relating the opinion of Valerias Antias). The confusion seems caused by the chronological proximity of the institution of reserved seats for senators and equestrians, which is placed by various sources in one of these two years. Livy rejects Antias on the date of the *ludi scenici Megalenses*, even while accepting Antias' account concerning reserved seating. See further Bernstein (1998), 191–195, and p. 159–60 in this chapter.

34. Ov., *Fast.* V.327–330. Velleius Paterculus (1.14.8) claims that the first games for Flora were celebrated in 241, but Ovid makes clear that the games celebrated by the plebeian aediles the Publicii in either 241 or 238 B.C.E. were not annual (V.287–295). The problem of dating the aedileship of the Publicii need not concern us; see Broughton *MRR*, 219–221. In general on the *ludi Florales*, see Bernstein (1998), 206–223.

period, they had played only a relatively minor role in the Roman religious system. The *ludi Romani* and perhaps the *ludi plebeii* were celebrated annually, and on infrequent occasions special *ludi* were vowed by magistrates in response to a specific crisis. By way of comparison, four of the festivals marked in capital letters on the *fasti*, assumed to be the oldest festivals, were celebrated more than once every year: the Agonalia are marked four times each year, the Lemuria are marked on three nonconsecutive days in May, and the Carmentalia, Consualia, Lucaria, Vinalia, and Tubilustrum are indicated on two dates each. Yet by 170 B.C.E., the situation had been dramatically altered; the Romans went from having one or possibly two annual celebrations of *ludi* to having six such celebrations. Along with the expansion in the number of annual *ludi* celebrated in Rome came an expansion in the number of days on which *ludi* were celebrated. In part, this was a natural process; more *ludi* naturally occupied more days of the year. But this natural process was augmented by attaching additional days to existing celebrations of *ludi*. Thus the *ludi Romani*, which had occupied four days in 367, ran for ten days beginning during the Second Punic War; the *ludi plebeii* expanded to four days by 190, and the *ludi Apollinares*, introduced only in 208, had already grown from one day to three. As a result, where in 367 four days were occupied with annual *ludi* and an additional one or at most two might be celebrated for special *ludi*, in 170 twenty-nine days were occupied with annual *ludi*, and special *ludi* had become more common, as they were often celebrated at the dedication of a new temple or vowed by generals on campaign.[35] *Ludi* had taken their place as perhaps the most characteristic Roman rite, and it should not cause surprise that *ludi* were one of the primary means by which Sulla, Caesar, and Augustus attempted to convey messages of victory in the struggles of the first century B.C.E.[36]

This rapid expansion of *ludi* during the middle Republic has not been lost on those studying Roman culture and religion, and various explanations have been offered for this phenomenon. Early interpreters of Roman religion spoke in terms of the decline of a pure and primitive religion and saw in the increased number of games a sign of moral decline.[37] In this attitude, they found much support among the Roman moralizers; it is well known that Roman authors often ascribed the fall of the Republic to the luxury introduced in the wake of Roman imperialism of the late third and early second centuries.[38] Juvenal's

35. Cf. Taylor (1937), 285–291.

36. On the *ludi Victoriae (Sullanae)* and the *ludi Victoriae Caesaris*, see Bernstein (1998), 313–350.

37. E.g., Warde Fowler (1911); Latte (1960).

38. For a survey of Roman theories on Rome's moral decline, cf. Earl (1967), esp. 17ff.

lament about *panem et circenses* shows the continuing vitality of this theme well into the Empire. These moralizing views of Roman religion, often spurred by the imposition of modern views on what religion is, have been rightly rejected and need not be considered here.[39] A second option observes the closely intertwined relationship of religion and politics at Rome and suggests that the increased number of games is a sign of the political manipulation of religion at Rome: more games means more opportunities for leading politicians to curry electoral favor with the populace through lavish displays of entertainment, as well as more opportunities for the nobility as a class to demonstrate their fitness to run the state.[40] Certainly, this was the general view taken by Polybius in his famous excursus on Roman religious practices in Book VI of his work, where the historian suggests that the nobility deliberately fostered pomp and circumstance in religious observations to keep the populace in check.[41] But despite the high esteem that Polybius is accorded as a historian, his opinions on the Roman constitution have rightly been criticized for failing to fully comprehend the nuances of the system.[42] While it is clear that the Roman nobility was aware of the political ramifications of their religious actions, it is also clear that they were not cynical and unbelieving manipulators of the religious system; crises such as repeated prodigies or even the Bacchanalia reveal both a concern for their own position and a concern for the state. So a purely political explanation for the expansion of *ludi* will not suffice, but neither will a purely religious explanation; the acknowledged bonds between religion and politics mean that there is no such thing as a purely religious action at Rome. The Romans were constantly presented with situations that might seem to an outside observer to demand a religious response: wars, famines, plagues, prodigies, and other crises. Yet not every situation was resolved through a religious action, and even fewer resulted in a religious innovation, such as a new festival, temple, games, or other ritual. Given the nature of the Roman system, innovations ought to respond to a newly perceived need; the connection between religion and politics makes the religious system a good map of Roman society, revealing its hierarchies, its fears, and its needs. So while there may have been a religious occasion for the introduction of each new set of *ludi*, we must look at the surrounding context for these actions to uncover these underlying factors. Why did the Romans choose to respond to these situations with the inauguration of new *ludi* rather

39. Cf. North (1976) and especially Scheid (1987).
40. Quinn-Schofield (1967b); Cels-Saint-Hilaire (1977). For the now outdated view of political manipulation of religion in general during this period, see Scullard (1951).
41. Polyb. 6.56.
42. Cf. Walbank (1957); Morgan (1990), 14–16.

than repeating rituals from the past, constructing new temples, or even cele-brating a single nonannual set of *ludi?* What were the extenuating circum-stances that led the Romans to increase the number of annual *ludi* sixfold beginning in the late third century B.C.E.?

One response to the expansion of *ludi* has been to see it as part of a series of innovations connected with the stresses of the Hannibalic War.[43] Certainly the war, and particularly the major Roman defeats during the war's initial stages, led to a series of religious actions, and these are fully described by Livy in his account. These actions in just the first two years of the war included both repetitions of existing rituals, including sacrifices, a *novemdiale sacrum*, *lectisternia*, and *supplicationes*, as well as innovations, including the erection of temples to new divin-ities, the vowing of a *ver sacrum*, and "the least Roman rite," according to Livy, a human sacrifice.[44] But it would be a mistake to explain Roman religious activity at this time solely as a response to the Hannibalic War; several of these actions have been discussed in earlier chapters.[45] This is especially the case with the proliferation of *ludi*, as only one set of *ludi* was actually added during the war. The *ludi Apollinares* in 212 B.C.E. might well be seen as a response to the military crisis, considering that the outlook for the war continued to be as bleak as ever: Hannibal had recently captured Tarentum, the Romans had yet to reconquer either Syracuse or Capua, and the Romans were also engaged with Philip V on their own, as the Aetolian alliance had not yet been concluded. But the *ludi Plebeii* and the *ludi Ceriales* both seem to have been instituted prior to the outbreak of war. Even if both were instituted on the very eve of war, as suggested by some scholars, the argument that these games responded to the impending war still contains serious gaps.[46] One is the question of whether the Romans felt the war to be a threat in 220, an issue that modern historians have been (and will continue to be) unable to resolve; without an anticipation of war, there would have been no crisis to which to respond. The argument that these games anticipated the needs of the Romans during the war reads backward our knowledge of Hannibal's extraordinary invasion and early successes; the Romans in

43. This was the approach of Warde Fowler (1911), 261–263; Bayet (1957), 136. Cf. Toynbee (1965), 2.374–415.

44. See Livy 21.62 for the religious activity of 218 (following Trebia); Livy 22.1.14–20 for religious activity at the beginning of 217; Livy 22.10 for activity following Trasimene in 217; Livy 22.57 for the human sacrifice (*minime Romano sacro*) following Cannae.

45. Cf. pp. 71–76,122–127.

46. This suggestion has been raised by Bernstein (1998), p. 162 (*ludi Plebeii*) and 166 (*ludi Ceriales*).

220 or even 219 would have had no reason to suspect that the bulk of any impending war would be fought on Italian, rather than Spanish, soil. The position of the Romans in 218 or 217 was dramatically different from that of 220, and the religious attitude of those later years cannot be projected back even two years. Last, it would be atypical of Roman practice to have responded in this fashion in advance of a crisis; the approach of war was not a cause for panic, not for a state that spent the bulk of its existence engaged in war. Only defeat or another negative result was cause for concern, and Roman religious practice tended to respond to such crises after the fact, as they did following those defeats in the early years of the war.[47] Without question, Roman diplomatic attention had focused on Hannibal by the time the games were initiated, but the Hannibalic War cannot be posited as the direct impetus for the institution of the first new sets of annual *ludi* in at least a century.

For the *ludi Megalenses* and the *ludi Florales*, it is more evident that the Second Punic War does not provide the appropriate context for the addition of *ludi* to the ritual calendar. To be sure, the temple to the Magna Mater was vowed during the course of the war's latter stages, and the black stone thought to represent the goddess was brought to Rome in 204.[48] Interpretations of the reasons for the importation of this goddess have varied widely, as discussed earlier, from a response to continued apprehension over the outcome of the Second Punic War to a diplomatic maneuver looking ahead to the world after the conclusion of that war.[49] However the introduction of the goddess is viewed, the games themselves bear only the most tenuous connection to the Hannibalic War, for they were not instituted until well past the conclusion of the war. Games celebrated at the construction of a temple were an increasingly common occurrence during the second century, but this is the only instance when such games became an annual occurrence, making it difficult to see the institution of annual *ludi Megalenses* as a result of the Hannibalic War. And it is quite clear that the *ludi Florales* have no

47. The Romans did on certain occasions make forward-looking vows, as when the incoming consuls ascended the Capitoline hill and made vows to Jupiter for the continued health and safety of the Roman state. But these are not responses to a crisis, and the vows do not involve innovations in Roman religious practice. In the second century, we know the Romans did make vows at the beginning of a war for its successful conclusion, such as in 200 against Philip V (Livy 31.9.10). But this custom was itself an innovation, it is explicitly connected with the declaration of war, and the vow was for a single set of *ludi magni*, not the institution of a new annual set of *ludi*. On these vows connected with the declaration of war, cf. Bernstein (1998), 155–157.

48. See Livy 29.10–11; 29.14.

49. Cf. Burton (1996), 36–63; Gruen (1990), 5–33.

connection to the war, for they were not instituted as an annual rite until nearly thirty years after the war's conclusion. The Second Punic War is the most dramatic event of the period in which the number of annual *ludi* exploded and one of the most dramatic in all of Roman history, and yet it cannot be considered as the inspiration for the expansion of *ludi*.

The key to understanding the proliferation of *ludi* should be sought not in a single dramatic event, but in the processes set in motion as part of the transformation of Rome from a city-state into a world power. As demonstrated in earlier chapters, as part of their absorption of defeated peoples, the Romans adopted many cultural elements from outside the state, including religious elements. In the fifth and fourth century, this openness presented little challenge to Roman identity; Rome was still what we might call a traditional city-state, and a Roman lived in or just outside the city of Rome, participated in the civic structures of the Roman state, and fought for Rome in her battles against neighboring states. In the third century, however, Rome began to outgrow those structures, particularly as she began to engage in warfare further afield and to control territory overseas, and Rome became home to a variety of practices that blurred the boundaries between Roman and non-Roman. If Rome continued to expand and continued to maintain her traditional openness toward foreigners, she needed to find a new way to define the Roman community, to distinguish between Roman and non-Roman practices as she took her place on the world stage. We have seen some of these tensions between maintaining open boundaries and yet a clear sense of those boundaries in earlier chapters, especially with the haruspices and the Magna Mater.[50] The rapid increase in the number of annual *ludi* in Rome responded to the same conundrum in a different fashion, not by marking a practice as foreign, but by establishing a practice as a quintessentially Roman type of celebration. While a wide variety of religious practices continued to be utilized in Rome, *ludi* came to be identified as a typical Roman practice, and participation in *ludi* was part of the definition of Roman citizenship, such that in 122 the consul C. Fannius could argue against granting citizenship to the Latins on the following grounds:

> If you give citizenship to the Latins, I suppose you think that you will continue to have space in public meetings and you will take part in *ludi* and festivals in the same way. Do you not think that they will occupy everything?[51]

50. See chapter 3.

51. Halm *Rhetores Latini* 402: *Si Latinis civitatem dederitis, credo, existimatis vos ita, ut nunc constitistis, in contione habituros locum aut ludis et festis diebus interfuturos. Nonne illos omnia occupaturos putatis?*

As Fannius sees it, participation in the political and religious life of Rome is the essential element of Roman citizenship, and *ludi* are singled out as especially representative of Romanness.

Ludi in fact present several unique factors that made them an ideal vehicle for both expressing Roman identity and continuing to present an openness toward the outside world. As noted earlier in our analysis, both ancients and moderns have struggled to define *ludi circenses* or *ludi scenici* as indicative of either Greek or Etruscan influence on Roman society, but that debate obscures the broader picture, the distinctness of the Roman practice. To see this fact more clearly, one should consider the entirety of the ritual, the *pompa* as well as the circus competitions and/or stage plays. The procession, as described by Dionysius of Halicarnassus, consisted first of the magistrates, followed by the youth of Rome, and then the charioteers and the contestants in the games; three groups of dancers—men, youths, and boys—came next, accompanied by musicians, and finally came the statues of the gods carried on men's shoulders.[52] As Florence Dupont has recently argued, the dance of the *ludii* was seen as the core of the *ludi*; that element defined the ritual.[53] In elevating the dance to this position as the defining element, the Romans invested this aspect of the ritual with a significance that it may not have held elsewhere. Whether this aspect of the ritual can be paralleled elsewhere becomes less important; its investment by the Romans with such significance helped create a cultural distinction, for anthropologists have observed that the emphasis that a society gives to a particular cultural trait has significance for their identity over and above any supposed uniqueness of that trait.[54] *Ludi* as a ritual are different from ceremonies in either Etruria or Greece, and that difference allowed the Romans to claim a cultural distinctness and to reaffirm their own identity.

It is significant that even where the Romans eventually developed their own culturally distinctive practice, they began by accepting elements from

52. Dion. Hal. *Ant. Rom.* 7.70–73. Although Dionysius is at pains in his analysis to point out how similar the Roman custom is to the Greek, as part of his effort to convince the reader of the essential similarity between Roman and Greek, his description may be broadly accepted. See further Thuillier (1975).

53. Dupont (1993), 199. Cicero (*Har. resp.* 23) notes that if the dancer stopped, an *instauratio* would be necessary to confirm the essential need for this aspect of the ritual, and according to Festus (436–438 L), the Roman proverb *Salva res est dum saltat senex* referred to a dancer who continued this essential activity, even as the spectators were called away to arms.

54. As noted in the Introduction, it is the investment of certain traits with significance by a society that vests them with the ability to create distinctions. Cf. Smith (1991) and Hall (1997), 20–23, with the literature cited there.

neighboring communities and then invested those elements with a different significance. The incorporation of components related to *ludi* from outside Rome continued the tradition of openness that has been visible in the introduction of foreign cults and foreign priests throughout the early Republic. Frank Bernstein has recently illuminated the ways in which the development of *ludi* in the third and second centuries laid stress on the connections to Greek culture, especially by emphasizing *ludi scenici* over *ludi circenses* in this period. This development is seen as part of the attempt by the Roman governing class to indicate their participation in the wider cultural world still dominated by Greeks.[55] Recent discussions of Rome's cultural relationship with Greece have emphasized that embracing a Greek cultural custom does not betray cultural dependence but might even allow the Romans to present themselves as superior, as they adapted Greek cultural elements to serve their own purposes.[56] For our purposes, the significance lies in the fact that the Romans did not slavishly imitate and adopt the Greek custom, but developed their own approach that was recognizably different. The desire to draw a distinction between Greek and Roman practice may even be seen in the controversy over the origins of *ludi* in Rome. As noted before, many Roman authors, including Livy, Valerius Maximus, and Tacitus, connect the origins of the *ludi scenici* to the Etruscans rather than to the Greeks. Florence Dupont has suggested that these texts reveal that the Romans were concerned to avoid situating Roman theater in the Greek tradition, precisely to make clear that the Romans were not simply copying from the Greeks.[57] This emphasis on drawing a clear distinction between Greek and Roman theater, while still clearly absorbing elements from Greek theater, speaks directly to the issue of identity that we have been addressing; drawing a line between Greek and Roman tradition enabled the Romans to assert an independent identity. The proliferation of *ludi* in the late third and early second centuries may have simultaneously served two purposes: on the one hand, it facilitated Roman entrance into the Greek cultural world by expanding a ritual with which the Greeks were familiar and turning more toward Greek models, and on the other it established a distinctive Roman practice that could mark the boundaries between the Greek and Roman worlds. *Ludi* were thus particularly valuable for demonstrating the boundaries of Romanness and also that those boundaries are still permeable and thus that Rome was still accessible to outsiders.

55. Bernstein (1998), passim.
56. Cf. Gruen (1992).
57. Dupont (1993), especially her conclusions on 209–210. Dionysius of Halicarnassus, of course, does connect Roman theater to the Greek world, hardly surprising given his overall attempt to paint Rome as a Greek *polis*.

Analyzing this celebration from a slightly different angle suggests that *ludi* were particularly well suited to function as a ritual that created a sense of community, especially a community that was open to change. Dupont has suggested that since the gods and humans took pleasure in the staged activities at the same time and at the same place, the gods from their couches and the humans from wherever they were, status distinctions were dramatically lessened.[58] Georges Devallet, by comparing the *pompa circensis* with triumphal and funeral processions, arrived at similar conclusions: the procession had the function of *creating* a temporary communal space for the celebration of the ritual that followed.[59] *Ludi* provided a ceremony where the hierarchies and order of everyday life no longer existed, a place of *communitas*, to use Victor Turner's formulation.[60] Turner suggests that this state of undifferentiation is a typical feature of the liminal state involved in many religious rituals, and further that these periods do not merely provide a respite from the structures of everyday life, but provide an opportunity to review the values of the community that can often bring fundamental change to the society. *Ludi* are thus ideally suited to incorporate new members of the Roman community, especially since many of the individual elements of the ritual came themselves from outside Rome and had been incorporated into a Roman ritual. As so often with Roman religion, developments in the religious sphere parallel developments in the political sphere and elsewhere in Roman society.

The twin natures of the activity connected with *ludi*—to assert a sense of Romanness while still maintaining openness toward outsiders—become especially clear if we examine again the new sets of *ludi* introduced in the critical period at the end of the third century and the divinities to whom they were dedicated: Ceres, Apollo, the Magna Mater, and Flora. Although Ceres and Apollo had been worshipped in Rome since the fifth century, these cults appear to have undergone significant changes in the period just before the addition of *ludi* to their rites. Ceres had received her first temple in Rome in 493; the divinity introduced at this time was not yet considered the Roman equivalent of Demeter, but an old Italic goddess.[61] However, during the third century, the process of assimilating Ceres to Demeter apparently began; third-century representations of Ceres show considerable Greek influence, and new rites were added, also

58. Dupont (1993), 200.
59. Devallet (1989).
60. See, in particular, Turner (1969).
61. Cf. Spaeth (1996), 7–8; Le Bonniec (1958), 292–305.

following Greek models.[62] But as the cult took on these Greek aspects over the course of the third century, the Romans also added *ludi* at the end of the century that helped emphasize the Roman nature of this cult. The Greek elements adopted recently, and even the potential Greek influence on *ludi scenici*, which may have dominated the *ludi Ceriales*, indicated the Romans' receptivity to the Greek cultural world, but *ludi* were a distinctly Roman touch; the Thesmophoria, the Greek festival to Demeter that seems most closely related to the new Roman rites, were not a venue for stage productions. So the addition of the *ludi Ceriales* should serve as a signal that the changes in the cult over the course of the third century should not be taken as the Hellenization of the Roman Ceres, but rather as part of a continuing Romanization of the Greek Demeter now welcomed at Rome.

A similar phenomenon is evident in regard to Apollo and the *ludi Apollinares*. The first temple to Apollo was built in the fifth century as a response to a plague in Rome, though some evidence indicates that Apollo was worshipped even before the construction of this permanent shrine.[63] As with Ceres, the character of Apollo underwent significant changes at Rome in the third century. Late in the century, the Romans developed a much closer acquaintance with the Delphic oracle, delivering a golden bowl in 222 following the victory of Marcellus over the Gauls, sending Fabius Pictor as part of an embassy to consult the oracle after the battle of Cannae in 216, and both dedicating spoils from the battle at the Metaurus and consulting the oracle concerning the Magna Mater in 205.[64] These actions show Rome establishing her credentials in the Greek world; dedicating trophies of war was a long-established Greek custom, and Delphi the most prominent panhellenic site for such dedications. These contacts with Delphi fall on either side of the institution of the *ludi Apollinares*, which Livy

---

62. A *sacrum anniversarium Cereris* was interrupted after the battle of Cannae (Livy 22.56.4), Festus (s.v. Graeca sacra) links this festival to the Greek myth of Proserpina, and special priestesses were brought up from Magna Graecia to officiate (Cic. *Balb.* 55). See Spaeth (1996), 11–13, for a summary of the Middle Republican history of the cult of Ceres.

63. Temple: Livy 4.29.7; worship prior to temple is suggested by Livy 3.63.7, where the historian speaks of a precinct known as the Apollinar. See, in general, J. Gagé (1955).

64. The golden bowl in 222 is noted by Plut. *Marc.* 8.6; the embassy of 216 led by Fabius Pictor by Livy, 22.57.4–5 and 23.11. The events of 205 are recounted by Livy, 28.45.12 on the spoils and 29.10.6 on the consultation about the Magna Mater to Rome. Though earlier embassies to Delphi are reported in Roman sources, many of these, such as the mission of Brutus in 509 B.C.E. (Livy 1.56), are likely to be apocryphal.

notes were instituted for the purpose of gaining victory, not health, as most people thought.[65] This shift marks a move away from the original focus of the cult, which was founded as a healing sanctuary. While the healing aspect to Apollo is well known in Greece, both in cult and in mythology, victory was not a major aspect of Apollo's persona in Greece.[66] In the late third century, therefore, the strands that were evident in the development of Ceres are also evident in connection with Apollo: a move toward embracing Hellenic culture, as seen in the embassies to Delphi, but also an emphasis on establishing a Roman form of celebration. Despite the repeated trips to Delphi, with regard to the cult as practiced in Rome, the Romans made no attempts to emphasize the oracular nature of Apollo in Rome, certainly the most prominent feature of his cult in Greece, or his connection to the lyre or other musical arts; that transformation would occur under Augustus.[67] Rather, the Romans treated the cult of Apollo according to their own needs. The very introduction of the *ludi Apollinares* was prompted by distinctly Roman causes: the praetor, a civilian magistrate, brought the *carmen* of a certain Marcius to the attention of the Senate, which referred the matter to the *decemviri sacris faciundis*; written prophecies of this type seem to have been a distinctly Roman or Italian phenomenon.[68] The response that Fabius Pictor brought back from Delphi in 216 also falls in line with the Roman style of prophecy as exemplified by the Sibylline Books; it provided a list of actions to be performed to

65. Livy 25.12.15: *Haec est origo ludorum Apollinarium, victoriae non valetudinis ergo, ut plerique rentur, votorum factorumque.* Bernstein (1998), 181–182, argues that the connection of Apollo to victory was a later construction of the Sullan period, projected backward to connect with the praetor of 212, P. Cornelius Sulla. But while Livy's text does indicate the existence of an alternative tradition connecting the *ludi Apollinares* to health, Livy consciously rejected that interpretation, and there is no good reason to substitute our judgment for his here.

66. The connection of Apollo to healing is evident already in the *Iliad*, where it is Apollo who sends the illness among the Greeks in response to the prayer of Chryses. Additionally, Apollo was the father of Asclepius, the preeminent god of healing, whom the Romans imported at the beginning of the third century. It is, of course, possible that Livy's emphasis on Apollo as bringer of victory in 212 is a late retrojection of this aspect, intended to provide a Republican precedent for the behavior of Augustus following the triumph at Actium, but our knowledge of the relationship between Livy and Augustus does not suggest such a close cooperation.

67. The closest connection to Apollo as worshipped in Greece would be the theatrical performances connected with the *ludi Apollinares*, but it is difficult to see this as a special connection to Apollo when *ludi scenici* formed part of the other *ludi* as well. On Augustus and Apollo, see pp. 211–14.

68. Cf. North (2000).

remedy the *pax deorum*, rather than offering divine approval or disapproval for a proposed course of action, as with most Greek consultations of the oracle. Thus even in utilizing the Hellenic custom of consulting the Delphic oracle, the Romans handled the procedure in a typically Roman fashion. The *ludi Apollinares* formed a part of this Romanization of Apollo, emphasizing the Roman nature of the cult. The Romans again showed their willingness to participate in Greek cultural traditions, yet also an ability to stake their own claim as to the proper cultivation of the favor of the gods.

The *ludi Megalenses* may provide the clearest indication of how the Romans took a foreign divinity and arranged a distinctively Roman style of worship in her honor. The Magna Mater was clearly a foreign cult, arriving in Rome toward the end of the Second Punic War, and she represents a new addition to the Roman pantheon, so we are not forced to reconstruct the history of the cult in Rome prior to this moment. Our concern here is not with the cult's introduction from Asia Minor or with the priests of the cult, both of which have been discussed earlier, but with the arrangement of cult activities by the Romans upon the arrival of the cult. In Asia Minor, the cult of the Magna Mater was apparently attended by eunuch priests who marched accompanied by drums and clanging cymbals, occasionally whipping themselves into an ecstatic frenzy culminating in bloodshed.[69] But in Rome, such activities were off-limits to Roman citizens: only the Phrygian priests brought with the cult were allowed to engage in such activities, and then only in a specified procession on a specified day. Roman citizens by law were not allowed to participate in these rites.[70] These actions have seemed contradictory to many scholars, but rather than focusing on what the Romans did not allow, it is instructive to examine how the Romans did pay honor to this goddess. The Roman elite set up *sodalitates* to dine among themselves in honor of the goddess, and the Roman populace at large was invited to *ludi* in honor of the goddess.[71] Neither of these activities can be paralleled in Asia Minor or Greece; the *sodalitates* seem to be an innovation of the Romans.[72] The significance of *ludi* as the typical Roman form of worship becomes clear

69. See Catull. 63.1–38; Ov. *Fast.* 4.179–246; Lucr., 2.598–643. For a modern discussion of the cult, see Vermaseren (1977).

70. Dion. Hal. *Ant. Rom.* 2.19.4–5.

71. For the sodalitates, see Cic. *Sen.* 45; Ov., *Fast.*, 4.353–356. See also the *Fasti Praenestini* for April 4 (*Inscr. Ital.* 13.2, p. 127).

72. The suggestion of Bernstein (1998), 192, that *sodalitates* may have been modeled on Greek *thiasoi* seems unlikely; the differences between what we know of the two institutions seem greater than the similarities, which seem limited to the fact that both are groups of people gathered for worship.

in conjunction with the new Roman institution of *sodalitates*; Roman citizens would worship the Great Mother in a Roman fashion, even while appreciating the power of the goddess and observing the local style of worship. These forms of worship, along with the restrictions concerning the Phrygian style of worship, were intended precisely to identify and to define the boundaries of Romanness in terms of religious practice.[73] The *ludi Megalenses* functioned as the direct counterpart of the wild and orgiastic dance of the *galli*; the former were as Roman as the latter was foreign.

The *ludi Florales* present a more complicated picture, yet they also show the importance of understanding games as a Roman style of celebration. Unlike the other divinities honored with *ludi* in this period, Flora was an old Italic divinity; furthermore, games in her honor had first been celebrated in the middle of the third century. More than fifty years had passed since that first celebration of *ludi* in her honor, and more than twenty years since the last annual games had been added to the calendar, raising questions of why these *ludi*, the last annual games to be established in Rome until the games instituted by the military dynasts of the first century B.C.E., should have been instituted at this time. The lack of an apparent military context has led some scholars to posit that these games in particular were instituted for political purposes, to provide an additional means for politicians to gain name recognition and popularity for higher office.[74] M. G. Morgan has criticized this view, arguing that scholars should not be so quick to see political manipulation of religion by the Romans and that there were good religious grounds in the Roman view for instituting these games on an annual basis.[75] Yet even granting that there was a crop problem or a similar crisis in the mid-170s that may have called for a religious response, it is still significant that the Romans chose to respond not only by celebrating *ludi* but also by making a permanent addition to the religious calendar.

An answer may be sought in the social and cultural issues with which the Romans were grappling at this time. In the 170s, Rome's attention was no longer predominantly focused on her relationship to Greek culture; issues of Rome's relationship with her Italian allies, which had been simmering since the end of the Second Punic War, had risen to the forefront, particularly those revolving around citizenship. Following the war, Rome had resumed

---

73. Cf. the suggestion of North (1993), 137–138. For a fuller discussion of how the Roman treatment of the Magna Mater helped illuminate the difference between Roman and foreign, see Beard (1994), 164–169.

74. Cf. in particular Cels-Saint-Hilaire (1977).

75. Morgan (1990).

her policy of sending out colonies, though increasingly these were citizen colonies rather than Latin ones, and at the same time Rome extended the franchise to select communities: Arpinum, Formiae, and Fundi were raised to full citizenship in 188, the same year in which the Campanians were given the *ius conubium*.[76] The status of other Italian *municipia* remains uncertain, but it is clear that the relationship between Rome and her Latin and Italian allies consumed a large part of the Senate's attention, even as Rome continued to wage war in Greece and Asia Minor. In 187, Latin communities, apparently faced with loss of population through migration to Rome, asked the Senate to send home those Latins living in Rome without Roman citizenship. According to Livy, 12,000 Latins were expelled from the city, and a similar action followed in 177, just four years prior to the institution of annual *ludi Florales*.[77] In the very same period when the Romans were removing Latins from Rome, they honored an old Italian deity with the characteristic Roman rite, suggesting that the Roman attention toward Italy at this time remained friendly. It is important to bear in mind that the deportation of Latins from Rome took place on the request of Latin communities themselves. Like the previous additions of annual *ludi*, this action served to indicate both openness, in this case to Rome's Italian neighbors, and the distinctiveness of Rome. In the wake of the adoption of so many Hellenic elements within the Roman religious system, the *ludi Florales* offered similar recognition to Italic elements that had long been part of that system.[78]

The expansion of *ludi* may have played an additional role in providing a religious ceremony that facilitated the creation of a Roman sense of identity. As the Roman state expanded, more and more citizens of Rome would not have not lived close enough to Rome to attend the various religious ceremonies, *ludi* and otherwise, held throughout the course of the year.[79] In part, this may have presented a religious problem; low attendance at the games may have been felt to imperil the *pax deorum*.[80] But it also presented a problem in terms of the social function performed by religious rituals; these ceremonies on behalf of the Roman state provided an opportunity for the entire citizenry to come together

76. Livy 38.36.7. Sherwin-White (1973), 77–79; cf. pp. 210–214 for Sherwin-White's examination of the issues surrounding Italian citizenship at this time.

77. Livy 39.3 (187); Livy 41.8 (177).

78. Perhaps this is what Ovid had in mind at *Fasti* 5.303–329, when he has Flora complain that the Senate neglected her, leading her to abandon her care of the countryside until the Senate voted her an annual festival; Italic cults had been comparatively neglected in favor of Hellenic influences.

79. Morgan (1990), 33–34.

80. Morgan (1990), 30–31.

and recognize their part in their common enterprise. The dispersal of citizens throughout Italy made gatherings of Romans more difficult, and the Roman state lacked other mechanisms for helping its citizens imagine their community. The growth of *ludi* may have helped to address this issue in two ways. As noted before, the expansion in the number of *ludi* was accompanied by an expansion in the number of days for each festival; a three- to seven-day festival, sometimes grouped with other such festivals and perhaps followed by markets, might make the journey worthwhile and have thus offset, to some degree, the diffusion of the citizen body.[81] The more people who came to Rome for the *ludi*, the more people who might have the opportunity to feel themselves a direct part of the Roman state. This practical consideration may have played a large role in the expansion in the number of days allotted to each festival, just as the ideological consideration of defining Roman identity contributed to the expansion in the number of annual *ludi*. Second, *ludi* as a ritual were "exportable." While the *ludi Megalenses* or *Apollinares* were specifically Roman festivals tied to locations in the city of Rome, *ludi* as a ritual could be celebrated anywhere, and increasingly were celebrated in other cities throughout Italy. *Ludi* provided an opportunity, either in Rome or elsewhere in Italy, for a typically Roman form of celebration and thus for individuals to participate and identify themselves with other members of the Roman community who might be celebrating in the same fashion.

The challenge that the extension of this communitarian ritual posed for the traditional ways Romans defined themselves may be seen in one other innovation of this period related to *ludi*. Most likely in 194, separate seats were reserved for senators for the first time.[82] Livy's account of the comments engendered by this innovation is revealing:

> To some it appeared as a tribute which had been due long before to the highest order in the State, while to others it seemed that whatever was added to the greatness of the patricians took away from the

---

81. Note the close proximity of the *Ludi Cereales* (April 4–10 in the early Empire) and the *Ludi Megalenses* (April 12–19). *Mercatus* is marked on several *fasti* following the *Ludi Apollinares*, the *ludi Romani*, and the *ludi plebeii*. Cf. Morgan (1990), 35.

82. Livy 34.54.3. There is some confusion as to whether separate seats were introduced in 194 or 191; Livy, followwng Valerias Antias, is clear in placing the reform at the *ludi Romani* of 194, but Cicero (*Har. resp.* 24) and Valerius Maximus (2.4.3) both connect the reserved seating with the *ludi Megalenses*, which were probably celebrated for the first time in 191. See further Ungern-Sternberg (1975). The exact date has little impact on the argument here.

dignity of the people, and that all such distinctions by which the orders in the State were set apart diminished both concord and liberty equally. For five hundred and fifty-eight years, all the spectators had sat mixed together: what had happened so suddenly that the senators did not wish to have the commons intermixed with them in the theatre?[83]

The terms of this debate, even if constructed by Livy after the fact, are revealing, confirming that the theater had been a place where the ordinary hierarchies of Roman society did not apply. To answer Livy's rhetorical question, what had changed were the boundaries that had previously regulated Roman life. With the expansion of *ludi* and the inclusion of so many foreign peoples and foreign elements in Roman society, the traditional categories used by the Romans to create social order were increasingly being challenged. The need to insert categorization into a ritual that had previously dispensed with such arrangements suggests the degree to which the boundaries that had given shape to Roman society up to this point had become unstable.[84] The very success of *ludi* in making the boundaries of Romanness permeable led the Romans to use that same ritual to reaffirm the importance of such boundaries.

The development of *ludi* offers significant insight into the approach favored by the Romans as they moved from the status of a single city among the inhabitants of the ancient Mediterranean to a dominant imperial power. From the third century onward, the Romans attempted to balance two concerns that might occasionally come into conflict: a continued openness to foreigners and a need to assert their own uniqueness. Prior to the third century, Rome had been a smaller state whose primary concern was continued growth, and the emphasis in her religious reactions to foreign cultures had been acceptance and incorporation. But as the res publica grew in size, her concerns shifted; no longer was it sufficient merely to adopt and adapt foreign religious elements, and a more complicated procedure was necessary. It was important for the Romans to identify certain practices as Roman

83. Livy 34.54: *Aliis tandem quod multo ante debuerit tributum existimantibus amplissimo ordini, aliis demptum ex dignitate populi quidquid maiestati patrum adiectum esset interpretantibus et omnia discrimina talia quibus ordines discernerentur et concordiae et libertatis aequae minuendae esse: ad quingentesimum <quinquagesimum> octauum annum in promiscuo spectatum esse; quid repente factum cur immisceri sibi in cavea patres plebem nollent?*

84. For a slightly different approach, cf. the comments of Gruen (1992), 205, who sees the seating reform as "a visible reminder of the ascendancy of the *nobiles*."

while at the same time maintaining a sense that their boundaries were still open to outsiders. This process is observable already in the third century, with the inclusion of foreign priests within the system and the simultaneous marking of some of those priests as outsiders. *Ludi* provide a different manifestation of this phenomenon, and it is evident, even within the roughly fifty years that marked the dramatic expansion of this ritual, that the Romans were increasingly grappling with the need to reestablish a clear sense of Romanness in the wake of their sudden explosion onto the world stage. As we will see in the next chapter, Roman attempts to draw clear lines of demarcation between themselves and other cultures come to occupy an increasingly prominent place during the second century.

6

Establishing Boundaries in the Second Century

The previous chapters have focused on illuminating two important aspects of Roman society and their relationship to Roman religious practice. On the one hand, the Romans had developed a tradition of incorporating foreigners into their community, whether the foreigners were individuals, entire communities, or particular cultural elements. Roman actions, including and perhaps especially those relating to religious practice, enabled residents of the Italian peninsula to imagine themselves as Romans in perhaps the most important sense of the word: the willingness to die for the community. The open boundaries of the Roman state clearly contributed to the Romans' ability to build a large territorial empire and then to defend that territory from Hannibal's invasion. On the other hand, that very openness presented challenges to the Romans' sense of their own identity; if cultural practices and even people from far away could find a place in Roman society, how was one to distinguish between the acceptable and the unacceptable, between Roman and non-Roman? The inclusion of foreign peoples and foreign practices within the Roman community raised questions of exactly where these boundaries lay. The discussion of expiations and foreign priests suggests that already in the third century the concern with drawing a clearer line between Roman and non-Roman became manifest, even as the Romans continued to suggest the permeability of that line. But a series of noteworthy incidents in the early second century have led many scholars to suggest that the Roman elite made a conscious effort to restrict the entry of foreign elements into Rome, to close these metaphorical boundaries.[1] A careful analysis, however, will reveal that while the Romans paid increasing attention to the line between Roman and non-Roman, this period did not see the reversal of the open attitude that marked Rome's previous five hundred years. The actions that the Romans took in the second century were often more symbolic than practical, aimed at clarifying *how* the boundary between Romans and non-Roman was to be drawn, and *where* it was to be drawn, rather than closing it to further foreign integration. Although the frequency of incidents during this period attests to heightened interest in this issue, the underlying Roman attitudes in the first part of the second century were largely similar to those of the third century and earlier.

The relationship of Rome to Greek culture has attracted much of the analysis of this period, and analysis of the Roman actions in this regard can illustrate some of this continuity. John Scheid's discussion of the *Graecus ritus* suggests one way in which Greek culture served as a useful foil for the Romans as they attempted to redefine their identity, but it also points toward a model useful for understanding Roman behavior throughout the second century.[2] Scheid suggests that the *Graecus ritus*, a style of sacrificing that seems to have involved, among other elements, sacrificing with a bare head, rather than covered as in a standard Roman sacrifice, was not an archaic practice, but rather emerged sometime in the third century B.C.E.; the first mention comes in a speech of Cato the Elder.[3] More significantly, the *Graecus ritus* was not used exclusively and consistently with cults of Greek origin; the cult of Saturn, an old Italian deity, employed the *Graecus ritus*, as did Greek cults such as Hercules or Apollo, but other Greek cults such as Aesculapius or Castor and Pollux did not. Scheid concludes that the *Graecus ritus* "was not a foreign body inside Roman religion, it was considered, and as a matter of fact was, typically Roman."[4] The Greek rite thus demonstrates, and was intended to demonstrate, the openness of the Roman state, using an avowedly Greek sacrificial style as an integrated part of the Roman religious mechanism. But the use of this rite also served to highlight that the Roman

---

1. Cf., e.g., Beard, North, and Price (1998), 88–91; also Fowler (1911), 350; Altheim (1938), 316–317; Bayet (1957) 152–155. Dumézil (1970), 512–525, sees this period as one of "thrusts and resistances."

2. Scheid (1995). The phrase is attested in Livy 1.7.3 and 25.12.10 and 13; as well as on the inscription recording the celebration of the *Ludi Saeculares* under Augustus; see Pighi (1965), 155 line IV, 6; 162, line Va, 49.

3. Cato, *ORF* 77. Cf. Scheid (1995), 29.

4. Scheid (1995), 19.

way of sacrificing was a distinct and unique practice; although, as Scheid suggests, both were part of the *patrius mos*, it suggests that there was a clear distinction between the Greek rite and the Roman rite, even if the difference consisted only in a number of minor details. Greek cultural practice served as the foil against which the Romans could define their own style, and hence their own sense of identity, and as we will see, the Romans made use of this opposition repeatedly, especially in the first half of the second century.

There is, however, a further significance to the development of a "Greek rite" within Roman religion in the third and second centuries B.C.E. Livy's text suggests that other rituals in Rome, particularly archaic ones supposedly founded by Romulus, might be celebrated *Albano ritu*, according to the Alban ritual.[5] The reference point in this instance is another city, as also with the *cinctus Gabinus*, a particular way of wearing a toga.[6] The *Graecus ritus*, however, refers not to another city, but to another country or *ethnos*. As Scheid points out, this fact suggests that the development of the *Graecus ritus* was "related to a particular self-consciousness, opposing the Romans and their allies, as an *ethnos*, to the Hellenic part of Italy and to the world seen as a whole."[7] This observation, while particularly appropriate to Roman religion, can be extended more broadly to the renewed intensity of the Roman encounter with Greek culture. The Greeks provided a backdrop against which the Romans could define their own identity, rejecting or adapting elements of Greek culture according to Roman desires.[8] But the fact that they took these actions in opposition to an *ethnos* as opposed to a *polis* suggests that they had come to think of themselves in terms of the larger agglomeration of people; in this conception, the Romans and their allies formed a single *ethnos*.[9] The earlier chapters of this study, as well as Scheid's analysis of the *Graecus ritus*, have suggested that the extension of the Roman *ethnos* to encompass Italy began long prior to the

---

5. E.g., Livy 1.7.3.

6. Cf. Scheid (1995), 19–20.

7. Scheid (1995), 29.

8. For studies of the Roman encounter with Greek culture in the second century, see Gruen (1990, 1992).

9. This formulation is not meant to suggest that such an ethnos came into being at this point, or that Italy was sufficiently Romanized to be considered an extension of Rome; Mouritsen (1998), 59–86, in particular has argued against the notion that Italy underwent "romanization" in the second century. The point here is rather that the Romans began to conceive the existence of an *ethnos*, not necessarily that one began to exist or that their allies began to perceive it.

second century.[10] The incidents of the second century reveal that process coming to fruition, sometimes even expanding inclusion in the *ethnos* to parts of Italy that may not have been initially enclosed, as well as exposing problems remaining in the construction of a new sense of Romanness.

Perhaps the most remarkable religious episode of the second century B.C.E., and certainly the one most discussed by modern commentators, was the Bacchic affair of 186, and this episode already suggests the tensions inherent in Roman society in this period. While many features of this episode remain obscure because our sole literary source, Livy, has elaborated his account and probably fabricated many details to heighten the impact of his moralizing aims, the main points can be established with enough certainty to proceed with our interpretation.[11] According to Livy's account, in 186 B.C.E. an obscure Greekling (*ignobilis Graecus*) from Etruria brought to Rome his secret nocturnal rites, which promoted both sexual debauchery and criminal activity, ranging from fraudulent wills to murder. Eventually, rumors of this behavior reached the ears of the consul Sp. Postumius, who, after gaining sufficient confirmation from a patriotic freedwoman courtesan, laid the matter before the Senate. The *patres* expressed alarm for public safety and invested the consuls with special authority to seek out the perpetrators in Rome and throughout Italy. Seven thousand people of both sexes were reportedly implicated as participating in Bacchic rites; many people committed suicide, a great number were convicted of capital offenses and executed, and a smaller number were imprisoned. The consuls then turned to the destruction of Bacchic shrines throughout Italy, excepting only those of great antiquity, and the Senate decreed that in the future there should be no Bacchic rites in Rome or Italy except under strict conditions. Further investigations continued in Tarentum in 184 and in Apulia in 181.[12]

This incident, unique and seemingly out of character in its repressive nature, has called forth numerous attempts to explain this reaction to the worship of Bacchus. The hypotheses have ranged from a reaction against

10. The question of precisely *when* Roman Italy became conceptualized as a unit has generated its share of discussion. For recent treatments, see Williams (2001), 127–137, and Bispham (2008), 53–68, who both identify the Pyrrhic Wars as an important moment in this conceptualization. Cato's *Origines* and Polybius, especially 2.14–23, bear on this question and are discussed by both authors, with further references. See also Mouritsen (1998), 45–58, on the historiographical problems created by the use of the word *Italia*.

11. Cf. Livy 39.8–19. For discussion of the reliability of this account and its rhetorical turns, see in particular Festugière (1954); Cova (1974); Scafuro (1989); Walsh (1996); Dubourdieu and Lemirre (1997); Briscoe (2003); Pagán (2005), 50–67.

12. Livy 39.41.6, 40.19.9.

the influx of Greek cults, to the ways in which this cult may have represented a social, economic, and/or political challenge to the Roman state, to
the Senate's fear of allowing members of a religious group to swear allegiance to each other or its desire to extend its control of religion over all of
Italy.[13] Because many of the most basic facts relating to this incident remain
open to doubt, it may not be possible to establish an overarching explanation for this affair, and it may be best to set aside some of the most conten-
tious issues. But recent scholarship has shed light on several points of
relevance for our investigation. It can no longer be argued that the Roman
reaction was caused by the sudden appearance of a foreign cult that was
leading the Romans to abandon their traditional ways.[14] Livy's presentation of this episode suggests that the historian saw the incident in these
terms, as he placed a speech in the mouth of the consul Postumius that
emphasized the threat to ancestral practice posed by the Bacchanalia.[15]
Postumius' speech recalls an earlier passage in Livy's narrative, an episode
from 213 in which the historian reported that petty sacrificers and prophets
had distracted the people so that they no longer used the ancestral rite, and
the Senate ordered that prophetic books be turned in to the praetor.[16] The
close linguistic parallels between the two passages suggest not only that he
has the earlier incident in mind but also that he has consciously modeled
his narrative of the two episodes in order to emphasize his point about
foreign religious traditions.[17] These passages are evidence of Livy's concerns with foreign religions and suggest that questions of the Romanness
of religious practices posed a live issue in his day, a topic to which we return
in the next chapter.[18] However, these passages cannot be used to ascribe
motivations more than 150 years earlier, especially as examination of the
available evidence has shown that worship of Bacchus was well known and

---

13. For a selection of the most important recent studies, with older bibliography, cf.
Gallini (1970); North (1979); Luisi (1982); Rousselle (1982); Voisin (1984); Pailler (1988,
1998); Gruen (1990), 34–78; Cancik-Lindemaier (1996); Flower (2000); Takács (2000).

14. See in particular Luisi (1982); Rouselle (1982).

15. Livy 39.15–16. Cf. especially 39.16.7–8.

16. Livy 25.1.6–12.

17. In 213, Livy reports on *sacrificuli ac uates* who were *in foro* and not sacrificing
patrio more and notes the Senate's edict against *libros uaticinos*. In Postumius' speech,
the consul notes the prohibition of *sacrificulos uatesque foro circo*, the seeking out of
libros uaticinos, and the abolition of all modes of sacrificing except *Romano more*. Note
also that the only previous antecedent cited by Livy is the episode of 213, despite Postumius' rhetorical claim of numerous incidents.

18. See p. 208ff. On Livy's approach to religion, see Levene (1993); Davies (2004),
esp. 21–85.

widespread in Rome prior to 186.[19] Participation in foreign rites, whatever Livy might want to say, was not the main problem, and there is now widespread consensus that the senatorial action in regard to the cult of Bacchus was not motivated simply by opposition to a foreign cult.

In fact, one of the striking elements of the senatorial actions in 186 is precisely that they did not permanently ban the worship of Bacchus. Although Livy's account leaves the impression that Bacchic worship was to be eradicated throughout Italy, even the historian acknowledges that it was permitted to continue, and we are fortunate to have inscriptional evidence that corroborates this central point on a copy of the senatorial decree recovered from Tiriolo.[20] Livy's account notes that Bacchanalian shrines where there was an ancient altar or a sacred image were not destroyed, and the inscription offers a mechanism for those who desire a place devoted to the worship of Bacchus, by applying to the urban praetor. Bacchic rites were permitted to groups of no more than five persons (two men and three woman), provided that there was no organization or common fund, no oaths sworn between the participants, and no man serving as priest; provisions were even made for applying to the Senate to waive some of these restrictions. Even the punishments doled out by the consuls do not focus on religious behavior; according to Livy himself, the people executed were those who were convicted of murder, giving false evidence, forging seals and wills, or other fraudulent practices.[21] While it may be rightly questioned whether in practical terms people would be able to successfully appeal the restrictions, the fact is that despite Livy's presentation of the cult as eradicated, worship of Bacchus was allowed to, and did, continue long past 186 B.C.E. Were it not for Livy's slanted account, our impression of the Roman actions in regard to Bacchus might be very different, for the restrictions placed on the worship of Bacchus are not fundamentally different from those placed on the worship of the Magna Mater, whose temple in Rome had been dedicated only five years previously: Romans were not to become priests, and the places at which the rites were performed were carefully circumscribed, but cult activity was permitted. The primary difference was that the Magna Mater had been admitted as part of the state religion while Bacchus continued to be

19. The evidence has been collected by Bruhl (1953), 58–81; the case against seeing the Bacchic cult as an innovation of the second century has been made most forcefully by North (1979). Cf. also Gruen (1990), 48–54.

20. *ILLRP* 511.

21. Cf. Livy 39.18.4.

worshipped outside the structures of the formal state religion, but the foreignness of the latter was not the reason for its absence.

Issues of foreignness may play a role in our understanding of the Bacchic incident, but in a manner suggested by the comparison to the Magna Mater. Just as the Romans marked the Magna Mater as "non-Roman" both by placing restrictions on the foreign aspects of her cult, such as the *galli*, and by instituting a Roman style of worship for the goddess, so one concern of the Romans in regard to Bacchus was to insist on a Roman style of worship. Several commentators on the Bacchanalia have noted that one result of the senatorial actions regarding the cult was to place it very closely under the control of the Senate.[22] The Senate both decreed conditions for the cult's worship and insisted on approving any deviations from those conditions at a Senate meeting with at least one hundred members (perhaps a third of the total body). This insistence is very much in keeping with traditional Roman practice, where the Senate served as the final arbiter for religious matters. While the cult was to be permitted, worship was to be conducted in accord with a Roman decree and not according to Greek practice. Greek *thiasoi* were not allowed, but men and women could worship together, at least in limited numbers, as was common in Rome. It is not necessary to see the Senate's action as a response to a social or political movement on behalf of the lower classes to recognize that the Senate always reserved for itself the prerogative to determine what constituted Roman practice. The real wrath of the Senate in the 180s fell on those who violated trust (and the laws) by committing murder or fraud, but they also took the opportunity to assert their position as the authority on Roman religious practice. The Senate's actions regarding Bacchus should be seen as consistent with activity over the previous half-century, both open to allowing the worship of a foreign deity and concerned to delineate a proper Roman style of worship.

Two actions involving Roman religion taken in the wake of the Bacchic incident reveal further attempts of the Roman governing class to define their sense of Romanness while also suggesting a continued openness to foreign religious traditions. In 181, two unusually large chests were discovered at the foot of the Janiculum, which the inscriptions on the side claimed held the body of King Numa, Rome's mythical lawgiver, as well as books

22. Cf., e.g., McDonald (1944), 30–32; Gallini (1970), 65–73; Gruen (1990), 65–77. Though differing on the motivations for the Senate's actions, all note the control of the Senate as a dominant feature of the episode.

belonging to the king.[23] When the chests were opened, they were found to contain two sets of seven books, one set in Latin on pontifical law and the other in Greek, said to be Pythagorean. As knowledge of the books began to spread, word reached the urban praetor Q. Petilius, who read the books and concluded that both sets of books should be destroyed. The Senate stood behind the praetor's judgment without even looking at them, and the books were duly burned in the *comitium* with the assistance of the *victimarii*. In the same year, Livy reports that a temple to Venus Erycina, which had been vowed during the Ligurian war three years previously by L. Porcius, was dedicated near the Colline gate by his son of the same name.[24]

The burning of the Books of Numa presents many challenges of interpretation, not least because of the large number of unusual and seemingly too convenient details. The episode, in fact, offers a staged quality similar to the Bacchanalia, and while some similarities may be due to Livy's presentation of the two incidents, it is hard to escape the conclusion that the entire episode was stage-managed by the Senate.[25] This episode may have served several purposes. I have argued elsewhere that one purpose was to assert the preeminence of senatorial oral authority over written authority in matters of Roman religion.[26] But the episode also called attention to the tradition that connected Numa, the legendary founder of Roman religion, with the Greek philosopher Pythagoras, despite the chronological impossibility of any direct connection between the two men.[27] The

23. The episode is recounted by Livy 40.29. Other accounts include Plin., *HN* 13.84–87, citing Cassius Hemina; August., *De. Civ. D.*, 7.34, citing Varro; Val. Max. 1.12 and Plut., *Numa* 22, both drawing from Livy and Valerias Antias.

24. Livy 40.34.4.

25. Some of the convenient details include the appearance of the books as "brand-new"; a relationship of dependence between the urban praetor and the scribe on whose property the chests were found; and the Senate's willingness to simply accept the word of the praetor about what the books contained. Livy viewed both the Bacchic episode and the Numa episode as tending to the "dissolution of proper religious behavior" (39.16.9: *dissolvendae religionis*; 40.29.11: *dissolvendarum religionum*).

26. Orlin (2000), 76–81. For other interpretations of this incident, cf. Rosen (1985); Pailler (1988), 623–703; Gruen (1990), 163–170. The notion that this episode represented a serious attempt to introduce Pythagorean precepts to Rome, as suggested by earlier studies [e.g., Ferrero (1955); Prowse (1964)] has now been thoroughly rejected.

27. For the connection, see Dion. Hal., *Ant. Rom.* 2.59.1–2, Diod. Sic. 8.14; Cic. *Rep.* 2.28–29; Livy 1.18.1–3; Ov. *Fast.* 3.151–54 and *Met.* 15.1–8, 60–72. Dionysius, Livy, and Cicero in particular are at pains to refute the story, which serves only to show how strong a hold the story had in the Late Republic. The origin of the legend is uncertain but may have been established by the time of the Samnite wars, when a statue of Pythagoras was erected in the *comitium* (Plin. *HN* 34.26; Plut. *Numa* 8.10), or in the course of the next century as Romans confronted the statue in the marketplace. See Gruen (1990), 158–162.

miraculous unearthing of texts in both Latin and Greek highlighted the distinctions between Roman and Greek traditions: Numa's writings on pontifical law concerned traditional Roman religious practice, and the Pythagorean teachings involved the Greek philosophical tradition. At the same time, the joint discovery suggested the possibility that Numa's precepts may have been influenced by Pythagorean principles, another reminder of the openness that characterized Roman society: even the founder of the Roman religious tradition was not averse to utilizing Greek ingredients. The destruction of both sets of books makes clear that the Senate's intent was not to close the door on the incorporation of foreign cultural elements in Rome; preserving the books of Numa while destroying the writings of Pythagoras would have accomplished that goal more effectively. The Senate instead declared that Roman tradition, as it had developed over the centuries and as embodied in the Senate's own decisions, was superior to those writings as a guide to Roman religious practice.[28] The foundation of the second temple to Venus Erycina, a cult that apparently incorporated more of the foreign elements present in the cult's home on Mount Eryx, underscored this point; Rome remained open to foreign religious traditions, even in the wake of the Bacchic episode.[29] The events of 181 provided a coda to the incident involving the worship of Bacchus; it served as a reminder of Roman openness but evinced a concern with drawing boundaries between Greek and Roman and with proclaiming the Senate as the ultimate authority for defining what religious practices should be considered Roman, even in the face of the founder of Roman religion. The religious events of the 180s demonstrate how cultural elements from overseas, especially Greece, provided a context in which the Roman elite attempted to define what it meant to be Roman.

Challenges to Roman identity came not only from overseas but also from Italy itself, as the wars of the late third and early second centuries posed questions about the status of the Italian communities in regard to Romanness, and these issues loom large in the first decades of the second century. Many of these communities had fought and died side by side with Roman forces throughout the long years of the Hannibalic War, raising the question about the place of these people, especially the communities that had joined up with Hannibal, within the Roman enterprise. Cato's *Origines* provides a glimpse into the attempt of one member of the Roman elite to come to grips with this issue in the immediate

28. Cf. Gruen (1990), 168–170, who suggests that through this event "the ruling class once again asserted its cultural independence."

29. I have discussed this temple more fully elsewhere; see Orlin (2000). The temple was called an ἀφίδρυμα by Strabo (6.272), and the presence of prostitutes at the temple (Ov. *Rem. Am.* 549; *Fast.*, 4.865–872) is reminiscent of the temple prostitutes of the Eryx cult.

aftermath of the Second Punic War; the attempt to establish the origins of every Italian community might help in establishing whether a particular community should be considered a friend or an enemy.[30] The question of Roman identity in Italy became even more acute as Rome resumed planting colonies throughout the peninsula: eight separate colonies in 194 including at Puteoli and Croton; at Copia in 193; Vibo Valentia in 192; Bononia in 189; Potentia and Pisaurum in 184; Parma, Mutina, and Saturnia in 183, Gravisca and Aquileia in 181; Pisa in 180; and Luna in 177.[31] These colonies are scattered throughout Italy, with the earlier ones mostly in the south, apparently intended to solidify control in the region that had showed some support for Hannibal during the war, and the later ones in the north most likely to be connected with the campaigns in Cisalpine Gaul and Liguria. The Roman concern with the question of Roman status can be seen in the issue of whether to make these colonies Roman or Latin; Livy specifically reports a debate on the Senate concerning the character of Aquileia, which was eventually founded as a Latin colony.[32] What is striking about the colonial foundations of this period as opposed to earlier phases is the increasing number of Roman colonies; indeed, the foundation of Aquileia is the last recorded instance of a Latin colony. While the reasons for this development are worth exploring, our concern here lies with the result.[33] Over these twenty years, increasing numbers of people with full Roman citizen rights found themselves living well outside the ambit of the city; at least nine thousand such citizens were added to these ranks during this period of colonial foundation.[34] These colonial foundations presented a new challenge to the conceptualization of Roman identity: large numbers of full Roman citizens who found themselves, like noncitizens, living outside the city and, like noncitizens, fighting on behalf of Rome, elided the distinctions between Roman and non-Roman. It became increasingly obvious that citizenship was no longer defined by residence in the near vicinity of Rome, and even that Romanness may not have been defined by citizenship.

30. Cf. Williams (2001), 75–79, 88; Bispham (2008), 58.

31. Eight colonies in 194: Livy 34.45; Copia: Livy 35.9; Vibo: Livy 35.40.5–6; Bononia: Livy 37.57.7; Potentia and Pisaurum: Livy 39.44.10; Parma, Mutina, and Saturnia: Livy 39.55.6–9; Gravisca and Aquileia (the latter initially voted in 183; cf. Livy 39.55.5): Livy 40.29.1 and 40.34.2; Pisa: Livy 40.43.1; Luna: Livy 41.13.4–5.

32. Livy 40.34.5–6.

33. For discussions of this period of Roman colonization, see Sherwin-White (1970), 77–80; Salmon (1970), 95–109, and (1982), 94–97; Bispham (2006).

34. The colonies at Parma, Mutina, and Luna are specified as consisting of 2,000 men, and three of the colonies sent out in 194 (Puteoli, Volturnum, and Liternum) comprised 300 men. Assuming the lower figure for all the unspecified colonies yields a figure of 9,000 additional Romans living outside of Rome; the actual number was probably higher.

Issues of citizenship appear prominently in the historical record in the first half of the second century, offering a glimpse of these problems as the Romans began to grapple with issues surrounding Latin and Italian communities. In 189, the Campanians, who had been deprived of citizen rights in 211 because of their support of Hannibal, were allowed to register at Rome, and in the following year, they were granted the right to marry Roman women and to have marriages to Roman women prior to this time recognized as valid.[35] In this instance, a city that had fought on the wrong side during the Hannibalic War was reincorporated into the Roman state. In the next year, 187, the Senate heard a complaint from Latin communities that too many of their citizens had migrated to Rome; in consequence, the Senate ordered that anyone who had been registered in a Latin community after 204 should return to the city of his registration, and Livy reports that 12,000 Latins returned home as a result.[36] A similar episode occurred a decade later: the Latin allies appealed to the Senate, complaining that so many men had migrated to Rome that they might soon be incapable of meeting their military obligations to Rome.[37] The Senate responded by attempting to close the loopholes through which many Latins had obtained Roman citizenship and by sending those who had already taken advantage of the loopholes back to their cities. Several points might be made in connection with these incidents. First, at this time Roman actions cannot be ascribed to a Roman desire not to share the benefits of citizenship with Latins. The Roman action was spurred by the Latin communities themselves; the Romans were acceding to Latin requests, not proactively choking off Latin immigration.[38] Second, it is clear that legal citizenship was increasingly becoming a desired end, as the attempt by so many individual Latins to obtain Roman citizenship indicates. Yet there does not seem to have been a push by Latin communities as a whole to agitate for Roman citizenship for the community; the concern as expressed in these incidents is the negative impact the emigration to Rome was having on their ability to fulfill their obligations under their present status, not agitation for a change in status.[39] In 187, the Latin communities

35. Livy 38.28.4; 38.36.5–6.

36. Livy 39.3.4–5.

37. Livy 41.8.6–12.

38. For a counterargument, see Frezouls (1981).

39. Broadhead (2008) has recently argued that the Roman expectation of geographical fixity combined with the reality of geographical mobility in second-century Italy to present these obstacles for the functioning of the Roman state. That question may be left to the side here; whatever the causes of these incidents, they forced the Romans to confront the question of who should be considered a Roman and how residents of Italy should be treated.

may have held back from such agitation because the Romans had just raised three Volscian towns—Arpinum, Formiae, and Fundi—to full citizen status, so it may be that they hoped further promotions would be forthcoming without making demands.[40] Yet by 177, another decade had passed in which Livy does not record the granting of full citizen status to any other communities; indeed, the grants to the Volscian communities are the last recorded extensions of full citizenship to a community until the Social War.[41] This absence may suggest that Roman citizenship may not have been a goal for communities at this time, however much individuals may have desired it; we should not be too quick to read the Italian complaints of the Social War back into the early second century. Issues of citizenship would come to dominate the discourse between Romans and the Italian communities in the second century, and eventually have to be resolved through bloodshed, but they are only one piece of the relationship between Rome and these communities, and we should not let them obscure other elements in the development of a sense of Romanness.

Financial matters provide another area in which the Romans were challenged to work out a new way of defining the position of Latins and Latin communities vis-à-vis Rome. By the beginning of the second century, moneylenders had discovered that they could evade the stricter Roman laws regulating their practices by transferring the debts to a citizen of an allied state, who would therefore not be bound by Roman law but by local restrictions. The legal distinction that existed failed to match the reality of the situation in practice, and in this case, the Romans responded by formally erasing the legal distinction: the *lex Sempronia* of 193 provided that the laws of lending money should be the same for the allies and those of the Latin name as for Rome.[42] While the legislation was apparently drawn up to protect Roman citizens, the result was that all Italy fell under the same legal system as pertained to moneylending. A similar sequence occurred later in the century in regard to sumptuary laws, an issue that concerned the Roman elite from the beginning of the century. The *lex*

40. For Arpinum, Formiae, and Fundi, see Livy 38.37.6–9.

41. Sherwin-White (1970), 210–214, discusses the problem of the enfranchisement of the Italian municipia, including the lack of attestation for the period following 188. He suggests that the silence of Livy for the period up to 167 should carry weight, and that there are no reasons to suggest a general enfranchisement prior to the Social War. Cf. Salmon (1982), 117–118, who suggests that in general the Romans were not averse to upgrading communities, even if they might be reluctant to extend the franchise; he blames internal politics for the absence of subsequent upgrades.

42. Livy 35.7.2–6.

Fannia of 161 had placed a series of limits on the amount of money that could be spent on various festival days; in 143, this law was followed by the *lex Didia*, which explicitly provided that the law should apply to all of Italy, for, as Macrobius writes, there were "Italians who believed that the Fannian law did not apply to themselves, but only to citizens of the city."[43] The extension of Roman laws over the entire peninsula may have been intended as a demonstration of Roman authority and domination, but the effect was to treat Romans, Latins, and allies as members of a single community, with a single set of laws. In fact, that these laws were not designed to create a single community of Romans, Latins, and Italians is highly revealing; it suggests that at one level the Roman authorities believed that the residents of the Italian peninsula and other territories controlled by the Romans were, in an important sense, already Roman.

These actions in the legal sphere regarding the Latin and Italian communities provide the backdrop for understanding the Roman religious activity of this period. We have already examined the response to the Bacchic incident in terms of its implications for the Roman reaction to Greek culture, but it also has implications for the Roman relationship with Italian communities. Livy's account of the Bacchanalia makes it clear that the Senate's response was not limited to Rome itself, but included Roman allies in Italy: the consuls were instructed to seek out Dionysiac priests "not only at Rome, but throughout all the *fora* and *conciliabula*."[44] Furthermore, the senatorial decrees were to be sent "through all Italy" (*per totam Italiam*), and indeed, the one copy of the decree that we possess was found in Tiriolo in the very foot of Italy. The decree itself is explicit in insisting on a public reading of the Senate's instructions in the marketplace and the public display of the decree.[45] While Rome had long been the dominant power on the Italian peninsula, this type of intervention by the Roman Senate is unprecedented. Earlier interventions had involved insisting on the expiation of prodigies and occurred either at colonies, such as Ardea, or at locations where the Romans had a special relationship, such as the shrine of Juno Sospita in Lanuvium.[46] Here the Senate expanded its jurisdiction over all the municipalities of Italy, and it did so by permanently limiting the autonomy of those communities to perform

---

43. Macrob. *Sat.* 3.17.6: *prima et potissima, ut universa Italia, non sola urbs, lege sumptuaria teneretur, Italicis existimantibus Fanniam legem non in se sed in solos urbanos cives esse conscriptam.*

44. Livy 39.14.7: *non modo Romae sed per omnia fora et conciliabula conquiri.*

45. *ILLRP* 511, line 2. Cf. lines 22ff.

46. See chapter 1.

ritual activities according to their own wishes.[47] Indeed, it has been suggested that the demonstration of Roman control over Italy may have been one of the Senate's primary aims in this affair.[48] Whatever the motivation for the Senate's action in extending the regulations concerning Bacchus far afield from Rome, the result was that the Senate treated the Italian municipalities in the same manner that it treated Rome; the distinction between Roman and Italian was elided in this context.[49] The episode of the Bacchanalia reveals the conception of a single community of all the inhabitants of Italy, activated here by distinctions between Roman and Greek religious practice.

The extension of Roman religious practices throughout Italy seen in the Bacchic incident is visible in the same period in less repressive situations as well, further suggesting the extension of a sense of identity between Rome and the inhabitants of Italy. Though both incidents have been discussed earlier in the context of expiations performed throughout Italy during the Second Punic War, a brief reminder is worthwhile to provide the context for Roman behavior at this time; the continuance of this practice in the second century confirms that the earlier behavior was not merely due to the exigencies of war. In 181, the decemviri recommended the celebration of a three-day *supplicatio* and *feriae* throughout all Italy (*per totam Italiam*) in response to a prodigy at the temple of Juno Sospita in Lanuvium, the first time that a ritual had been extended in this fashion.[50] In the following year, in response to a severe pestilence, the decemviri advised that a *supplicatio* be held for two days in Rome and in all the *conciliabula* and *fora*.[51] In the exact places where the Senate insisted on publishing its decree concerning Bacchic rites and at the same time as investigations continued into Bacchic worship, the Senate now insisted that a religious rite be performed for the sake of health. As discussed in the chapter on expiations, these rites were performed for the sake of the community. Even if the health with which the authorities were concerned was primarily of the people living in Rome, the

47. Whether the Senate was legally justified in expanding its jurisdiction in this fashion is a moot point; the Italian communities were not in a position to challenge Rome's authority here. For discussion of this issue, see, e.g., Accame (1938); McDonald (1944); Levi (1969).

48. Gruen (1990), 66–73.

49. Mouritsen (1998), 55, although denying that the *Sc de Bacchanalibus* "constitutes proof of Roman law and jurisdiction being extended to the allies," sees the decree as "an internal Roman document," which would support the idea that the Romans at least viewed Rome and the allied parts of Italy in the same way.

50. Livy 40.19.5.

51. Livy 40.37: *in urbe et per omnia fora conciliabulaque.*

inclusion of the Italian municipalities in the rites strongly suggests that they were considered an integral part of the community; without their participation, presumably the rite would have been ineffective. The rites performed in these two years, along with the theoretically uniform practice in regard to the worship of Bacchus, might have enabled the residents of Italy to imagine themselves as a single community: in all the *fora conciliabulaque* of Italy, individuals just like them were performing the same rites. These episodes suggest a growing Roman interest not only in defining Roman religious practice but also defining the relationship between Rome and Italy.

A cause célèbre of 173 allows us to see tensions within the Roman elite in regard to the relationship with Italian communities, but in the end this incident reinforced the messages of senatorial control and of inclusiveness that we have seen in the episodes of the 180s. One of the censors of 173, Q. Fulvius Flaccus, was engaged in building the temple to Fortuna Equestris that he had vowed during his campaigns in Spain eight years previously.[52] Desirous of building the most magnificent temple in Rome, Flaccus had the marble roof tiles taken off the temple of Juno Lacinia in Croton and brought to Rome. This temple was an important regional sanctuary, the original headquarters for the Italiote League and still important in this period and possessed of significant resources.[53] Livy reports that complaints arose in the Senate, centered on criticisms that a censor responsible for public morals and keeping temples in good repair should have been responsible for damage to a sanctuary of an allied city, "as if the immortal gods were not the same everywhere."[54] A vote that was eventually taken required that the roof tiles be returned to Croton and expiatory offerings be made to Juno Lacinia; unfortunately, says Livy, no workmen could be found who knew how to reinstall the tiles, so they had to be left upon the ground at the temple.

---

52. For the account of events, see Livy 42.3.

53. The wealth of the sanctuary at this time is attested by Livy 23.3; continued wealth at a later date by Plut., *Pomp.* 24 and Strabo, 6.1.1. On its use as a federal sanctuary, see de Sensi Sestito (1984).

54. Livy 42.3.6–9: *templum augustissimum regionis eius, quod non Pyrrhus, non Hannibal violassent, violare parum habuisse, nisi detexisset foede ac prope diruisset. detractum culmen templo, nudatum tectum patere imbribus putrefaciendum. ad id censorem moribus regendis creatum? cui sarta tecta exigere sacris publicis et locare tuenda more maiorum traditum esset, eum per sociorum urbes diruentem templa nudantemque tecta aedium sacrarum vagari! et quod, si in privatis sociorum aedificiis faceret, indignum videri posset, id eum templa deum immortalium demolientem facere, et obstringere religione populum Romanum, ruinis templorum templa aedificantem, tamquam non iidem ubique di immortales sint, sed spoliis aliorum alii colendi exornandique!*

Interpretation of this episode is made particularly difficult because of the highly rhetorical nature of Livy's presentation, which culminates some chapters later with the suicide of Fulvius in the following year, the result, said popular opinion, of the anger of Juno Lacinia over the despoliation of the temple.[55] Thus, one should not place too much stock in the notion that the Romans felt that all gods were the same, and possibly not even that the complaints against Fulvius revolved around the despoliation of a sanctuary important to the allies. We have seen before in discussing sumptuary legislation that ostentatious display was definitely a concern to the Senate in trying to maintain some equilibrium among the aristocracy, and it is certainly possible that the real concern of the Senate in regard to Fulvius lay in the grandiloquence of the temple and especially in its use of marble as a construction material. Marble temples are not found in Rome until the middle of the second century, when three went up in rapid succession, clearly serving as part of a struggle for individual glory among three major generals of the time.[56] The Senate may well have been trying to maintain a limit on the opulence of new temples, but even so, the discourse reported by Livy may represent the publicly announced reasons for the Senate's actions, as the desire to rein in a flamboyant senator would not be proclaimed openly. In responding to Fulvius, the Senate was apparently willing to acknowledge that Fulvius' action involved not just the magistrate but the entire Roman people in a religious obligation (*obstringere religione populum Romanum* in Livy's phrasing) and that therefore the state bore responsibility for the proper worship of an important Italian deity, even one at the very edge of the peninsula. This episode thus provides another incident where the distinction between Roman and Italian was elided in view of the other aims of the Roman Senate.

The activity of Fulvius here is as revealing as that of the Senate, if only because it provides a glimpse of a competing vision of Rome's relationship to Italy. In the wake of the increasingly frequent despoliation of

---

55. Livy 42.28: *vulgo Iunonis Laciniae iram ob spoliatum templum alienasse mentem ferebant.* This part of the story was evidently a standard moralizing lesson by the early imperial period, for Val. Max. 1.1.20 tells the same story. Mueller (1998), 251–252, suggests that by ascribing this version to the mob, Livy discredited it, attributing Fulvius' suicide instead to the death and illness of his two sons in that same year.

56. The first marble temple was that of Jupiter Stator, dedicated by Q. Caecilius Metellus around the time of his consulship in 143; cf. Val. Max. 1.11.3. L. Mummius' temple to Hercules Victor and D. Iunius Brutus' temple to Mars followed within fifteen years; all three politicians seem to be combating the prominence of Scipio Aemilianus; cf. Ziolkowski (1988), 326–329.

sanctuaries in Sicily and Greece following Marcellus' sack of Syracuse in 212, Fulvius' action turned that behavior toward an important Italian sanctuary.[57] The attitude underlying Fulvius' behavior may be seen in one of two ways: either Fulvius recognized the Croton sanctuary as an important Italian site but decided that his own personal desire as a Roman for the roof tiles outweighed the claims of the Italian allies, or he simply may have treated the sanctuary at Croton in the same fashion as recent generals had treated overseas sanctuaries, without recognition that it held any special status as a locus for allied religious behavior. Croton, after all, had deserted the Romans after the battle of Cannae and had not returned to Roman control until the departure of the Carthaginians; we have already noted that a colony was planted on the site in 194, likely to ensure the loyalty of the inhabitants. For Fulvius to have treated the city as a defeated enemy is not unthinkable, though Livy's suggestion that the local population was cowed by the censor's authority suggests a civil rather than military rationale. The critical point is that under either scenario Fulvius' action served as a declaration that the religious communities of the Italians and the Romans were not coterminous. In this view, the Roman community was naturally more important and possessed the unlimited right to employ elements, even active elements, of local Italian sanctuaries for strictly Roman, or even personal, purposes.[58] Fulvius' other activity during this year further suggests that he was concerned to highlight the importance of Roman status throughout Italy; his censorship was notable for its building projects throughout Italy and not just in Rome, but without exception his activity was confined to colonies with full Roman status.[59] Ultimately the Senate overruled Fulvius in regard to the temple at Croton, but the episode suggests that the nature of the relationship between Rome and her Italian allies continued to serve as a source of controversy and contestation.

The location and history of Croton suggests further that this may be a particularly valuable incident for understanding the increasing ambiguity of the

---

57. Livy 24.3.3 provides a digression on the temple, calling it a temple nobler than the city itself and sacred to all the surrounding peoples: *templum ipsa urbe nobilius Laciniae Iunonis, sanctum omnibus circa populis.*

58. Cf. Jaeger (2006), 407.

59. Cf. Livy 41.27: "Fulvius Flaccus, acting alone, built a temple to Jupiter at Pisaurum and at Fundi and brought water to Placentia. He also paved a street at Pisaurum with flint. At Sinuessa he added some suburban residences with aviaries, constructed sewers, enclosed the place with a wall, built colonnades and shops all round the forum, setting up three statues of Janus there." Cf. Bispham (2006), 121, who also notes Fulvius' focus on Roman colonies.

boundary between Roman and Italian. Not only was Croton the site of the temple to Juno Lacinia but also it was the home of Pythagoras after his emigration from Samos; the respect shown to the temple reinforced the message that the burning of the Pythagorean texts in 181 did not represent a rejection of the culture of Magna Graecia. Furthermore, Mary Jaeger has recently suggested that Livy's treatment of the temple of Juno at Croton, located at the very edge of Italy, forms an important part of the historian's narrative concerning the creation of a unified peninsula under Roman control.[60] For example, the apparent ease of movement in the episode of the roof tiles, in which Fulvius begins in Rome, goes to the very foot of Italy, and then returns with the roof tiles, while the roof tiles themselves move from Croton to Rome and back again, suggests that Italy has become a single geographic unit.[61] Furthermore, the sanctuary at Croton was important not only as a religious site for the surrounding people but also for an event that occurred there toward the end of the Second Punic War. Just before leaving Italy, Hannibal, having been summoned home, massacred those of his Italian allies who refused to follow him to Africa and who had taken refuge in the temple of Juno Lacinia.[62] Livy's account suggests that these men were killed simply on account of belonging to the Italian race (*Italici generis*), thereby positing that a unified Italian race existed; Jaeger notes that Livy may have intended to call attention to this act as the foundational sacrifice of a unified peninsula.[63] While the Romans of Fulvius' day may not have viewed the massacre in this fashion, they were certainly aware of the slaughter that had occurred in the sanctuary; Livy's account of the senatorial complaints about Fulvius' despoliation of the sanctuary may indicate as much, for it includes a remark that not even Hannibal had been guilty of such impiety.[64] Senatorial support for the sanctuary of Croton in 173, even if that support turned out to be symbolic since the roof tiles could not ultimately be reinstalled on the temple, served as a mark of respect. Rather than a declaration that the local population was no longer sufficiently alive or important to warrant an intact sanctuary, the Senate affirmed their importance, even in diminished circumstances, to the Roman state. The inability to restore the roof tiles may even have called special attention to the suffering of the Italians and to the concern of the Roman Senate,

60. Jaeger (2006).

61. Jaeger (2006), 406–407.

62. Livy 30.20.5–7.

63. Jaeger (2006), 401–402. Cf. Levene (1993), 74. Appian's account (*Hann.* 7.9.59) of the same event suggests that Hannibal subdivided his Italian allies into groups and also that although the massacre was an act of cruelty, it had a military purpose that is absent from Livy's account. These differences suggest that Livy has indeed constructed his account carefully to suit his purposes.

64. Livy 42.3.6.

by leaving behind a monument to those Italians who had sacrificed themselves rather than go overseas to fight their coinhabitants of the peninsula. A casual visitor to the sanctuary, knowing that the most famous event in the sanctuary's history was the slaughter of the Italian allies of Hannibal, and seeing the roof tiles on the ground and the increasingly dilapidated temple, might associate the two events and be reminded of Hannibal's action. A more sophisticated visitor, or one with a good guide, might know that a Roman magistrate was responsible for the condition of the temple but would also know that the roof tiles had been returned by the Roman Senate; the pile of roof tiles would serve as a reminder that the action was that of a rogue magistrate, and the return of the tiles was reflective of the importance attached to the site by the Roman elite. Paradoxically, the despoliation of the temple of Juno Lacinia, perhaps intended as a demonstration that the sanctuary was foreign to Rome, may have turned it into an enduring reminder of an essential unity between Romans and Italians.

The new temple foundations in Rome itself in the first half of the second century confirm the Roman interest in suggesting that the Roman religious community extended throughout Italy. This period saw a burst of new temple construction that is unparalleled by any other period in Roman history: fifteen new temples were definitely dedicated between 194 and 173, and a further three temples are first attested in this period, though they might have been constructed earlier.[65] A remarkable aspect of these new temples is how many were dedicated to important divinities from the Italian peninsula; the Magna Mater, whose introduction originated during the Second Punic War, finally saw her temple dedicated in 191, and the second temple to Venus Erycina, as discussed previously, was dedicated in 181, but apart from these two examples, only the temple of Hercules Musarum in the early 170s had its roots overseas. The inclination to focus on Italian deities was demonstrated at the very outset of the period in question, for in 194, the Romans finally dedicated a temple to Juno Sospita, whom they had worshipped in common with the people of Lanuvium since 338.[66] The foundation of the temple in Rome did not involve a transfer of the rites performed at the sanctuary in Lanuvium, for it is clear from Cicero that Roman magistrates continued to make the journey to perform sacrifices in Lanuvium.[67] The temple in Rome thus added to the veneration already shown by the Romans to this goddess,

65. See Orlin (1997), 201, for a list of the temples.

66. Livy 34.53. The historian errs in identifying the goddess in this passage as Juno Matuta; he correctly names her as Juno Sospita when reporting the vow that led to the temple by C. Cornelius Cethegus in 197 (32.30).

67. Cic. *Mur.* 90.

without detracting from the importance of her Lanuvian home. Three other temples were dedicated in Rome in the same year: to Faunus, to Fortuna Primigenia, and to Vediovis.[68] Faunus was an ancient Italic god of the countryside whom mythology turned into the father of Latinus, aetiological father of the Latins, and although the identity of Vediovis and his potential relationship to Jupiter remain problematic, there is little doubt that this god was worshipped from a very early date in Italy.[69] Fortuna Primigenia offers a more significant example of the reconception of the Roman religious community. Less than fifty years earlier, the Senate had apparently declared the foreignness of this goddess worshipped at Praeneste, just twenty-five miles from Rome. In 241 B.C.E., the Senate had refused to allow the consul of that year, Q. Lutatius Cerco, to consult the oracle at Praeneste on the grounds that he should use ancestral, not foreign-born (*alienigenis*), auspices.[70] In this short span of time, Fortuna Primigenia moved from being a goddess the Senate did not trust to a home on the Quirinal hill, inside the *pomerium* of Rome itself. Although these temples had been vowed in different years, the dedication of four temples to important Italian deities in the same year, three of them within forty-five days, is striking.[71] This trend would continue over the next twenty years, with temples built to Vediovis (again), Ops, Diana, and Juno Regina, among others. The construction of temples to Italian deities need not be read as a sign of Roman conservatism, but rather of the Romans' interest in expressing a commonality with Italy. These new temples provide an important reminder that the relationship between Rome and peninsular Italy needed to be resolved just as much as the relationship between Rome and Greece needed to be worked out.

68. Livy 34.53. The *fasti* know this god as Vediovis, but the historian identifies the recipient of the temple dedicated in 194 as Jupiter, while at the time of the vow six years earlier (31.21.12) he gave the name as Diiovis, though the text is corrupt and may originally have read Vediovis. See further Degrassi (1963), 388; Briscoe (1973), 112.

69. On Vediovis, see Scullard (1981), 56–58, who discusses both the derivation of the name Vediovis as well as the evidence for Iron Age worship of the god.

70. Val. Max. 1.3.2: *Lutatius Cerco, qui primum Punicum bellum confecit, a senatu prohibitus est sortes Fortunae Praenestinae adire: auspiciis enim patriis, non alienigenis rem publicam administrari iudicabant oportere.* Cf. Champeaux (1982), 78–80, on the hostility between Rome and Praeneste evidenced by this incident.

71. It is worth noting that three of the four temples were dedicated in rapid succession: Vediovis on January 1, Juno Sospita on February 1, and Faunus on February 13; in a space of forty-five days the Romans witnessed three processions and ceremonies focused on Italian deities.

An incident from later in the second century indicates that the Romans continued to be concerned to define Romanness in religious terms yet also that the ground may have shifted significantly by the second half of the century. According to Valerius Maximus, in 139 the praetor Cornelius Hispanus by an edict ordered the "Chaldaeans" to leave the city, accusing them of misleading simple minds by a false interpretation of the stars; in the same year, he also expelled the Jews from the city, on the grounds that they were infecting Roman customs.[72] Scholars have generally assumed that by "Chaldaeans" Valerius denoted astrologers, the ethnic meaning of the term having been discarded by this time; this translation makes sense of Valerius' reference to the misinterpretation of the stars.[73] Yet even so, this notice is not without its problems. For instance, the names preserved in the epitomes of both Paris and Nepotianus are confused, with Paris naming the praetor as Cornelius Hispalus, confusing the praetor Hispanus of 139, the consular year of M. Popillius Laenas and Cn. Calpurnius Piso, with his father, the consul of 176, and further misidentifying the consul of 139 as L. Calpurnius.[74] Moreover, the epitome of Paris claims that the Jews tried to infect Roman customs with the cult of Jupiter Sabazios, though the Jews were not adherents of this cult, a syncretistic combination of Jupiter with an Asia Minor deity often connected with Dionysius; confusion with the Jewish Sabbath has been posited as the most likely source of the confusion.[75] Nepotianus claims only that the Jews tried to pass their religion on to the Romans, a more reasonable claim but still one more appropriate to the imperial context of the epitomator than the mid-second century B.C.E.[76] Despite the fact that it is unlikely that Jews were actively proselytizing in mid-second-century Rome, it is possible and even likely that there was a Jewish presence in Rome by this time, especially in the wake of the Roman victory over Antiochus in 188.[77] Despite the problems presented by the text, therefore, scholars have generally accepted the factual basis lying at the root of this

72. Val. Max. 1.3.3.

73. Most texts (e.g., the recent Loeb edition) simply translate Chaldaeans as astrologers. Cf. Wardle (1998), 149.

74. See further Wardle (1998), 148.

75. See Wardle (1998), 150–151; Gruen (2002), 16.

76. Cf. Gruen (2002), 16–17.

77. Leon (1960), 3–4, notes the likely presence of Jews in Rome in the second century but suggests the group expelled were merely temporary inhabitants, such as merchants. This suggestion has generally been rejected; cf., e.g., Slingerland (1997), 39–46. On Jews in Rome, see also Westenholz (1995).

account, that these two groups were expelled from the city in 139.[78] Given the problems with Valerius' text, the challenge has been to explain this incident.

Both astrologers and Jews were expelled from the city several additional times, particularly in the imperial period, leading some interpretations to focus on the nature of these groups. Astrologers were particularly suspect in the eyes of the Roman state, attracting the wrath already of Cato the Censor.[79] The epitome of Paris suggests that the concern in 139 was the astrologers' attempt to profit from their art or that astrology led to false predictions, but the major concern of the Roman elite with astrology appears to have been that it placed religious knowledge in the hands of people not controlled by the Roman Senate; members of the Roman elite and even emperors might on occasion employ astrology without reproof.[80] Regarding the Jews, some have seen in the expulsion of 139 an early manifestation of anti-Semitism, but the fact that astrologers were evicted from Rome at the same time as the Jews suggests that the Jews were not singled out here, and we have already discarded the notion that Jews might have been proselytizing and thereby causing disruptions in the city at this early date. Furthermore, one may well question the importance attached to the efficacy of the measures taken in 139, for the repetition of expulsion measures in succeeding generations suggests that both Jews and astrologers found their way back to Rome. The measures of 139 cannot be read as an attempt by the Senate to eradicate either Judaism or astrology from the city of Rome.

Rather than focusing on the groups expelled in 139, it may be more profitable to focus on the act of expulsion itself. The Romans do not seem to have employed this procedure prior to the second century, and the expulsions of Latins from the city in the 180s and 170s, which were previously discussed, seem to have been the first widespread expulsion of non-Romans from the city.[81] Although those particular evictions occurred at the behest of Latin communities, the Senate seems to have begun to use this tool more proactively in the ensuing years, and these instances may provide

---

78. Lane (1979) has suggested that rather than assuming a simple exchange between Jews and worshippers of Sabazius in Valerius, *both* groups were expelled from Rome in 139, in addition to the astrologers. While this is possible, it cannot be definitively established; more important, the addition of Sabazius worshippers to the groups expelled in 139 does not change the nature of the argument here.

79. Cato, *Agr.* 5.4.

80. On Roman attitudes to astrology, see Beard, North, and Price (1998), 161 and 231–233; Cramer (1954), 233–248. Cf. also Wardle (1998), 149.

81. On expulsions from Rome in general, see Noy (2000), 37–47.

insight into the Roman behavior. In 171, when the Romans decided that they would have to fight against Perseus, they demanded that the ambassadors from Perseus leave Italy within thirty days, but they also apparently proclaimed the same expulsion for all Macedonian residents.[82] Ten years later, the praetor Pomponius gained the approval of the Senate to remove all philosophers and rhetors from the city, and two individual Epicurean philosophers were evicted from the city during the consulship of L. Postumius, which must be either 173 or 154.[83] As with the expulsion of astrologers and Jews in 139, none of these expulsions can have been effective in completely removing a targeted group from Rome or eradicating an unwanted behavior. The need to repeat the expulsion of Italians points in this direction, the presence of rhetors and philosophers in Rome after 161 is well attested, and the token expulsion of two Epicureans can hardly have had a significant practical impact. Yet the fact that the Senate continued to periodically issue expulsion decrees suggests that they did not find the ineffectiveness of these decrees problematic or, better yet, that the primary purpose in passing these decrees may not have been simply the physical removal of a group from the city of Rome.[84] Rather, it may be more profitable to see these actions as symbolic, as the Senate's attempt to draw boundaries between Roman and non-Roman. Creating distinctions between themselves and what they perceived to be foreign cultures, or what they wanted to be perceived as such, remained a continuing theme for the Roman Senate throughout the second century. Just as with the Magna Mater or Bacchus, the effect was to define certain practices or groups as non-Roman, even if their presence in the city was tolerated or encouraged; in 139, the Senate focused attention on two groups, astrologers and Jews, whose practices could easily be defined as foreign.[85] Religion again served as a key arena in which to mark the boundaries of Romanness.

It is difficult to pin down a single specific cause for the decision to act in 139, but the historical context does provide some suggestive clues to the contributing factors. If one source for the arrival of numerous Jews in Rome was the defeat of Antiochus III, that event had occurred fifty years earlier, so it is hard to see the praetor's edict as a response to a sudden

82. App. *Mac.* 11.9 reports the general expulsion of Macedonians; Polyb. 27.6 and Livy 42.48.1–4 report only on the expulsion of the ambassadors.

83. Pomponius: Suet. *Rhet.* 1.2; Epicureans: Ath. 12.547a; Ael. *VH* 9.12.

84. Cf. the discussion of these expulsions by Gruen (1990), 170–179, who sees the expulsions as a "symbolic resistance to Greek morals and manners," while pointing out that "philosophers were not, in fact, unwelcome at Rome" (174).

85. Cf. the conclusions of Gruen (2002), 19.

influx of Jews; the same is true for astrologers in Rome, who are attested as far back as the third century. The suggestion of unrest over Laelius' land bill, proposed and then withdrawn in 140, has only chronological coincidence to recommend it; there is no evidence to suggest that astrologers or Jews were in any way connected to this incident.[86] An embassy from the Hasmonean king Jonathan of Judaea is reported to have visited Rome at approximately this time, probably in 142, but the embassy had received favorable treatment, making hostility in the wake of this visit an implausible explanation.[87] Perhaps an answer may be sought more broadly in the historical context of the period; in 146, Roman generals had conquered and sacked two of the major cities of the Mediterranean basin, Corinth and Carthage. Apart from removing the last vestiges of a threat from these quarters, the victories brought unprecedented amounts of booty, in the form of money, slaves, and artwork, into Rome over the next few years. The Senate may have felt a public restatement of Romanness at this time would serve as an important symbolic reminder of the boundaries between Roman and non-Roman. In this regard, the Judean embassy may have been significant in raising the profile of the Jewish community in Rome such that Jews would be a recognizable example of non-Romanness.

It is suggestive to note that the action in 139 focused on ethnic groups from the east but did not involve Greeks, despite the recent influx of material objects from Corinth. In the wake of Mummius' victory over Corinth, the victor had exhibited large numbers of bronze and marble statues as well as numerous paintings of his triumph, and he also built a votive temple of marble to Hercules Victor, which he apparently dedicated as censor in 142.[88] This marble temple followed very closely on the heels of the first marble temple in Rome, which was constructed by Q. Metellus following *his* campaigns in Greece in the year before Mummius arrived to take command.[89] Yet this sudden influx of Greek art and Greek architectural styles, even affecting the design of religious buildings, did *not* occasion a reaction in regard to Greek culture from the Roman Senate. Jews and "Chaldaeans" filled the role of non-Roman that Greeks had filled earlier in the century, in the case of the Bacchic controversy and philosophers. This development suggests that while the Roman elite continued to define the boundaries of Romanness through religious actions, drawing distinctions between Roman and Greek culture was no

86. For the suggestion, Cramer (1954), 235, rejected by Wardle (1998), 149.

87. For the embassy, see 1 Macc. 14.17–18, 14.24, 14.40; Joseph. *AJ* 13.5.8. Cf. Wardle (1998), 150–151; Gruen (2002), 17.

88. Triumph: Livy *Per.* 52; Eutr. 4.14. Temple to Hercules Victor: *CIL* I².626.

89. Vell. Pat. 1.11.3.

longer their primary concern. Greek elements were seen once again to fit comfortably within the boundaries of Romanness.

Even as Greek cultural elements came to fit comfortably within the definition of Romanness by the end of the second century, significant questions remained about the place of Italian communities, despite (or perhaps because of) their greater geographical proximity. While the Roman religious actions in the first half of the second century explored here point to the Romans' underlying sense of a shared community between themselves and the other inhabitants of Italy, other actions, such as the periodic expulsions of those other people from the city, reveal a significant gap between that underlying sense of identity and the overt recognition of the place of Latins and Italians, especially in regard to citizenship. This question of legal status was not significant in the case of the Greeks, who could not contemplate going to Rome to vote in elections, a traditional prerogative of citizens, and who were not asked to fight on Rome's behalf, a traditional responsibility of citizens. In the case of the residents of the Italian peninsula, on the other hand, the possibility that they might indeed participate in the Roman political process raised a possible threat to the Roman elite's collective control of the process, a possibility that took visible form with the rise of the Gracchi. In a similar fashion, the distance and continuing cultural differences between Romans and Greeks may have made the incorporation of Greek cultural elements less of a threat to Roman identity; the very closeness of Romans and Italians may have made it harder to create distinctions with each passing year, causing the Italians to present a greater challenge to a clear sense of Roman identity. These questions revolving around social identity and legal status would prove difficult for the Romans to resolve.

The tension can be clearly seen in two expulsions of non-Romans from the city in the latter part of the second century, in the period following the tribunate of Tiberius Gracchus. In 126, a law proposed by the tribune M. Junius Pennus barred *peregrini* from the city, and four years later a similar banishment of all those who were not Roman occurred; the repetition again reveals the practical ineffectiveness of these measures.[90] Plutarch, our source for the latter expulsion, explicitly relates this decree to the strife engendered by the reform program of Caius Gracchus, claiming that "when a throng came together from all parts of Italy for his support, the senate prevailed upon the consul Fannius to drive out of the city all who were not Romans."[91] In this account, the Senate is presented as

90. Cic., *Off.* III.11.47, remarks on the expulsion carried out by Pennus, whom at *Brut.* 109 he dates to the year 126.

91. Plut. *C. Gracch.* 12: ὄχλου δὲ πανταχόθεν αὐτῷ συνιόντος ἔπεισεν ἡ βουλὴ τὸν ὕπατον Φάννιον ἐκβαλεῖν τοὺς ἄλλους πλὴν Ῥωμαίων ἅπαντας.

unwilling to share the prerogatives of being a Roman with those who were not legally citizens; a fragment from Fannius' speech, where Fannius explicitly links participation in the political process and in religious festivals with citizenship, confirms this interpretation of Fannius' behavior.[92] The difference between this expulsion and the expulsion of Italians from Rome earlier in the century, discussed in the previous chapter, is notable. Whereas the expulsions of the 180s and 170s were apparently prompted by the Italian communities themselves, concerned about emigration, those of the 120s were initiated by the Romans themselves, worried about immigration.

Yet we should not allow a focus on the legal status to dominate the question of the Romanness of other peoples inhabiting the Italian peninsula. The legal definition of citizenship might be important to a definition of social identity insofar as both Italians and Romans *saw* it as central to that definition, and the emphasis placed by our sources on questions of citizenship at this time may indicate that the legal definition of citizenship was in fact being used as a means of differentiation at this time.[93] But while the Roman elite seems to have been unwilling to consider the residents of the Italian peninsula as Roman citizens prior to the Social War, Latins and Italians did not suddenly become Roman with the passage of the *lex Julia de Civitate Latinis et Sociis Danda* in 90 and the *Lex Plautia Papiria de Civitate* the following year. Indeed, in light of the religious activity of the third century and first half of the second century discussed previously, the process had been under way for some time and had clearly reached different stages in different parts of Italy. The variety in the degree of integration may be reflected in the level of enthusiasm for the revolt; Etruria and Umbria, although they were on the verge of joining the revolt, nevertheless maintained their loyalty to Rome when the Senate granted them

92. Halm *Rhet. Lat.* 402. See chapter 5, pp. 150–51.

93. Studies of ethnic identity have stressed that characteristics such as language or religion (or citizenship) are not significant for determining group identity until they are *invested* with such significance by the group in question; cf. Hall (1997), 19–24, with further bibliography. The topic of Roman citizenship and the Italian communities is obviously too vast to be tackled in a mere footnote, but it is possible that a contributing factor to the struggles of this era was that over the course of the second century, citizenship may have evolved into a means of differentiating Rome from Italy, a new boundary to identify Romans; the events of the late second and early first centuries might thus be read as finding a way to make that boundary permeable as well, while still retaining a clear sense of Romanness. Fuller discussion of the issues leading up to the Social War can be found in Gabba (1954); Brunt (1965); Sherwin-White (1973), 134–149; and more recently Mouritsen (1998), among others; in particular, Mouritsen has argued that citizenship was not the initial aim of the allies.

citizenship, while the Samnites and Lucanians remained the most hostile to Rome.[94] This degree of integration may be seen in the religious actions of the Romans up to this point; although there is little evidence of the formal integration of Samnite or Lucanian religious elements, temples to deities popular in Etruria and Umbria had long been accepted in Rome, and the haruspices had been an established part of the Roman religious system for many years. For the people to whom the Romans had long been extending the boundaries of Romanness, the legal grant of citizenship in the first century did not so much create Romans out of whole cloth as recognize the facts on the ground.[95]

Roman religious actions in the years preceding the Social War reflect the varying relationships with Italian communities and the intense interest in defining their place in the Roman system at this time. If the reports of Julius Obsequens may be accepted, a large number of prodigies were accepted by the Senate from Etruria in the years preceding the war. We have seen how expiations often served to help demarcate the boundaries of Romanness, as prodigies are accepted from those places the Romans are willing to consider part of Rome; these reports from Etruria have been read as an attempt by the Roman Senate to shore up support among the Etruscan population.[96] Another religious action at this time suggests that even the place of the Latin communities came into question during this time of crisis. In 90 B.C.E., on the very eve of the Social War, the Senate responded to a dream of Caecilia Metella by ordering the restoration of the temple of Juno Sospita, the goddess whom the Romans had held in common with the Lanuvians since 338 B.C.E.[97] Unfortunately, our sources do not specify whether the temple rebuilt was the Lanuvian shrine or the one erected in Rome in 194, leading to much difficulty for us in

94. For Etruria and Umbria, see App. *B. Civ.* 1.49; for the Samnites and Lucanians, see App. *B. Civ.* 1.53, 1.68. See, however, Mouritsen (1998), 153–163, who suggests that the Etruscans and Umbrians may in fact have joined the revolt, only to be quickly defeated. At the least, Etruria and Umbria joined the hostilities late, suggesting some closer affinity to Rome than the other rebels.

95. Wallace-Hadrill (2008), esp. 451–452, offers another approach to the nexus between legal status and social position, arguing for the transformation of the very concept of Roman citizenship "from a reciprocal bundle of rights to a form of social dignity" and noting that in such circumstances, "it becomes more urgent to define culturally what 'being Roman' is about."

96. MacBain (1982), 78–79. See chapter 4, p. 135–36. It should be noted that prodigies were also accepted from the Vestini in 94 and 91; these may indicate a similar sense of acceptance by the Romans of a people whose territory bordered on Sabine country, although the Vestini nonetheless actively opposed the Romans during the war.

97. Cic. *Div.* 1.4; cf. Obsequens 55.

determining how this particular action should be interpreted.[98] Kragelund has argued for the Lanuvian site, interpreting the action as a means sponsored by the consul of 90 B.C.E. of "ensuring divine sanction for the policy of compromise" that was enacted by the *lex Iulia de civitate*.[99] Schultz, however, suggests that the temple in question must have been the Roman one, the position argued by most previous studies, and sees the action as a reminder to the Romans and the Latins of the earlier result of the conflict between the two parties, as well as a bid for the support of Juno in the upcoming hostilities.[100] Whichever temple was involved, the decision indicates a desire on the part of the Senate to restate the relationship between Rome and Lanuvium, which surely reflects uncertainty over the latter's status at this time; the question at stake is whether the action indicates that Lanuvium was or was not considered Roman. One might also note that prodigy reports from Lanuvium increased dramatically at this time, suggesting again concern about the place of this Latin city in the Roman world. In this light, even if the temple rebuilt was the one located in Rome, the decision to rebuild the temple of an important Latin deity may indicate a recognition of the special place held by the Latins within the Roman community. It could function simultaneously as a reminder of the special bonds between Romans and Latins and as a reminder of the result on the last occasion when the Latins had taken up arms against the Romans. The ambiguous position of the Latins, as both Roman and non-Roman simultaneously, and the challenges it posed for the Romans at the outset of the Social War are clearly revealed by this incident.[101]

The issue of whether the Italian communities, Latin and otherwise, would be given Roman citizenship was settled by the Social War, but one should not make the mistake of believing that the conclusion of the Social War automatically brought to a close the evolution of the Roman relationship with Italian towns. While the Social War marked a critical turning point in the relationship of Rome and the rest of Italy, numerous questions about the Romanness of the new Italian citizens remained. That the position of the Latins, the residents of the Italian peninsula who were perhaps closest to being considered

---

98. For the temple in Rome, see Livy 34.53; see also earlier here.

99. Kragelund (2001), esp. 169.

100. Schultz (2006b), 227. For earlier comments, see Gordon (1938), 25; Palmer (1974), 31; Chiarucci (1983), 73; and Richardson (1992), 217.

101. Mouritsen (1998), 159–161, has argued that Roman struggles in the first year of the Social War may be due to the reticence of the Latins to fully join with the Romans, a sign of the challenges faced by the Romans and suggesting that the Latins also felt the ambiguity of their position.

fully Roman, was uncertain on the very eve of the war suggests that resolution with all the peoples of Italy would not happen overnight. Although the Romans wanted to consider the Italians as part of the Roman enterprise, the degree to which they were willing to consider them Roman in every sense remained an open question.[102] To take an example from the legal perspective, the Romans certainly did not raise their allies to full political equality, even though they had granted them citizenship. The distribution of the new citizens only among ten new tribes rather than through the thirty-five existing ones significantly diminished their political rights, and the tensions created in attempting to resolve these legal and political questions ultimately demanded resolution further down the road. One reason that the question of the status, both legal and social, of the Italians proved so difficult was because it involved the very nature of Romanness: how was it to be defined? At the close of the Social War, this must have been the most pressing issue of the day, but it was soon eclipsed by an even more fundamental question: *who* would define it? In the wake of the Social War, the Romans embarked on another series of internal conflicts that again involved the very nature of Romanness, a conflict that overshadowed, in our sources at least, the Italian question. In the end, the resolution of the Roman civil wars, with the triumph of Octavian some sixty years later, brought resolution to both questions and set the course for the subsequent centuries. The challenges to Roman identity posed by that civil war, fought among the Romans themselves, and the role played in it by the Roman reaction to foreign religious traditions form the subject of the next chapter.

102. It is, of course, also an open question how much the Italians would have considered themselves Roman, or how much they wanted to do so. See further the remarks in the conclusion.

7

The Challenges of the First Century

More than questions about resolving the place of Italians, the Late Republic was marked by the increasingly violent competition among the Roman aristocracy for internal supremacy. This competition wreaked havoc not only on the consensus that had for so long marked the supremacy of the Roman Senate in the Roman state but also on the definition of Romanness. Indeed, from the point of view of identity, the most salient aspect of this period is its complete loss of coherence. In addition to the challenges posed by the expansion of citizenship to the Italian communities following the Social War, there was no longer any agreed-upon (if unwritten) sense of what comprised a true Roman among the Roman elite, but the very definition of Roman often constituted the most contested arena in the struggles among Roman politicians.[1] Were the followers of Sulla true Romans, even though they marched on the city? Or the followers of Marius, often willing to cast aside the traditional Roman governing processes? Were Pompey's followers, and later Brutus and Cassius' supporters, the true Romans, defending the Republic against the encroachment of a tyrant? Or was Caesar the true Roman, defending the prerogatives of the tribune and by extension the governmental structure of the state from, as Augustus put it, "the despotism of a faction"?[2] The impact of these struggles was felt throughout Roman society, in religious matters as well as elsewhere, and

1. Cf. the comments of Wallace-Hadrill (2000), 294–295.
2. Augustus *Res Gestae*, 1.1: *dominatione factionis.*

posed a grave challenge to the Romans' ability to define Romanness. Incidents such as the sacrilege of the rites of the Bona Dea and Clodius' subsequent acquittal and Bibulus' famed "watching the heavens" in an effort to obstruct Caesar's legislation during the momentous year of their consulship continued to call into question the sources of authority for interpreting the will of the gods. Religious developments of this period have long been an object of study, and the view that this period of the Late Republic represents the final stages in the decline of Roman religion has at last been supplanted by the recognition that the nature of Roman religion means that political struggles should naturally have been reflected in religious affairs.[3] In these circumstances, the Roman response to foreign religious elements can no longer be read as reflective of a sense of Romanness. The continued importance of religious activity to Roman politicians demonstrates the vitality of Roman religion, but this activity lacks coherence precisely because Roman identity itself lacks coherence in this period. The Roman response to foreign religious elements in this period provides not a view of the development of Romanness, but a window through which to observe the conflict revolving around who should be included as Roman, and who should determine who should be included.

The Gracchi are often viewed by modern historians as marking a critical turning point in Roman history, the first time, as Plutarch famously noted, that a political dispute had ended in internal bloodshed, and the religious actions following the deaths of the Gracchi brothers already reveal significant contrasts with earlier religious behavior. Cicero reports that in the aftermath of Tiberius Gracchus' death, numerous prodigies led the Senate to order a consultation of the Sibylline Books, "where it was found that the most ancient Ceres needed to be placated. Thus priests of the Roman people from the most distinguished decemviral college, although in our city there was a most beautiful and magnificent temple, nevertheless they set out for Henna."[4] Cicero highlights the unusual aspect of this mission, that when the Romans first decided that Ceres needed to be propitiated, they elected to do so at her sanctuary in Sicily, despite the fact that a temple to Ceres had stood in Rome since the early fifth century.

3. Most early studies of Roman religion tended to look at the late Republic as a period of declining religiosity; see, for instance, Taylor (1949) and Dumézil (1970), 526–550. This paradigm has been effectively destroyed by numerous recent studies; see, in particular, Beard, North, and Price (1998) 10–13, 114–134; Scheid (1987, 2003).

4. Cic., *Verr.* 2.4.108: *ex quibus inventum est Cererem antiquissimam placari oportere. Tum ex amplissimo collegio decemvirali sacerdotes populi Romani, cum esset in urbe nostra Cereris pulcherrimum et magnificentissimum templum, tamen usque Hennam profecti sunt.* Cicero's purpose in emphasizing the sanctuary in Henna is, of course, to emphasize Verres' impiety, but the embassy to Henna is confirmed by Val. Max. 1.1.1.

The decision to use this overseas sanctuary undermines the notion that placating Ceres, a goddess with close ties to the plebeians, was meant to placate the lower classes in the wake of Tiberius' death.[5] Extending an olive branch in this fashion would have been more effective at the Roman site, both because of that cult's already established links to the plebs and because its presence in the city of Rome would have made the gesture immediately visible to the intended audience. Another explanation for the selection of Henna has to be found.

On the one hand, the decision to propitiate Ceres on the island of Sicily reveals continuity with the actions undertaken earlier in the second century, extending to Sicily the sense of what counted as Roman from the religious standpoint. The Sicilian context is important here. Henna had been the locus of the Sicilian slave revolt led by Eunous, which must have been quelled only months before the embassy to Henna was dispatched.[6] This revolt came at a time when the Romans were beginning to organize the exploitation of Sicily's agricultural potential; indeed, the Roman general Rupilius, in the immediate aftermath of his success in suppressing the revolt, put in place regulations for the island with the help of ten commissioners sent from Rome. The mission to Henna may have been intended to demonstrate renewed Roman control of the sanctuary after the revolt, and thus the restoration of Roman power in Sicily. It may also have drawn attention, in typical Roman fashion, to the anger of the goddess as an explanation for the troubles in Rome at this time.[7] More significantly for our purposes, however, the acceptance that the despoliation of a Sicilian sanctuary by slave rebels affected the Roman relationship with their gods acknowledged the inclusion of the sanctuary within the boundaries of "Roman." In this way, the embassy can be seen as extending to an overseas territory, even if only just across a narrow strait, a similar treatment that had been extended to various Italian communities over the past fifty years.

Viewed from a different perspective, however, the embassy to Henna marks a departure from previous practice and a foreshadowing of religious activity over the next century. It is difficult to escape the conclusion that the embassy to Henna represented an effort by the senatorial opponents of Tiberius to justify the killing of the tribune. Several scholars have drawn attention to the fact that Scipio Nasica pulled the hem of his cloak around his head as

---

5. For the suggestion that the embassy was meant as an overture to the plebs, see Le Bonniec (1958), 367–369; Astin (1967), 227; Stockton (1979), 87–88; MacBain (1982), 38–39. The suggestion is firmly rejected by Spaeth (1990).

6. Cf. Flower (2006), 71–72.

7. Flower (2006), 73–74.

he encouraged his supporters to the forum and that this gesture is significant coming from the *pontifex maximus*.[8] Barbette Spaeth has convincingly argued that Scipio's action should be understood as an attempt to indicate that this action was a *consecratio capitis*, a justified response to an individual who violated the laws of *sacrosanctitas*, as Tiberius had arguably done in regard to the deposition of Octavius, and attempted a tyranny.[9] She suggests that the embassy to Henna served as part of the senatorial campaign to support this interpretation of the events of 133, because Ceres was the goddess involved in the *consecratio* ritual. The choice of Henna as the location for expiation makes sense in this context precisely because of the plebeian associations of the Roman temple; an attempt to bolster the senatorial position through the use of this plebeian stronghold would undoubtedly have been met with hostility and possibly with more violence. The result, however, had significant implications. On the one hand, the status of the Roman temple was undermined in favor of an overseas sanctuary, challenging the very notion of what a Roman sanctuary was; the Senate's action suggested that in certain contexts the Henna sanctuary might be more appropriate for a Roman ceremony than the traditional sanctuary in Rome. The particular context here is significant as well; according to his opponents, Tiberius had been killed for behaving in an un-Roman fashion, calling for a crown and seeking to become a king.[10] In suggesting that the sanctuary in Henna was more Roman than the Aventine, the senatorial elite may also have been suggesting that some Romans, and their followers, were not truly Roman. What is significant in this situation is how the religious activity functioned to drive a wedge into Roman society. While religious activity had long been a part of political competition in Rome, a primary feature of Roman religious behavior during the Republic up to this point had been the remarkable degree of consensus it represented among the aristocracy. Individuals might compete for positions of primacy, but that competition concerned the status of individuals in regard to their position within the Roman aristocracy, while maintaining the collective values and power of the aristocracy.[11] If Roman religious activity of the third and second centuries reflects how the Romans struggled to develop a sense of Romanness

8. The detail is recounted by Plutarch (*Ti. Gracch.* 19) and by Appian (*B.Civ.* 1.16).

9. Spaeth (1990). See also Badian (1972), Linderski (2002), and most recently Clark (2007).

10. Cf. Plutarch's account of Tiberius' death (19), where Tiberius' opponents interpret his hand gestures as calling for a crown, and also the story preserved in Plutarch (14) that Tiberius had been presented with a royal diadem and a purple robe by Eudemus of Pergamum.

11. Cf. Orlin (1997). On aristocratic competition in Rome, see also Wiseman (1985), 3–20; Rosenstein (1990).

in regard to overseas cultures, the action of sending the embassy to Henna reflects the beginning of the struggle to redefine that sense of identity in regard to their own community.

This shift is even more evident in the religious activity following the death of Caius Gracchus twelve years later. Like his older brother, Caius was killed as a result of violence that arose in connection with the political struggle over his reform program, and the sources present the fighting that claimed his life as far more premeditated on both sides than the violence that resulted in the death of Tiberius.[12] And as with his older brother, there was a religious aspect to the Senate's behavior after his death; although no source implies a *consecratio* to Ceres or Jupiter, the bodies of Caius, Fulvius, and three thousand of their followers were thrown into the Tiber, and their property was seized and sold, elements that recall the *consecratio*. More clearly, the consul Opimius performed a *lustratio* to purify the city of the bloodshed and erected a temple to Concordia, possibly at the behest of the Senate.[13] The temple of Concordia reveals the changed atmosphere of the period; in suggesting that Concordia needed to be propitiated at a time when clearly no harmony existed in the state, the sponsors suggested that those who continued their opposition were at fault and risked the wrath of the goddess. That *concordia* could be seen to exist only among the supporters of the victorious side not only is evident to us but also was apparently clear to contemporaries, for according to Plutarch, someone carved the following remark below the inscription on the temple: "A work of mad discord produces a temple of Concord." The graffiti reveals the competing visions of Roman society, made more explicit by Plutarch's further commentary on how the temple was received by the people: "It was felt that he [Opimius] was priding himself and exulting and in a manner celebrating a triumph in view of all this slaughter of citizens."[14] The building of a temple after the conclusion of a successful military campaign over an enemy was a well-known tradition in Rome; if Opimius' temple was indeed likened to a manubial temple, it would only underscore the Senate's view that the defeated party—Caius Gracchus, Fulvius Flaccus, and other clearly Roman citizens—was not in fact Roman at all, but a foreign enemy. This representation, too, was challenged by the people, who, again according to Plutarch, consecrated the places where the Gracchi were slain, brought offerings and made sacrifices at those places, and fell

12. For the narrative of the end of Caius' life, see Plut. *C. Gracch.* 13–17; App. *B. Civ.* 1.25–26.

13. Appian *B. Civ.* 1.26 reports that the Senate ordered the temple; Plutarch *C. Gracch.* 17 says only that Opimius erected the temple.

14. Plut. *C. Gracch.* 17.

down before statues erected of the brothers "as though they were visiting the shrines of gods."[15] The supporters of Gracchus thus also had recourse to a religious action to express their views. The religious activity following the death of Caius Gracchus, even more than the embassy to propitiate the Ceres of Henna that followed the death of Tiberius, reflects contestation over the very notion of who was a Roman that was emerging at this time.[16]

The importance of trying to define Roman behavior in the midst of these clashes is revealed in a senatorial action from just prior to the outbreak of the Social War. In 97 B.C.E., the Senate passed a decree banning human sacrifice, by which no man might be immolated.[17] If we take Pliny's language literally, practices that moderns might consider to be human sacrifice, such as the punishment of errant Vestal Virgins by burying them alive, do not seem to have been part of the ban, which referred specifically to the burning of the victim. The Senate thus determined to isolate certain forms of the ritual killing of human beings as non-Roman, even as they allowed other forms, and even though the Romans themselves had performed the now-outlawed style of human sacrifice in the forum on several occasions, as recently as 114/113.[18] Human sacrifice from this point forward became a marker of "bad" religion for the Romans. For instance, the ancient sources are full of stories about Carthaginian child sacrifice, but there is no evidence that such accusations of human sacrifice were a contemporary charge at the time of the Punic Wars; Livy and Polybius make no mention of this accusation. It appears in the first century B.C.E., after the Senate's ban, in the writings of Cicero and Diodorus Siculus and is especially picked up by Christian authors, eager to discredit pagan religious practices.[19] In Roman sources, human sacrifice is frequently associated with the Gauls; Julius Caesar comments on the practice in the later first century B.C.E., as do Pomponius Mela and Pliny in the first century C.E.[20] In light of the campaigns led by Marius and Catulus in the last decade of the second century B.C.E., the Senate's ban on human sacrifice seems oriented more toward the Gauls; that religious practice was henceforward defined as non-Roman, even if the Romans previously had no qualms about it. It is possible to see this action as also precipitated by internal Roman struggles; just three years earlier, during the disturbances associated with Saturninus, the Roman Senate had declared a tribune, a praetor, and a

15. Plut. *C. Gracch.* 18.

16. Cf. the remarks of Flower (2006), 77–78.

17. For the ban, see Plin. *HN* 30.3.

18. The incident in 113 is reported by Plutarch (*Quaest. Rom.* 83). See Rives (1995), 77–80, and also Beard, North, and Price (1998), 233–234.

19. Cic. *Rep.* 3.13–15; Diod. Sic. 20.24; Tert. *Apol.* 9.6–8; Min. Fel., *Oct.* 30.2.

20. Caes., *B. Gall.* 6.16.1; Mela, 3.18; Plin., *HN* 30.3.

quaestor to be public enemies, and these three, along with others, had been stoned to death by a mob.[21] This battle again brought the question of Romanness to the fore, as these officers of the Roman state were decreed to be no longer citizens worthy of the protection of the law. The ban on human sacrifice demonstrates the ability of the Roman Senate to continue to define some practices as non-Roman and thus, in the broadest strokes, provide an image of Roman identity, even as the struggles to define more exactly who counted as a Roman wreaked havoc on that image. It is worth noting that the effort to place human sacrifice outside the bounds of Romanness was so successful that within a century, Livy could write about the sacrifice of two Greeks and two Gauls in 216 that it was *minime Romano sacro*.[22] Amid the conflict of the Late Republic, this practice was one on which all factions could agree.

The ensuing years saw not only the increasing division of the Roman elite into camps based on allegiance to one leader or another but also sharper lines being drawn in the battle over Romanness that make the interpretation of actions in regard to foreign religions even more problematic. The divisions expanded both internally, between Romans in the struggle between Marius and Sulla, and externally, between Romans and Italians in the Social War. In 88 and 87, Sulla and Marius took turns labeling each other as *hostes* or enemies, formally declaring that the other and his followers should no longer be considered Roman citizens and entitled to the protection of the laws, and these declarations were enforced by arms.[23] The contest over defining Romanness could not be starker; these declarations for the first time marked some members of the Roman elite as legally non-Roman, based on nothing more than political affinity, and as such escalated the contest and the implications of being Roman. The contest between Marius and Sulla took place at almost the same time as Rome's Italian allies took up arms against the state, driven in no small part by the refusal of the Roman government to extend the privileges of citizenship to those who had fought for centuries on behalf of Rome's imperial conquests, as discussed in the previous chapter.[24] The religious activity of this period, especially in regard to non-Roman religious elements, needs to be understood against the backdrop of these challenges to the notion of Roman identity.

Marius and Sulla have been noted as among the first Romans to claim an individual connection with a divinity, and a foreign one at that, as a

21. App. *B.Civ.* 1.32.

22. Livy 22.57.6.

23. On the declarations of *hostis*, see Plut. *Sull.* 22; App. *B. Civ.* 1.73, 77, 81. For discussion see Ungern-Sternberg von Pürkel (1970), 74–78; Nippel (1988), 91–92.

24. On the Social War, see Wulff Alonso (2002); Mouritsen (1998), 129–171; Brunt (1988), 93–143; Gabba (1976), 70–130.

means of elevating themselves above other Roman politicians.[25] Despite the best efforts of the Senate to prevent politicians from using divination to advance their own political careers, both Marius and Sulla made use of foreign oracles to build support for themselves. Marius apparently maintained a prophetess named Martha in his entourage, carried in a litter with such pomp that Plutarch claims the soldiers questioned whether Marius really believed in her prophecies or was merely pretending to do so in order to gain support.[26] Two points about this woman are worth noting: Plutarch reports that she hailed from Syria and also that the Senate had rejected her when she wished to prophesy before them concerning the war with the Cimbri and Teutones. Here we can see the contest moving to the realm of who might define appropriate sources of divinatory authority. The Senate's decision to reject the authority of Martha's prophecies as valid for the Romans was challenged by Marius, who triumphed via force of arms; Marius' victory at Aquae Sextiae is what lent legitimacy to the prophecies. The foreignness of the prophetess used by Marius and rejected by the Senate is noteworthy, but the meaning is elusive; since the traditional Roman forms of divination, such as the haruspices or the Sibylline Books, were strictly controlled by the Senate to ensure its dominant position in religious affairs, Marius' use of a Syrian prophetess may reflect merely the use of an available avenue for a more personal source of divination. It may thus represent a challenge to the Senate's authority, rather than any specific attitude toward Syrian culture.[27] It would also not be wise to derive the Senate's attitude toward foreign sources of divination from its rejection of Martha, especially as Plutarch records that at approximately the same time, Bataces, a priest of the Magna Mater, came to Rome with a prophecy that the Romans were going to be victorious, a prophecy the Senate accepted.[28] It may be that the place of Asia within the Roman system had long been accepted, or again it may be that the Magna Mater was a goddess who had been introduced by the Senate through the medium of the Sibylline Books and so was seen as an acceptable source of prophecy. These episodes clearly reveal the sharp divisions over the ability to define legitimate sources of divinatory authority, but it is impossible, in light of the factional struggles of the time,

25. Scipio Africanus seems to have fostered a relationship with the gods unlike that of any previous Roman, but apparently not to the extent cultivated by Marius and Sulla. For the evidence, see Poly., 10.2.20; also Gell. *NA* 6.1; Livy 36.19 Cf. Tondriau (1949); Walbank (1967); Beard, North, and Price (1998), 84–86.

26. Plut. *Mar.* 17.1–3.

27. For Roman forms of divination and the Senate's careful control of these avenues, see North (1990).

28. Plut. *Mar.* 17.5.

to read these actions as statements of the Roman elite either in favor of or against particular foreign sources of divination.

Nor was Marius alone in seeking to use divination in this fashion, for Sulla responded similarly, also utilizing the favor of foreign sources of divination. Plutarch reports that during his time in Cappadocia in the 90s, Sulla encountered a Chaldaean soothsayer who remarked that Sulla was destined to become the greatest man in the world.[29] Although this incident may have been a chance meeting rather than an attempt to formally employ Chaldaeans on his behalf, Sulla found the Chaldaeans important enough to include their utterances in his memoirs, making it likely that he advertised their prophecies of his good fortune earlier in his career as well.[30] In regard to religious support from foreign traditions, Sulla is most frequently connected with the Cappadocian goddess Ma. Plutarch records two occasions on which Ma prophesied success for Sulla: once prior to his fateful march on Rome, when the goddess appeared to him in a dream (another form of prophecy favored by Sulla) and helped him defeat his enemies with a thunderbolt, and a second time during the civil war of 83, when a slave declared that he brought Sulla triumph and victory from the goddess.[31] It has been suggested that Sulla was responsible for the introduction of Ma to Rome, though it is more likely that she was already known in Rome and that Sulla's connection to her merely added to her popularity.[32] It seems that Sulla may have constructed one or more shrines to Ma-Bellona, though the assimilation to Bellona makes it difficult to definitively establish the presence of the Cappadocian goddess in these shrines. It is important to note, however, that even if Sulla were responsible for the construction of one or more shrines to Ma, the *fasti* give no indication of the addition of Ma to the state

29. Plut. *Sull.* 5.5. Cf. also Vell. Pat. 2.24.3, where the word *magi* is used to denote the prophets.

30. On the citation of the Chaldeans in his memoirs, see Plut. *Sull.* 37.2. Cf. Keaveney (1983), 50.

31. Plut. *Sull.* 9.6; 27.11. For the latter episode, see also August. *De. Civ. D.* 2.24. In the latter episode, the goddess is called Bellona, but since Plutarch indicates in the first passage that the goddess was called variously Luna, Minerva, or Bellona, it has been universally assumed that this second message also came from the Cappadocian goddess.

32. The notion that Sulla was responsible for bringing Ma to Rome was argued by Alföldi (1976), esp. 150–151, based on coin evidence; Fishwick (1967), 152–154, and Keaveney (1983), 65, suggest the evidence is too thin to bear the weight of the conclusion. Sulla's dreams are indeed the earliest mentions of Ma in a Roman context, but imperial inscriptions call her a *pedisequa* of the Magna Mater, raising the possibility that Ma followed Cybele, another goddess from Asia Minor, at some point in the second century. For the inscriptions, unfortunately undated, see *CIL* VI.30851; Dessau, *ILS* 3084.

festival calendar.[33] If these shrines did exist, therefore, they do not seem to have become part of the state religious system and so again tell us only that Sulla on his own personal authority recognized this goddess as a legitimate religious authority; that status was clearly contested by others and did not formally become part of the Roman system. That both Marius and Sulla felt comfortable identifying themselves with, and depending upon, foreign religious authorities, even in the midst of their struggles to present themselves as legitimate Romans and their opponents as *hostes*, provides a striking confirmation of the Romans' willingness to absorb foreign elements—and also of the growing challenges to determining what elements could now be considered as Roman.

Even elements that had long been accepted as part of the Roman religious system came under renewed scrutiny during this period. The episode involving Marius and the priest of the Magna Mater points in this direction; when Bataces wanted to come before the people, he was prevented by the tribune Aulus Pompeius, contesting the legitimacy of the prophecy and calling Bataces an impostor.[34] As discussed earlier, the Magna Mater had been installed as part of the state religion since 204, when the Roman Senate voted to import the black stone representing the goddess from Asia Minor.[35] This episode again speaks to the highly contested nature of prophetic utterances in the Late Republic, here extended to the priest of a cult that had long been part of the Roman religious system. The epilogue to the story is interesting in its own right: Aulus died of a fever within a week, which according to Plutarch lent credence to the position of Bataces. Presumably the Magna Mater was thought to have intervened and caused the death of Aulus, and in this way the position of the cult was reaffirmed. But the cult

33. Dio Cass. (42.26.2) refers to an Ἐννεῖον that was destroyed in 48 B.C.E., which would provide a *terminus ante quem* for the goddess if in fact Ma was worshipped here. He reports that jars of human flesh were discovered in the shrine, leading to the opinion, expressed in Platner and Ashby and Richardson (1992), among other modern texts, that this building must have been a temple to Ma-Bellona, but this is hardly Dio's usual word for a temple. The shrine was apparently part of a larger sanctuary of Isis and Sarapis, since it was discovered during the destruction of that sanctuary, which further suggests that Ma, even if worshipped here, was not part of the state religion but was tolerated in this location along with other deities from the East.

A separate temple to a Bellona Pulvinensis is known exclusively from inscriptions (Dessau, *ILS* 4080–4082) and is thought to have stood near the Porta Collina; the name of the goddess and the location have led Palmer (1975), 660, and Richardson (1992), 58, to suggest that this temple was also dedicated by Sulla to the Cappadocian Ma in thanks for his victory in the civil wars.

34. Plut. *Mar.* 17.5.

35. As discussed previously, pp. 76–82.

of the Magna Mater continued to be a focal point for skirmishing among Roman politicians. According to Cicero, Clodius engineered the expulsion of a priest of the Magna Mater from Rome while serving as tribune of the plebs.[36] Cicero provides no context for this action, using it merely to cast aspersions on Clodius' impiety, so it is impossible to know whether Clodius' action represents a reaction against the cult of the Magna Mater by a certain segment of the Roman population or whether this expulsion was simply a tool Clodius used in pursuit of other political goals. Yet as much as Clodius may have attacked the cult, Cicero felt as comfortable defending it, placing the expulsion of the priest on the same level as an attack on the auspices. The divisions among the Roman elite can clearly be read in these actions regarding a cult that had been part of the state religion for over a century, making Romanness increasingly hard to discern.

Sulla's religious behavior offers another window into activity that was to have a profound effect on Roman identity, an action that during the Late Republic sowed additional disunity but was eventually to become a source of renewed stability. Sulla was among the first Roman politicians to claim a direct personal relationship with a divinity that favored him and the first, apparently, to claim Venus in that role.[37] Sulla's use of the cognomen *Epaphroditos* is well known, and Appian indicates that the Roman Senate confirmed his right to use this name.[38] Interestingly, the term was used in the eastern part of the Roman world, while its counterpart in Rome was *felix*, a term not exactly synonymous in meaning. It has been suggested that Sulla's use of the term in the East was meant to help him, and the Romans, resume the exploitation of the Greek East in the wake of the Mithridatic Wars, drawing the Greek elites into closer cooperation by a reminder of their cultural links.[39] Appian also records a response given to Sulla by an oracle, most likely Delphi, that emphasized the relationship between Aeneas and the Romans, acknowledged that Venus favored the Romans, and called upon Sulla to make an offering at Aphrodisias at the sanctuary of the goddess. This initiative, while not reflective of the Roman aristocracy as a whole, set precedents that cut in several directions. On the one hand, the connection to Venus would become one of the stabilizing elements of Roman identity, as Sulla's use of Venus and the Aeneas myth would be more fully exploited by Augustus. On the other, this result was possible only because of Augustus'

36. Cic. *Sest.* 56.
37. On the phenomenon in general, see Tondriau (1949). On Sulla, see Keaveney (1983), 56–64, especially 60–64 on Venus.
38. Plut. *Sull.* 34.4; App. *B. Civ.* 1.97.
39. Santangelo (2007), 199–213, esp. 210–213.

military triumph in the civil wars; in the Late Republic, associations with Venus were profoundly destabilizing, as both Pompey and Caesar would later seek to present themselves as specially favored by Venus, both generals building temples in honor of the goddess.[40] The behavior of the dynasts in the generation after Sulla reveals the increasing struggle over defining the "true Roman"; the person who could claim the favor of Venus, ancestor of the Roman people, might have the better claim to that title, but that claim was contested by all parties.

Even in the light of the increased competition for power, Roman religious behavior in the late Republic and early Empire shows marked continuities with earlier periods. The willingness of the Roman elite to consider foreign elements as integral to Roman identity, even as they continued to grapple with the very question of Romanness, is perhaps the clearest indication of this continuity. The very fighting between Roman forces that took place on Sulla's return to Italy provides the backdrop for a clear example. During the fighting in 83 B.C.E., the temple of Jupiter Optimus Maximus was burned, along with the Sibylline Books that had long been stored in a chest in the temple's cella.[41] The Sibylline Books themselves, reputedly purchased by Tarquin the Proud from an unknown old woman, represent one of the most prominent foreign elements in Roman religion and were responsible for the introduction of a number of foreign elements, including several temples already discussed.[42] Their placement in the temple of Jupiter on the Capitoline hill, the central temple of the Roman religious system, indicates the degree to which the Romans accepted the books as Roman. The Romans kept no copies of the original Sibylline Books, so in 76 B.C.E., the Senate authorized a mission to search for replacements. The results of this mission might seem surprising; while Vergil and other authors of the Augustan period locate the Sibyl's true home at Cumae in southern Italy, the Senate voted specifically to send three

40. Pompey's temple of Venus Victrix was connected with his famous theater; Caesar's temple to Venus Genetrix was erected in his new forum. Plutarch suggests that some people interpreted the maneuvering concerning Venus in this light; in relating Pompey's dream (Plut. *Pomp.* 68) before the battle of Pharsalus that the temple of Venus Victrix was being decorated with spoils, the biographer indicates that some accounts related that Pompey was encouraged by the omen, but others that he was depressed, feeling that the omen presaged success for the offspring of Venus.

41. On the burning of the temple, see Cic. *Cat.* III.9; Sall. *Cat.* 47.2; Tac. *Hist.* III.72; App. *B. Civ.* I.83, 86; Plut. *Sull.* 27; on the loss of the Sibylline books, see Dion. Hal., *Ant. Rom.* IV.62. Sulla apparently began the rebuilding (cf. Val. Max. IX.3.8; Tac. *Hist.* 3.72), but the new temple was not dedicated until 69 (Livy *Ep.* 98; Plut. *Publicola* 15).

42. On the Sibylline Books in general, see Orlin (1997), 76–115; Parke (1988), 136–152, 190–215.

envoys to Erythrae in Asia Minor, thus clearly accepting those oracles as authentic.[43] While this decision clearly reflects the continued Roman confidence about the absorption of foreign religious elements, it may also reflect two additional impulses relevant to the sense of Roman community at this time. On the one hand, it may suggest the continuing tensions following the conclusion of the Social War. While the war ended with the extension of the franchise to most of peninsular Italy, the voting power of the new citizens was diluted by confining them to the rural tribes, a clear indication of the unease Romans felt in regard to the position of the Italians. Campania had been a hot bed of resentment, and Cumae, on the coast west of Naples, may have been considered insufficiently settled, or perhaps too close to Samnite territory, one of the regions that remained uneasily integrated into the Roman community.[44] On the other hand, the Romans had serious concerns with Asia; the First and Second Mithridatic Wars had only recently been concluded, and the tensions that would erupt in the Third Mithridatic War were building. Mithridates felt sufficiently confident in his control of Erythrae in the 80s that he sent hostages taken from rebellious cities to the city. For the Romans to indicate that they considered the Sibylline oracles from Erythrae to be the most authentic announced the importance that they attached to that city, as well as to the rest of western Asia Minor, as members of the Roman community. As noted earlier, this statement may have been easier for the Romans to make in regard to Asia, as those relationships were not encumbered with the complications of citizenship. But it is nonetheless remarkable that even in this period, when the very notion of Romanness was challenged on so many fronts, both internal and external, the Senate was still able to declare that Erythrae was possessed of authentically "Roman" Sibylline oracles. The challenges to Roman identity posed by the civil wars did not lead to an inward turn.

Roman behavior in regard to the Egyptian goddess Isis, the foreign cult that has attracted the most scholarly attention in this period because of its

43. Dion Hal. *Ant. Rom.* 4.62. While Dionysius does note that other oracles came from cities in Italy, he does not mention any by name, and he follows the mention of the Senate and Erythrae by indicating that some came transcribed by private citizens and that some of those were easily determined to be false. The implication is clearly that those from Erythrae were not only thought to be authentic but also, uniquely, had the senatorial seal of approval. Cf. also Tac. *Ann.* 6.12.4, who also mentions Erythrae in addition to several other locations, but makes no specific mention of any location in Italy.

44. That the Augustan writers saw Cumae as the true home of the Sibyl is no obstacle here; such views merely Augustus' efforts, and success, in fully integrating the Italian communities into the Roman state.

later prominence in Roman political and cultural history, reflects a continuation of similar attitudes. Worship of this goddess had been established by
the early part of the first century B.C.E., as attested particularly by a funerary
inscription listing a priest of Isis.[45] The earliest literary mention of Isis
derives from Varro, who described how in 59 Sarapis, Isis, Harpocrates, and
Anubis had been banned from the Capitol by the Senate, and how the altars,
destroyed by order of the Senate, were restored by popular resistance.[46] The
end of this story recounts that on the first day of the following year, the new
consul Gabinius apparently gave grudging permission for sacrifices in
response to the popular outcry but continued to forbid the construction of
altars. Five years later, Dio reports that the Senate ordered that shrines that
had been erected at private expense should be torn down, and five years
after that, in 48 B.C.E., in response to an omen at a statue of Hercules, the
Senate ordered that all precincts to Isis and Sarapis should be completely
dug up.[47] Several points from the literary sources are worth noting here. The
most obvious is the acceptance of Isis in Rome prior to 59 B.C.E., to the
point that altars actually stood on the Capitoline hill, the religious heart of
the city; this point squares well with the inscriptional evidence. We might
also note the increasing severity of the measures taken against the cult, from
removal of one set of altars to destruction of shrines to the complete digging
up of the precincts. At the same time, it is clear that these measures did not
result in the total elimination of Isis worship; M. Volusius, aedile in 43,

45. *CIL* VI.2247 = Dessau, *ILS* 4405 = *ILLRP* 159. The date of between 90 and 60
B.C.E., suggested by Coarelli (1984), is the most widely accepted. But see also Degrassi in
ILLRP, who preferred 58 B.C.E., and Malaise (1972), who proposes 48 B.C.E.

46. Tert. *Ad. Nat.* 10.

47. 53: Dio Cass. 40.47; 48: Dio Cass. 42.26. The language of the final action in 48
may be significant; Dio says τεμενίσματα κατασκάψαι, a phrase that may translate
the Roman *exauguratio*, a formal Roman ceremony for transforming a religious locale
back into a secular one—a much stronger action than simply razing a sanctuary to the
ground.

An incident related by Valerius Maximus (1.3.4) has sometimes been considered in
this context. According to Valerius, the consul L. Aemilius Paullus took an axe to the
doors of a shrine of Isis and Serapis, and the consul of 50 has been identified as the most
likely candidate, in light of the other senatorial actions mentioned previously. However,
four earlier consuls of the same name are possible, and Coarelli (1984), 463, has suggested the early second century, when actions were taken against the Bacchic cult in
Rome, as a likely context. Coarelli's suggestion would obviously mean that the cult of
Isis was known in Rome as far back as 168 B.C.E. In the absence of corroborating evidence for any date, it seems best to leave this incident to the side, but its absence has no
impact on the argument presented here; in the context of the Late Republic, it would
simply provide one additional example of an action taken against the cult of Isis.

managed to escape proscription by dressing as a priest of Isis; in the same year, the triumvirs apparently vowed a temple to Isis.[48]

Note that these actions took place prior to Cleopatra's rise to prominence and so cannot be connected to the queen's self-representation as Isis or the Senate's response to her ambitions. Rather, these actions are more likely to be connected to the prominence of Egyptian affairs in Roman politics at this time. The status of Egypt seems to have been an open question since 87 B.C.E., when Ptolemy Alexander bequeathed his kingdom to Rome, though in 63, it seems that the Romans had not yet formally accepted the bequest.[49] Ptolemy Auletes, who had taken the throne in the meantime, had been attempting to gain acknowledgment of his status for many years and in 59 provided Julius Caesar a large sum of money in exchange for recognition as a friend and ally of the Roman people.[50] In 58, Clodius, as tribune, pushed a bill through the assembly annexing Cyprus, ostensibly part of Egypt, thereby depriving Ptolemy of part of his territory. When the Alexandrians showed their displeasure with Auletes through rioting, the king thought it best to leave Egypt and to seek further support in Rome, where he arrived in 57. The issue of restoring Auletes proved highly controversial, as both Pompey and Lentulus Spinther sought the command, and a Sibylline oracle was found that, conveniently, forbade the restoration of an Egyptian king by Roman troops. Ultimately, the very same Gabinius who had blocked the use of altars for Isis in 58 restored Auletes to the throne in 55 while serving as governor of Syria. Gabinius was subsequently accused and acquitted of leaving his province without permission, although he was convicted of accepting a bribe from Ptolemy to come to his rescue.

These political machinations and the shifting political alliances in Rome provide the context within which the measures against the worship of Egyptian divinities were taken and make it impossible to regard those actions as reflective of Roman thinking about the place of Egypt within the Roman system. The Romans were clearly divided in their responses, and Egypt offered

48. Volusius: App. *B. Civ.* 4.47; Val. Max. 7.3.8. Triumvirs' vow: Dio Cass. 47.16. There is no evidence this vow was fulfilled; it may well have been a casualty of the ensuing conflict between Antony and Octavian. As the vow predated Antony's meeting with Cleopatra, however, the original vow must be understood on its own terms, not as part of the battle between the dynasts.

49. The information comes to us from Cic. *Leg. agr.* 2.41, where he says that there was an *auctoritas senatus* that the bequest should be accepted, but that apparently did not translate into a formal acceptance of the bequest. See Shatzman (1971) for a good summary of this and subsequent events.

50. For Caesar's role in 59, see Cic. *Att.* 2.16.2; *Rab Post.* 6; Caesar, *B. Civ.* 3.107; Suet. *Iul.* 54.3; Dio Cass. 39.12.1.

simply another venue in which Roman politicians played out their struggles, each attempting to define themselves as representative of Roman authority. Thus, while many analyses of these measures have tended to see them as anti-Egyptian, these incidents have also been examined from the perspective of who might have gained a short-term political advantage from these repeated assaults on Isis. Connections have been posited between Isis and Pompey and between Isis and Clodius, leading scholars to suggest that actions against Isis should be seen as political moves designed to weaken one or the other of these leaders.[51] Analysis along the lines of immediate political concerns might make sense of the actions of Gabinius, who opposed the altars to Isis in Rome in 58 but was willing to use Roman legions to restore Ptolemy Auletes to his throne in 55; Gabinius can certainly not be seen as an implacable opponent of all things Egyptian. Yet the evidence is too sparse and Roman loyalties too transient for us to determine which Roman politicians might have sought to suppress the worship of Egyptian deities and what purposes they might have hoped to accomplish.

Indeed, interpretations based on attitudes toward Egypt or political advantage may not be as productive as a consideration of the role of the Senate in examining the series of actions in regard to Isis. The Senate in our sources is generally presented as unified in opposition to the cult of Isis, which appears to have drawn many of its adherents from the nonelite; Tertullian's account certainly suggests that the Egyptian divinities were popular with the lower classes.[52] The inscription mentioned as the earliest evidence for the cult of Isis in Rome may leave the same impression; eight of thirteen people listed on the inscription are freedmen.[53] Worship of Egyptian divinities was clearly well established in Rome prior to the 50s, though not in any official manner, and Gabinius' action may well have been an attempt to reassert senatorial authority in matters of religion, one of the traditional spheres of senatorial control; Gabinius' argument against

51. The connection to Clodius was suggested by Coarelli (1984); Hayne (1992) proposed, less plausibly, a connection to Pompey. Takács (1995) avoids a strictly political reading.

52. The incident noted by Valerius Maximus, 1.3.4, might also lend support to this hypothesis: the consul Aemilius Paullus is forced to wield the axe himself because he could find no laborer willing to take action against the goddess. On the problems of dating this incident, see n. 46. On the popularity of Isis with the lower classes, see further Versluys (2002), 459.

53. CIL VI.2247 = Dessau, ILS 4405 = ILLRP 159. See Takács (1995), 51–56, for a recent discussion; she argues that the presence of so many freedmen should *not* be read as a sign of the cult's appeal to the 'socially disadvantaged,' since some of the *gentes* represented on the inscription were among the most prominent in Rome.

the cult, as related by Tertullian, is that he valued the decision of the Senate higher than the impulse of the mob.[54] At a time when its collective authority was being challenged with increasing regularity, the Senate may have taken this opportunity to attempt to reestablish itself as the central decision-making authority in Roman society.[55]

It is instructive to consider the reaction to Isis at the tail end of the Republic with another incident from the early days of Rome's appearance as a world power. The parallels with the Bacchanalia are striking: a foreign cult that had existed in Rome for many years, a Senate concerned that individuals were wielding too much authority, and actions that demonstrated the power of the Senate but did not result in, and probably did not aim at, the eradication of the cult in question. Perhaps the single most significant difference between the action in this era as opposed to the early second century was that the Senate was not successful at the time of Caesar and Pompey in reestablishing its authority. We should not, however, let that result color our impression of the activity at this time and see the senatorial actions in regard to Egyptian religions as a serious attempt to eliminate their worship in Rome. As the new collection of Sibylline oracles in the 70s demonstrated, the Romans remained open to foreign religious traditions even as they strove to define for themselves who had the authority to define Romanness.

The willingness of the Romans to integrate foreign elements thus appears as a consistent feature of their religious system, from the early Republic through the challenges of war and expansion, and even during the most intense struggles between Pompey and Caesar and their followers. This study has examined the challenges posed to Roman identity, first by that rapid expansion of Rome into a world power, an expansion that wrought changes in every aspect of Roman life, and then by those internal conflicts that themselves were a result of that expansion. It has become evident that the willingness to absorb and incorporate foreign religious elements, both people and cultural practices, contributed greatly to the Romans' ability to become an imperial power and to maintain that position yet also contributed to their difficulty in defining a sense of their own unique identity. Roman reactions to foreign cults and foreign priests, and the development of their own religious behavior in regard to foreign cities, reflect both the sense of Romanness that emerged in the fourth, third, and second centuries B.C.E. and the challenges that

54. Tert. *Ad. Nat.* 10: *potiorem habuit senatus censuram quam impetum uulgi.*
55. Cf. Takács (1995), 65–66, who offers this as an "extremely plausible reason for the senatorial decree." See also Ciceroni (1992), 106; Arena (2001), 302–303.

arose in the first century, when civil wars rather than external forces threatened Roman identity. Religious reform and cultural borrowing, which provide two characteristic means of ethnic self-renewal, played a vital role in the third and second centuries, while a third important factor, a sense of ethnic election or chosenness, came to have a more prominent place in Roman thinking in the second and especially the first centuries B.C.E.[56] The Romans claimed to be the most religious of all peoples, which, in light of the Roman formulation of the relationship between themselves and the gods, suggests that the Romans believed that they were uniquely favored by the gods.[57] It may not be coincidence that the first recorded instance of this claim comes in a letter from the Roman Senate to the people of Teos dated to 193 B.C.E., precisely the period, as we have seen, in which the Romans were beginning to redefine their identity.[58] This statement then became a common refrain in the late Republic, as Cicero, Sallust, and Livy all take it as an established fact and clearly one of the defining pieces of Roman identity.[59] The strife of the second and first centuries clearly did nothing to dampen this sense, and indeed, the efforts of all the military dynasts from Marius down to Octavian to suggest that each was uniquely favored by the gods reveals just how deep-seated this conception had become. It might have been an open question throughout most of the first century as to exactly which person or persons were most favored by the gods, but no one disputed that *those* people were the true Romans.

The military triumph of Octavian ended the contest for supremacy but did not resolve the nature of the state that would remain for the victor to govern; it answered the question of who would define Roman identity but not how that identity would be defined. Outlawing practices such as human sacrifice may have painted a very broad outline of Romanness, but the problem still demanded resolution; given the collapse in the coherence of Roman identity during the Late Republic, reconstructing a clear sense of that identity was one of the primary tasks facing the new emperor. The political transition from republic to empire had been every bit as disruptive to Roman identity as the growth to territorial empire had been, which

56. Smith (1991), 25ff. Cf. earlier in this chapter.

57. The notion of *do ut des*—that if the humans performed their rituals correctly, the gods would grant their prayers—suggests that the people who best performed religious rituals would receive the most favor from the gods.

58. *IGRom.* 4.1557. One should, of course, be wary of equating the first surviving instance of a claim with the first *actual* claim, but the fact that the Romans were making this claim by this point shows remarkable self-awareness.

59. Cf. Cic., *Nat. D.* 2.3.8 and *Har. resp.* 19; Sall., *Cat.* 12.3; Livy, *praef.* 6.

the examples in this chapter have shown, and the clarification of Roman identity was every bit as necessary. A concern with Romanness is visible in many aspects of Roman culture during the Augustan period; the discourse is evident in Roman literature, and Vitruvius makes clear that the discourse extended to architectural forms as well.[60] Roman religious practice, and the Roman understanding of those practices, naturally served as an important locus for this debate; as noted in the introduction, distinguishing between Roman and foreign practices was a primary concern of Livy, especially in his treatment of the late third and early second centuries.[61] This period also saw attempts to regularize and categorize Roman practices: Varro's activities extending back into the Late Republic are well known, but one should not overlook Verrius Flaccus, who attempted to define the *sacra peregrina* (wrongly, as I argued at the outset of this study).[62] As with the other dynasts of the first century, Octavian's actions may reveal more about his own conception of Roman identity than a consensus view, but his unquestioned supremacy enabled him to impose his vision on the Roman governing elite and the Roman state; his vision became the Roman vision. The transition from republic to empire did not shatter the link between religion and politics but caused it to operate in a new fashion, reflecting the decisions of one man rather than the consensus decisions of a governing aristocracy. Augustus' membership in all of the religious colleges, an act contrary to Republican practice, as well as the enhanced importance of the position of *pontifex maximus*, provides a sharp reflection of the changed nature of the connection between religion and politics under the Principate; the connection is very much present, but religious decision making, like political decision making, revolved around the figure of the *princeps*.

The triumph of Octavian thus makes religious activity once again an appropriate lens through which to view Roman identity, as that identity was projected by those in power. Octavian could utilize the various mechanisms at his disposal to promote his vision of Roman religion and to affect the notion of Roman identity promoted by the Roman state. Religion, for reasons that have been repeatedly discussed in this study and elsewhere, occupied a special place at Rome that made it particularly well suited to the dissemination of the new imperial culture.[63] In many areas, the new emperor picked up threads that had been developing during the Republic and brought them to

60. On Vergil, see Toll (1997); on Horace and Ovid, see Habinek (1998), chapters 4 and 8. On Vitruvius, see Wallace-Hadrill (2000), 300–305. Even Greeks might take part in this conversation; on Strabo, see Van der Vliet (2003).

61. See the introduction, pp. 8–10.

62. See the introduction, pp. 9–12.

63. Cf. Cooley (2006), 229.

fruition; this practice fit well with the emperor's claims to be keeping with Republican traditions. The inclusion of the Italian municipalities inside the boundaries of Romanness was one such thread. As Ronald Syme noted long ago in his magisterial study, the reign of Augustus marked the final inclusion of the Italian municipalities into the res publica.[64] The activity explored throughout this study has suggested that the development of a Roman national identity that might include Italians and others living outside the city had been under way since the Middle Republic. The package of religious activity undertaken by Augustus, the so-called program of restoration, needs to be analyzed in this light: not as the restoration of a system in danger of collapse, but as a restoration of Roman identity that helped to redefine the place of the Italian communities.[65] Just as Republican religious activity, especially in regard to foreign cults, helped us understand Roman self-perception in the Middle Republic, the religious activity of Octavian provides us with insights into the new contours of Romanness and its inclusion of the Italian communities. Because the Augustan religious program was so multifaceted, it cannot be treated here in the detail it deserves, but a glance at the Augustan religious program will highlight the continued contribution of religious activity to constructing a new sense of Romanness and to setting the stage for the *longue durée* of the Empire.

One place to explore the emperor's conception of Romanness is his celebrated reconstruction of eighty-two temples in the city of Rome. On the *Res Gestae*, Augustus lists this accomplishment under his sixth consulship, 28 B.C.E., a date only two years removed from his final victory in Egypt and before he had fully begun to promote the notion of the restored Republic.[66] While it would be impressive even to have started work on eighty-two temples in a single year, it is most unlikely that all eighty-two temples were completely rebuilt in this year, and indeed, we know of some temples presumably counted among the eighty-two that were rededicated long after this date.[67] A curious feature of these reconstructions is that the first temples rededicated were not always those that would seem at first glance to be most important, but rather those, such as Jupiter Feretrius, Victoria, and Saturn, that could be connected to Rome's deep mythohistorical past rather

64. Syme (1939), especially chapters 20 and 24. We are still exploring the full implications of this insight. See the collections of essays in Toher and Raaflaub (1990); Habinek and Schiesaro (1997); Millar (2000).

65. For some recent comments along these lines, see Scheid (2005); Cooley (2006).

66. *Res Gestae* 20.

67. Unfortunately, we do not even know all eighty-two temples that were reconstructed, as only a handful are mentioned by name or have been shown through archaeological work to have been repaired by the emperor.

than to the more documented history of the Middle and Late Republic.[68] Similarly, festivals marked on the numerous stone *fasti* that date from the early Empire tend to cluster either toward the Augustan or the Romulean eras, with only a scattering from the period between those two poles.[69] By evoking Rome's earliest history with the first temples to be rebuilt in Rome, Augustus harked back to a period that was unquestionably Roman but also one in which neighboring peoples participated equally in the building of the Roman state.[70] According to Roman tradition, firmly established by the time of Augustus, Romulus opened an asylum on the Capitoline to attract new strength to Rome, made an alliance with Titus Tatius to incorporate the Sabines into the Roman state, and after his death, was succeeded by a Sabine, Numa Pompilius.[71] Among other factors that made Romulus so attractive to Augustus as a model was the original founder's willingness to consider Sabines and other non-Romans as fully Roman. With his choice of temples to be rebuilt earliest, Augustus as the second founder of Rome directed attention to his similar embrace of the inhabitants of Italy.

In the same year of 28 B.C.E., Augustus took two further actions that also suggest a redrawing of the boundaries of Romanness. In that year, he issued an edict banning the worship of Isis and Sarapis from within the *pomerium* and also provided for rebuilding their shrines outside that religious boundary, and at the same time he dedicated a new temple to Apollo in close proximity to his own house on the Palatine hill. These actions contributed to clarifying a sense of Roman identity while at the same time reinforcing the notion of Rome as open to foreign cultural elements.[72] The insistence on moving the shrines of Isis and Sarapis outside the *pomerium* marked these cults as non-Roman, as Augustus apparently invented a tradition that foreign cults should be located outside that religious boundary.[73] Such an action should not be surprising, especially only two years removed from the final surrender of Alexandria. Augustus' personal involvement in the restoration of shrines to these Egyptian deities is remarkable, however, and again calls attention to the openness of the Roman state. The temple to Apollo underscored both points made by the treatment of the Egyptian cults. The erection of a temple to a Greek god, with emphasis on the Hellenic aspects of his cult, served as another sign of the openness of the Roman state, and the temple's location

---

68. Cf. Gros (1976), 26.

69. Wallace-Hadrill (1987), 226.

70. I have developed this point more fully elsewhere; see Orlin (2007).

71. For these stories, see Livy 1.6–8, 1.13, and 1.18.

72. I have discussed these events more fully in Orlin (2008).

73. On the *pomerium* and foreign cults, see Orlin (2002); on Augustus and his possible invention of tradition here, see also Beard, North, and Price (1998), 180.

on the Palatine hill, inside the *pomerium*, called attention to the permeability of the boundaries of Romanness; the Greek cult was marked as Roman, in contrast to the Egyptian cults. The fuller inclusion of Greek culture in Roman society further demonstrated Roman openness to Greeks as well as to the Italian municipalities, who themselves had become fully conversant with Greek culture over the previous centuries.

The concern of the *princeps* to include Italy within the boundaries of Romanness can be seen in other religious activity where his action in regard to Italy parallels a similar action undertaken in Rome. A reform of Augustus that had a widespread impact on the residents of Rome was his restructuring of the city in 7 B.C.E. to divide it into 14 *regiones* and 265 *vici*.[74] These *vici* contained numerous shrines at crossroads dedicated to the *Lares Compitales*, which often dated far back into the Republic and had become a focal point for political activity in the Late Republic.[75] During Augustus' reorganization of the city, these shrines were transformed into cults of the *Lares Augusti*, so that in every neighborhood rituals were performed on a regular basis to deities connected with the emperor, perhaps even his ancestors.[76] Paralleling his activity in Rome, Augustus reorganized Italy into eleven *regiones*, and just as the cult of the *Lares Augusti* provided a means for a broader segment of society in Rome to demonstrate their devotion to the emperor, so the appearance of *Augustales* throughout Italy provided a means for local residents to express a similar loyalty.[77] Although the *Augustales* may not be directly connected with the imperial cult, residents of the towns of Italy who held this position thereby connected themselves to Augustus and performed religious rituals on a regular basis that supported the res publica. The creation of this office provided residents of Italy with the same opportunity to forge a connection to the ruling family.

In addition to the creation of the *Augustales*, a series of other religious actions demonstrate Augustus' interest in furthering the integration of Italian communities with Rome. John Scheid has highlighted a number of

74. For discussion, see Liebeschuetz (1979), 69–71; Fraschetti (1990) 204–273; Lott (2004), 81–127.

75. On the *compitales* in the Republic, see Lintott (1968), 80–83.

76. See Beard, North, and Price (1998), 139, 184–186. Lott (2004), 106–110, rejects the notion that these cults represented an extension of the private family cult of Augustus but rather simply "pulled the neighborhoods, their religion, and their inhabitants into the new system of the Principate."

77. On the organization of space by the first emperor, see Nicolet (1991), especially pp. 173–178 and 194–204 on the Italian and Roman *regiones*. On the *Augustales* in Italy, see Ostrow (1990), who explicitly compares developments in Rome with those in Italy. Cf. Duthoy (1978) on the same topic.

actions taken by the emperor that affected sanctuaries outside Rome: the transformation of the *lucus Feroniae*, an ancient Italic cult site, into a more elaborate complex; the granting of Roman colony status to a sanctuary of Fortuna in Umbria; the confirmation of privileges and a grant of autonomy to the sanctuary of Diana Tifatina in Campania; and the foundation of a colony at Hispellum in Umbria with the specific responsibility of over-seeing the nearby sanctuary of Clitumnus.[78] In light of the extensive building projects undertaken in Rome by the emperor, Scheid suggests that these actions were designed to show that not just Rome, but Italy also received material benefits from the Augustan program of restoration. Fur-thermore, the symbolic value of these actions may be as important as the physical benefits brought to the local communities. The respect shown by Augustus for these important Italian sanctuaries parallels the respect given to Roman sanctuaries; to some extent, the Italian sanctuaries were treated as Roman, as the emperor himself took the responsibility to care for these shrines. Augustus' actions recall those of the Senate in regard to the temple of Juno Lacinia at Croton: the Roman state indicating that proper ritual observance at an Italian sanctuary affected the well-being of the Roman state. By his actions, Augustus confirmed that the boundaries of Roman-ness had been irrevocably altered to allow for a fuller participation by the people who had fought a desperate civil war against Rome only sixty years earlier: what was formerly just Italian was now Roman as well.

Any discussion of the Augustan religious program cannot be complete without a discussion of the *ludi saeculares*, and this celebration provides us with one more opportunity to observe the Augustan reshaping of Roman identity. The Augustan celebration claimed to be the third occurrence of a ritual first celebrated in 249 at the Tarentum in the Campus Martius, although, as discussed in chapter 2, the earlier observances may not have been intended to be celebrated on a 100-year (or 110-year) cycle.[79] The first celebration of this ritual had occurred during the First Punic War, and the second in connection with the wars against Carthage and Greece in 146 B.C.E.; that is, both were con-nected with wartime crises and thus specifically tied to the expansionist his-tory of the Roman state. The games of Augustus, despite the professions of restoration from the *princeps*, represent a sharp break from past practice, both in adopting the aspect of marking a *saeculum* and in the celebration them-selves.[80] As is well known, Augustus altered the primary deities to whom the

78. Scheid (2005).

79. See chapter 2, p. 67ff.

80. Cf. Schnegg-Köhler (2002), 129, who argues that the very prayers of the *ludi saeculares* were new, even while adopting a traditional-sounding form.

festival was dedicated from Dis and Proserpina to Jupiter, Juno, Apollo, and Diana. Even the nighttime ceremonies paid honor to the Fates (Moirai), goddesses of childbirth (Ilythiae), and Mother Earth (Terra Mater) rather than the gods of the underworld. These changes effectively dissociated the festival from its previous incarnation and allowed it to help create a new community; that an individual was not part of the community that had celebrated this rite during earlier incarnations no longer mattered. The *ludi Saeculares* marked the beginning of a new area of Romanness, not narrowly tied to the historical community of the past but to the community as constituted by the *princeps*.[81] The gods invoked demonstrate the breadth of the Roman community at this time: the newly Hellenized Apollo, to whom sacrifices were made at his new temple on the Palatine, and his sister Diana, alongside the Cretan Ilythiae and the Greek *moirai*. The rituals themselves further suggest the nature of the Roman community: *ludi* were, not surprisingly, a central aspect of the ritual, but these games apparently took several forms. According to the inscribed record of events, during one part of the celebration, "games were celebrated by night on a stage without the additional construction of a theater and without the erection of seating," while on the following day there were "Latin games in a wooden theater which had been erected on the Campus Martius next to the Tiber."[82] Later in the seven days of games that closed the celebration, Greek shows were held in both the Theater of Pompey and the Circus Flaminius, as well as additional Latin games on the Campus Martius. The juxtaposition of a style supposedly deriving from Rome's deep past alongside those from neighboring communities and from the Greek East is striking. The religious festivity, which more than any other single moment symbolized the founding of a newly imagined Roman community, centered on a ceremony that represented the quintessential Roman ritual, combined deities and rituals from a wide spectrum of societies, and unified those elements into a single new Roman celebration. There is no better illustration of how Roman religious practice reflected the development and redefinition of Roman identity.

81. Cooley (2006), 230–237, discusses the celebration of the Secular Games in these terms and suggests that "the role of the Latins in the Centennial Games was to present a favorable image of the integration of conquered peoples into the Roman Empire." She suggests that the ability of the Latins to serve as a paradigm for this integration, since they were the first people conquered, may explain their presence in the prayers of the ceremony.

82. *CIL* 6.32323 = Dessau, *ILS* 5050: *ludique noctu sacrificio confecto sunt commissi in scaena quoi theatrum adiectum non fuit nullis positis sedilibus. . . . Deinde ludi latini in theatro ligneo quod erat constitutum in campo secundum tiberim sunt commissi.*

Conclusion

This book has explored how the oft-noted willingness of the Romans to incorporate foreign religious elements into their religious system—cults, priests, practices—both reflected and contributed to changes in the sense of their own identity as they expanded from a city-state on the banks of the Tiber to a Mediterranean empire. A fundamental feature of the Roman state, and a key element in their successful expansion during the Republic, was the permeability of the boundaries of Romanness. To varying degrees and in varying ways, they allowed foreigners to participate in the Roman enterprise, and tracing the incorporation of the specifically religious foreign elements has been the focus of this study. The Roman approach to empire building, however, posed a potential challenge to Roman identity; by accepting so many outside elements into their society, they risked blurring the distinction between Roman and non-Roman. The particular cults and practices that the Romans accepted and, more important, the ways in which those practices were incorporated into the Roman system reveal transformations in their sense of Romanness. The case of the Magna Mater provides perhaps the best example of this phenomenon and hence has figured in several chapters of this study. The cult, coming from Asia Minor with its self-mutilating priests and frenzied ritual celebrations, surprisingly did not present a genuine challenge to maintaining an understanding of what it meant to be Roman, for the Romans regulated the role of the priests, added *ludi* along with other Roman forms of celebration, and so shaped the worship of the Magna Mater in Rome to their needs. Not only did the Roman alteration of cult practices serve to highlight the "Roman" and "non-Roman" elements of the cult but also its presence called attention to two elements that the Romans, from the second century B.C.E. onward, saw as increasingly central and distinctive of their character: their Trojan heritage and their willingness to incorporate foreigners. Even the occasional complaints lodged against the cult by various literary and political figures served only to emphasize the non-Roman aspects of it. The discourse itself about the contours of Romanness served as perhaps the most important element in the maintenance of clear boundaries for the Romans. The success of the Roman approach can be seen not only in the construction of an empire but also in its longevity, for the pattern that developed in the Republic came to be firmly established by the emperor Augustus and continued throughout the imperial period.

Though the focus of this study has been on the Roman side of the story, the story of the Italian communities and the other outsiders poses issues of equal interest. The arguments advanced in this book should not be taken to imply that a coherent identity to which these people subscribed came into existence during the era of Augustus, at the end of the period under study here. While the Romans may have tried to project an image of themselves as open to outside influences, the Roman sense of themselves as building an ethnos that could include others may not have been reciprocated by the communities of the Italian peninsula. Cicero, in an oft-cited passage, suggests that people from the *municipia* might consider themselves to have dual identities, one by birth and one by citizenship.[1] Cicero wants to have it both ways, acknowledging the importance of the birth homeland but still insisting that such persons were part of the Roman people and, indeed, that the Roman aspect of their identity was greater and included the local one within it. Cicero's perspective, while offering one possible approach to the issue, may be of limited use to us for understanding Italian attitudes more broadly. As an Arpinate who moved to Rome and attained for himself the highest position in the Roman state, he might remember and value his roots in Arpinum, but his perspective is that of a member of the Roman elite. The townsmen he left behind in Arpinum might not have perceived their identity in the same way.

Indeed, it seems clear that local identities remained important and that any Italian identity remained incomplete for many years, even after the inauguration of the Principate.[2] Several recent studies have emphasized that while Roman expansion left a clear mark on the landscape and on the

1. Cic., *Leg.* 2.5
2. Gabba (1994); Giardina (1997); Bradley (2006, 2007).

communities of Italy, the spread of Roman (and Greek) cultural influence should not be read as "a progressive erosion of local cultural identities."[3] Archaeologists working outside Rome have been particularly active in addressing the question of the Italian reaction to Roman culture, questioning whether Romanization or Hellenization is a more appropriate term, and unpacking the implications of these terms.[4] The notion that one culture dominated or subsumed the other, as implied by the term "Romanization," has gradually been discarded, often in favor of "creolization," a mixing of the two cultures. For another alternative, Andrew Wallace-Hadrill has suggested that the model of "bilingualism" may be the most appropriate lens through which to view Roman Italy; this model posits the existence of one culture side by side with the other, and the choice to use one language or the other carries implications for both cultures.[5] This conclusion is not the place to explore these questions in the detail they deserve, but it may be worthwhile to glance at a few developments in the first centuries B.C.E. and C.E. to gauge, at least in part, the impact of the Roman behavior traced in this study.

The appearance of inscribed stone calendars known as *fasti* from many communities in Italy provides one suggestive piece of evidence. These calendars, which date almost exclusively to the end of the Republic and the Augustan period, describe the Roman festival year, listing single-day celebrations such as the Lupercalia, multiday festivals such as the *ludi Romani*, and the dedication days of specific temples located in Rome; some even marked the day on which Rome was said to be founded. It is unlikely that the primary intent of these calendars was for people to make a pilgrimage to Rome to participate in these festivals, yet the existence of the calendars indicates that it was important for the residents of Antium or Praeneste to know what festivals were being celebrated in Rome. The local residents were in some measure able to participate in the rituals taking place in Rome through their knowledge of when they were being held; they could imagine themselves as part of the Roman religious community. The fact that local magistrates were listed on these *fasti* alongside Roman ones suggests that these calendars were commissioned locally; it was not the Roman elite who insisted on the diffusion of Roman customs, but the local elite who wanted to present their town as part of the Roman community. Sharing of time thus became one important means by which people residing outside Rome were linked to those living in the city; it has been said that with the publication of the calendar "Roman time

3. Wallace-Hadrill (2008), 128.
4. Curti, Dench, and Patterson (1996); Terrenato (1998); Keay and Terrenato (2001); Bradley (2007).
5. Wallace-Hadrill (2008), 9–14.

becomes the property of all Romans."[6] The dual implications of this statement are important; not only is Roman time available to people living outside
Rome but also "all Romans" includes those living outside the *urbs*.

Another development of particular interest is the apparent decline or
disappearance of local religious sanctuaries during the last two hundred
years of the Republic. The archaeological evidence suggests that many
sanctuaries of local or regional significance, from major sites such as Pietrabondante to lesser ones such as Gabii or Schiavi d'Abruzzo, declined or fell
into disuse.[7] Interpretation of this phenomenon is challenging, and more
work needs to be done in this area.[8] The increasing urbanization of Italy
must have played a significant role, not only in the movement of people
into cities and towns but also in the disruption of the society on which
these extraurban sanctuaries depended.[9] As one piece of evidence that the
disruption was not limited to areas that had only recently come into the
Roman ambit, we might consider the situation at Lavinium, another
extraurban sanctuary. At a site that had been an important Roman sanctuary for more than three hundred years, an artificial priesthood had to be
established under the Principate to enable Roman magistrates to continue
performing their annual rituals, apparently because the town had been
largely abandoned.[10] It seems clear that the decline of rural Italian sanctuaries should not be ascribed to direct Roman interference with local customs, but rather to broader trends affecting the whole of the peninsula. In
this regard, the impact of the Romans lay not so much in conscious actions
in the religious sphere as in the simple fact of Roman expansion, which
forced people to adjust to a new way of life throughout much of Italy.

Not all of the rural sanctuaries in Italy disappeared under the Empire,
and Lavinium may again prove to be a particularly instructive example of
how the emperors continued to use the model that had developed during the
Republic. Just as that sanctuary became Roman in the Republic and then
survived into the Empire because of Roman intervention, so, too, activity
continued elsewhere in sanctuaries where the Romans took a special interest
in the site. Augustus in particular took action in several instances, explicitly
assigning responsibility for the maintenance of a sanctuary to a particular

6. Wallace-Hadrill (2005), 61.
7. See Crawford (1996), 987, for a summary of the evidence.
8. The number of factors at play makes it difficult to read the decline of local religious sanctuaries as an example of straightforward Romanization, where an important
element of the local religious system was simply abandoned in favor of the Roman
system. Future work hopefully will untangle these factors.
9. Cf. Crawford (1996), 427.
10. Thomas (1990).

town. The veteran colony at Hispellum, already favored by the first emperor with new city walls, was given responsibility for the famous Umbrian cult at the Lacus Clitumnus nearby.[11] Similarly, the Etruscan religious festival at the Fanum Voltumnae was reorganized, perhaps under Augustus, into a joint Umbrian-Etruscan festival to be held alternately at Hispellum and Volsinii; a rescript of Constantine attests that celebrations continued in this fashion into late antiquity.[12] These sanctuaries in Umbria and Etruria show a pattern similar to Lavinium; while the Lacus Clitumnus or Fanum Voltumnae never became incorporated into Roman origin myths, we once again see the Romans selecting particular local sanctuaries for exceptional treatment. How we should interpret these actions is less clear. Just as we know little about how the Latins viewed the Roman involvement at Lavinium, we know little about the Etruscan response to the Augustan sponsorship of Fanum Voltumnae; it is not even known whether Roman magistrates participated at Fanum Voltumnae as they did at Lavinium. While the meaning that the ceremony held for the participants must have changed over this period, the implications for our understanding of local identities remain to be worked out. From the Roman perspective, the support for these local sanctuaries again conveys the openness of the Roman state, and further exploration of this phenomenon would help us understand the continued development of Roman identity during the Empire.

Because boundaries do not remain static and need to be repeatedly defined and redefined to ensure their maintenance, it is hardly surprising that religious activity during the Empire continued to mark out the contours of Romanness. While much scholarly attention on religion during the Empire has focused on emperor worship as the primary shared religious experience and thus a focal point for Roman identity, a reconsideration of that view may be overdue. On the one hand, the presumed commonality of the so-called imperial cult can easily be overstated; a tremendous diversity of practices were associated with the imperial cult, and in many instances, these practices were closely intertwined with a local practice, such that it might be better to speak of imperial cults.[13] On the other hand, the appearance of Capitolia outside the city of Rome and oaths sworn in Spain to the Penates suggest that religious actions unrelated to the imperial cult but still recognizably Roman could be practiced all over the empire.[14] These examples

11. Plin., *Ep.* 8.8. Another example is provided by the sanctuary of Hercules Curinus assigned to the city of Sulmona. Cf. Bradley (2007), 308–310.

12. *CIL* 11.5215. See further Coarelli (2001) and Bradley (2007), 312–313.

13. See the work of Friesen (1993, 2001), among others.

14. Cf. Ando (2008), 95–119.

and others indicate that some elements of religious behavior did come to be shared throughout the empire. Just as important, this religious activity during the imperial period reveals the continuation of a discourse about being Roman. A Capitolium is not just a temple to Jupiter; it is the Roman temple to Jupiter. Such a foundation is concerned to announce itself as Roman; it serves to identify the town and its residents with the other towns and people who worship that particular incarnation of the sky god, most notably Rome. The evolution of Roman religion during the Late Republic thus points the way toward a method for creating a Roman empire, of developing a sense of Romanness that could be shared not just in the city of Rome, but throughout the Roman world.

Bibliography

Accame, S. 1938. "Il senatus consultum de Bacchanalibus." *Rivista di filologia* 66, 225–234.

Alföldi, A. 1954. "Isiskult und Umsturzbewegung im letzten Jahrhundert der römischen Republik." *Schweizer Münzblätter* 5, 25–31.

Alföldi, A. 1965. *Early Rome and the Latins*. Ann Arbor: University of Michigan Press.

Alföldi, A. 1976. "*Redeunt Saturnia regna V*: zum Gottesgnadentum des Sulla." *Chiron* 6, 143–158.

Allély, A. 2003. "Les enfants malformés et considérés comme "prodigia" à Rome et en Italie sous la République." *Revue des études anciennes* 105, 127–156.

Altheim, F. 1938. *A History of Roman Religion*. London: Methuen.

Anderson, B. 1983. *Imagined communities: reflections on the origin and spread of nationalism*. London:Verso.

Ando, C. (ed.). 2003. *Roman Religion*. Edinburgh: Edinburgh University Press.

Ando, C. 2008. *The Matter of the Gods: Religion and the Roman Empire*. Berkeley: University of California Press.

Andren, A. 1939–40. *Architectural Terracottas from Etrusco-Italic Temples*. Acta Instituti Romani Regni Sueciae 6, Leipzig.

Armstrong, J. 1982. *Nations before Nationalism*. Chapel Hill: University of North Carolina Press.

Arena, A. 2001. "Romanità e culto di Serapide." *Latomus* 60, 297–313.

Aronen, J. 1989. "Il culto arcaico nel Tarentum a Roma e la gens Valeria." *Arctos* 22, 19–39.

Astin, A. E. 1967. *Scipio Aemilianus*. Oxford: Oxford University Press.

Badian, E. 1971. "Roman Politics and the Italians (133–91 B.C.)." *Dialoghi di Archeologia* 4–5, 373–421.

Badian, E. 1972. "Tiberius Gracchus and the Beginning of the Roman Revolution." *Aufstieg und Niedergang der Römischen Welt* I.1, 668–731. Berlin: W. de Gruyter.

Barth, F. (ed.). 1969. *Ethnic Groups and Boundaries*. Boston: Little Brown.

Basanoff, V. 1947. *Evocatio. Etude d'un rituel militaire romain*. Paris: Presses universitaires de France.

Bauman R. A. 1983. *Lawyers in Roman republican politics. A study of the Roman jurists in their political setting, 316–82 BC*. Munich: C.H. Beck'sche Verlagsbuchhandlung.

Bauman, R. A. 1992. *Women and Politics in Ancient Rome*. London: Routledge.

Bayet, J. 1926. *Les origines de l'Hercule romain*. Paris: E. de Boccard.

Bayet, J. 1957. *Histoire politique et psychologique de la religion romaine*. Paris: Payot.

Beard, M. 1987. "A Complex of Times: No More Sheep on Romulus' Birthday." *Proceedings of the Cambridge Philological* Society 33, 1–15.

Beard, M. 1990. "Priesthood in the Roman Republic." In *Pagan Priests: Religion and Power in the Ancient World* (M. Beard and J. North, eds.), London: Duckworth, 17–48.

Beard, M. 1994. "The Roman and the Foreign: The Cult of the "Great Mother" in Imperial Rome." In *Shamamism, History and the State* (N. Thomas and C. Humphrey, eds.), Ann Arbor: University of Michigan Press, 164–190.

Beard, M., J. North, and S. Price. 1998. *Religions of Rome*. Cambridge: Cambridge University Press.

Beaujeu, J. 1988. "Jeux latins et jeux grecs (à propos de Cic. Fam. VII,1 et Att. XVI,5)." In *Hommages à Henri Le Bonniec* (Collection Latomus 201), Brussels: Latomus, 10–18.

Bendlin, A. 1997. "Peripheral Centres—Central Peripheries: Religious Communication in the Roman Empire." In *Römische Reichsreligion und Provinzialreligion* (H. Cancik and J. Rüpke, eds.), Tübingen: Mohr Siebeck, 35–68.

Bendlin, A. 2000. "Looking beyond the Civic Compromise: Religious Pluralism in Late Republican Rome." In *Religion in Archaic and Republican Rome and Italy: Evidence and Experience* (E. Bispham and C. J. Smith, eds.), Edinburgh: Edinburgh University Press, 115–135.

Bernstein, F. 1997. "Verständnis- und Entwicklungsstufen der archaischen Consualia : römisches Substrat und griechische Überlagerung." *Hermes* 125, 413–446.

Bernstein, F. 1998. *Ludi Publici: Untersuchungen zur Entstehung und Entwicklung der öffentlichen Spiele im republikanischen Rom*. Stuttgart: Franz Steiner.

Bettini, M. 2007. "Forging Identities. Trojans and Latins, Romans and Julians in the *Aeneid*." In *Herrschaft ohne Integration? Rom und Italien in republikanischer Zeit* (M. Jehne and R. Pfeilschifter, eds.), Frankfurt am Main: Verlag Alte Geschichte, 269–291.

Bilde, P., I. Nielsen, and M. Nielsen. 1993. *Aspects of Hellenism in Italy: Towards a Cultural Unity?* (Acta Hyperborea 5), Copenhagen: Museum Tusculanum.

Bispham, E. 2006. "*Coloniam deducere*: How Roman Was Roman Colonization during the Middle Republic?" In *Greek and Roman Colonisation: Origins, Ideologies and Interactions* (G. J. Bradley and J.-P. Wilson, eds.), Swansea: Classical Press Of Wales, 73–160.

Bispham, E. 2008. *From Asculum to Actium: The Municipalization of Italy from the Social War to Augustus*. Oxford: Oxford University Press.

Bloch, R. 1963. *Les prodiges dans l'antiquité classique*. Paris: Presses universitaires de France.

Bloch, R. 1972. "Héra, Uni, Junon en Italie centrale." *Comptes rendus de l'Académie des inscriptions et belles-lettres*, 384–396.

Bloch, R. and Foti, G. 1953. "Nouvelles dédicaces archaïques à la déesse Feronia." *Revue de philologie* 27, 64–77.

Blomart, A. 1997. "Die evocatio und der Transfer 'fremder' Götter von der Peripherie nach Rom." In *Römische Reichsreligion und Provinzialreligion* (H. Cancik and J. Rüpke, eds.), Tübingen: Mohr Siebeck, 99–111.

Borgeaud, P. 2004. *Mother of the Gods: From Cybele to the Virgin Mary* (L. Hochroth, trans.). Baltimore: Johns Hopkins University Press.

Boyce, A. A. 1937. "The Expiatory Rites of 207 B.C." *Transactions of the American Philological Association* 68, 157–171.

Bradley, G. 2001. *Ancient Umbria: State, Culture, and Identity in Central Italy from the Iron Age to the Augustan Era*. Oxford: Oxford University Press.

Bradley, G. 2006. "Colonization and identity in Republican Italy." In *Greek and Roman Colonisation: Origins, Ideologies and Interactions* (G. J. Bradley and J.-P. Wilson, eds.), Swansea: Classical Press of Wales, 161–87.

Bradley, G. 2007. "Romanization: The End of the Peoples of Italy?" In *Ancient Italy: Regions Without Boundaries* (G. Bradley, E. Isayev, and C. Riva, eds.), Exeter: Exeter University Press, 295–322.

Bradley, G., E. Isayev, and C. Riva (eds.). 2007. *Ancient Italy: Regions without Boundaries*. Exeter: Exeter University Press.

Brass, P. 1991. *Ethnicity and Nationalism*. London: Sage.

Bremmer, J. 1987. "Romulus, Remus and the Foundation of Rome." In *Roman Myth and Mythography* (Bulletin of the Institute of Classical Studies Supplement 52, J. N. Bremmer and N. M. Horsfall, eds.), London: Institute of Classical Studies, 25–48.

Breuilly, J. 1993. *Nationalism and the State*, 2nd ed. Manchester: Manchester University Press.

Brind'Amour, P. 1978. "L'origine des jeux séculaires." *Aufstieg und Niedergang der Römischen Welt* II.16.2, Berlin: W. de Gruyter, 1334–1417.

Briquel D. 1986. "Ludi/lydi: jeux romains et origines étrusques." *Ktèma* 11, 161–167.

Briquel, D. 1993. "Une opinion hétérodoxe sur l'origine des jeux équestres Romains." In *Spectacles sportifs et scéniques dans le monde étrusco-italique* (Collection de l'École française de Rome 172), Rome: École française de Rome, 121–140.

Briscoe, J. 1973. *A commentary on Livy, Books xxxi–xxxiii*. Oxford: Oxford University Press.

Briscoe, J. 2003. "A. Postumius Albinus, Polybius and Livy's Account of the 'Bacchanalia.'" In *Hommages à Carl Deroux* 4 (P. Defosse, ed.), Brussels: Latomus, 302–308.

Broadhead, W. 2008. "Migration and Hegemony: Fixity and Mobility in Second-Century Italy." In *People, Land, and Politics: Demographic Developments and the Transformation of Roman Italy 300 BC–AD 14* (L. de Ligt and S. Northwood, eds.), Leiden: Brill, 451–470.

Bruhl, A. 1953. *Liber pater; origine et expansion du culte dionysiaque à Rome et dans le monde romain*. Paris: E. de Boccard.

Brunt, P. A. 1965. "Italian Aims at the Time of the Social War." *Journal of Roman Studies* 55, 90–109.

Brunt, P. A. 1988. *The Fall of the Roman Republic and Related Essays*. Oxford: Oxford University Press.

Burkert, W. 1985. *Greek Religion: Archaic and Classical*. Trans. J. Raffan. Oxford: Oxford University Press.

Burton, P. J. 1996. "The Summoning of the Magna Mater to Rome (205 B.C.)." *Historia* 45, 36–63.

Cancik, H. 1999. "The Reception of Greek Cults in Rome." *Archiv für Religionsgeschichte* 1 (2), 161–173.

Cancik, H., and J. Rüpke (eds.). 1997. *Römische Reichsreligion und Provinzialreligion*. Tübingen: Mohr Siebeck.

Cancik-Lindemaier, H. 1996. "Der Diskurs Religion im Senatsbeschluss über die Bacchanalia von 186 v. Chr. und bei Livius (B. XXXIX)." In *Geschichte—Tradition—Reflexion: Festschrift für Martin Hengel zum 70. Geburtstag* 2 (H. Cancik, ed.), Tübingen: Mohr Siebeck, 77–96.

Capdeville, G. 1993. "Jeux athlétiques et rituels de fondation." In *Spectacles sportifs et scéniques dans le monde étrusco-italique* (Collection de l'École française de Rome 172), Rome: École française de Rome, 141–187.

Capdeville, G. 1995. *Volcanus: recherches comparatistes sur les origines du culte de Vulcan*. Rome: École française de Rome.

Cartledge, P. 1993. *The Greeks: a portrait of self and others*. Oxford: Oxford University Press.

Castagnoli, F. 1972–1975. *Lavinium*. Rome: De Luca.

Castagnoli F. 1977. "Roma arcaica e i recenti scavi di Lavinio." *La Parola del Passato* 32, 340–355.

Castagnoli, F. 1982. "La leggenda di Enea nel Lazio." *Studi Romani* 30, 1–15.

Castagnoli, F. 1984. "Il tempio romano: questioni di terminilogia e tipologia." *Papers of the British School at Rome* 52, 3–20.

Catalano, P. 1978. "Aspetti spaziali del sistema giuridico-religioso romano." *Aufstieg und Niedergang der Römischen Welt* II.16.1, Berlin: W. de Gruyter, 440–553.

Cels-Saint-Hilaire, J. 1977. "Le fonctionnement des *Floralia* sous la République." *Dialogues d'histoire ancien* 4, 253–286.

Champeaux, J. 1982. *Fortuna: recherches sur le culte de la fortune à Rome et dans le monde romain des origines à la mort de César*. Collection de l'École française de Rome 64. Rome: École française de Rome.

Chapple, E., and C. Coon 1942. *Principles of Anthropology*. New York: Henry Holt.

Chiarucci P. 1983. *Lanuvium*. Rome: Paleani Editrice.

Chirassi Colombo, I. 1975. "Acculturation et cultes thérapeutiques." In *Les syncrétismes dans les religions de l'antiquité (Études préliminaires aux religions orientales dans l'Empire romain* 46, F. Dunand and P. Lévêque, eds.), Leiden: Brill, 96–111.

Ciceroni, M. 1992. "Introduzione ed evoluzione dei culti egizi a Roma in età repubblicana: la testimonianza delle fonti letterarie." In *Roma e l'Egitto nell'antichità classica* (G. Carratelli, ed.), Rome: Istituto Poligrafico e Zecca dello Stato, 103–7.

Clark, Albert. 1907. *Q. Asconii Pediani Orationum Ciceronis quinque enarratio*. Oxford: Oxford University Press.

Clark, Anna J. 2007. "Nasica and Fides." *Classical Quarterly* 57, 125–131.

Clavel-Lévéque, M. 1986. "L'espace des jeux dans le monde romain; hégémonie, symbolique et pratique sociale." *Aufstieg und Niedergang der Römischen Welt* II.16.3, Berlin: W. de Gruyter, 2405–2563.

Coarelli, F. 1977. "Il comizio dalle origini alla fine della repubblica: cronologia e topografia." *Parola del Passato* 32, 166–238.

Coarelli, F. 1984. "Iside Capitolina, Clodio e i mercanti di schiavi." In *Alessandria e il mondo ellenistico-romano, Studi in onore di Achille Achiani* (N. Bonacasa and A. di Vita, eds.), Rome: L'Erma di Bretschneider, 461–475.

Coarelli, F. 1986. *Fregellae, II: Il santuario di Esculapio.* Rome: Quasar.

Coarelli, F. 1993. "Note sui ludi saeculares." In *Spectacles sportifs et scéniques dans le monde étrusco-italique* (Collection de l'École française de Rome 172), Rome: École française de Rome, 211–245.

Coarelli F. 2001. "Il rescritto di Spello e il santuario 'etnico' degli umbri." In *Umbria Cristiana. Dalla diffusione del culto al culto dei santi (secc. iv–x),* Spoleto: Il Centro Italiano di Studi sull'Alto Medioevo, 737–747.

Cole, S. 1965. *Races of Man.* London: Trustees of the British Museum (Natural History).

Colin, G. 1905. *Rome et la Gréce.* Paris: Fontemoing.

Combet-Farnoux, B. 1980. *Mercure Romain.* Rome: École française de Rome.

Cooley, A. E. 2006. "Beyond Rome and Latium: Roman Religion in the Age of Augustus." In *Religion in Republican Italy* (C. Schultz and J. Harvey, eds.), Cambridge: Cambridge University Press, 228–252.

Cornell, T. J. 1975. "Aeneas and the Twins: The Development of the Roman Foundation Legend." *Proceedings of the Cambridge Philological Society* 201, 1–32.

Cornell, T. J. 1977. "Aeneas' Arrival in Italy." *Liverpool Classical Monthly* 2, 77–83.

Cornell, T. J. 1995. *The Beginning of Rome. Italy and Rome from the Bronze Age to the Punic Wars (c.1000–264 B.C.).* London: Routledge.

Cousin, J. 1942–43. "La crise religeuse de 207 av. J.-C." *Revue de l'histoire des religions* 126, 15–41.

Cova, P. V. 1974. "Livio e la repressione dei baccanali." *Athenaeum* 52, 82–109.

Cramer, F. 1954. *Astrology in Roman Law and Politics.* Philadelphia: American Philosophical Society.

Crawford, M. 1983. *Roman Republican Coinage.* Cambridge: Cambridge University Press.

Crawford, M. 1996. "Italy and Rome from Sulla to Augustus." In *Cambridge Ancient History* vol. 10 (2nd ed.), Cambridge: Cambridge University Press, 414–443.

Crowther, N. B. 1983. "Greek Games in Republican Rome." *L'Antiquité Classique* 52, 268–273.

Cumont, F. 1911. *The Oriental Religions in Roman Paganism.* Chicago: Open Court.

Curti, E. 2000. "From Concordia to the Quirinal: Notes on Religion and Politics in Mid-Republican/Hellenistic Rome." In *Religion in Archaic and Republican Rome and Italy: Evidence and Experience* (E. Bispham and C. J. Smith, eds.), Edinburgh: Edinburgh University Press, 92–107.

Curti, E., E. Dench, and J. Patterson. 1996. "The Archaeology of Central and Southern Roman Italy: Recent Trends and Approaches." *Journal of Roman Studies* 86, 170–189.

Davies, J. 2004. *Rome's Religious History: Livy, Tacitus and Ammianus on their Gods.* Cambridge: Cambridge University Press.

de Cazanove, O. 2000. "Some Thoughts on the 'Religious Romanisation' of Italy before the Social War." In *Religion in Archaic and Republican Rome and Italy: Evidence and Experience* (E. Bispham and C. J. Smith, eds.), Edinburgh: Edinburgh University Press, 71–76.

Degrassi A. 1947. *Inscriptiones Italiae, vol. XIII—Fasti et elogia, fasc. I—Fasti Consulares et Triumphales.* Rome: Libreria dello Stato.

Degrassi, A. 1963. *Inscriptiones Italiae, vol. XIII—Fasti et elogia, fasc. II—Fasti anni Numani et Iuliani.* Rome: Libreria dello Stato.

Dench, E. 1995. *From Barbarians to New Men: Greek, Roman, and Modern Perceptions of Peoples of the Central Apennines.* Oxford: Oxford University Press.

Dench, E. 2005. *Romulus' asylum: Roman identities from the age of Alexander to the age of Hadrian.* Cambridge: Cambridge University Press.

Dessau, H. 1892–1926. *Inscriptiones Latinae Selectae.* Berlin: Wiedmann.

Devallet, G. 1989. "*Pompa circensis* et constitution d'un espace ludique romain." *LALIES. Actes des sessions de linguistique et de littérature 7,* 299–305.

Diamond, J. 1994. "Race without Color." *Discover* 15, 200–206.

Diels, H. 1890. *Sibyllinische Blätter.* Berlin: G. Reimer.

Dougherty, C., and L. Kurke. 2003. *The Cultures within Ancient Greek Culture. Contact, Conflict, Collaboration.* Cambridge: Cambridge University Press.

Dubourdieu, A. 1989. *Les origines et le développement du culte des pénates à Rome.* Collection de l'École française de Rome 118, Rome: École française de Rome.

Dubourdieu, A., and E. Lemirre. 1997. "La rumeur dans l'affaire des Bacchanales." *Latomus* 56, 293–306.

Dumézil, G. 1970 (reprinted 1996). *Archaic Roman Religion.* Chicago: University of Chicago Press.

Dupont, F. 1993. "Ludions, *Lydioi*: Les danseurs de le *pompa circensis*." In *Spectacles sportifs et scéniques dans le monde étrusco-italique* (Collection de l'École française de Rome 172), Rome: École française de Rome, 189–210.

Dury-Moyaers, G. 1981. *Enee et Lavinium. A propos des decouvertes archeologiques recentes.* Brussels: Latomus.

Dury-Moyaers, G. 1986. "Réflexions à propos de l'iconographie de *Iuno Sospita*." In *Beiträge zur altitalischen Geistesgeschichte. Festschrift Gerhard Radke zum 18. Februar 1984* (R. von Altheim-Stiehl and M. Rosenbach, eds.), Münster: Aschendorff, 83–101.

Duthoy, R. 1978. "Les *Augustales*." *Aufstieg und Niedergang der Römischen Welt* 2.16.2, Berlin: W. de Gruyter, 1254–1309.

Earl, D. C. 1967. *The Moral and Political Tradition of Rome.* London: Thames and Hudson.

Eder, W. 1990. "Augustus and the Power of Tradition: The Augustan Principate as Binding Link between Republic and Empire." In *Between Republic and Empire: Interpretations of Augustus and His Principate* (M. Toher and K. Raaflaub, eds.), Berkeley: University of California Press, 71–122.

Edwards, C. 1996. *Writing Rome.* Cambridge: Cambridge University Press.

Enea nel Lazio. Archeologia e mito. 1981. Rome: Palombi.

Eriksen, T. H. 1993. *Ethnicity and Nationalism.* London: Pluto.

Erkell, H. 1969. "Ludi saeculares und ludi Latini saeculares. Ein Beitrag zur römischen Theaterkunde und Religionsgeschichte." *Eranos* 67, 166–174.

Evans, A. J. 1886. "Recent Discoveries of Tarentine Terra-Cottas." *Journal of Hellenic Studies* 7, 1–50.

Evans, J. K. 1991. *War, Women and Children in Ancient Rome.* London: Routledge.

Fantham, E. 1992. "The Role of Evander in Ovid's *Fasti*." *Arethusa* 25, 155–171.

Farney, G. 2007. *Ethnic identity and aristocratic competition in Republican Rome*. Cambridge: Cambridge University Press.

Fears, J. R. 1981. "The Theology of Victory at Rome. Approaches and Problems." *Aufstieg und Niedergang der Römischen Welt* II.17.2, Berlin: W. de Gruyter, 736–826.

Feldherr, A. 1998. *Spectacle and Society in Livy's History*. Berkeley: University of California Press.

Ferrary, J-L. 1988. *Philhellénisme et impérialisme*. Rome: École française de Rome.

Ferrero, L. 1955. *Storia del Pitagorismo del mondo Romano*. Turin: Universita di Torino.

Festugière A. J. 1954. "Ce que Tite-Live nous apprend sur les mystères de Dionysos." *Melanges de l'Ecole Francaise de Rome. Antiquite* 66, 79–99.

Fishwick, D. 1967. "Hastiferi." *Journal of Roman Studies* 57, 142–160.

Flower, H. 2000. "Fabula de Bacchanalibus: The Bacchanalian Cult of the Second Century BC and Roman Drama." In *Identität und Alterität in der frührömischen Tragödie* (G. Manuwald, ed.), Würzburg: Ergon, 23–35.

Flower, H. 2006. *The Art of Forgetting. Disgrace and Oblivion in Roman Political Culture*. Chapel Hill: University of North Carolina Press.

Forsythe, D. 1989. "German Identity and the Problem of History." In *History and Ethnicity* (E. Tonkin, M. McDonald, and M. Chapman, eds.), London: Routledge, 137–156.

Fowler, D. 1990. "Deviant Focalisation in Virgil's *Aeneid*." *Proceedings of the Cambridge Philological Society* 36, 42–63.

Fowler, W. W. 1911. *The Religious Experience of the Roman People*. London: MacMillan.

Fraschetti, A. 1990. *Roma e il Principe*. Rome: Editori Laterza.

Frézouls E. 1981. "Rome et les Latins dans les premières décennies du II siècle av. J.C." *Ktèma* 6, 115–132.

Friesen, S. 1993. *Twice Neokoros. Ephesus, Asia, and the Cult of the Flavian Imperial Family*. Leiden: Brill.

Friesen, S. 2001. *Imperial Cults and the Apocalypse of John: Reading Revelation in the Ruins*. Oxford: Oxford University Press.

Gabba, E. 1954. "Le origini della Guerra sociale e la vita romana dopo l'89 a. C." *Athenaeum* 32, 41–114 and 293–345.

Gabba, E. 1976. *Republican Rome, the Army, and the Allies* (P. J. Cuff, trans.). Oxford: Oxford University Press.

Gabba, E. 1994. "Il problema dell' 'unità' dell'Italia romana." In *Italia romana* (E. Gabba, ed.), Como: New Press, 17–31.

Gagé, J. 1934. *Recherches sur les jeux séculaires*. Paris: Les belles Lettres.

Gagé, J. 1955. *Apollon romain: essai sur le culte d'Apollon et le développement du ritus Graecus à Rome des origines à Auguste*. Paris: E. de Boccard.

Gagé, J. 1973. "Une consultation d'haruspices: sur les tabous étrusques de la statue dite d'Horatius Cocles." *Latomus* 32, 1–22.

Galinsky, K. 1969. *Aeneas, Sicily and Rome*. Princeton: Princeton University Press.

Galinsky, K. 1996. *Augustan Culture: An Interpretive Introduction*. Princeton: Princeton University Press.

Gallini, C. 1970. *Protesta e integrazione nella Roma antica*. Bari: Laterza.

Galsterer, H. 1976. *Herrschaft und Verwaltung im republikanischen Italien*. Munich: Beck.

Gauthier, P. 1974. "'Générosité' romaine et avarice grecque: sur l'octroi du droit de cité." In *Melanges William Seston*, Paris: E. de Boccard, 207–215.

Geiger, F. 1920. "Sacra." *Paulys Real-encyclopädie der classischen Altertumswissenschaft* I. A 2, Stuttgart: J.B. Metzler, 1656–1664.

Gellner, Ernest. 1983. *Nations and Nationalism*. Oxford: Oxford University Press.

Giardina, A. 1997. *L'Italia Romana: Storia Di Un'identità Incompiuta*. Rome: Laterza.

Gillis, J. (ed.). 1994. *Commemorations: The Politics of National Identity*. Princeton: Princeton University Press.

Girard, J.-L. 1980. "Interpretatio romana: questions historiques et problèmes de méthode." *Revue d'histoire et de philosophie religieuses* 60, 21–27.

Glazer, N., and D. Moynihan (eds.). 1975. *Ethnicity: Theory and Practice*. Cambridge: Harvard University Press.

Gordon, A. E. 1938. *The Cults of Lanuvium*. University of California publications in Classical Archaeology 2, Berkeley: University of California Press.

Graillot, H. 1912. *Le culte de Cybèle, mère des dieux, à Rome et dans l'empire*. Paris: Macon.

Gras, M. 1987. "Le temple de Diane sur l'Aventin." *Revue des Études Anciennes* 89, 47–61.

Gros P. 1976. *Aurea templa. Recherches sur l'architecture religieuse de Rome à l'époque d'Auguste*. Paris: École française de Rome.

Grosby, S. 1991. "Religion and Nationality in Antiquity: The Worship of Yahweh and Ancient Israel." *European Journal of Sociology* 32, 229–265.

Gruen, E. 1990. *Studies in Greek Culture and Roman Policy*. Leiden: Brill.

Gruen, E. 1992. *Culture and National Identity in Republican Rome*. Ithaca: Cornell University Press.

Gruen, E. 2002. *Diaspora: Jews amidst Greeks and Romans*. Cambridge: Harvard University Press.

Gustafsson, G. 2000. Evocation deorum: *Historical and Mythical Interpretations of Ritualised Conquests in the Expansion of Ancient Rome*. Uppsala: Uppsala University.

Habinek, T. 1998. *The Politics of Latin Literature*. Princeton: Princeton University Press.

Habinek, T. and Schiesaro, A. (eds.). 1997. *The Roman Cultural Revolution*. Cambridge: Cambridge University Press.

Hall, E. 1989. *Inventing the barbarian: Greek self-definition through tragedy*. Oxford: Oxford University Press.

Hall, Jonathan. 1997. *Ethnic Identity in Greek Antiquity*. Cambridge: Cambridge University Press.

Hall, Jonathan. 2002. *Hellenicity: Between Ethnicity and Culture*. Chicago: University of Chicago Press.

Hall, John, III. 1986. "The Saeculum Novum of Augustus and Its Etruscan Antecedents." *Aufstieg und Niedergang der Römischen Welt* II.16.3, Berlin: W. de Gruyter, 2564–2589.

Hallett, J., and M. Skinner (eds.). 1997. *Roman Sexualities*. Princeton: Princeton University Press.

Hanson, J. A. 1959. *Roman Theater Temples*. Princeton: Princeton University Press.

Harmon, D. 1978. "The Public Festivals of Rome." *Aufstieg und Niedergang der Römischen Welt* 2.16.2, Berlin: W. de Gruyter, 1440–1468.

Harris, W. V. 1971. *Rome in Etruria and Umbria*. Oxford: Oxford University Press.

Hartog, F. 1988. *The mirror of Herodotus: the representation of the other in the writing of history*. Berkeley: University of California Press.

Hastings, A. 1997. *The Construction of Nationhood: Ethnicity, Religion and Nationalism*. Cambridge: Cambridge University Press.

Hayne, L. 1991. "The First Cerialia." *L'Antiquité classique* 60, 130–138.

Hayne, L. 1992. "Isis and Republican Politics." *Acta Classica* 35, 143–149.

Henderson, J. 2000. "The Camillus Factory: Per Astra ad Ardeam." *Ramus* 29, 1–26.

Hobsbawm, E. 1990. *Nations and Nationalism since 1780: Programme, Myth, Reality*. Cambridge: Cambridge University Press.

Hobsbawm, E., and T. Ranger (eds.). 1983. *The Invention of Tradition*. Cambridge: Cambridge University Press.

Hoffmann, W. 1933. *Wandel und Herkunft der Sibyllinischen Bücher*. Leipzig: Edelmann.

Hölkeskamp, Karl-Joachim. 1993. "Conquest, Competition and Consensus." *Historia* 42, 12–39.

Holloway, R. 1994. *The Archaeology of Early Rome and Latium*. London: Routledge.

Holloway, S. 2001. *Assur Is King! Assur Is King! Religion in the Exercise of Power in the Neo-Assyrian Empire*. Leiden: Brill.

Hölscher, T. 1990. "Römische Nobiles und hellenistische Herrscherr." In *Akten des XIII Internationalen Kongresses für klassische Archäologie Berlin 1988*, Mainz: P. von Zabern, 73–84.

Horowitz, D. 1975. "Ethnic Identity." In *Ethnicity: Theory and Experience* (N. Glazer and D. Moynihan, eds.), Cambridge: Harvard University Press, 111–140.

Horsfall, N. 1987. "The Aeneas Legend from Homer to Virgil." In *Roman Myth and Mythography* (Bulletin of the Institute of Classical Studies Supplement 52, J. N. Bremmer and N. M. Horsfall, eds.), London: Institute of Classical Studies, 12–24.

Jaeger, M. 1997. *Livy's Written Rome*. Ann Arbor: University of Michigan Press.

Jaeger, M. 2006. "Livy, Hannibal's Monument, and the Temple of Juno at Croton." *Transactions of the American Philological Association* 136, 389–414.

Jones, C. 1999. *Kinship Diplomacy in the Ancient World*. Cambridge: Harvard University Press.

Just, Roger. 1989. "The Triumph of the *Ethnos*." In *History and Ethnicity* (Elisabeth Tonkin, Mayron McDonald, and Malcolm Chapman, eds.), London: Routledge.

Keaveney, A. 1983. "Sulla and the Gods." In *Studies in Latin Literature and Roman History*, Vol. 3, Brussels: Latomus, 44–79.

Keay S., and N. Terrenato (eds.). 2001. *Italy and the West: Comparative Issues in Romanization*. Oxford: Oxford University Press.

Kedourie, E. 1960. *Nationalism*. London: Hutchinson.

Kienast, D. 1989. *Augustus: Prinzeps und Monarch*, 3rd ed. Darmstadt: Wissenschaftliche Buchgesellschaft.

Kragelund, P. 2001. "Dreams, religion and politics in Republican Rome." *Historia* 50, 53–95.

Kraus, C. 1994. "'No Second Troy': Topoi and Refoundation in Livy Book V." *Transactions of the American Philological Association* 124, 267–289.

La Rocca, E. 1974–1975. "Due tombe dell'Esquilino. Alcune novità sul commercio euboico in Italia centrale nell' VIII secolo a. C." *Dialoghi di archeologia* 8, 86–103.

La Rocca, E. 1977. "Note sulle importazioni greche in territorio laziale nell' VIII secolo a. C." *Parola del Passato* 32, 375–397.

Lambrechts, P. 1951. "Cybèle, divinité étrangère ou nationale?" *Société royale belge d'anthropologie et de préhistoire* 62, 44–60.

Lane, E. N. 1979. "Sabazius and the Jews in Valerius Maximus: A Re-examination." *Journal of Roman Studies* 69, 35–38.

Latte, K. 1960. *Römische Religionsgeschichte*. Munich: Beck.

Laurence, R., and J. Berry (eds.). 1998. *Cultural Identity in the Roman Empire*. London: Routledge.

Le Bonniec, H. 1958. *Le culte de Cérès à Rome, des origins à la fin de la République*. Paris: C. Klincksieck.

Le Gall, J. 1976. "Evocatio." In *L'Italie préromaine et la Rome republicaine: mélanges offerts à J. Heurgon* I, Rome: École française de Rome, 519–524.

Leon, H. J. 1960. *The Jews of Ancient Rome*. Philadelphia: Jewish Publication Society of America.

Levene, D. S. 1993. *Religion in Livy*. Leiden: Brill.

Levi, M. A. 1969. "Bacchanalia, foedus e foederati." *Klearchos* 11, 15–23.

Liebeschuetz, J. H. W. G. 1979. *Continuity and Change in Roman Religion*. Oxford: Oxford University Press.

Linderski, J. 1986. "The Augural Law." *Aufstieg und Niedergang der Römischen Welt* 2.16.3, Berlin: W. de Gruyter, 2146–2312.

Linderski, J. 2002. "The Pontiff and the Tribune: The Death of Tiberius Gracchus." *Athenaeum* 90, 339–366.

Lindsay, W. M. 1913. *Sexti Pompei Festi. De uerborum significatu quae supersunt cum Pauli Epitome*. Leipzig: Teubner.

Lintott A. W. 1968. *Violence in republican Rome*. Oxford: Oxford University Press

Liou-Gille, B. 1980. *Cultes "heroiques" romains. Les Fondateurs*. Paris: Les Belles Lettres.

Liou-Gille, B. 1992. "Une tentative de reconstitution historique: les cultes federaux latins de Diane Aventine et de Diane Nemorensis." *Parola del Passato* 47, 411–438.

Liou-Gille, B. 1996. "Naissance de la ligue latine: mythe et culte de fondation." *Revue belge de philologie et d'histoire* 74, 73–97.

Liou-Gille, B. 1997. "Les rois de Rome et la Ligue Latine: definitions et interpretations." *Latomus* 56, 729–764.

Lomas, K. 1993. *Rome and the Western Greeks, 350 BC—AD 200: Conquest and Acculturation in Southern Italy*. London: Routledge.

Lott, J. B. 2004. *The neighborhoods of Augustan Rome*. Cambridge: Cambridge University Press.

Luce, T. J. 1977. *Livy: The Composition of his History*. Princeton: Princeton University Press.

Luisi, A. 1982. "La lex Maenia e la repressione dei Baccanali nel 186 A. C." *Contributi dell'Istituto di storia antica* 8, 179–185.

MacBain, B. 1982. *Prodigy and Expiation: A Study in Religion and Politics in Republican Rome*. Brussels: Latomus.

MacMullen R. 1991. "Hellenizing the Romans: (2nd century B.C.)." *Historia* 40, 419–438.

MacMullen, R. 2000. *Romanization in the Time of Augustus*. New Haven: Yale University Press.

Malaise, M. 1972. *Inventaire préliminaire des documents égyptiens découverts en Italie (Études préliminaires aux religions orientales dans l'Empire romain* 21). Leiden: Brill.

Malavolta, M. 1996. "I *Ludi* delle *Feriae Latinae* a Roma." In *Alba Longa: mito, storia, archeologia* (A. Pasqualini, ed.), Rome: Istituto italiano per la storia antica, 255–273.

Malkin, I. (ed.) 2001. *Ancient Perceptions of Greek Ethnicity*. Cambridge: Harvard University Press.

Mark, Ira. 1993. *The Sanctuary of Athena Nike in Athens: Architectural Stages and Chronology*. Princeton: Princeton University Press.

Massa-Pairault, F.-H. 1993. "Aspects Idéologiques des *Ludi*." In *Spectacles sportifs et scéniques dans le monde étrusco-italique* (Collection de l'École française de Rome 172), Rome: École française de Rome, 247–279.

McDonald, A. H. 1944. "Rome and the Italian Confederation (200–186 B.C.)." *Journal of Roman Studies* 34, 11–33.

McInerney, J. 1999. *The Folds of Parnassos: Land and Ethnicity in Ancient Phokis*. Austin: University of Texas Press.

Miles, G. 1986. "The Cycle of Roman History in Livy's First Pentad." *American Journal of Philology* 107, 1–33.

Miles, G. 1988. "*Maiores, Conditores*, and Livy's Perspective on the Past." *Transactions of the American Philological Association* 118, 185–208.

Miles, G. 1995. *Livy: Reconstructing Early Rome*. Ithaca: Cornell University Press.

Millar, F. (ed.). 2000. *La révolution romaine après Ronald Syme*. Geneva: Fondation Hardt.

Millett, M. 1990. *The Romanization of Britain : An Essay in Archaeological Interpretation*. Cambridge: Cambridge University Press.

Mitchell, R. 1990. *Patricians and Plebeians: The Origin of the Roman State*. Ithaca: Cornell University Press.

Momigliano, A. 1942. "Camillus and Concord." *Classical Quarterly* 36, 111–120.

Momigliano, A. 1967. "L'ascesa della plebe nella storia arcaica di Roma." *Rivista Storica Italiana* 79, 297–312 (reprinted in A. Momigliano, *Quarto Contributo alla storia degli studi classici e del mondo antico*, Rome, 1969, 437–454).

Mommsen, T. 1859. "Die Ludi Magni und Romani." *Rheinisches Museum für Philologie* 14, 79–87 (reprinted in *Römische Forschungen* II, Berlin, 1879).

Mommsen, T. 1879. *Römische Forschungen*, Vol. 2. Berlin: Weidmann.

Mommsen, T. 1887. *Römische Staatsrecht*, 3rd ed. Leipzig: Hirzel.

Mommsen, T. 1912. "Epistula de Romanorum Prodigiis ad Ottonem Jahnium." In *Gesammelte Schriften* 7, Berlin, 168–174.

Montanari, E. 1988. *Identità culturale e conflitti religiosi nella Roma repubblicana*. Rome: Edizioni dell'Ateneo.

Morgan, M. G. 1990. "Politics, Religion and the Games in Rome, 200–150 B.C." *Philologus* 134, 14–36.

Mouritsen, H. 1998. *Italian Unification. A Study in Ancient and Modern Historiography*. (Bulletin of the Institute of Classical Studies Supplement 70). London: Institute of Classical Studies.

Müller, C. 1882. *Sexti Pompei Festi De uerborum significatione quae supersunt cum Pauli Epitome*. Leipzig: Teubner.

Mueller, H.-F. 1998. "*Vita, Pudicitia, Libertas*: Juno, Gender, and Religious Politics in Valerius Maximus." *Transactions of the American Philological Association* 128, 221–263.

Mueller, H.-F. 2002. *Roman Religion in Valerius Maximus*. London: Routledge.

Münzer, F. 1920. *Römische Adelsparteien und Adelsfamilien*. Stuttgart: Metzler.

Musial, D. 1990. "Sur le Culte d'Esculape à Rome et in Italie." *Dialogues d'histoire ancienne* 16, 231–238.

Mustakallio, K. 1990. "Some aspects of the story of Coriolanus and the women behind the cult of Fortuna Muliebris." In *Roman eastern policy and other studies in Roman history: proceedings of a colloquium at Tvärminne, 2–3 October 1987* (H. Solin and M. Kajava, eds.), Helsinki: Commentationes Humanarum Litterarum, 125–131.

Neel, J. 1970. "Lessons from a 'Primitive' People." *Science* 170, 815–822.

Nicolet, C. 1980. *The World of the Citizen in Republican Rome* (trans. P. S. Falla). Berkeley: University of California Press.

Nicolet, C. 1991. *Space, Geography, and Politics in the Early Roman Empire*. Ann Arbor: University of Michigan Press.

Nippel, W. 1988. *Aufruhr und "Polizei" in der römischen Republik*. Stuttgart: Klett-Cotta.

Nock, A. D. 1934. "Religious Development from the Close of the Republic to the Death of Nero." In *Cambridge Ancient History* vol. 10 (2nd ed.), Cambridge: Cambridge University Press, 465–511.

North, J. 1976. "Conservatism and Change in Roman Religion." *Papers of the British School at Rome* 44, 1–12.

North, J. 1979. "Religious Toleration in Republican Rome." *Proceedings of the Cambridge Philological Society* 25, 85–103.

North, J. 1990. "Diviners and Divination at Rome." In *Pagan Priests* (M. Beard and J. North, eds.), Ithaca: Cornell University Press, 49–71.

North, J. 1993. "Roman Reactions to Empire." *Scripta Classica Israelica* 12, 127–38.

North, J. 2000. "Prophet and Text in the Third Century BC." In *Religion in Archaic and Republican Rome and Italy: Evidence and Experience* (E. Bispham and C. J. Smith, eds.), Edinburgh: Edinburgh University Press, 77–91.

Noy, D. 2000. *Foreigners at Rome: Citizens and Strangers*. London: Duckworth.

O'Brien, C. 1988. *God-Land: Reflections on Religion and Nationalism*. Cambridge: Harvard University Press.

Ogilvie, R. M. 1970. *A commentary on Livy, books 1–5*. Oxford: Oxford University Press.

Orlin, E. 1997. *Temples, Religion and Politics in the Roman Republic*. Leiden: Brill.

Orlin, E. 2000. "Why a Second Temple for Venus Erycina?" In *Studies in Latin Literature and Roman History*, Vol. X, Leiden: Brill, 70–90.

Orlin, E. 2002. "Foreign Cults in Republican Rome: Rethinking the Pomerial Rule." *Memoirs of the American Academy in Rome* 47, 1–18.

Orlin, E. 2007. "Augustan Religion and the Reshaping of Roman Memory." *Arethusa* 40, 73–92.

Orlin, E. 2008. "Octavian and Egyptian Cults: Redrawing the Boundaries of Romanness." *American Journal of Philology* 129, 231–253.

Ostrow, S. E. 1990. "The Augustales in the Augustan Scheme." In *Between Republic and Empire: Interpretations of Augustus and His Principate* (M. Toher and K. Raaflaub, eds.), Berkeley: University of California Press, 364–379.

Pagán, V. 2005. *Conspiracy Narratives in Roman History*. Austin: University of Texas Press.

Pailler, J.-M. 1988. *Bacchanalia. La répression de 186 av. J.C. à Rome et en Italie. Vestiges, images, tradition*. Paris: École française de Rome.

Pailler, J.-M. 1998. "Les Bacchanales, dix ans après." *Pallas* 48, 67–86.

Palmer, R. E. A. 1970. *The Archaic Community of the Romans.* Cambridge: Cambridge University Press.

Palmer, R. E. A. 1974. *Roman Religion and Roman Empire: Five Essays.* Philadelphia: University of Pennsylvania Press.

Palmer, R. E. A. 1975. "The neighborhood of Sullan Bellona at the Colline Gate." *Mélanges d'archéologie et d'histoire de l'École Française de Rome* 87, 653–665.

Parke, H. W. 1988. *Sibyls and sibylline prophecy in classical antiquity.* London: Routledge.

Pasqualini, A. 1996. "I miti albani e l'origine delle Feriae Latinae." In *Alba Longa. Mito, storia, archeologia* (A. Pasqualini, ed.), Rome: Istituto italiano per la storia antica, 217–253.

Pensabene P. 1982. "Nuove indagini nell'area del tempio di Cibele sul Palatino." In *La soteriologia dei culti orientali nell'impero romano. Atti del Colloquio internazionale, Roma, 24–28 settembre 1979* (U. di Bianchi and M. J. Vermaseren, eds.), Leiden: Brill, 68–108.

Pensabene, P. 1985. "Area sudoccidentale del Palatino." In *Roma: archeologia nel centro* (A. M. Bietti Sestieri et al., eds.), Rome: De Luca, 179–212.

Pensabene, P. 1988. "Scavi nell'area del Tempio della Vittoria e del Santuario della Magna Mater sul Palatino." *Archeologia Laziale* 9, 54–67.

Petrochilos, N. 1974. *Roman attitudes to the Greeks.* Athens: National and Capodistrian University of Athens.

Piganiol, A. 1923. *Recherches sur les jeux romains: notes d'archéologie et d'histoire religieuse.* Strasbourg: Librairie Istra.

Pighi, J. B. 1965. *De Ludis Saecularibus populi Romani quiritium.* Amsterdam: P. Schippers.

Platner, S. B. and Ashby, T. 1929. *A topographical dictionary of ancient Rome.* London: Oxford University Press.

Poucet J. 1979. "Archéologie, tradition et histoire. Les origines et les premiers siècles de Rome." *Les Études Classiques* 47, 201–214 and 347–363.

Poucet, J. 1978. "Le Latium protohistorique et archaique a la lumiere des decouvertes archeologiques recentes." *L'Antiquité classique* 47, 566–601.

Poucet, J. 1985. *Les origines de Rome—tradition et histoire.* Brussels: Latomus.

Poucet J. 1986. "Albe dans la tradition et l'histoire des origines de Rome." In *Hommages à Josef Veremans* (F. Decreus and C. Deroux, eds.), Brussels: Latomus, 212–236.

Poucet, J. 1989. "La difusion de la legende d'Enee en Italie centrale et ses rapports avec celle de Romulus." *Les Études classiques* 58, 227–254.

Poucet, J. 1992. "Troie, Lavinium, Rome et les Pénates." *L'Antiquité classique* 61, 260–267.

Prowse, K. R. 1964. "Numa and the Pythagoreans: A Curious Incident." *Greece and Rome* 11, 36–42.

Quinn-Schofield, W. K. 1967a. "*Ludi, Romani magnique uarie appellati.*" *Latomus* 26, 96–103.

Quinn-Schofield, W. K. 1967b. "Observations upon the *Ludi Plebeii.*" *Latomus* 26, 677–685.

Rasmussen, S. 2003. *Public Portents in Republican Rome.* Rome: L'Erma di Bretschneider.

Rawson, E. 1974. "Religion and Politics in the Late Second Century B.C. at Rome." *Phoenix* 28, 193–212.

Rawson, E. R. 1971. "The Prodigy Lists and the Use of the *Annales Maximi.*" *Classical Quarterly* 21, 158–169.

Renfrew, C. 1987. *Archaeology and Language: The Puzzle of Indo-European Origins.* London: J. Cape.

Rich, J. W. 2008. "Treaties, Allies and the Roman Conquest of Italy." In *War and Peace in Ancient and Medieval History* (P. De Souza and J. France, eds.), Cambridge: Cambridge University Press, 51–75.

Richard, J.-C. 1978. *Les origines de la plèbe romain. Essai sur la formation du dualisme patrico-plébéien.* Paris: École française de Rome.

Richardson, J. S. 1980. "The Ownership of Roman Lands: Tiberius Gracchus and the Italians." *Journal of Roman Studies* 70, 1–11.

Richardson, L., Jr. 1992. *A New Topographical Dictionary of Ancient Rome.* Baltimore: Johns Hopkins University Press.

Rives, J. 1995. "Human Sacrifice Among Pagans and Christians." *Journal of Roman Studies* 85, 65–85.

Rizzo, G. E. 1946. *Monete greche delle Sicilia.* Rome: Forni.

Roller, L. 1997. "The Ideology of the Eunuch Priest." *Gender & History* 9, 542–559.

Roller, L. 1999. *In Search of God the Mother: The Cult of Anatolian Cybele.* Berkeley: University of California Press.

Romanelli, P. 1963. "Lo scavo al tempio della Magna Mater sul Palatino." *Monumenti Antichi* 46, 201–330.

Romanucci-Ross, L. and De Vos, G. 1995. *Ethnic identity : creation, conflict, and accommodation.* Walnut Creek: Altamira.

Rosen, K. 1985. "Die falschen Numabücher." *Chiron* 15, 65–90.

Rosenberger, V. 1998. *Gezähmte Götter. Das Prodigienwesen der römischen Republik.* Stuttgart: Franz Steiner.

Rosenstein, N. 1990. *Imperatores Victi.* Berkeley: University of California Press.

Rousselle, R. 1982. *The Roman Persecution of the Bacchic Cult.* Diss. Binghamton.

Rüpke, J. 1990. *Domi militiae: die religiöse Konstruktion des Krieges in Rom.* Stuttgart: Franz Steiner.

Rüpke, J. 2005. *Fasti sacerdotum,* 3 vols. Stuttgart: Franz Steiner.

Rüpke, J. 2007. *The Religion of the Romans.* Cambridge: Cambridge University Press.

Sabbatucci D. 1982. "L'extra-romanità di Fortuna." *Scritti in memoria di Angelo Brelich* (*Religioni e civiltà,* Vol. 3), 511–527.

Salmon, E. T. 1970. *Roman Colonization under the Republic.* Ithaca: Cornell University Press.

Salmon, E. T. 1982. *The Making of Roman Italy.* London: Thames and Hudson.

Santangelo, F. 2007. "Pompey and religion." *Hermes* 135, 228–233.

Saulnier, C. 1984. "*Laurens Lauinas.* Quelques remarques à propos d'un sacerdoce équestre à Rome." *Latomus* 43, 517–533.

Saunders, C. 1944. "The Nature of Rome's Early Appraisal of Greek Culture." *Classical Philology* 39, 209–217.

Scafuro, A. 1989. "Livy's Comic Narrative of the Bacchanalia." *Helios* 16, 119–142.

Scheid, J. 1985. *Religion et piété à Rome.* Paris: Découverte.

Scheid, J. 1987. "Polytheism Impossible; or, the Empty Gods: Reasons behind a Void in the History of Roman Religion." In *The Inconceivable Polytheism* (F. Schmidt, ed.), *History and Anthropology* 3, 303–325.

Scheid, J. 1995. "*Graeco Ritu*: A Typically Roman Way of Honoring the Gods." *Harvard Studies in Classical Philology* 97, 15–31.

Scheid, J. 2003. *An Introduction to Roman Religion* (trans. Janet Lloyd). Bloomington: Indiana University Press.

Scheid, J. 2005. "Augustus and Roman Religion: Continuity, Conservatism, and Innovation." In *The Cambridge Companion to the Age of Augustus* (K. Galinsky, ed.), Cambridge: Cambridge University Press, 175–193.

Scheidel, W. 2007. "The Demography of Roman State Formation in Italy." In *Herrschaft ohne Integration? Rom und Italien in republikanischer Zeit* (M. Jehne and R. Pfeilschifter, eds.), Frankfurt am Main: Verlag Alte Geschichte, 207–226.

Schilling, R. 1954. *La religion romaine de Vénus, depuis les origines jusqu'au temps d'Auguste.* Paris: École française de Rome.

Schilling, R. 1960. "Les Castores romains à la lumière des traditions indo-européennes." In *Hommage à Georges Dumézil* (*Collection Latomus* 45), Brussels: Latomus, 177–192.

Schnegg-Köhler, B. 2002. *Die augusteischen Säkularspiele.* Archiv für Religionsgeschichte 4, Munich: K. G. Saur.

Schultz, C. 2006a. *Women's religious activity in the Roman Republic.* Chapel Hill: University of North Carolina Press.

Schultz, C. 2006b. "Juno Sospita and Roman insecurity in the Social War." In *Religion in Republican Italy* (C. Schultz & P. Harvey, eds.) New Haven: Yale University Press, 207–227.

Scullard, H. H. 1951. *Roman Politics 220–150 B.C.* Oxford: Oxford University Press.

Scullard, H. H. 1981. *Festivals and Ceremonies of the Roman Republic.* London: Thames and Hudson.

Sensi Sestito, G. de. 1984. "La funzione politica dell'Heraion del Lacinio al tempo delle lotte contro i Lucani e Dionisio I." *Contributi dell'Istituto di Storia antica dell'Università del Sacro Cuore* 10, 41–50.

Shapiro, H. A. 1998. "Autochthony and the Visual Arts in Fifth-Century Athens." In *Democracy, Empire, and the Arts* (Deborah Boedeker and Kurt Raaflaub, eds.) Cambridge: Harvard University Press, 127–151.

Shatzman I. 1971. "The Egyptian questions in Roman politics (59–54 B.C.)." *Latomus* 30, 363–369.

Sherwin-White, A. N. 1973. *The Roman Citizenship.* Oxford: Oxford University Press.

Slingerland, H. Dixon. 1997. *Claudian Policymaking and the Early Imperial Repression of Judaism at Rome.* Atlanta: Scholars Press.

Smith, A. D. 1986. *The Ethnic Origin of Nations.* Oxford: Oxford University Press.

Smith, A. D. 1991. *National Identity.* Harmondsworth: Penguin.

Smith, A. D. 2001. *Nationalism.* Cambridge: Cambridge University Press.

Sommella, P. 1972. "Heroon di Enea a Lavinium: recenti scavi a Practica di Mare." *Rendiconti della Pontificia Accademia di archeologia* 44, 47–74.

Sommella, P. 1974. "Das Heroon des Aeneas und die Topographie des antiken Lavinium." *Gymnasium* 81, 283–297.

Spaeth, B. 1990. "The goddess Ceres and the death of Tiberius Gracchus." *Historia* 39, 182–195.

Spaeth, B. 1996. *The Roman Goddess Ceres.* Austin: University of Texas Press.

Stambaugh, J. 1978. "The Functions of Roman Temples." *Aufstieg und Niedergang der Römischen Welt* 2.16.1, Berlin: W. de Gruyter, 554–608.

Stangl, T. 1912. *Ciceronis orationum scholiastae.* Leipzig: Freytag.

Staples, A. 1998. *From Good Goddesses to Vestal Virgins.* London: Routledge.

Steinby, E. M. 1993–2000. *Lexicon Topographicum Urbis Romae.* Rome: Quasar.

Stockton, D. 1979. *The Gracchi.* Oxford: Oxford University Press.

Sydenham, E. A. 1952. *The Coinage of the Roman Republic.* London: Spink.

Syme, R. 1939. *The Roman Revolution.* Oxford: Oxford University Press.

Szemler, G. 1972. *The Priests of the Roman Republic: A Study of Interactions between Priesthoods and Magistracies.* Brussels: Latomus.

Takács, S. 1995. *Isis and Sarapis in the Roman World.* Leiden: Brill.

Takács, S. 2000. "Politics and Religion in the Bacchanalian Affair of 186 B.C." *Harvard Studies in Classical Philology* 100, 301–310.

Taylor, L. R. 1931. *The Divinity of the Roman Emperor.* Middletown: American Philological Association.

Taylor, L. R. 1934. "New Light on the History of the Secular Games." *American Journal of Philology* 55, 101–120.

Taylor L. R. 1937. "The opportunities for dramatic performances in the time of Plautus and Terence." *Transactions of the American Philological Association* 68, 284–304.

Taylor, L. R. 1939. "Cicero's Aedileship." *American Journal of Philology* 60, 194–202.

Taylor, L. R. 1942. "The Election of the Pontifex Maximus in the Late Republic." *Classical Philology* 37, 421–24.

Taylor, L. R. 1949. *Party Politics in the Age of Caesar.* Berkeley: University of California Press.

Tengström, E. 1977. "Theater und Politik in Kaiserlichen Rom." *Eranos* 75, 369–375.

Terrenato, N. 1998. "Tam firmum municipium: The Romanization of Volaterrae and Its Cultural Implications." *Journal of Roman Studies* 88, 94–114.

Thomas, G. 1984. "Magna Mater and Attis." *Aufstieg und Niedergang der Römischen Welt* II.17.3, Berlin: W. de Gruyter, 1499–1535.

Thomas, Y. 1990. "L'institution de l'origine: *sacra principiorum populi Romani*." In *Tracés de fondation* (M. Detienne, ed.), Leuven: Peeters, 143–170.

Thuillier J.-P. 1975. "Denys d'Halycarnasse et les jeux romains. Antiquités romaines VII,72–73." *Mélanges d'archéologie et d'histoire de l'École Française de Rome* 87, 563–581.

Thuillier, J.-P. 1981. "Les Sports dans les Civilisation Étrusque." *Stadion* 7, 173–202.

Thuillier, J.-P. 1985. *Les Jeux Athletiques dans la Civilization Étrusque.* Rome: École française de Rome.

Toher, M. and Raaflaub, K. (eds.). 1990. *Between Republic and Empire: interpretations of Augustus and his principate.* Berkeley: University of California Press.

Toll, K. 1991. "The *Aeneid* as an Epic of National Identity: *Italiam Laeto Socii Clamore Salutant*." *Helios* 18, 3–14.

Toll, K. 1997. "Making Roman-ness and the Aeneid." *Classical Antiquity* 16, 34–56.

Tondriau J. 1949. "Romains de la république assimilés à des divinités." *Symbolae Osloenses* 27, 128–140.

Torelli, M. 1975. *Elogia tarquiniensia.* Florence: Sansoni.

Torelli, M. 1984. *Lavinio e Roma. Riti iniziatici e matrimonio tra archeologia e storia.* Rome: Quasar.

Torelli, M. 1990. "Comments on Wallace." In *Staat und Staatlichkeit in der frühen römischen Republik* (W. Eder, ed.), Stuttgart: Franz Steiner, 303–305.

Torelli, M. 1995. *Studies in the Romanization of Italy*. Edmonton: University of Alberta Press.

Torelli, M. 1999. *Tota Italia. Essays in the Cultural Formation of Roman Italy*. Oxford: Oxford University Press.

Toynbee A. J. 1965. *Hannibal's legacy*. Oxford: Oxford University Press.

Turner, V. 1969. *The Ritual Process: Structure and Anti-Structure*. Chicago: Aldine.

Turner, V. 1974. *Dramas, Fields, and Metaphors: Symbolic Action in Human Society*. Ithaca: Cornell University Press.

Ungern-Sternberg, J. von. 1970. *Untersuchungen zum spätrepublikanischen Notstandsrecht. Senatusconsultum ultimum und hostis-Erklärung*. Munich: Beck.

Ungern-Sternberg, J. von. 1975. "Die Einführung spezieller Sitze für die Senatoren bei den Spielen (194 v. Chr.)." *Chiron* 5, 157–163.

Van der Vliet, E. 2003. "The Romans and us: Strabo's "Geography" and the construction of ethnicity." *Mnemosyne* 56, 257–272.

Van Son, D. W. L. 1963. "The Disturbances in Etruria during the Second Punic War." *Mnemosyne* 16, 267–274.

Vanggaard, Jens H. 1988. *The Flamen. A Study in the History and Sociology of Roman Religion*. Copenhagen: Museum Tusculanum.

Vermaseren, M. J. 1977. *Cybele and Attis, the Myth and the Cult*. London: Thames and Hudson.

Versluys, M. 2002. *"Aegyptiaca Romana": Nilotic scenes and the Roman views of Egypt*. Leiden: Brill.

Veyne, P. 1990. *Bread and Circuses: Historical Sociology and Political Pluralism* (trans. B. Pearce; French ed., 1976). London: A. Lane, The Penguin Press.

Voisin, J. L. 1984. "Tite-Live, Capoue et les Bacchanales." *Mélanges de l'Ecole française de Rome* 96, 601–653.

Wagenvoort, H. 1951. "The Origin of the Ludi Saeculares." *Meded. Kon. Ned. Akad. V. Wetensch. Afd. Lett. N.R.* 14, no 4 (reprinted in *Studies in Roman Literature, Culture, and Religion*, Leiden: Brill, 1956), 193–232.

Walbank, F. W. 1957. *A Historical Commentary on Polybius*, 3 vols. Oxford: Oxford University Press.

Walbank, F. W. 1967. "The Sciponic Legend." *Proceedings of the Cambridge Philological Society* 13, 54–69.

Wallace, R. W. 1990. "Hellenization and Roman Society in the Late Fourth Century B.C. A Methodological Critique." In *Staat und Staatlichkeit in der frühen römischen Republik* (W. Eder, ed.), Stuttgart: Franz Steiner, 278–292.

Wallace-Hadrill, A. 1987. "Time for Augustus: Ovid, Augustus and the Fasti," In *Homo Viator: Classical Essays for John Bramble* (Michael Whitby, Philip Hardie, and Mary Whitby, eds.), Oak Park: Bolchazy-Carducci, 221–230.

Wallace-Hadrill, A. 2000. "The Roman Revolution and Material Culture." In *La révolution romaine après Ronald Syme* (F. Millar, ed.), Geneva: Fondation Hardt, 283–313.

Wallace-Hadrill, A. 2005. "*Mutatas Formas*: The Augustan Transformation of Roman Knowledge." In *The Cambridge Companion to the Age of Augustus* (K. Galinsky, ed.), Cambridge: Cambridge University Press, 55–84.

Wallace-Hadrill, A. 2008. *Rome's Cultural Revolution*. Cambridge: Cambridge University Press.

Walsh, P. G. 1961. *Livy: his historical aims and methods*. Cambridge: Cambridge University Press.

Walsh, P. G. 1996. "Making a Drama out of a Crisis: Livy on the Bacchanalia." *Greece & Rome* 43, 188–203.

Warde Fowler, W. 1911. *The Religious Experience of the Roman People*. London: Macmillan and Co.

Wardle, D. 1998. *Valerius Maximus: Memorable Deeds and Sayings: Book I*. Oxford: Oxford University Press.

Wardman, A. 1982. *Religion and Statecraft among the Romans*. London: Granada.

Warrior, V. 2006. *Roman Religion*. Cambridge: Cambridge University Press.

Weinstock, S. 1957. "Victor and Invictus." *Harvard Theological Review* 50, 211–247.

Weinstock, S. 1960. "Two Archaic Inscriptions from Latium," *Journal of Roman Studies* 50, 112–118.

Weinstock, S. 1971. *Divus Julius*. Oxford: Oxford University Press.

Weiss P. 1973. "Die 'Säkularspiele' der Republik, eine annalistische Fiktion? Ein Beitrag zum Verstandnis der kaiserzeitlichen Ludi saeculares." *Mitteilungen des Deutschen Archäologischen Instituts, Römische Abteilung* 80, 205–217.

Westenholz, J. (ed.) 1995. *The Jewish Presence in Ancient Rome*. Jerusalem: Bible Lands Museum.

Williams, C. 1999. *Roman Homosexuality: Ideologies of Masculinity in Classical Antiquity*. Oxford: Oxford University Press.

Williams, J. H. C. 2001. *Beyond the Rubicon: Romans and Gauls in Republican Italy*. Oxford: Oxford University Press.

Wiseman, T. P. 1985. *Roman Political Life 90BC—69AD*. Exeter: Exeter University Press.

Wiseman, T. P. 1995. *Remus*. Cambridge: Cambridge University Press.

Wiseman, T. P. 2005. *"Origines Ludorum."* In *Roman Crossings: Theory and Practice in the Roman Republic* (K. Welch and T. W. Hillard, eds.), Swansea: Classical Press Of Wales, 49–58.

Wissowa, G. 1912. *Religion und Kultus der Römer*, 2nd ed. Munich: Beck.

Wolters, P. 1925. "Götter oder Heroen?" In *Festschrift P. Arndt*, Munich: F. Bruckmann.

Woolf, G. 1998. *Becoming Roman: The Origins of Provincial Civilization in Gaul*. Cambridge: Cambridge University Press.

Wuilleumier, P. 1932. "Tarente et le Tarentum." *Revue des études latines* 10, 127–146.

Wuilleumier, P. 1938. "Tarente et le *Tarentum*." *Revue des études latines* 16, 139–145.

Wuilleumier, P. 1939. *Tarente, des origines à la conquête romaine*. Paris: E. de Boccard.

Wulff Alonso, F. 2002. *Roma e Italia de la Guerra social a la retirada de Sila*. Brussels: Latomus.

Wülker, L. 1903. *Die geschichtliche Entwicklung des Prodigienwesens bei den Römern*. Leipzig: E. Glausch.

Yavetz, Z. 1969. *Plebs and Princeps*. Oxford: Oxford University Press.

Zanker, P. (ed.). 1976. *Hellenismus in Mittelitalien*. Göttingen: Vandenhoeck und Ruprecht.

Zanker, Paul. 1998. *Pompeii: Public and Private Life* (trans. by D. Schneider). Cambridge: Harvard University Press.

Zeitlin, F. 1982. "Cultic Models of the Female: Rites of Dionysus and Demeter." *Arethusa* 15, 29–57.

Ziolkowski, A. 1988. "Mummius' Temple of Hercules Victor and the Round Temple on the Tiber." *Phoenix* 42, 309–333.

Ziolkowski, A. 1992. *The Temples of Mid-Republican Rome and Their Historical and Topographical Context.* Rome: L'Erma di Bretschneider.

INDEX

Aeneas, 20–22, 34, 45–47, 51, 73–75,
    80, 126, 201
Aesculapius, 12, 27, 59, 62–70, 72, 76,
    83–84, 163
ager Romanus, 114–16
Agonalia, 146
Alba Longa, 45–49, 51, 53
Alban mount, 44, 49, 50, 56, 118–19
Albano ritu, 164
Alexander the Great, 60
Alexandria, 205
Annales maximi, 96
Antemnae, 54
Antiochus III, 182, 184
anti-Semitism, 183
Antium, 63, 64, 124, 125, 217
Anubis, 204
Aphrodisias, 201
Aphrodite, 73, 126
Apollo (see also *ludi Apollinares*), 11, 17,
    28, 36, 66, 113, 153–56, 163, 211, 214
Appian Way, 125
Apulia, 165
Aquae Sextiae, 198
Aquileia, 171
Ardea, 49, 54, 125, 126, 128, 174
area Lucinae, 41

Aricia, 119
Ariminum, 94
Arpinum, 24, 132, 158, 173, 216
Ascanius, 45, 51
Asia Minor, 79, 100, 156, 158, 182, 198,
    200, 203, 215
astrologers, 182–85
asylum, 20, 211
Athens, 5, 16, 18, 60
Attalus of Pergamum, 77, 80, 81, 82, 100
Attis, 80
augurs, 87, 99, 100
Augustales, 212
Augustus (Octavian), 8, 25–26, 29–30, 67,
    85, 103, 146, 155, 190–91, 201, 208–19
auspicia, 99
autochthony, 21
Aventine hill, 37, 40, 123, 126, 129, 194

Bacchanalia, 7, 28, 132, 133, 147, 165–69,
    174–75, 185, 207
Bacchus, 35, 133, 165–68, 170, 175–76, 184
Barth, Fredrik, 14
Bataces, 198, 200
Bellona, 199
Beneventum, 124
Bible, Hebrew, 15

Bibulus, M. Calpurnius, 192
Bona Dea, 192
Bononia, 171
boundaries, 13–19, Ch. 6 *passim*
  permeability of, 14, 36, 83, 126, 152,
    160–62, 215, 219
  pomerium as, 82, 126, 211
  prodigies as transgression of,
    120–21, 188
  between Roman and non-Roman, 5,
    24, 104, 150, 163, 184–85
  between Roman and Greek, 28, 109,
    152, 170, 185–86, 211–12
  between Roman and Italian, 179, 188,
    210–213
  of Romanness, 26, 28–30, 83, 104,
    109–10, 121, 152, 157, 160–62,
    184–85, 188, 193, 210–213
  significance for group identity,
    13–19, 24, 84, 121, 150, 215–219
  walls as, 5, 22, 94, 121
Brutus, M. Junius, 191

Cacus, 33–34
Caecilia Metella, 188
Caere, 116, 123–24
calendar, 16, 31, 37, 39, 56, 104, 138,
    145, 149, 157, 200, 217
Cales, 115, 124
Calliphana, 106
Campania, 43, 115, 172, 203, 213
Campus Martius, 68–69, 213–14
Cannae, 105, 126, 154, 178
Capena, 116, 127–28
Capitolia, 219
Capitoline hill, 20, 34, 37, 60, 72,
    75–76, 84, 96–97, 125, 128, 202,
    204, 211
Cappadocia, 199
Capua, 42, 124, 148
carmen Marciana, 155
Carthage, 23, 74, 185, 213
Carthaginians, 69, 71, 74, 78, 124, 130,
    178, 196
Cassius Longinus, C., 191
Castor and Pollux, 3, 35, 36, 163, 222
Cato, M. Porcius, 163, 170, 183
  Origines, 170

Ceres, 3, 27–28, 35, 104–10, 144, 153–55,
    192–96, 222
  Graeca sacra festa Cereris, 105–6
  ieiunium Cereris, 91
  sacrum anniversarium Cereris, 105
Chaldaeans, 182, 185, 199
Cicero, M. Tullius, 24, 44, 54, 79–80,
    93, 98, 100, 105–7, 140, 180, 192,
    196, 201, 208, 216
Cimbri and Teutones, 198
cinctus Gabinus, 164
Circus Flaminius, 140, 142, 214
Circus Maximus, 137, 139, 142
citizens, Roman (see also colonies,
    Roman)
  living outside Rome, 4, 22, 42–43, 55,
    95, 115–16, 158–59, 171–74
  rights, 4, 19, 132, 171–72
citizenship, Roman (see also: openness;
    Romanness)
  contested nature of during Late
    Republic, 196–98
  expansion comes to halt, 24, 132, 158,
    172–73
  as marker of identity, 4–5, 18–20,
    27, 95, 104–10, 115, 150–51, 171–74,
    186–90, 216
  as reward, 42–43, 115–116
  and Social War, 135, 150, 158, 171–74,
    187–90, 203
  willingness to extend, 4, 18–19, 22, 33
Claudia (sister of P. Claudius Pulcher),
    108
A. Claudius Caecus, 108
A. Claudius Crassus, 37
Cleopatra, 205
Clitumnus, 213, 219
P. Clodius, 192, 201, 205–06
colonies, 4, 64–65, 174, 178, 213, 219
  Latin, 115–16, 125–28, 158, 171,
  Roman citizen, 22, 94–95, 108, 158, 171,
    178, 213
communitas, 121, 153
Concordia, 195
consecratio capitis, 194–95
Consualia, 139, 146
Copia, 171
Corinth, 185

Coriolanus, C. Marcius, 41
Cn. Cornelius Hispanus, 182
Croton, 171, 176, 178–79, 213
Crustumerium, 133
Cumae, 202–3
Cybele, *see* Magna Mater
Cyprus, 205

decemviri sacris faciundis, 72, 78, 87, 89,
    90–91, 93, 98, 100, 123, 125–29,
    132–33, 155, 175
P. Decius Mus, 8, 63, 88
Delphi, 17, 19, 77, 154, 155, 201
Demeter, 35, 105, 153–54
devotio, 8, 88
Diana, 119, 181, 213–14
    Diana Tifatina, 213
dies natalis, 88, 102, 140
Dionysius, 182
Dionysius of Halicarnassus, 51, 99, 101,
    105, 151
Dioscuri. *See* Castor and
    Pollux
Dis, 27, 68–69, 70, 214
divination, 91, 120, 198–99
Drepana, 69, 108
duodecim populi Etruriae, 93

Egypt, 205–6, 210
    deities, 203, 205–07, 211
    as 'Other', 30, 205–6, 211–12
elogia Tarquiniensa, 93, 98
Epicureans, 184
Epidaurus, 63, 65
Erythrae, 203
Eryx, 71, 73–74, 126, 170
Esquiline hill, 41
ethnos, 164–65, 216
ethnic groups, 12–25, 49, 94–95, 182,
    184–85, 208
Etruria
    prodigies from, 123–24, 127–31, 136,
        188
    Roman concern to integrate,
        37, 89, 92, 94, 124, 127–131,
        136, 188, 219
    and Social War, 136, 187–88
    victories over, 37–39, 108

Etruscan (see also haruspices; Juno
    Regina)
    elements in Rome, 20, 27, 37, 55, 88–92,
        95, 129–30, 137–40, 143, 151–52, 165
    as ethnic group, 94–97
    foreignness of, 97–99, 108–9, 152
    religious expertise, 91–92, 98, 129
Etrusca disciplina, 92, 97–98
eunuchs, 101, 104
Evander (Arcadian king) 33–34
evocatio, 26, 36–38, 40, 42, 56, 92, 126
expiatory rituals, 28, 78, 89, 90, 91, 98,
    111, 113, 114, 120–31, 134, 136, 174, 176,
    194
expulsions from Rome, 186
    of astrologers (Chaldaeans), 182–84
    of Latins and Italians, 158, 183–87
    of Jews, 182–84
    of Macedonians, 184
    of *peregrini*, 186
    of philosophers and rhetors, 184
    of priest of Magna Mater, 201

Q. Fabius Gurges, 73, 108
Q. Fabius Maximus, 60, 71–72
Q. Fabius Pictor, 84, 154–55
Q. Fabius Rullianus, 63
Falerii, 54
C. Fannius, 150–51, 186–87
Fanum Voltumnae, 219
fasti (see also calendar), 61, 79, 146, 199,
    211, 217
    Praenestini, 41, 217
Faunus, 181
feriae (ritual), 132–33, 175
feriae Latinae, 44–50, 55, 95, 118
Feronia, 116, 119, 127
fetiales, 87
ficus Ruminalis, 66–67
Figulus, T. Marcius, 134
flamen Dialis, 87
C. Flaminius, 45
Flora, 28, 145, 153, 157
foreignness, paraded, 100, 109,
    196–97
Formiae, 24, 43, 115, 116, 132,
    158, 173
Fors Fortuna, 124

Fortuna, 41, 123, 124, 176, 181, 213
    Equestris, 176
    Muliebris, 41
    Primigenia, 181
Forum Boarium, 33–34
freedwomen, 127
Fregellae, 134, 135, 136
Frusino, 129
fulgural lore, 91, 98, 129
M. Fulvius Flaccus, 195
Q. Fulvius Flaccus, 176–79
Fundi, 24, 43, 132, 158, 173
M. Furius Camillus, 10, 36, 39, 40,
    42, 45, 51, 143

Gabii, 218
A. Gabinius, 204–6
Galatia, 79
galli, 27, 79, 82, 100–110, 157, 168
Gauls, 63, 71, 154, 171, 196–97
    sack of Rome, 39–40
Genucius (gallus), 101
Gracchus, C., 23, 186, 192, 195–96
Gracchus, T. Sempronius (the Elder),
    99–100
Gracchus, T. Sempronius, 72, 98, 186,
    192–96
Graecus ritus, 29, 34, 163–64
Gravisca, 171
Greece
    religious practice in, 36, 59, 61–62, 106,
        109, 138, 151, 154–56, 211
    Roman hegemony over, 23, 28, 185
Greeks (see also Graecus ritus, Magna
        Graecia)
    culture in Rome, 26–28, 34–36, 59–67,
        83–84, 104–5, 130, 137–38, 151–54, 163,
        166
    as ethnic group, 12 n. 25, 16–19, 29,
        164
    foreignness stressed, 5, 23, 26, 30,
        151–52, 163–64, 168–70, 175
    integration stressed, 5, 109–10, 185–86,
        201, 211–212

Hadria, 94
Hannibal, 4, 28, 71, 73, 78, 122–23, 127,
    130–31, 148–49, 162, 170–72, 179–80, 222

Harpocrates, 204
haruspices, 27, 88–103, 107–110, 122, 129,
    131, 136, 150, 188, 198
Hasmonean, 185
Hellenistic world, 59–62, 74, 79
Hellenization, 5 n. 5, 154, 217, 222
Henna, 192–96
Hephaestus, 35
Hercules, 3, 33–35, 42, 61–62, 163, 180, 185,
    204
    Ara Maxima, 33–34, 61
    Invictus, 62
    Musarum, 180
    Victor, 62, 121, 153, 185
hermaphrodite, 111, 113, 120
Herodotus, 16, 19
Hispellum, 213, 219
Forum Holitorium, 125
Horatius Cocles, 96–97
human sacrifice, 148, 208
    Senatorial ban on, 196–197

identity
    Augustus restores Roman, 208–215
    challenges to Roman, 5–6, 150, 162–63,
        170–71, 186, 191–92, 197, 207–8
    civic, 5, 22, 150
    ethnic, 13–17, 20–22
    means of defining, 14–25, 121, 151–52,
        208
Ilythiae, 214
imperialism, military, 4, 32–33, 36, 59, 83,
    92, 129, 146, 160, 207
imperialism, 'religious,' 39, 42, 92–93, 115
instauratio, 45
Interamna, 94
intercessio, 123
Isis, 203–7, 211
Italian
    deities, 35, 62, 76, 104, 131, 145, 153,
        157–58, 163, 180–81, 213
    Roman integration of, 28–30, 114–16,
        120, 123, 127–33, 138, 174–76, 180,
        210–213
    and Social War, 135, 173, 187–89, 191,
        197
    status of, 19, 24, 83, 131, 157, 170–79,
        184, 186–190, 203, 210, 216

Jews, 15, 182–85
Jonathan (King of Judaea), 185
C. Julius Caesar, 146, 191–92, 196, 202, 205, 207
M. Junius Pennus, 186
L. Junius Pullus, 71
Juno
  on the Alban mount, 118
  in Italy, 54, 56, 62, 76
  Lacinia, 176–80, 213
  Lucina, 41, 42
  Regina, 12, 26, 36–42, 44, 55–56, 65, 76, 90, 92, 95, 126–30, 181
  Sospita (in Lanuvium), 43–46, 54–56, 95, 118, 123–25, 131, 174–75, 180, 188–89
  Sospita (in Rome), 43, 123, 125, 180, 188
Jupiter, 24, 60, 66, 72, 89, 116, 118–19, 128, 129, 181, 182, 195, 214, 220
  Feretrius, 210
  Latiaris, 54, 118
  Optimus Maximus, 12, 60, 70, 72, 87, 125, 139–140, 202
  Sabazios, 182
  Victor, 60
Juvenal, 101, 146

C. Laelius (Sapiens), 185
Lake Regillus, battle of, 35–36
Lake Trasimene, battle of, 45, 71, 124
Lanuvium, 43–46, 54–56, 95, 118–19, 123–28, 131–32, 174–75, 180, 189
lares Compitales, 212
Latin League, 5, 42, 54, 94, 125–26
Latin Revolt of 338 BCE, 4, 22, 26, 50, 54, 56, 59, 115–16, 118, 125, 222
Latins (see also colonies, nomen Latinum), as ethnic community, 19, 49, 54–56, 123
  literature, 23, 84
  regional sanctuaries of, 49, 54, 126, 132, 189
  relations to Rome, 5, 26, 43, 55–56, 59, 95, 116, 123, 188–89
Latinus (eponymous founder), 181
Latium
  Roman hegemony over, 57–58, 94
  Roman integration of, 4, 110

prodigies in, 115, 123–25
Lavinium, 35, 44–56, 126, 218–19
lectisternium, 72, 123, 143, 145, 148
Lemuria, 146
lex
  Didia, 174
  Fannia, 174
  Hortensia, 108
  Iulia de civitate, 187, 189
  Licinia et Sextia, 139, 141
  Ogulnia, 65, 67
  Plautia Papiria de Civitate, 187
  Sempronia, 173
Lightning (as prodigy), 89, 90–91, 96, 98, 111, 113, 115, 116, 118–19, 129
Liguria, 171
liminality, 113, 121, 153
Livius Andronicus, 84, 129, 143
Livy (T. Livius), 8–11, 21–24, 36–53, 56, 60–63, 78–80, 90–91, 96, 105–6, 112, 120, 130, 134, 139–44, 148, 152, 154, 158–60, 164–79, 196–97, 208–9, 222
Lucania, 65, 188
Luceria, 94
lucus Feroniae, 127, 213
ludi
  and Greek culture, 132, 138, 151–54, 156
  origins of, 28, 139–142
  as typical Roman rite, 27–28, 92, 104, 137–38, 146, 150–52, 156–57, 160–61, 215
  Apollinares, 28, 144–48, 154–56, 159
  Ceriales, 28, 143–44, 148, 154
  circenses, 137, 151–52
  Florales, 145, 149, 157–58
  Megalenses, 28, 102–3, 145, 149, 156–59
  plebeii, 140–43, 146, 148
  Romani (Magni), 72, 139–40, 146, 217
  saeculares, 59, 67–70, 213–14
  scenici, 113, 137, 142–43, 151–52, 154
  Tarentini, 27, 68–69, 143
Luna, 171
Lupercalia, 217
lustratio, 90, 92, 121, 123, 195
Q. Lutatius Cerco, 181

Marcellus, M. Claudius, 83
Ma, 199
Macedonia, 131

Macedonian War, First, 81
Macrobius, 174
Magna Graecia, 22, 27, 34–36, 59–61,
    64–71, 83, 104–5, 107, 127–30, 179, 202
Magna Mater (see also *ludi Megalenses*,
    galli), 12, 27–28, 59, 65, 76–84, 100–7,
    145, 149–50, 153–57, 167–68, 180, 184,
    198, 200–1, 215
T. Manlius Torquutus, 97
C. Manlius Vulso, 79
Marcellus, M. Claudius, 154, 178
Marica, 116
C. Marius, 191, 196–200, 208
Mars, 21, 72, 88
Martha (prophetess), 198
Mater Matuta, 116
matronae, 106, 109, 127, 129
Matronalia, 41
C. Memmius, 144
Mens, 72
Menturnae, 116
Metaurus, battle of, 78, 154
Metellus, Q. Caecilius, 185
Mettius Fufetius, 48
Minerva, 119, 128
Mithridatic Wars, 201, 203
Moirai, 214
monetales, 103
mons Algidus, 123–24
L. Mummius, 185
municipia, 128, 158, 216
Mutina, 171

nomen Latinum, 49, 173
Norba, 54
novemdiale sacrum, 78, 120, 123, 148
Numa Pompilius, 20, 28, 168–70, 211
numen, 24

Obsequens, Julius 75, 108, 113, 188
Odysseus, 38
Odyssey, 84
Q. Ogulnius, 63, 65
Olenus Calenus, 96
openness,
    as aid in expansion, 4, 41, 57, 61, 138
    as challenge to identity, 26–28, 84, 150,
        160–62

ideology of, 7, 26–27, 54, 61, 67, 76, 88,
    101, 110, 126, 138, 151–53, 158, 163, 170,
    211–12, 219
political, 4, 20, 41, 87, 95
religious, 4, 26–27, 31, 57, 168
L. Opimius, 195
ordo haruspicum, 93–94
orthopraxis, 86
Oscan, 135
the 'Other', 16–17, 109, 121, 217
Ovid, 54, 79, 80, 106

Paestum, 94
Palatine hill, 27, 60, 65, 77, 80–84, 103–4,
    145, 211–14
Palladium, 38
Parma, 171
Pater Indiges, 51
patrius mos, 29, 164, 166
pax deorum, 24, 37, 45, 87, 111, 113, 121, 124,
    156, 158
Peace of Phoenice, 81
Penates, 44–45, 47–48, 50–52, 56, 219
Pergamum, 77, 81, 100
Persephone, 105
Perseus (king of Macedon), 90, 134, 184
Pessinus, 77–80
Q. Petilius, 169
Philip V, 77, 148
Phrygia, 77–80, 102, 109, 156–57
Picenum, 123
Pietrabondante, 218
Pisa, 171
Pisaurum, 171
plebeians, 8, 22, 40, 65, 67, 107, 108, 193
Pliny the Elder, 35, 41, 66, 96, 196
Plutarch, 75, 186, 192, 195, 198–200
polis, 5, 18, 20, 164
politics and religion, 4, 7, 25, 32, 43, 55,
    59, 63, 82–83, 112 n. 7, 114–15, 126, 136,
    147, 151–53, 192–94, 209
Polybius, 71, 147, 196
pomerium, 82, 88, 99, 126, 181, 211, 212
pompa, 151, 153
Pompeius, A. (trib. 102), 200
Pompey the Great, 191, 202, 205–7
    Theater of, 214
M. Pomponius (pr. 161), 184

Pomponius Mela, 196
pontifex maximus, 87, 194, 209
pontiffs, 44, 87, 122, 127, 129
L. Porcius, 169
L. Postumius Megellus, 60
Sp. Postumius, 165–66
L. Postumius Albinus, 184
Potentia, 171
Practica di Mare, 51
Praeneste, 41, 43, 124, 125, 181, 217
priests (see also *galli*; *haruspices*;
    decemviri)
    colleges in Rome, 87–88, 93, 97, 111,
        120, 192
    foreign in Rome, Ch. 3 *passim*
    temples and, 39, 187–88
    and Roman aristocracy, 87–89, 96
prodigies, 28, 63, 78–79, 89–91, 98–99,
    Ch. 4
    passim, 147, 174, 192
    androgyne, 90, 130
    as means of building community, 28,
        114–126, 131–134, 188
    as transgression of boundaries, 111–113,
        121
    lists of, 112–114
    non suscepta, 134–35
    peregrine, 114–116, 118, 123–25, 134–35
    during Second Punic War, 78,
        118–120
    and Social War, 136, 188
Proserpina, 27, 68, 69, 70, 214
Ptolemy Alexander, 205
Ptolemy Auletes, 205, 206
Punic Wars, 196
    First, 27, 69, 71–75, 108, 213
    Second, 27–28, 71, 74–78, 102, 113, 118,
        122, 126, 129–34, 146, 148–50, 156–57,
        171, 175, 179–80
Puteoli, 171
Pyrrhus, 65, 74, 96, 115
Pythagoras, 66, 169, 170, 179

Quirinal hill, 181
Quirinus, 88

religio, 24, 106 n. 62, 169 n. 25, 177
Remus, 21, 46, 66–67

Res Gestae, 210
rites of passage, 120
rogator, 99
Romanization, 5 n. 5, 7, 154, 156, 217,
    222
Romanness (see also: boundaries.)
    attempts to define, 2–8, 18–20, 27,
        82–85, 157, 168, 182, 191–95,
        207–8
    Augustan reassertion of, 209–214
    not defined by citizenship, 171–73,
        186–88, 197
    discourse on, 103–4, 166, 216
    paraded, 109, 151
    of practices, 70–71, 76, 109, 151–60,
        166, 203
    questions about, 98–99, 170–71, 178–79,
        186–92, 197
Romulus, 20–22, 34–35, 46, 66–67, 82, 139,
    164, 211
P. Rupilius, 193

Sabines, 20, 34–35, 68, 123, 127,
    139, 211
sacerdotes Lanuvini, 44
sacra peregrina, 9, 209
sacrosanctitas, 194
salii, 87
Samnite Wars, 59, 63–66, 188, 203
Samnium, 108, 135
    and Social War, 188, 203
Samos, 179
Sant' Omobono sanctuary, 34
sanctuaries, regional, 19, 52–54, 116, 119,
    128, 132, 176–79, 218
Sarapis, 204, 211
Saticula, 94
Satricum, 54, 116
Saturn, 163, 210
Saturnalia, 125
Saturnia, 171
Saturninus, L. Appuleius, 196
Scipio Africanus, P. Cornelius, 77
Scipio Nasica, P. Cornelius (cos. 138),
    193–94
Secular Games. See *ludi saeculares*.
Segesta, 74, 75
Sena, 94

Senate, Roman
    arbiter of legitimate religious practice,
        10, 168–69, 181, 184, 196–98, 203,
        206–7
    as body in control of Roman religion,
        87–90, 111–14, 133, 168–69, 174–76,
        194, 198, 206–7
Sentinum, 60–63
septemviri epulones, 87
Servius Tullius, 124
shower of stones, 78, 100, 118, 120, 123
Sibylline Books, 63, 65, 76, 78–79, 87, 100,
    122, 155, 192, 198, 202–3, 205, 207
Sicily, 27, 71, 73, 74, 75, 108, 125, 126, 178,
    192, 193
Social War, 29, 114, 132, 135–36, 173,
    187–91, 196–97, 203
sodalitates, 103–4, 156, 157
Soracte, 127
Struggle of the Orders, 41, 66, 141, 143
Suessa, 94
Sulla, L. Cornelius, 87, 93, 146, 191, 197,
    198, 199, 200, 201, 202
P. Sulpicius Galba, 131
Summanus, 89
supplicatio, 72, 90, 92, 123, 127–34, 148,
    175
Syme, Ronald, 210
Syracuse, 84, 92, 148, 178
Syria, 198, 205

Tarentum, 60, 64, 65–70, 148, 165, 213
Tarquinius Priscus, 20, 88, 139, 140, 202
Tarracina, 119, 127
Teos, 208
theology, Roman, 31–32, 37–38, 60–62,
    120
Thesmophoria, 106, 109, 154
Tiber island, 23, 63, 68, 124, 195, 214, 215
Tibur, 43
Tiriolo (inscription), 167, 174
Titus Tatius, 20, 34, 211
toga, 23, 164
tota Italia, 30, 132–33, 174–75

Trebia, battle of, 71, 78
Trojan War, 38, 46
Troy
    Roman origins from, 24, 45–47, 51,
        74–76, 79–82, 216
    Veii compared to, 37–39, 45, 47, 51, 81
Tullus Hostilius, 98
Turner, Victor, 121–22, 153
Tusculan rite, 42
Tusculum, 42–43, 124

Umbria, 63, 187–88, 213, 219
Uni (Etruscan goddess), 37, 39

C. Valerius Flaccus, 106
Valerius Maximus, 62, 68, 101, 105, 140,
    142, 152, 182
P. Valerius Publicola, 70
Varro, M. Terentius 204, 209
Vediovis, 181
Veii, 26, 36–40, 43–44, 55–56, 92–95, 126
Velia, 106
Veliterni, 43
Venus, 52, 54, 108, 126, 169–70, 180, 201–2
    Erycina, 71–84, 180
Venusia, 65, 94
ver sacrum, 72, 148
Vergil, 3, 24, 45, 73, 202
M. Verrius Flaccus, 9, 11, 41, 96, 209
Vesta, 45, 50, 87
Vestal Virgin, 87, 103
Vestini, 135, 136
Vibo Valentia, 171
Victory
    goddess, 60–1, 65, 73, 145
    theology of, 32, 59–62, 112, 146
Vinalia, 75, 146
vitium, 100
Vitruvius, 209
Volcanal, 34
M. Volusius (aedile), 204
Volscian, 173
Volsinii, 219
Vulcan, 34–35